Southern Legal Studies

SERIES EDITORS

Paul Finkelman, *Albany Law School*
Timothy S. Huebner, *Rhodes College*

ADVISORY BOARD

Alfred L. Brophy, *University of North Carolina School of Law*
Lonnie T. Brown Jr., *University of Georgia School of Law*
Laura F. Edwards, *Duke University*
James W. Ely Jr., *Vanderbilt University Law School*
Sally E. Hadden, *Western Michigan University*
Charles F. Hobson, *College of William & Mary*
Steven F. Lawson, *Rutgers, The State University of New Jersey*
Sanford V. Levinson, *University of Texas at Austin, School of Law*
Peter Wallenstein, *Virginia Polytechnic Institute and State University*

Slavery and Freedom in Texas

Slavery and Freedom in Texas

STORIES FROM THE COURTROOM, 1821–1871

Jason A. Gillmer

The University of Georgia Press
ATHENS

© 2017 by the University of Georgia Press
Athens, Georgia 30602
www.ugapress.org
All rights reserved
Set in Minion Pro by Graphic Composition, Inc., Bogart, Georgia

Most University of Georgia Press titles are
available from popular e-book vendors.

Printed digitally

Library of Congress Cataloging-in-Publication Data

Names: Gillmer, Jason A., author.
Title: Slavery and freedom in Texas : stories from the courtroom,
    1821–1871 / Jason A. Gillmer.
Other titles: Southern legal studies.
Description: Athens : The University of Georgia Press, [2017] |
    Series: Southern legal studies | Includes bibliographical references
    and index.
Identifiers: LCCN 2016055423 | ISBN 9780820351339 (hardback : alk. paper) |
    ISBN 9780820351636 (pbk. : alk. paper) | ISBN 9780820351322 (ebook)
Subjects: LCSH: African Americans—Legal status, laws, etc.—Texas—
    Cases. | Slaves—Legal status, laws, etc.—Texas—Cases. | Freedmen—
    Legal status, laws, etc.—Texas—Cases. | Slaveholders—Legal status,
    laws, etc.—Texas—Cases. | Slavery—Law and legislation—Texas—
    Cases. | Trials—Texas.
Classification: LCC KFT1611.5.A34 G55 2017 | DDC 342.76408/7—dc23
    LC record available at https://lccn.loc.gov/2016055423

For Kristene, Sophia, and Maxwell

CONTENTS

List of Illustrations   xi
Acknowledgments   xiii

INTRODUCTION White Slaves and Ownership Rights in Central Texas   1

CHAPTER ONE Sex, Race, and Family on the Gulf Coast   13

CHAPTER TWO Slave Resistance and Class Conflict in the Redlands   53

CHAPTER THREE A Free Family of Color on the Borderland   89

CHAPTER FOUR Lawyers and Slaves on Galveston Island   133

CONCLUSION Telling Stories of Slavery and Freedom   175

Notes   181
Bibliography   225
Index   239

ILLUSTRATIONS

MAPS

Texas, 1856   2
The Gulf Coast, 1856   14
Wharton County   19
East Texas, 1856   54
Southeast Texas, 1856   90
Orange County   99
Galveston Island, 1856   134
City of Galveston   142

PHOTOGRAPHS

J. Pinckney Henderson   76
William Pitt Ballinger   152

ACKNOWLEDGMENTS

It is hard to remember all the people who have helped shape the stories in this book. When you work on a project for over a decade, your memory about some of the specifics tends to fade. If you consider that many people played a role even before I first thought about writing a history of slavery and freedom in Texas, the task becomes even harder. With that in mind, I would like to thank Adrienne Davis first. Adrienne was my professor in law school, and she has provided encouragement, advice, and guidance at just about every step in my career. If not for her, I doubt that I would be writing this today. William "Terry" Fisher and Kenneth Mack also deserve early recognition. They were my advisors at Harvard while I worked on my LLM, and they showed me how to be a legal historian, teaching me about substantive areas and various methodologies while they supervised my work. I would also like to thank Ariela Gross. I reached out to Ariela years ago, and we have remained in contact ever since. Her approach to writing about race has always inspired me, delving into local records to upend traditional assumptions, and I continue to draw on her advice, mentorship, and support.

My interest in Texas's history started when I took my first tenure-track job at Texas Wesleyan (now Texas A&M) Law School. Before then, I had not spent much time in Texas except to visit my wife's family. The longer we lived there, however, the more intrigued I became with how Texas seemed to be both a real and an imagined place, the sum of the many stories people told about it. As I started to dig into these stories, my law school provided me with summer grants, travel money, and research assistance. During that time, Constance Mims, one of my research assistants, helped immensely, trekking about locally to find various sources, as well as drafting memos that I still rely on today. My colleagues from that time were wonderful. Stephen Alton, Susan Ayers, Michael Green, Keith Hirokawa, Earl "Marty" Martin, Huyen Pham, Susan Phillips, and Aric Short are a few of the people on the current or former faculty who read drafts of early articles and offered support.

I have since accepted a position at Gonzaga Law School and moved to Spokane, Washington. Despite my new location, my interest in the history of Texas continued unabated. Fortunately, Gonzaga recognized the worth of my project and supported me as I tried to uncover the lost stories of the people in the book. My former dean George Critchlow and my current dean Jane Korn provided funds for travel, research, and conferences, for which I am deeply grateful. Sean Harkins, Paige Holly, Morgan Napieralski, Katherine Naulty, and Jacob Stillwell are among the research assistants who located obscure sources and helped with citations. They are among those deserving thanks. A number of my current and former colleagues, especially Patrick Charles, Mark DeForrest, Gerry Hess, Brooks Holland, Kim Pearson, Kevin Michels, and Mary Pat Treuthart, also deserve my gratitude. They read drafts and offered assistance and suggestions at various points along this journey.

In traveling the state of Texas in search of materials, I have encountered so many people willing to help that I cannot possibly name them all, so I'll settle on acknowledging their support by mentioning the places in which they work. In Fort Worth, I am grateful for the help at the Amon Carter Museum, where the staff let me arrive early and stay late to scroll through the microfilm of newspapers before they were digitized and made available on the Portal to Texas History. In Waco, I want to thank the staff at the McLennan County Courthouse, as well as the librarians at Baylor Law School, for helping me recover the story from the introduction and the conclusion. In Wharton, I want to thank the staff at the Wharton County Courthouse and the Courthouse Annex for patiently listening to my questions and helping me to locate many of the sources in chapter 1. I am also grateful to the employees at the Wharton County Historical Museum. I am especially appreciative of that moment after I said I was writing about John C. Clark, and the staff member pointed to John's powder horn prominently displayed in the museum, illustrating for me how real the story had become. The staff there also put me in touch with George "Bud" Northington, a descendant of the Heard and Northington families of Wharton County, including W. J. E. Heard, who bought his property from John Clark long ago. Bud sent me information about the family and showed me a restored home on his property that helped me visualize the cabin in which John Clark and Sobrina lived. Finally, I am grateful that Barbara Byers—a descendant of F. Gray Franks, who represented the children in the dispute over John Clark's estate—contacted me. Barbara pointed me in the direction of a number of sources that helped me appreciate the role Franks played.

I would also like to thank the staff at the East Texas Research Center, located at Stephen F. Austin University in Nacogdoches. They were incredibly helpful as I sought to reconstruct the story in chapter 2. I was in Nacogdoches when my wife's grandfather, "Papa," died. As I left Nacogdoches and drove down from East Texas to Houston, where Papa lived most of his life, I kept thinking about how lucky I was that my wife's family, who had descended from slaves in Texas, had welcomed me into their home. My in-laws Keith and Alice, my new sister Kim, my new uncles and aunts, my new cousins, and my new grandparents graciously accepted me in their lives. The memory of my wife's grandmother carrying around that old, tattered copy of my first law review article to show her friends at church is enough to make this whole project worth it.

The people who helped reconstruct the story in chapter 3 are also too numerous to name. I received assistance from the staff at the Jefferson County Courthouse, as well as at the Tyrrell Historical Library, in Beaumont. Several miles away in Orange, the staff at the Orange County Courthouse also helped me navigate the old record books. The same is true of the people at the Sam Houston Regional Library and Research Center in Liberty, where a lot of the old case files, tax records, and minute books from Jefferson and Orange Counties can be found. The story of the Ashworths is a very personal one for the descendants of the family, many of whom still live in the area. A number of the family members have reached out to me over the years after reading an early article I'd written about the family or after hearing about my current project. I regret that I will not be able to name all those I have spoken to, but I would like to mention Sharon Jarrell, Verna Thompson, Rachel Stinson, and Ken Williams. These descendants and others have shared pieces of information about the family with me, pointed out a few of my errors, and, without exception, shown deep appreciation for my efforts to bring their remarkable family's story to light.

I am also grateful for the help excavating the story in chapter 4. I spent time in the Dolph Briscoe Center for American History at the University of Texas in Austin, as well as in the Rosenberg Library in Galveston, reading through William Pitt Ballinger's diary and his papers, along with other, more obscure sources. The professionals in both libraries were exceptional and deeply knowledgeable. I also would like to thank the staff at the Galveston County Courthouse.

Finally, I would like to recognize the staff at the Texas General Land Office and at the Texas State Library and Archives Commission, both in Austin. There I found critical pieces of each story, and I am grateful for the insight and patience of the many people who helped explain sources and steer me in the right direction.

A number of my friends and colleagues have read drafts, offered suggestions, and provided support. I am especially grateful to Daniel Sharfstein. Dan, one of the best writers I know, read every page of my manuscript, and his comments unquestionably made the final product better. Dan also brought me to Vanderbilt University to present my work at the Circum-Atlantic Studies Seminar, headed by the inestimable Jane Landers. Jane and her colleagues were incredibly gracious, and while their imprint is most noticeable in the introduction, it can also be felt elsewhere in the book. Another close colleague who provided immeasurable support is Alfred Brophy. Several times Al encouraged me to keep going, reminding me of the possibilities and potential of my project. He offered advice, suggestions, and good cheer. I would also like to thank Randolph "Mike" Campbell. Mike, whose knowledge of Texas history is unmatched, has read versions of a number of the stories in the book and has provided welcome feedback.

Parts of the stories in the book were published elsewhere. A version of the story in chapter 1 was published as "Base Wretches and Black Wenches: A Story of Sex and Race, Violence and Compassion, during Slavery Times," *Alabama Law Review* 59, no. 5 (2008): 1501–54. A brief version was also part of a chapter, "Telling Stories of Love, Sex, and Race," in *Loving in a Post-Racial World: New Legal Approaches to Interracial Marriages and Relationships*, edited by Kevin Noble Maillard and Rose Cuison Villazor (New York: Cambridge University Press, 2012), 29–45. A version of the story in chapter 3 was published as "Shades of Gray: The Life and Times of a Free Family of Color on the Texas Frontier," *Law and Inequality: A Journal of Theory and Practice* 29, no. 1 (2011): 33–106. Finally, a version of the story in chapter 4 was published as "Lawyers and Slaves: A Remarkable Case of Representation from the Antebellum South," *University of Miami Race and Social Justice Law Review* 1, no. 1 (2011): 47–76.

I have presented versions of the stories in the book at a number of schools and conferences over the years. It is impossible to name all the people who have commented and offered suggestions, so a list of the events and places will have to suffice: Lewis & Clark Law School, Seattle University School of Law, Southern Methodist University School of Law, Stetson University College of Law, Texas A&M University School of Law, UC Davis School of Law, University of Toledo College of Law, University of South Carolina School of Law, Washington University School of Law, Association for the Study of Law, Culture, and the Humanities, Law and Society Association, LatCrit, Southeastern Association of Law Schools, Dallas Bar Association, and Texas State Historical Association. Along the way, and in between these presentations, others provided comments and insight to my work. I hope you forgive me for not naming everyone individually, even though I greatly appreciate your support.

I am also grateful for the assistance, guidance, suggestions, and support of the team at the University of Georgia Press. Walter Biggins had the initial vision to see what this book could add to the historiography of slavery in Texas. His enthusiastic embrace of my narrative approach was also deeply rewarding. Jon Davies provided superb copyediting and production support. Deborah Oliver also carefully read every sentence and every endnote. Her insightful comments and suggestions made the book better in numerous ways. Two anonymous reviewers also offered cogent thoughts about how to tighten the argument and improve the analysis. After all of the hard work at the Press, any remaining errors, weak spots, or awkward transitions rest solely with me.

Finally, I would like to thank my family. My parents, Dick and Kay, have always been there for me, supporting me in the ways only parents can do, as have my brothers and sister and their families. My children, Sophia and Maxwell, have grown up listening to me talk about these stories. They served as daily inspirations for the book, as well as for everything else in life. My wife, Kristene, has participated in this project in many ways. She kept me company on research trips, she read drafts, and she found sources. She traveled to conferences when her schedule allowed, and she drove me to the airport when it did not. She talked me through the ups and downs, pushed me to consider different angles and new ideas, and encouraged me to keep going when I felt like giving up. How do words capture how much she has sacrificed and what she has done? I dedicate this book to her and to my children.

Slavery and Freedom in Texas

INTRODUCTION

White Slaves and Ownership Rights in Central Texas

In the spring of 1856, just after the last brick was laid in the new courthouse in Limestone County, Texas, the trial over Ann, an enslaved girl who looked white, was set to begin. Men and women hardened by a life in the wilderness had begun gathering in the town square earlier that morning, eagerly awaiting a rarity of frontier life—a spectacle. Located in Central Texas, just east of McLennan County and the emerging town of Waco, Limestone County was an unforgiving place at the time of the trial. The county had been formed in 1846, after locals carved out an area in the rolling prairies along the Navasota River and called the region their own. They named Springfield the county seat, a settlement of about 120 people that grew to include five general stores, two hotels, two schools, a newspaper, and a Masonic hall. Although there were a few wealthy planters and a handful of professional men who settled in the county, most of those who came to see Ann were self-sufficient farmers who made the most out of what little they had.[1]

The men and women camped outside the Springfield courthouse had taken the day off from spring planting, having come from remote farms to contemplate the questions raised by the trial. While most of the spectators did not own slaves, almost all were southern born and had come to view the institution as part of the natural order of things. They spoke of blacks as being less than human, destined by God to serve whites for the betterment of (white) society. The racism they spouted, flowing so easily off their tongues, found support in the laws and policies of Texas, where people of color were reduced to property and denied all but the most basic rights. It is safe to say that if this trial had involved a black person asserting a right to freedom, the individuals in the square would have overwhelmingly supported the rights of the owner.

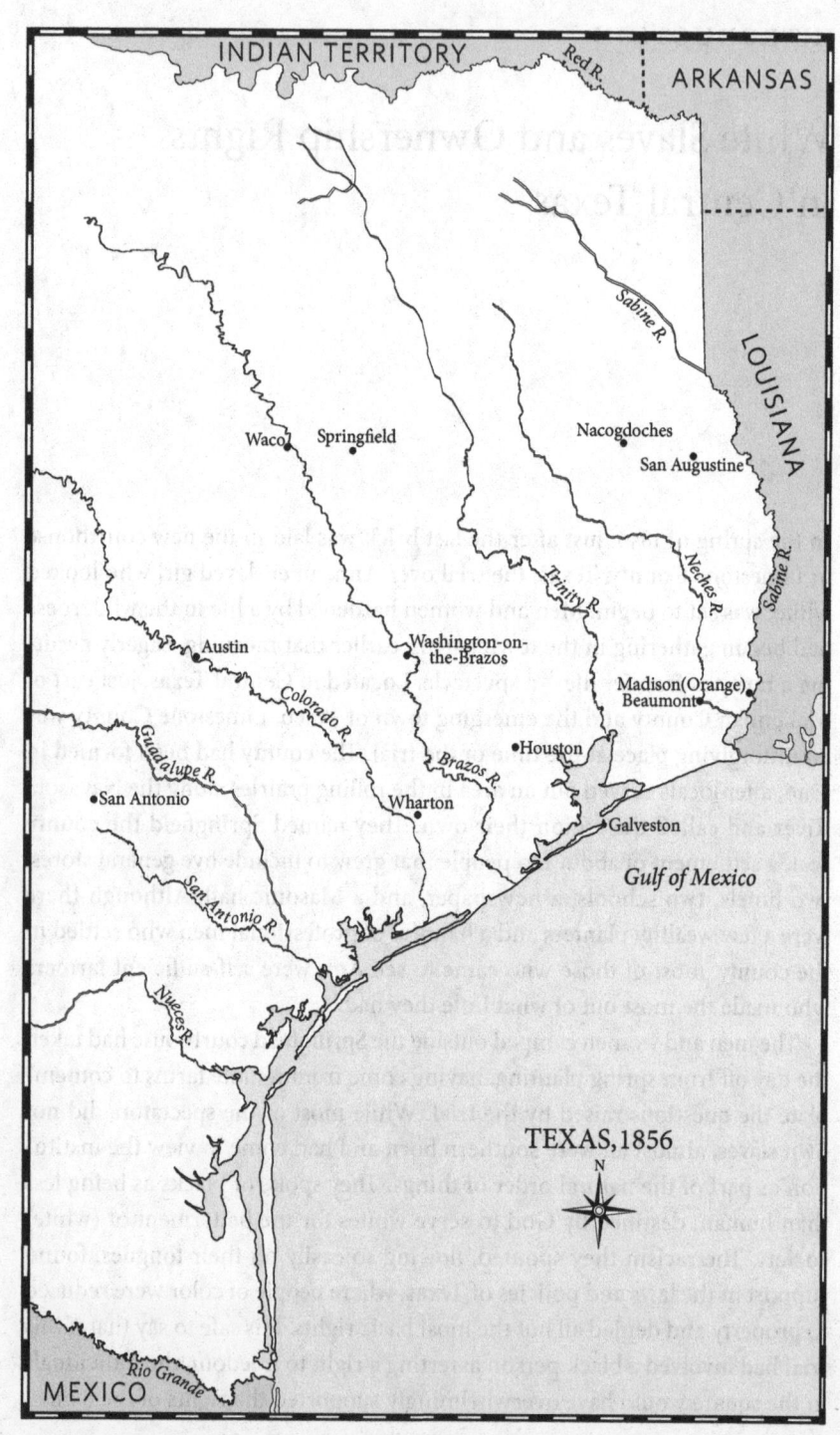

But this was no ordinary case. Not only did the young woman who sought to be free look white, but the man claiming her as his own—a Choctaw Indian named George Gaines—looked brown.[2]

The case of *George Gaines v. William Thomas* got its start a year earlier, in the summer of 1855. Evidently, George was passing through on Springfield Road, the main road of travel between North Texas and Houston, when the confrontation occurred. George was not a resident of Limestone County. He was a citizen of the Choctaw Nation in the Indian Territory, in what is now Oklahoma. In light of the historically poor relations the people of Limestone County had with the local tribes, it is hardly surprising that the residents were suspicious, even openly hostile, to George's ownership claims. Everyone in Limestone had either lived through or known about the time a large band of Comanche Indians and their allies raided Fort Parker in 1836, not too far from where Springfield now stood, killing five inhabitants and taking five more hostage. Among those taken were a young mother, Rachel Plummer, and a nine-year-old girl named Cynthia Ann Parker. Rachel was beaten and abused, starved, and held prisoner for over thirteen months before finally being rescued. Cynthia Ann lived with the Comanches for so long that she eventually became one, marrying a Comanche warrior. When George came through town, with Ann behind him, memories of these past atrocities came flooding to the forefront. As a member of a "Civilized Tribe," George may have spoken their language and adopted their ways, but to the people of Limestone County he was no different from the group that had raided their camps and caused them so much trouble. George was an outsider, a foreigner with dark skin and black hair, and the girl he claimed as his own reminded them too much of Rachel Plummer and Cynthia Ann. George had upset their understanding of the world, and they had no intention of allowing him to assert his dominance over a member of what they saw as the dominant race.[3]

After they stopped George in the road, William Thomas and several others forcibly took Ann and placed her in the safekeeping of the sheriff. George, comparing his experience to being robbed on the public highway, filed suit soon after, claiming to have been damaged in the amount of $1,500. The ensuing trial took place the following March, in 1856, pitting Ann's physical appearance against the records of her enslavement. George focused on the latter. He proffered the bill of sale and called on witnesses to describe how Ann was the daughter of Sarah, an enslaved "bright mulatto . . . said to be about one fourth African." George conceded that Ann's father may have been a white man and that Ann may have had even lighter skin than her mother, but there was no disputing the maternal connection. Ann's mother was a slave, and because slave women could give birth only to slave children, Ann was also a slave.[4]

With Ann's status now a central part of the trial, and with the answer affecting not just the defendants' liability but also Ann's future, William and the other defendants rejected the idea that Ann's background mattered and focused instead on her appearance. They said that Ann was "not a slave as set forth in [the] petition, but a free white girl." These men came from a tradition that insisted that race be tied to status, and anyone who *looked* white could not be enslaved, any more than someone who *looked* brown should not be free. All this talk about Ann's mother and the specifics of the sale was irrelevant to what these individuals could plainly see. The doctor they called as their expert offered an air of respectability to their assumptions. He examined Ann in preparation for trial and again in open court, and he could not "detect about the girl any of the distinguishing characteristics of the negro." He testified that "her complexion, color, features, hair, shape of the head, lips, chin, nose and general appearance was that of the white race." He admitted that he did not actually draw blood to see if an African past was coursing through her veins. But he was certain "that the child of a woman one fourth negro and a white man would show traces of the negro race" in her appearance, and Ann showed none. If there was any doubt, defense counsel received permission from the court to allow the twelve men on the jury to inspect Ann for themselves, ironically playing out the rituals of the slave market to prove what no (other) white woman would ever have to endure.[5]

Later that day, the jury returned a verdict in favor of freedom, finding that Ann was white and wrongly enslaved. Like the men who had stopped George on the road, the twelve jurors had disregarded the written rules of slavery, ignoring the uncontested evidence of descent, and righted a world that they saw as upside down. It made little sense to George or to anyone else who believed in the formal rule of law. He immediately appealed the decision to the Texas Supreme Court, where he found three justices far more sympathetic to the rights of a slaveholder than a slave. Focusing on Ann's history rather than her appearance, they promptly reversed the jury's verdict, finding that the "evidence in this case was clear and unequivocal, that the mother and grandmother of Ann were both slaves and of the African race." Stating that the rule was "too well settled to require a reference to authority," the court concluded that Ann's lineage meant that Ann was also a slave, and it remanded the case for a new trial. It was a major victory for George and a bitter loss for Ann, but the case was far from over. Three years later, on the cusp of the Civil War, it would be tried again, this time before a jury in McLennan County. George's fate, together with Ann's, would have to wait another day.[6]

~

The words "Gone to Texas," or "GTT," were fastened to the doors of countless homes and cabins throughout the second quarter of the nineteenth century. They were words of hope to a restless population in search of new opportunities and second chances. Mexico officially opened Texas to Anglo-American settlement at the end of 1821. For those who came early, the environment was harsh and each day brought new challenges. The sun beat down relentlessly in the summer, and cold and ice blew through in the winter. Basic supplies always seemed in short supply, and deaths from disease and encounters with the Indians were not uncommon even as the population grew. But for the hardy and industrious, few places offered the possibilities of Texas. Fertile land at extremely low prices stretched for thousands and thousands of miles, up the Sabine River in the east, along the Red River in the north, along the Gulf of Mexico in the south, and everywhere in between. "No country in North America," the popular *DeBow's Review* stated in 1851, "holds out such inducements to emigrants as Texas, both for the salubrity of its climate, the fertility of its soil, and the variety of its products." By the start of the Civil War, the population of Texas had soared from around seven thousand in 1820 to over six hundred thousand—still a tiny population in light of the state's size but a striking testament to the desirability of its riches.[7]

Not all those who came, of course, did so voluntarily. Of the 604,215 persons in the state in 1860, 182,566 (or 30 percent) were enslaved men, women, and children. Ann—the young woman on trial for her freedom—was among them. Ann was thirteen years old when the first trial began in 1856. A few years before, according to the plaintiff's testimony, she had been separated from all she knew. She had grown up on Joseph Hawkins's farm in Missouri, where her mother and her grandmother lived. Joseph passed her down to his son, Strother, who brought her to Fannin County in the far north of Texas, where he sold Ann to Joseph Cox. Joseph then sold her to George Gaines. Alone, with her family back in Missouri, she stumbled along behind George as he made his way through the sparsely populated prairies of Central Texas. By the time William Thomas stopped George to question him on the highway, Ann had experienced enough tragedy in her short life to fill a volume. The next several years, as she bounced from jail to the courtroom and back again, would only add more misery.[8]

Ann's story has never been told, at least not in any detail. Like countless other enslaved persons, her story of race and slavery and hardship has largely been lost in the larger historical narrative of Texas in the nineteenth century. Passed over in favor of more prominent names and more prominent events—Stephen F. Austin, Samuel Houston, Jim Bowie, and the Alamo—Ann's story and others like it feel more like a footnote, a nod in the direction of the institution but ultimately downplayed in light of the overall importance of other actors and moments. Twenty-five years ago, Randolph Campbell lamented the lack of modern historical research devoted to slavery in Texas, especially compared with other former slaveholding states. Campbell attributed the dearth in serious study in part to the ongoing narrative that Texas was more western than southern, the place of cowboys and cattle drives rather than of slave markets and whipping posts. The relatively short time slavery existed in Texas likely also contributed to the limited scholarly attention. Compared to a state like Virginia, where slavery had been active for over two hundred years, slavery in Texas felt like a mere historical blip.[9]

Campbell sought to reverse the trend, publishing *An Empire for Slavery: The Peculiar Institution in Texas, 1821–1865* in 1989. It was the first major effort to explore Texas's historical experience with slavery. Campbell's book highlighted the vital role slavery played in the state's history, from the time of Austin's colony through the Civil War. Debunking the myth that Texas was fundamentally western, Campbell showed how Texas before the Civil War identified with its southern neighbors both politically and culturally. Slavery may not have been around as long, and the percentage of the total U.S. slave population may not have been as large, but Campbell argued that the ideology, laws, and commitments of the ruling elite in Texas paralleled those in the rest of the South. His general account tracked slavery's time line, noted its role in the Texas War for Independence, discussed its economic impact, and explored more particular facets of the institution, such as working conditions and family life. Focusing in large part on the structural institutions that allowed for slavery to develop and that framed the institution, he ultimately concluded that "slavery in Texas did not differ in any fundamental way from the institution as it existed elsewhere in the United States."[10]

Since the publication of Campbell's book, a small body of work has grown up around the subject. Notable contributions from scholars like Alwyn Barr, Andrew Torget, Mark Carroll, and Dale Baum have added to Campbell's pioneering work to offer insight into African American life and the role of slavery in Texas. Though focused less on slavery than on Reconstruction, Barry Crouch has also written extensively about the experiences of African Americans in nineteenth-century Texas. The collective picture painted by these scholars has reinforced the notion that slavery—and its aftermath—played a critical role in the development of the state. More importantly, these efforts have revealed that Texas between the period of Anglo settlement and Reconstruction was a complex place, meshing Native American, Mexican, Anglo-American, and African American culture, traditions, and laws with the instability of the frontier. Both Carroll's book and Baum's book are particularly noteworthy in this regard. Using archival records in conjunction with legal texts, they highlight the synergy that exists between lived experience and formal law, opening up intriguing questions about the importance of local matters in shaping people's decisions and their responses to conflict.[11]

The opposite of slavery—freedom—has also slowly, if sporadically, garnered the interest of scholars of Texas. The early work of Harold Schoen and Andrew Forest Muir demonstrated the potential of studying the experiences of free people of color in Texas.[12] But, given how few there were and how difficult they were to trace, scholars focused on freedom for people of color have generally looked to places other than Texas.[13] In his 2014 article, John Garrison Marks notes the lack of attention paid to free people of color in Texas and begins the process of reinvigorating the subject by drawing on developing methodologies of historians examining free blacks in other areas. Like Carrol and Baum, Marks focuses on county and other archival materials that provide insight into the experiences of free people of color in Houston and Harris County. Measured against the body of work of other regions, these efforts add critical pieces to our understanding of how people experienced race and slavery in Texas, even as they serve as reminders of the work to be done.[14]

This book offers five discrete case studies of nineteenth-century trials that enrich our understanding of slavery and freedom and black and white in antebellum Texas. Each of these stories takes place at a boundary—between slave and free, black and white, rich and poor, old and new—as people who confounded rigid divisions forced legal institutions to deal with the conflicts they raised. Chapter 1 involves an early settler in a thirty-year relationship with an enslaved woman in a rural county along the Colorado River. Following his death and the end of the Civil War, their children brought suit maintaining they were his rightful heirs, forcing the community to consider the legitimacy of interracial relationships. Chapter 2 discusses a case from East Texas that arose after an owner refused to pay an overseer who shot one of her slaves, pitting the dynamics of wealth and class against the dynamics of race. Chapter 3 details the life and times of a pioneer family of color who carved out a place for themselves in the sparsely populated marshland of Southeast

Texas, before eventually losing their status and their land as new residents moved in and "civilized" the county. Chapter 4 involves an enslaved woman set free in her owner's will in comparatively urban Galveston and chronicles her relationship with her attorneys and the lengths they went to secure her rights. The conclusion picks up where the introduction left off, returning to Ann's case to discuss the second trial and complete the story of a white slave's suit for freedom.

Each of the stories detailed in the book illuminates the everyday experience of slavery and freedom in Texas. Each chapter unfolds gradually, beginning with a case or controversy that seems like an anomaly given our contemporary assumptions about race and slavery, but slowly comes to suggest broader implications for the institution as it existed in Texas. In many respects the narratives that follow support Campbell's thesis: Texas before the Civil War was far more southern than western in its outlook. Nineteenth-century Texans embraced the cotton culture with vigor, with the state trailing only slightly behind other regions of the Deep South in cotton production in the 1850s and 1860s. Texas politicians extolled the virtues of slavery. Legislatures passed laws supporting the institution, and the Texas Supreme Court handed down rulings that further entrenched proslavery ideals into the fabric of society. Moreover, as the Civil War approached, a majority of Texans made it clear that they stood with their southern counterparts rather than with the Union, and sixty or seventy thousand Texans would eventually fight on behalf of the Confederacy.[15]

The stories discussed in the book, however, also demonstrate that Texas's early connection to Mexico, combined with the realities of the frontier, shaped the experience of slavery and freedom in ways that distinguished Texas from other more established slaveholding states. From the perspective of the enslaved, life was not less harsh in the early days of Texas, but the parameters of slavery and freedom were less defined and—given Mexico's antislavery stance—less clear. People of color had more "liberty then," Abraham Kincheloe observed when discussing his experience in Austin's colony prior to the Texas War for Independence. Even as Texas evolved from a borderland society to a republic to a state, and enacted laws to firmly entrench slavery as an institution, the space between neighbors encouraged allowances in the formal law, and personal connections and common experience occasionally caused people to act in ways different from their beliefs. This does not mean that the institution was in danger of collapsing or that the legal rules underlining it were viewed with skepticism. To the contrary, even if people sided with—or even zealously advocated for—a slave or person of color, they still could fully embrace the system and all it stood for. What the following chapters demonstrate, however, is that out there in the Texas wilderness, and along the rivers and bayous, there was room on the margins for negotiations, that the law was flexible and fluid and able to adapt to everyday experiences, and that the story of slavery in Texas was one of fits and starts and messy transitions, even as it marched steadily in the direction of a slave society.[16]

∽

This book is a narrative history of slavery and freedom in Texas. Once a rarity, the list of historians drawing on legal and archival records to tell an individual story with race and slavery in the United States continues to grow. Michael Ross, author of *The Great New Orleans Kidnapping Case: Race, Law, and Justice in the Reconstruction Era*, captures the essence behind this approach when he references the poet William Blake's injunction that we "see a world in a grain of sand." Instead of offering an argument-driven analysis of multiple cases and materials, the narrative approach digs deep, presenting a richly textured discussion of a single individual or small group of people to offer perspective on a particular subject. As events and lives in the narrative unfold, readers gain an appreciation of what mattered most to the people from that time.[17]

The chapters that follow bring to life the events and the people that shaped the history of Texas. They are about real people using their own words and expressions, salvaged from trial records and court documents, the occasional memoir, census records, tax returns, deeds, cattle brands, and the pages of newspapers. People of color as well as white men and women, community members, planters, overseers, and attorneys weave their way in and out of the narratives. Like any good novel—and like life itself—the stories are not necessarily linear. They jump around as new parties are introduced or subplots are developed. Anyone who has been involved in a trial knows that good trial lawyers are good storytellers. The courtroom becomes a place where attorneys can shape a narrative to help further their client's cause. The book stays true to this form, allowing the reader to experience the story, to make it vivid and come alive.

The trials themselves were not chosen by accident. Several years ago, I endeavored to read and categorize every published case involving slaves and slavery from Texas. From there, I worked backward, reviewing trial transcripts and other local records for several different cases. The five cases selected for this book each add an intriguing perspective on the history of race and slavery in Texas. Each one was a hard case, forcing local communities to confront a situation that pitted ideological commitments against practical considerations. Each one also took place in a different region of Texas, under circumstances that arguably allowed for the controversy to arise. Individually, the cases might be dismissed as aberrations. Viewed collectively, they open a window into lived experience.

It has been said that trials and other legal disputes offer a unique view into the past. In comparison to statutes and other formal rules, which provide one of the best indications of how society thinks its members *ought* to behave, trials shine a light on those moments when the rules have come apart. Mining the legal documents of a trial can provide clues into what led to the breach, and, just as important, it can provide insight into the community as it responds. Held up against this framework, the stories in this book reveal both the power of formal law and its limitations in antebellum Texas life. Each chapter illustrates how the law played a critical role in the development of Texas. The law set up the rules for participating in community life and dictated the terms of belonging. At the same time, each chapter shows how, on the rough-and-tumble frontier, experience often competed with formal law, forcing Texans to adapt their legal institutions and committed ideologies to account for personal connections and common sense. The paradoxes are sometimes difficult to reconcile but should not be lost. As much as this book is about the contingencies and contradictions of slavery in Texas, and the promises of what might have been, it is also about the law's role in legitimizing that institution.[18]

Other considerations also dictated the stories in the book. In Texas, anytime a case was appealed, the lower court file was sent to the Texas Supreme Court. Unfortunately, a number of the files involving slaves and persons of color were taken from the Texas State Library and Archives Commission (TSLAC) in the early 1970s and have never been recovered. The five stories discussed in the book, however, managed to survive. The two inheritance cases discussed in chapters 1 and 4 were not filed until after the Civil War. They thus escaped the attention of the document thief, who evidently did not have the wherewithal to realize that slavery was being litigated long after it was formally over. The records for both are housed safely in TSLAC.[19]

The case file involving the overseer who shot a rebellious slave in chapter 2 had a different fate. It is among those missing from TSLAC. Fortunately, at the time the case was appealed, the county clerk kept a copy. It has survived all these years and is now on file in the East Texas Research Center at Stephen F. Austin State University.

The story of the pioneer family of color in chapter 3 also managed to escape the attention of the document thief. Their story is pieced together with trial records and court minutes, along with congressional petitions and other records of their lives. The reason the trial records still exist at TSLAC is because our protagonists were not slaves and their lawsuits did not directly invoke slavery. Freedom, it seems, was outside the interest of our thief.

Finally, the case files in TSLAC for the trials sketched in the introduction and conclusion, involving George Gaines and Ann, were among those that were evidently stolen. But, through the help of librarians at Texas A&M and Baylor Law Schools and the work of employees at the McLennan County Courthouse, copies of the records were located in the files of the courthouse. The employees at the courthouse located the records after discovering that they had been filed under a different case name than the one used on appeal. The difficulty of finding the records gives rise to the very real possibility that they have been sitting unread in the courthouse for 150 years, with only the occasional clerk noting their existence for purposes of record keeping.

~

The stories that follow are told from the perspective of the people involved. In re-creating their lives, I do my best to remain true to the record, using their own words when possible and other documentary evidence about the person or event. At times the work has been frustrating. Sometimes the trail ends, or never even starts, as when one hopes to find, but never does, a birth or death record, a marriage license, a deed of sale, or, in the case of an enslaved person, a last name. In the absence of direct evidence, I have relied on other material, including other primary-source records, the work of other historians, and my own personal observations and experience, scouting out the areas that serve as the setting for the stories.

In quoting people from the time, I have chosen to keep their language, including their misspellings, grammatical errors, and odd punctuation. I have also left their often problematic and offensive terminology on race. The point is to capture the words and beliefs of people from that era without running them through a modern filter. It sometimes leads to uncomfortable moments, but better to stay true to the record in order to shed light on the period than scrub the language clean.

In the writing of this book, one of the most important lessons I have learned is that, unlike a fictional story, real-life stories do not necessarily come neatly packaged with a beginning and an end. Even a favorable verdict—a substantial monetary award, a vindication of a right, a declaration of freedom—does not always translate into a comfortable living. I try to capture life's realities in the following chapters. Each one has several parts, or subchapters, that gradually pull together the story of the persons, the family, the community, and the society. Each one also ends with a postscript, after the case was over. All of the chapters illustrate how the law could play a powerful role in the lives of persons of color, providing them with an unprecedented voice. They also indicate how the law could be the cause of their undoing.

CHAPTER ONE

Sex, Race, and Family on the Gulf Coast

The Civil War was long over when Lourinda, Nancy, and Bishop sat down in the county courthouse in Wharton County to hear opening testimony in their suit against George W. Honey, the state treasurer. It was December 1871, and spectators had come from miles around to witness the latest developments in the ongoing dispute over the estate of John Clark, one of the wealthiest men in Texas. Everyone present was familiar with the case. A decade ago, John had died, leaving behind thousands of acres of land, over a hundred slaves, and more cattle than just about anyone in the county. Executors estimated his estate to be worth close to a half million dollars, an amount that surpassed the imaginations of practically everyone in the area. The problem was that John Clark had led a solitary life, miles away from his closest neighbor and even farther away from the life he left behind when he first ventured into the Texas wild forty years ago. Having long lost touch with his family, when he died no one stepped forward to claim the property. The local court had it inventoried and sold, including the human beings who resided on the plantation, and deposited thousands of bills and promissory notes in the state treasury.[1]

Word of the immense and unclaimed estate inevitably filtered out, and soon individuals from as far away as Virginia, Alabama, Indiana, and Iowa eagerly embraced the man they never knew. They spun different narratives of how they were John's next of kin—long-lost siblings, a nephew, maybe a niece—with none admitting "to be of kin as between themselves," lest they have to share in the estate of the "Texas Millionaire." The tangled web of stories and legal documents brought on by their claims, however, mattered little when Lourinda and her younger sister and brother walked into court. They

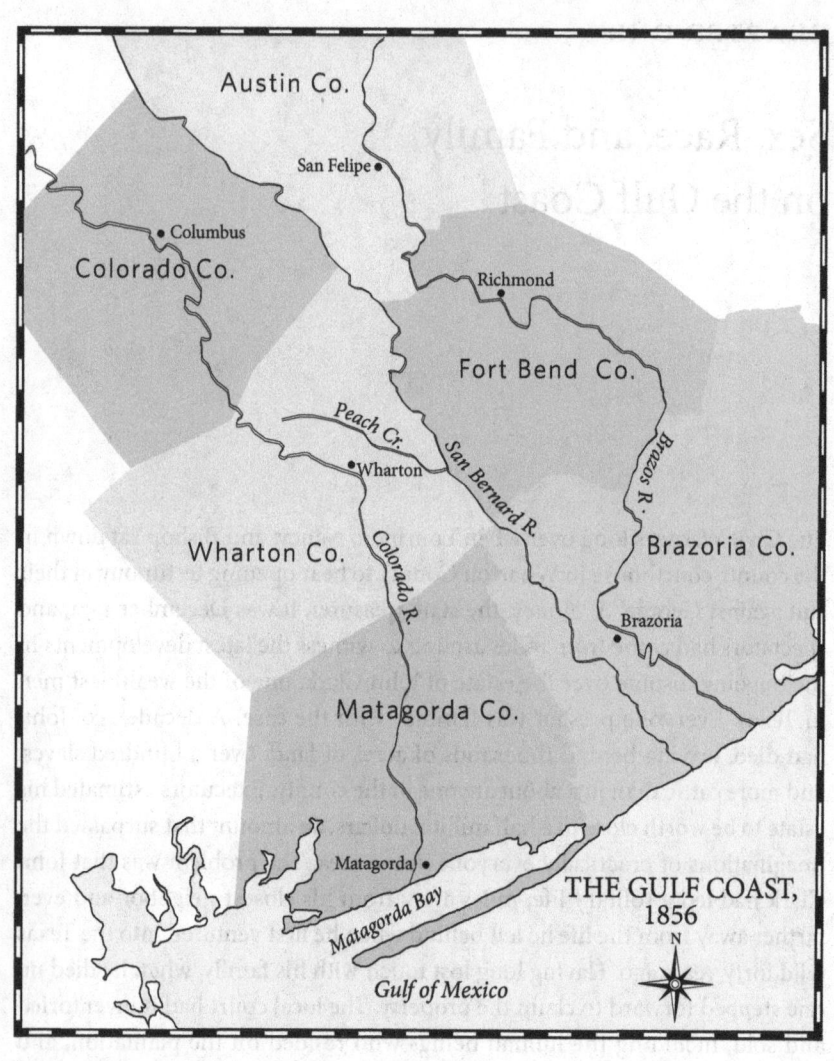

were John's children, and by the laws of intestacy they said that the estate and all its proceeds belonged to them.²

As simple as the assertion was, the children's case shook the foundation of some of the state's most deeply held convictions. A spectator casting a glance toward them could easily explain why. Lourinda, Nancy, and Bishop all possessed the light brown skin and soft, wavy hair that labeled them as "mulattoes," as their mother, Sobrina, had been one of John's first slaves. The reason for not coming forward at the time of John's death was therefore obvious. Under the laws of Texas, children followed the condition of the mother, meaning that all three were also John's slaves in 1861. Ten years later, at the time of the trial, their task had not grown much easier. No longer enslaved, they still faced the difficult burden of proving they were their father's lawful heirs. This required them to demonstrate something antithetical to the laws of slavery and ideals of the time. It required them to prove that John and Sobrina had been husband and wife.³

Much like now, people back then were invariably drawn to scandals, particularly those that involve sex, money, and power. The children's case involved all of that and more, pitting individuals who had known freedom for only six years against the powerful state treasurer. It was a first for Wharton County. In 1871, Wharton remained a small agricultural community a few days' journey on horseback from Houston, with only a few ramshackle buildings making up the county seat, also called Wharton. Residents had not yet established a newspaper, public education was dismal, and the railroad was still years away. Yet, even as time seemingly stood still, courtroom observers were being treated to a world turned upside down. Blacks were sitting on juries, whites were struggling to be heard, and the old was fighting the new.⁴

The trial of *Clark v. Honey* took place in the county courthouse, a two-story building that had been the pride of the town when it was constructed before the Civil War but now stood, like everything else in town, in need of repair. Inside the cramped and musty room, jurors and spectators shifted in their seats, trying to stay comfortable on the hard-backed wooden chairs and benches. It was a tense trial, with conflicting testimony barely hiding simmering disagreements about the future of the county. About the only thing on which people sitting in the courtroom could agree was that John Clark was different. The question was whether he was different enough to discard the sexual taboos that many residents sought to weave into the fabric of Texas life, and whether Sobrina was a willing partner in the endeavor. Following John's journey into the wide-open frontier, with boundaries made porous by the realities of daily life, the jury came to an unanimous conclusion. One side of the courtroom erupted in cheers.[5]

The Old Three Hundred

John Clark was adventurous. He left his native South Carolina as a young man—in his late teens, probably—joining the vast migration westward with little more than his trusty horse and a handful of provisions packed into a saddlebag. There was little reason for him to stay. He was born in 1798, by which time land in the Carolinas had grown tired from overuse, and opportunities, especially for those without, were few. Men and women of all stripes looked to the west in search of better fortunes. Land in the emerging states of the Deep South was cheap and plentiful compared to the Carolinas, and the invention of the cotton gin opened up new possibilities for profits and success. Settling into the saddle, John did not look back. People who knew him later in life said he rarely talked about his family. He never wrote letters to people back home or inquired about their goings-on. Galloping away, John had his eye on things to come.[6]

John might not have known where he was headed when he left South Carolina. Texas was not yet open for settlement, but wagon trains and cattle herds had succeeded in carving routes into the gentle plains of the Lower Mississippi Valley. Cotton fields had begun to dot the landscape next to cornfields and sugar plantations, with settlers and traders dragging along slaves, drenched in sweat in the summer and shivering in the winter, in the hopes that the humans they claimed as property would provide them with a comfortable living. John may have stopped for a while, deciding whether to set down roots among some of the emerging towns and communities. But in all likelihood he kept going, searching out the frontier's edge. John liked the freedom and independence that came from living on his own.[7]

Word that Stephen F. Austin was looking for colonists to immigrate to Texas began filtering out in early fall of 1821. Austin had taken over the colonization enterprise after his father, Moses, passed away, securing a grant from Spain and later Mexico to bring three hundred families to an area between the Brazos and Colorado Rivers in the Gulf coastal region of southeast Texas. "I do assure you on the word of a man that it is the most beautiful and fertile country I ever beheld in my life," Austin raved in a letter, seeking recruits. "The soil is a deep black mixed with sand, works very easy and produces immense crops, is well adapted to corn, sugar, rice, cotton, tobacco and wheat." Where John was when he first heard of Austin's enterprise is not known. By the spring of 1822, however, he had made his way to New Orleans, where William Kincheloe was organizing a party to sail to the mouth of the Colorado with plans to join a handful of others who had arrived the previous winter. John met a man named Alexander Jackson, and together they climbed aboard, settling down between barrels of flour and supplies of seed. Testing their guns as well as their mettle, they sailed out into the Gulf, intent on a prosperous future.[8]

John was used to the intense heat and humidity of the South. But somehow it felt more oppressive when he first disembarked and splashed ashore in June 1822, at the age of twenty-three or twenty-four. Some of those who had come in the previous winter were already turning back, overwhelmed by the sense of hopelessness of trying to carve a life out of the wilderness. Those who remained were half-starved, suffering from a lack of supplies and hoping for rain to salvage their first crops. Yet John kept his spirits up. All his life he had been in search of the frontier, and in Texas he had found it. Camped along the river, he chopped his way through giant river cane to gaze on untouched land that stretched for hundreds of miles. Wild oats and wild rye cast a golden hue along the river bottoms, with tall grasses gently waving on the prairies. Small creeks "whispered along through tall reeds" and water lilies sat undisturbed on the surface. Venturing out of the plains and into the woods, he found live oaks, pecans, ash, and other hardwoods in abundance, providing welcome shade from the sun, fuel for burning, and fertile hunting grounds. The frontier was, by definition, the edge of civilization, and some walked up to the edge and turned around. John thrived.[9]

That is, after he almost died. A few months after he arrived, John was paddling up the Colorado with two companions in a canoe loaded with corn. Without warning, members of the Karankawa tribe attacked. Austin had not informed immigrants that they would be settling on lands occupied by Indians, and colonists did here what they had always done. They tried to drive them out. The Karankawas, however, had no intention of leaving. Told from the perspectives of the settlers, the Indians were the aggressors, stealing horses and raiding camps. Today, we know that they were simply resisting encroachments on their grounds. When they saw John and two others on the river, they fired arrows with tips as sharp as knives. A few struck John. He dove into the water and started to swim to shore. As the Karankawas continued their attack, he felt the glancing blow of a few more. By the time he made it to the opposite side of the river and crawled out, he had been bloodied by seven arrows. He looked back toward his two companions. They were dead.[10]

After the battle on the river, John emerged in the lore as an Indian fighter of considerable proportions. Children whispered stories at night about him and the Old Three Hundred—the name given to the first three hundred families to settle in Austin's colony—and how they had fought Indians with bravery and resolve. In one story, handed down for generations, Karankawas raided the camp of John's neighbor Robert Kuykendall, killing a calf. About a dozen men, including John, formed a posse to follow their trail, spotting them on the west bank of the Colorado. The settlers plunged into the water with their horses, fending off arrows. When the posse emerged on the other side, their guns ready, the Indians fled into the woods. John and his traveling companion, Alexander Jackson, dismounted. As they did, an arrow flew from nowhere and struck Jackson in the arm. John spotted the shooter in the canebrake, raised his gun to his shoulder, and shot him dead. In a testament to his stature, his powder horn, tattered and worn, remains on display in the Wharton County Historical Museum.[11]

The Colorado River had a profound influence on John's life. The scene of his early encounter with the Karankawas, it also provided him access to the land he would eventually call his own. It was muddy and wide and gave off the appearance of a current much slower than it actually was. During strong rains it flooded surrounding areas, destroying vegetation and catching unsuspecting animals too slow to scamper to higher ground. But the many floods also deposited rich minerals into the ground, creating an alluvial soil ideal for growing crops. John had all of this in mind when he paddled up the river forty-five miles into the area that became Wharton County. By this time, Austin had confirmed his contract with Mexico and offered settlers a deal not found anywhere in the United States. For 12½ cents an acre, persons engaged in farming were entitled to at least one labor of land (about 177 acres), and those engaged in ranching were entitled to at least one *sitio* (about 4,428 acres). Though he had little to his name, John planned to make the most of his opportunity. He called himself a stock raiser and received a *sitio*—over 3½ square miles—of some of the most productive land he had ever known.[12]

John staked out the four corners of his property, carving his initials in trees and building mounds in the prairie to mark the boundaries. In the presence of government officials and assisting witnesses, he then "shouted, pulled grasses, threw stones, planted stakes and performed the other necessary ceremonies" to claim the land as his own. The east bank of the Colorado was the western boundary of his rectangular plot. Closer to the eastern boundary, Peach Creek flowed roughly parallel to the river. Laurels, with their distinctive leaves tasting like the kernel of a peach stone, grew near the creek and probably contributed to its name. A few miles downriver, John's closest neighbors

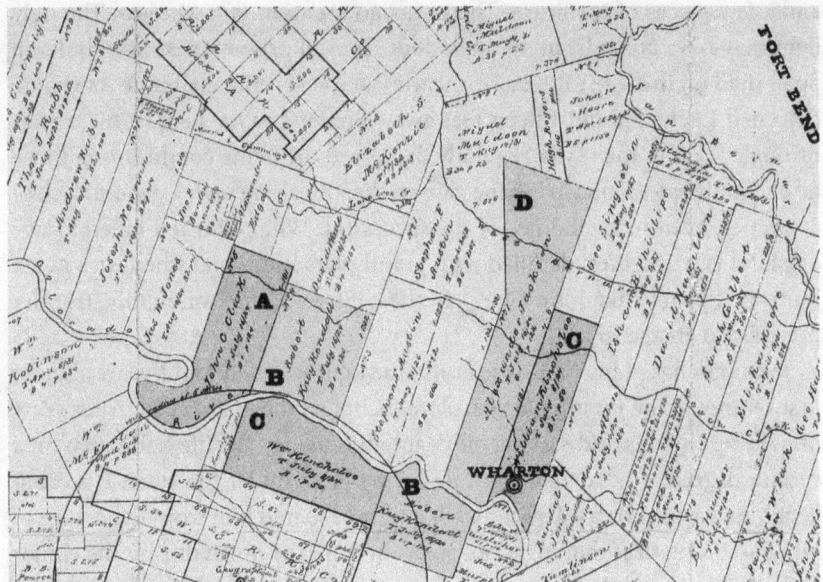

Wharton County. Landholdings: A. John C. Clark; B. Robert Kuykendall;
C. William Kincheloe; D. Alexander Jackson.
Texas Map Collection, di_03584, the Dolph Briscoe Center for American History,
the University of Texas at Austin

William Kincheloe and Robert Kuykendall laid claim to their own *sitios*, and Alexander Jackson was farther south. It was an isolated existence, to be sure, but the distance provided John with the independence he craved. Out here, his survival depended on his own skills and worth. He shot fat turkeys and roasted them on open fires. He used the skin from deer to make pants and shirts and blankets. He slashed and burned the underbrush and then poked holes in the ground with a sharpened stick to plant his first crop of corn. And, always, he kept a watchful eye on the river and the creek, learning their ebbs and flows and drawing on them for sustenance and life.[13]

A Slave Country

A true pioneer, John never desired to replicate the Old South, with its manor homes and landscaped estates, in his new home. Reason Byrne, who first knew John in 1835 and later passed by just before his death, recalled that John, even after he amassed a fortune, lived in a "very common log cabin," measuring about eighteen by twenty feet. It consisted of one room, with a plank floor and a few pieces of furniture. There was no mention of a window. The only light may have come from an open door. Typical of the times, John built an open shed on the side to store necessaries, and he eventually made a separate detached kitchen about fifteen feet away. Frederick Olmsted, in his travels through Texas in the 1850s, regularly dismissed the living conditions of those he encountered, emphasizing the gaps in the logs along with a general lack of amenities, even in the homes of the successful. What Olmsted failed to understand is that a lifestyle filled with grand plantations and fine tastes never motivated people like John Clark. To the contrary, John came to the frontier precisely to escape it.[14]

John purchased his first slave around 1830. It was only eight years after he first set foot at the mouth of the Colorado, but a lot had changed. After years of fighting Indians and staving off death and disease, his life had taken on a certain degree of normalcy. John no longer slept under the stars. His cabin kept him warm and dry. Its four walls and roof spared him from the deluge of rain and biting sleet that invariably blew in from the north during the winter and spring. John had also cleared a few acres of land over the previous years, and cornstalks grew tall in the summer and fall. Long ago he had traded some corn for a plow horse, easing some of the burden of turning the soil and hauling logs for fence rails. A few cows provided milk and butter. Hogs supplied meat. Bees supplied honey.[15]

Yet John's dream remained unfulfilled. As he stood in the shadow of his cabin and looked to the west, past the hog pens and cornfields, most of his land still looked the same as when he arrived. Eight years ago the wild grass waving in the wind opened John's eyes to possibilities. Now it reminded him of work to be done. Around him others were building up and tearing down. His neighbor William Kincheloe arrived with family members and two slaves, giving him several times the physical resources at John's disposal. When you add William's daughters to cook and help with chores around the house, the disparities became even more pronounced. There was no sense in trying to clear more land if it meant that existing crops would go unattended.[16]

John's opportunity to change his fortune came when a contingent of settlers from Alabama rolled into the colony in 1830. John offered to sell the western half of his *sitio*—the portion across Peach Creek, bordering the Colorado River—to William J. E. Heard, a man of considerable standing who would go on to prominence in the county. John drove a hard bargain. Those who knew him later in life referred to him as a "miserly" man. But "shrewd" is probably a more apt term. He had paid 12½ cents an acre for his land in 1824. Six years later, he sold it to Heard for eight times that amount, at one dollar an acre. Heard was no doubt pleased with his purchase. He paid $2,222 for 2,222 acres of rich and productive land, a price that was practically unheard of in Alabama. But John was the one who came out ahead. He kept the other half of his *sitio* for himself, and with over $2,000 in his pocket, his future looked bright.[17]

If John had misgivings about his decision to become a slaveholder, or suffered moral qualms about one person owning another, the record does not disclose it. To the contrary, like his neighbors, he probably looked on slavery as both natural and necessary. To be sure, slavery was not without controversy during this time, especially in Texas. Ever since the start of the colony, Mexico had made clear it disapproved of the institution. Mexico's position had come as somewhat of a surprise at first. Slavery had not been an issue when Austin's father negotiated his contract with Spain, but when Stephen ventured down to Mexico City to shore up his *empresario* (land agent) contract in the summer of 1822 he found himself fighting for slavery's survival. Mexican officials lashed out at the institution with the same vigor as some of the American revolutionaries, citing their own efforts to throw off the bonds of oppression when they declared independence from Spain. Austin therefore considered it a success when he helped negotiate the passage of the Imperial Colonization Law of 1823. The law prohibited the purchase and sale of slaves in the empire and mandated that all children born of slaves be free at age fourteen. But it also allowed current slaveholders to keep the slaves they had and allowed new immigrants to bring theirs with them.[18]

People like John's neighbor William Kincheloe undoubtedly greeted the law with relief. Their dreams of prosperity had always depended on slave labor. "We the Inhabitants of the lower part of the Brazos," a group of them wrote in 1824, "are unanously [sic] in favor of Slavery." Such strong support for the institution is hardly surprising. After all, while a few settlers may have harbored some doubts, most of Austin's colonists were southerners, and as such had come to see slavery as the best of all conditions. "The domestic Slavery of these States," the proslavery theorist James Henry Hammond once beamed, was "not only an inexorable necessity for the present, but a moral and humane institution, productive of the greatest political and social advantages." Not to be outdone, Texans carried their defense to extremes. "The people of the South, by birth, education, and habit, believe that [slavery] is right in every light in which it can be contemplated," insisted a fiery contributor to the *Marshall, Texas Republican*.[19]

For his part, Austin had been encouraging settlers to bring their slaves from the first days of the colony. In his mind the best way for the enterprise to succeed was to have extra hands to clear lands and build homes. He pointedly recruited slaveholders, promising additional land to anyone who brought slaves to the colony. People like Jared Groce, an Old South grandee with a thirst for adventure, joined the first group of settlers, crossing the Brazos in January 1822 with wagons full of furniture, spinning wheels, looms, and provisions. Trailing behind the train of white covered wagons were almost a hundred black slaves. Austin celebrated Groce's arrival by granting him an enormous amount of land—ten *sitios*—"on account of the property he has brought with him."[20]

Given the indeterminacy of history, it would be a mistake to assume that slavery in Texas was inevitable. But the avid determination of political leaders like Austin and the grassroots support of the majority of the colonists made it extremely likely. "It is in my opinion a matter of the greatest importance," Austin declared in 1825, after the Mexican legislature issued a decree prohibiting the slave trade, "to authorize the emigrants to bring in their Slaves and Servants; and that the right of property in these servants so introduced, as well as their descendants, be guaranteed to them by law." Austin was operating against a backdrop of a rising population, one that by 1826 had reached 1,800 total citizens, of which 443 (or one-quarter) were slaves. Austin understood that any risk to the rights of slave owners risked the enterprise itself. Texas could not survive if it became, in Austin's words, the place of "shepherds, or poor people," men who lacked (in his view) the fortitude and strong moral character of the slaveholding population.[21]

Austin's political guile as well as the determination of slavery's supporters became apparent in 1827 after Mexican leaders in the newly formed state of Coahuila and Texas sought to eliminate the institution gradually, first by the constitution and later by decree, by freeing at birth all children born to slaves and by prohibiting further importation of slaves into the colony. Rather than accept the notion that Texas would be a free country, Austin and others focused their efforts on keeping slavery alive. Patterning their talk around the system of Mexican peonage, they took to calling their slaves "indentured servants" and then bound the slaves and any children they had to a lifetime of service in exchange for their "freedom." The subterfuge, sufficient to satisfy the Mexican government several thousand miles away, fooled few others. "By the laws," one traveler to the area observed, "slavery is not allowed in the province; but this law is evaded by binding the negroes by indenture for a term of years. You will, therefore, find negro servants, more or less all over the country."[22]

Still, the institution's uncertain legal status unnerved a growing number of colonists. Most simply could not fathom a life that deprived them of a form of property that was not just legal but strongly encouraged in every state in the South. Mexico's position, no matter how inconsistently pursued, frustrated the plans of those already here and deterred others from coming. In 1830, tensions were again on the rise after the legislature signaled it was moving toward more restrictions. "The federal government and the government of each state," the legislature declared, "shall most strictly enforce the colonization laws and prevent the further introduction of slaves." Some colonists predictably ignored the edict, dismissing it along with other restrictions as, said one, the "puerilities" of a distant government. But for others it only contributed to the sense that conflict was inevitable. Talk of independence, earlier tapped down by political leaders, began to emerge in conversations throughout the region. Slavery was by no means the only grievance colonists lodged against the central government, but it helped solidify in the minds of many that Mexican rule had become intolerable. If it came to war, Texans would speak with a uniform voice. "*Texas must be* a slave country," Austin declared in 1835, shortly before the first shots in the Battle for Independence rang out. It is "no longer a matter of doubt."[23]

Sold

The slave market, with its holding pens and auctioneers, did not exist in Texas at the time John Clark decided to become a slaveholder. Frontier life and Mexican opposition meant that slave sales were handled more informally. Often a deal would take place between neighbors or at a sheriff's sale on the steps of a makeshift courthouse, with buyers squeezing the arms or hefting the breasts of their subjects before offering a price. Despite bans on the international slave trade during this time, a growing number of entrepreneurs made their way in and out of Texas, pulling a dozen or more men and women behind their horses in the hope of an easy sale. Jim Bowie, remembered for his valor at the Alamo, was one of the first to profit from this illegal venture. Just as the first colonists began to trickle in, Bowie and his brothers partnered with the famed pirate Jean Lafitte to sell Africans captured in international waters and smuggled onto Galveston Island. They marched their cargo to New Orleans, turned them over to the U.S. customs for a reward, and then bought them back at bargain prices. They subsequently sold them to new immigrants and made a fortune. A dozen years later, others were capitalizing on a largely unregulated slave trade, providing a steady supply of Africans to the newly arrived. Dilue Harris was a young girl when her father helped the notorious slave trader (and future legislator) Ben Fort Smith, who was lost and nearly starved when he showed up at their homestead in the early 1830s. Smith had with him "a large gang of negroes" that he was trying to sell.[24]

John Clark deserves no credit for rising above the institution. A white acquaintance once called him "humane," but such observations were standard fare among the institution's supporters and are worth very little in determining the type of man he was. A more telling description comes from Pleasant Ballard, one of John's slaves and the eventual husband of his daughter, Lourinda. John was not a very "indulgent" man, he said. The term captures John's disposition in more ways than one. John always appreciated the simple rather than the complex. Throughout his life he kept to himself, and at his death his estate listed the possessions of a man who needed little and wanted less—a few pieces of furniture, dishes, a gun, and a safe. Content with his rustic cabin, he had no brass candelabras or musical instruments, no stacks of the classics or bottles of French wine. Yet, for a man used to making it on his own, at his death he also owned more real and personal property than just about anyone in Texas.[25]

By the time he died, John owned over 8,700 acres of land. The total included his original grant on Peach Creek, which he called his "upper plantation," as well a "lower plantation." It also included thousands of undeveloped acres in various parts of Wharton County, which he evidently used primarily to graze cattle. The agricultural reports provide a glimpse into his success. In 1850 he harvested a total of 2,000 bushels of corn, 1,000 bushels of sweet potatoes, and 100 bales of cotton. In the same year, he owned over 2,000 head of cattle, more than anyone in the county. In 1860, a year before his death, he had better than doubled his production of cotton, producing 225 bales, and added to his production of corn, harvesting 2,500 bushels. He had 500 fewer cattle, but with 1,500 head he remained one of the largest ranchers in the county. During this entire period, he also owned milch cows, horses, mules, oxen, and pigs.[26]

John's holdings were not limited to land and livestock. As might be expected, he also owned human beings, whom he used to run his plantation and tend to his cattle. In 1840 he is listed as the owner of ten slaves. By 1850 he owned thirty-six. The latter number is striking. To provide some context, it is helpful to remember that Texas eventually paralleled other parts of the South in terms of the number of slaveholders and the size of their holdings. In Texas in 1860, a little over a quarter of the free population would own another person, roughly the same percentage as in other southern states. Of these, in both Texas and elsewhere, roughly half would own fewer than five and only 10 percent would own more than twenty. In Wharton the average size of slaveholdings was slightly larger than Texas as a whole, as it remained focused on production agriculture rather than subsistence farming. Even so, with thirty-six human beings, John easily qualified as one of the wealthier planters. The number of people he owned, moreover, would only continue to grow. In 1860, John counted 116 people as part of his holdings. And by his death in 1861, his administrators listed an astonishing 139 people belonging to his estate.[27]

John's rise in the slaveholding ranks defies common understandings of the market economy. For a man who started with so little, he ended up owning more people than 99.8 percent of all slaveholders in Texas. With that much wealth, those unfamiliar with the ways of the frontier puzzled over his decision to live as sparsely as he did. His cabin hardly looked better than the slave cabins down the lane, and his diet consisted of the same salt pork and stale cornbread eaten by those he owned. Frederick Olmsted encountered a planter in East Texas with a similar approach to life, someone who never had an interest in building fine homes or importing fancy silks. Talking with one of the planter's slaves, Olmsted determined that the family, living in a simple log cabin, cleared $3,000 in profits the year before. "What do people living in this style do with so much money?" he asked. "They buy *more negroes* and enlarge their plantations."[28]

The first person John ever purchased was a woman named Clarisa. Clarisa was probably in her fifties at the time—"I was grown and beginning to get grey," she said—and John's decision to buy her rather than, say, a prime field hand fits what his neighbors knew of him. John had no illusions about slaveholding. He did not enter the ranks in order to raise his standing in the community or because he thought it would give him more time for quiet reflection. His sole purpose was to shift the workload so that he could develop more land. With Clarisa, he could slash and burn and turn up new fields while she cooked, mended clothes, and fed the livestock. John's expectations of Clarisa quickly outpaced what she could do, however, and within a short while he purchased a young girl named Hannah to help with chores around the home. Hannah did not live long. The reason is not known, for the same reason that no other details of her life are known. She was a slave, a black child, and this was the frontier. No one bothered to write an obituary or mark her grave. Later generations know about her only because Clarisa remembered her over forty years later when she testified in the suit over John's estate. Clarisa was in her nineties by this time, but her memory was sharp. As his longtime house servant, she possessed an intimate knowledge of the details of John's habits and his comings and goings, as well as a general appreciation of life of Peach Creek. "Aunt" Clarisa's eyes and ears had seen and heard all.[29]

Clarisa remembered when John brought home Sobrina, his third purchase. She was a "dark mulatto" in her late twenties and already the mother of four children. It was in the early 1830s, maybe as early as 1831—no one could remember exactly, except to say that it was still while Texas was under Mexican rule. John purchased her from Preston Gilbert, who lived north of John on the Colorado and who was a member of the Old Three Hundred. Sobrina added an important piece to John's plans. She gave him the extra hand he needed around the home, and as a strong and healthy woman she also could be expected to work in the fields. But Sobrina also provided something that, because of their respective ages, neither Clarisa nor Hannah could. She provided John with sexual companionship.[30]

No one who spends much time studying the antebellum period can fail to appreciate the amount of sexual exploitation that took place throughout the South. Harriet Jacobs has penned perhaps the best-known account of what men can do, detailing in frank prose the depths of her owner's depravity and the lengths she took to escape him. But equally sobering accounts can be found in countless other sources, including from women and families who suffered through their own experiences in the Lone Star State. Betty Powers spoke many years later about how the "overseer and white mens took 'vantage of de women like dey wants to. De woman better not make no fuss 'bout sich. If she do, it am de whippin' for her." Elvira Boles said, "Iffen dey had a pretty girl dey would take 'em, and I'se one of 'em, and my oldest child, he boy by Boles, almost white." Rosa Maddox's remarks reflect why some scholars have concluded that every encounter between a white man and a black woman amounted to rape: she lacked the legal and practical power to refuse consent. "I can tell you," Rosa said, "that a white man laid a nigger gal whenever he wanted her."[31]

When John first brought Sobrina home, there is no reason to think that he was immune from the ideological justifications that allowed for white men to reduce black women to sexual property. As Clarisa explained it, "after Clark came home he put Sobrina in the house and stated he wanted her for his own woman." Everyone knew that John was a solitary man, and with the possibilities of a finding an eligible white woman in this remote frontier forever small, John turned to Sobrina. He even went so far as to warn neighboring male slaves to stay away from her. "Clark told me when he got Sobrina that she was his wife—and we boys must keep out of the way," Sharp Jackson recalled. She was pregnant within the year.[32]

Gray Franks

In 1861, ten years before the children's case came to trial, Wharton County ranked among the wealthiest and most productive counties in the state. John Clark, William J. E. Heard, and William Kincheloe helped lead the way, capitalizing on the rich soil and long growing season to produce significant amounts of cotton, sugar, corn, and beef. At the time, Wharton County was overwhelmingly rural, and most of the residents were African American. The 1860 census listed 646 whites and 2,734 blacks, all of whom were slaves. By 1870 the disparities between the races had only grown, with the number of blacks increasing to 2,910 and the number of whites falling to 514. As the county oriented around freedom, moreover, the tensions between whites and blacks were high. Records from the Freedmen's Bureau provide a glimpse of the violence. F. Gray Franks, who was the sheriff after the Civil War and later represented the children, reported in 1868 on "one of the most brutal murders ever perpetrated in Texas." Jim Jackson, "a freed boy," was tending to the horses of Alexander Jackson—John Clark's traveling companion from many years ago—when John Copeland rode up and, "without the least provocation of [sic] earth, shot him dead." After an hour, Copeland returned and "put a rope around his person, dragged him to a hole of water, mutilated him in a manner of which decency forbids further description, and then threw the body in." Franks held an inquest, but he was unable to capture the murderer.[33]

We need not speculate long on what motivated Copeland. Since the Civil War, for those who shared his sensibilities, it felt as if "a blight . . . seemed to rest upon" the region. Some former slaves, no longer interested in toiling for their former oppressors, left without so much as a by-your-leave, resulting in "one half the land formerly cultivated" lying fallow, to say nothing of the resentment. "Most of the labor is still performed by negroes," the *Texas Almanac* reported in the year of the trial, "though the farmers have great difficulty in getting them to work." Those who stayed made, in the minds of many whites, outrageous demands on the social order, insisting not just on fair wages but on educational and political opportunities. Many whites did what they could to maintain the status quo, but an aggressive U.S. Congress and successive droughts made it difficult. They hoped for a brighter future that returned them to the past.[34]

Gray Franks, the lawyer who represented the children, had been a resident of Wharton since the 1850s, when he arrived as a teenager with his family. Franks's father was not of the economic stature of John Clark, yet he did own land and nineteen slaves at the start of the Civil War. For someone like Copeland, Franks was hard to comprehend. He came from good stock. He was a southerner by birth. But by the end of the war he seemed more interested in incorporating the newly freed slaves into the fabric of Wharton than in keeping them in their place. People like Copeland took to calling Franks a radical and a "carpetbagger," labels that Franks would embrace with zest. He spoke at political rallies and aligned himself with the party of Lincoln. He supported Edmund J. Davis for governor over his Democratic rival, Andrew Jackson Hamilton, in the November election in 1869, and he also successfully ran for the Texas House of Representatives in the same cycle. Two years later he was elected to the Texas Senate, no doubt with the help of the African American community.[35]

By the standards of the time, Franks was a radical. He complained that others like him "were abused and cursed, called all sorts of names which decency forbids mentioning, simply because we were not rebels as they were, and were in favor of giving the colored people their rights." One of his first votes in the Texas legislature was to ratify the Fifteenth Amendment, prohibiting race discrimination in voting. Local whites were rankled by this and other positions. At a particularly tense time in the lead up to the 1870 election, an armed mob showed up at his home and demanded he account for his actions. He slipped out the back and holed up in the woods with two other local Republican officials, returning only after things settled down.[36]

Franks's decision to take the Clark case undoubtedly contributed to the general feeling that he had betrayed the community's values. The children approached him in September 1870, nine months after their mother, Sobrina, had died. Resentful that what they believed was theirs was still in the hands of others, they tried to impress on him that they had a winning case. Franks may have been skeptical at first, convinced, as were so many, that it "would not have done for any person to have introduced a black woman as his wife." But Franks was not naive. He knew that whites and blacks had been living together for two centuries, and he had enough sense to know that some of his fellow Texans had established strong bonds of affection with women of color. There were people like David and Sophia Towns from Nacogdoches, in East Texas. David was white and Sophia was a free woman of color, and they lived openly together as husband and wife with nine children. Closer to home, in neighboring Fort Bend County, A. H. Foster lived with a woman named Leah. He freed her and their children in Ohio and then moved the family to Texas, where they lived together "as man and wife." Downriver in Brazoria County, John Smelser lived with his former slave, a "nearly white" woman named Mary Ann Fraulis. They were visible enough with their affections that local officials decided to interfere, charging them with fornication. A jury convicted them, but the Texas Supreme Court reversed, on the curious ground that the couple "lived together in the same house, but occupied different rooms."[37]

Intimate relationships of the type described above were not supposed to happen in a world built on rigid rules of race. Texans had wasted little time in banning them. Right after they freed themselves from Mexican oppression, in 1837, they made it against the law for whites and blacks to marry, treating the act as a misdemeanor and declaring the marriage null and void. After they achieved statehood, in 1858, Texans increased the penalty to imprisonment of between two and five years. At the same time, Texans made clear that interracial sex would not be tolerated. Whites and blacks who were sexually intimate faced a fine of up to $1,000. But to declare intimacy illegal is one thing; to prevent it from happening is quite another. Simply put, while the law might be successful in regulating conduct, it is woefully inadequate in regulating emotion. As far back as the 1600s, as Edmund Morgan notes, blacks and whites sometimes found companionship, despite differences. "It was common, for example, for servants and slaves to run away together, steal hogs together, get drunk together. It was not uncommon," he adds, "for them to make love together." Franks, the radical Republican with ties to the black community, understood this as well as anyone. He met with the children again and asked them how they expected to pay for his services—they were landless sharecroppers in Wharton and Fort Bend Counties. With their firm promises that he would receive a fair share of whatever they recovered, and his growing confidence about the case, he walked into the courthouse in March 1871 to file their petition.[38]

Reminiscences of the Runaway Scrape

It is unlikely that John and Sobrina's middle child, Nancy, remembered the Runaway Scrape of March 1836. Even though she was "pretty large running around a chair," she was still only a "suckling child" of one or two years old. John and Sobrina's first child, Lourinda, had a better chance. She was a little older than her sister, already "about three feet high" at the time. At four or maybe five years old, she could sense the fear in her father and mother as they packed up their belongings into a wagon and fled east, with Clarisa, in the face of General Santa Anna's advancing army. Too young to understand why they were fighting the Mexicans, she was old enough to appreciate that their lives were in danger. She saw the clogged roads and discarded possessions and understood that tensions were high. The small entourage headed first to

Washington-on-the-Brazos, where men of importance were gathering to draft a declaration of independence and a new constitution. It was a town of only a few dozen buildings, feeling more like a settlement, but hundreds waited there to be ferried across the Brazos River, a chaotic scene repeated several days later once they reached the Trinity River. There, they stopped near the banks and made camp with a few other residents from Wharton, anxiously awaiting news of impending battles. Lourinda clung to her mother's skirt while her father talked in the distance with other men. James Montgomery, a black man from a neighboring plantation who was camped nearby, shared in a hushed voice what he had overheard.[39]

Once the news spread at the end of April that the Texas army had defeated Santa Anna at the Battle of San Jacinto, the camp turned into a festive place. Men talked about the spirit and courage of their fellow countrymen and remembered the Alamo dead, each embellishing the story until everyone fell a hero. Sobrina likely greeted the news with as much as relief as the men in the camp, knowing that her children were now out of danger. In the midst of the handshakes and whoops and hollers, however, a few people of color might have grasped the significance of the victory, knowing that, for them, the short-term securities were about to give way to a permanent loss of freedoms. A draft of the new constitution, which delegates at Washington-on-the-Brazos had just completed, formalized what Austin and others had fought so hard to preserve. Section 9 declared that all persons of color who were previously held as slaves were now formally slaves for life, and that the legislature could not force any slaveholder to free his slaves nor pass any law prohibiting immigrants from bringing their slaves into the republic. Texas was officially a slave country.[40]

The journey back to Peach Creek took almost as long as the flight out. The difference was in the faces of those they met. Gone were the looks of panic, the anxiety of waiting for hours if not days at the river crossings. People conversed once again not just about the present but also about the future, about what life under the Republic of Texas might look like. For all the heady talk, however, John was pleased to get back to his cabin on Peach Creek. John never had much interest in politics or the mechanics of government. He never parlayed his wealth into a political office or used his standing to give influential speeches. His focus was always on his land, and after a decade of working it, of clearing acres and tilling the soil, he understood its potential. Others considered him uneducated, ignorant even. Picking his teeth with his Bowie knife, John did not care. He knew what he had, and he planned to make the most of it.[41]

In the evenings, when he returned from the fields, John retired to his small cabin to take his meals with Sobrina. By this time they were also sleeping in the same bed. "Mr. Clark eat [sic] with her[,] slept with her and drank with her," Clarisa testified when Franks asked her about the relationship. Shortly after their return from the Runaway Scrape, Sobrina became pregnant with John's third child, a boy she named Bishop. Her pregnancy left John with some decisions. In addition to the bed he shared with Sobrina, the cabin had another bed where the girls slept with Clarisa. But a successful harvest left John contemplating how to grow his plantation, and he knew that he would have to build another cabin to house more hands. He considered what his neighbors might think if they discovered Sobrina and the children living with him rather than in a cabin with the other slaves. But in typical fashion he put those concerns aside. The chances of them visiting were rare, and he could always concoct some story to explain away their questions. Along with a new cabin, in his own cabin he started construction on either a loft or a separate room to afford some semblance of privacy in the otherwise open room.[42]

The Trial

In Wharton the air can be heavy in December. Although the temperature drops, the Gulf winds continue to blow moisture through the cracks in the buildings. The courthouse, like everything else, takes on a musty smell that ebbs and flows but never leaves. In 1871, when the children's case was called for trial, residents were familiar with the smell of humidity, perhaps even comfortable with it, providing for some a constant in a sea of change.

The Wharton County courthouse dated back to the 1850s. It was made of brick, forty feet square, with two stories. It was surrounded by a fence, which enslaved men and women of prominent citizens, hired out for the season, made by driving a hundred mulberry posts into the ground every eight feet. They then connected the posts with heart-pine planks. There was a fireplace in every room, and the court clerk promised to keep a fire going to cut the chill out of the December air. He also agreed to leave the doors open. The open doors would accommodate the larger-than-usual crowds, allowing those in the hall to hear what was going on even if they could not see it. They, in turn, could pass on tidbits of information to people camped in the square.[43]

From the outset, Gray Franks had an uphill battle. His unenviable task was to convince twelve men on the jury and a town full of onlookers that life on Peach Creek was not like it was supposed to be. He had to prove that John Clark never cared much for the conventions that bound other men, and that life on the river bottoms was fluid, organized around a frontier mentality where the only rules that mattered were the ones that helped a person survive.

Franks's first witness was "Aunt" Clarisa. "John Clark told me at the time he got her he had taken Sobrina for a wife and he would forsake all others for her," she announced early in her testimony. "Sobrina was after that the mistress of the plantation and I had to wait on her the same as if she was white."[44]

Franks had on his list nine witnesses for his case in chief, and three more ready for rebuttal. All but three were African Americans who had lived on or near John's plantation, either as his slaves or as the slaves of one of his neighbors. Clarisa's testimony revealed immediately Franks's strategy. He intended to focus on the humdrum of everyday life, dismissing the sweeping ideologies of the proper roles for whites and blacks in favor of personal knowledge and powerful anecdotes.

Where did John and Sobrina live? Franks asked Clarisa.[45]

"Sobrina and Clark lived in the same place until they died," she responded.

Where was that?

"They lived in the bottom in Wharton [County]."

What was their living arrangement, if you know?

"They used the same bed, the same table and everything as man and wife," Clarisa continued.

What makes you so certain?

"I carried the water and lights in to them and waited on him and Sobrina all the time."

You keep calling Sobrina his "wife." Who thought that?

"It was known by all on the plantation that Sobrina was his wife and it was known throughout the neighborhood."

How do you know? Did a priest ever officiate a wedding?

No. "There were very few priests in the country at that time."

Then how do you know?

"I have heard John C. Clark call Sobrina his wife, and have heard him tell her she was to do nothing but superintend and see things were right."[46]

Through Clarisa, Franks was beginning to lay the foundation for a common-law marriage. Since there was no official record of John marrying Sobrina, the only way to prove that they were husband and wife was to demonstrate that they held themselves out for a sufficient amount of time as a married couple. No priest officiated the wedding because there were no priests. But Clarisa knew about their relationship, and so did the others Franks planned to call.

John "always made much of her," Clarisa said. "Sobrina was always with him."

John's children with Sobrina were another key element of proof. A man who cared for his children lent further support to the notion that this was a family, with a father and mother who were husband and wife.

"I know they were Clark's children from the fact that they slept in the same room," Clarisa said.

Describe their appearance, if you could, Franks instructed.

"The children look like John Clark. The elder one is exactly like him," she said.

Could you describe how John treated the children?

"He always made a difference between his children and the colored children & slaves on the place."

You said he "made a difference." What do you mean?

He made "as much difference as there is between witness and counsel," Clarisa said, relieving some of the tension with a moment of levity. Laughter bubbled up in the courtroom, as an old black woman seemed to put a young white man in his place. Once the room was quieted by the sound of a gavel, Clarisa continued. "[I] have heard John C. Clark call the children his. I have seen [him] take the children up at the table and feed them the same as any person does their children and treat them in like manner."[47]

Clarisa's description of John's relationship with his children was not the type of testimony that people were used to hearing when it came to masters and their mixed-race offspring. Former slaves provided some of the most damning evidence. Owners and drivers "takes all de nigger gals dey wants," James Green, a former Texas slave, recalled many years later. The children were "brown and I seed one clear white one, but dey slave jus' de same." In light of such observations, and with former slaves in the audience all too familiar with the fate of mixed-race children, the portrayal of John's relationship with his children as more like a family than a typical master-slave arrangement became all that more important.[48]

What did the children call him? Franks asked James Montgomery, as he pursued the line of inquiry with other witnesses.

James had camped with the Clarks during the Runaway Scrape and had seen a lot of the family in the ensuing thirty years. His children called him "pappa," he said.[49]

Not "master" or "Mr. Clark"? he asked David Prophet, another witness.

David was responsible for getting up early on cold mornings and building a fire in John's cabin, and as such "had frequent occasion to see how they lived." No, David said, shaking his head. They called him "pappy."[50]

With each witness, the narrative that life on Peach Creek did not fit the mold of the typical slave plantation became more plausible. To be sure, there were cotton gins and slave cabins, acres of crops and assigned roles. But in the vast spaces, where there were rarely any white people around, the boundaries that Texans liked to draw between white and black seemed hazy at best.

When the children were young did you ever have occasion to see how John treated them? Franks asked Sharp Jackson.

Sharp had belonged to John's traveling companion, Alexander Jackson, when they boarded the schooner in New Orleans and first came to Texas in 1822. "I [saw] J. C. Clark nursing and petting the children," he said.[51]

Franks posed the same question to Albert Horton, who had lived on John's plantation since the Runaway Scrape.

"[I] have seen Clark take his meals with Sobrina & children a many time," he said. When Bishop was young, he added, "[he] was always in Mr. Clark's company & often in his lap." He called him "papa."[52]

Albert's testimony, like the testimony of the other black witnesses, added credibility to a theory that depended on personal knowledge. These individuals saw and heard what the white witnesses did not. They spoke from first-hand knowledge about life on a remote and isolated plantation, unconcerned about whether it matched people's preconceived notions about how white men and black women should act. The defense, of course, hoped that whites in the audience would reject the testimony. White Texans had long dismissed what black people said, convinced that they would lie just as quick as they would steal. Like others in the South, white Texans codified their beliefs into the rules of evidence in the years before the Civil War, prohibiting blacks from ever testifying when a white person was a party in a case. But the Civil War was over, and Aunt Clarisa, James Montgomery, David Prophet, Sharp Jackson, and Albert Horton all stood confidently in court to signal a new beginning, swearing under oath that what they said was true.[53]

Franks pressed Albert for more details about the children. "They were all treated different from slaves," he said. Asked for an example, Albert talked about how Pleasant Ballard, one of John's slaves, expressed an interest in John's daughter, Lourinda.

What did John do? Franks asked him.

"Mr. Clark objected because he was a negro & he wanted her to marry a gentleman."[54]

It was an intriguing opening, and Franks was determined to exploit it. He asked several witnesses about it, and they remembered how John refused to let them marry, as "he wanted no negro to marry his daughter."[55]

Franks followed up with Pleasant.

The "hands did not visit Lourinda & Nancy only by chance. Clark did not allow it," Pleasant confirmed.

Let's talk about your relationship with Lourinda, Franks said. What did John say, if anything, when he learned you wanted to marry his daughter?

He said "that he wanted her to marry a white man."

A white man? Franks asked, feigning incredulity to draw further attention to the answer. What was your response?

"I told him I was as good as Lourinda was."

What did John do next? Franks inquired.

"He got his gun to shoot me and I ran away."

After that?

"Mr. Clark sent me down to the lower plantation ten miles below Wharton . . . and I stayed down there about three years and a half as well as I can judge."

Did John ever change his mind? Did you ever take Lourinda's hand in marriage?

No he didn't. "[I] married her [after] Clark's death."[56]

This theme of race—that John treated his family as if they were "white"— was significant. "Nancy and Lourinda fared just like white girls," James Montgomery said. David Prophet used similar language. He said that John "made as much of [his children] as if they had been from a white woman." The message confirmed what Clarisa indicated at the outset. John's relationship with Sobrina and the children was different from his relationship with other hands. "Bishop was not compelled to work," David Prophet said, in coded language for the use of the whip. "He attended the stock." Pleasant Ballard agreed. No one was idle on a plantation. He had "seen Bishop plow and drive stock," but he had also "seen Mr. Clark work too." More telling, Pleasant had "seen Clark take [a] hoe away from Bishop and make another negro take his place." Asked for another example, Dan Owens passed along a story where John flew into a rage when someone hit Bishop. "He said God damn the man or boy that struck Bishop. When they strike him they strike my blood and if they set foot on my place I will blow a light hole through him."[57]

The Children's Case: Husband and Wife

Wealth cannot change the weather. Life along the river bottoms was difficult, no matter one's economic standing or social position. Northers blew in during the winter, and the temperature topped a hundred degrees for days on end during the summer. Many fell victim to yellow fever, malaria, various intestinal diseases, pneumonia, and rheumatism. Cholera and other diseases were known to decimate plantations, including eight on Charles Bolton's plantation, near John's, in 1852. When Sobrina took sick, therefore, John had reason for concern. He may have contacted a doctor, but medical care was so primitive that it may not have made much difference. What she needed was some fresh air, away from the stagnant bottoms on Peach Creek.[58]

John made the decision to bring Sobrina to Washington-on-the-Brazos, where they had crossed the river during the Runaway Scrape. The town was days away, but John thought the distance was worth the effort because it was considered one of the healthier places. It was still hot, humid, and muggy. But compared to the bottoms it was a veritable oasis. The town was positioned on the bluff, where gentle breezes helped cool residents even on the hottest days. Nearby, springs provided a freshwater supply, far cleaner than down near the muddy river.[59]

When John decided to make the multiday journey to Washington-on-the-Brazos for Sobrina's health, he brought the girls along. The reason was to provide them with an education. John was hardly a scholar. He knew how to read, but books never interested him much. Still he wanted to give the girls advantages that persons in their position rarely had. Perhaps he enrolled them in Timothy Hall's school. Hall ran an academy for girls in Washington. Over a five-month term, he would teach reading, writing, geography, arithmetic, history, botany, and chemistry. For additional fees, he would also teach the girls French, art, and how to play the piano. At the trial, the witnesses did not expound on the details of the girls' experience, probably because they did not know much about it. They only knew that the family stayed about a year, coming home after one of the girls fell ill.[60]

The time spent in Washington-on-the-Brazos had effects on Sobrina beyond her health. She saw some of the items only a town can provide—a shipment of new goods at Brown & McMiller's general store, or the medicine, "dye-stuff," and perfumeries that lined the shelves at James Ringgold's store. Back at home, she impressed on John a need for small luxuries, and John indulged her requests enough that others noticed. John "dressed her better than he did himself," Clarisa observed. He had "always treated her kindly," and the fright brought on by her illness may have been enough to break ever so slightly John's aversion to anything reminiscent of the old ways. He joked with her, calling her "dear" and his "old woman," and she responded by calling him her "old man."[61]

Stories like these animated Franks's case in chief. He had been laboring to prove something that few back then accepted as true—that a white man and black woman could view themselves as husband and wife. Yet as he closed in on his case in chief, he felt confident that he had made a strong case.

Sobrina gradually took over as "mistress of the plantation," Clarisa testified. She "carried the keys and had management of everything." Abraham Kincheloe, who adopted the surname of John's early neighbor, William Kincheloe, agreed. "Sobrina had charge of his keys & money and everything pertaining to the place," he said. Frontier marriages were hardly romantic affairs. They were, in many respects, marriages of convenience. Two people came to depend on each other for sustenance and care, with distinct roles defined by law, culture, and religion. John worried about cotton prices and how to make the most of his land. Sobrina "gave orders on the place" and kept the household running.[62]

Clarisa insisted that John and Sobrina were "as loving as any other people," as if to say that "love" played neither a larger nor a smaller role here than it did in other spots on the frontier. Like others, they "fell out a little," but they also "talk[ed] together as husband and wife." Olmsted's description of the wives he met in his Texas travels did not stray far from the descriptions of Sobrina. These were not southern belles. They worked as hard as their husbands, milking cows and slaughtering pigs before attending to the household. Sobrina "always took authority just like a white woman," people recollected, in what seemed a fair comparison to other women they knew. Sobrina "attended to everything on the place," Abraham Kincheloe said. She "acted as wives usually do," confirmed Reason Byrne, one of the few white witnesses to testify on behalf of the plaintiffs. Albert Horton remarked that she even had him whipped.[63]

When John approached the final days of his life in the summer of 1861, there were few beyond the plantation who gave it much notice. There was far more on the minds of many. Texas had seceded from the Union, and the Civil War had begun. Sobrina and Lourinda did what they could for him. But John had lived a full life, and they likely could do little beyond propping up a pillow or fetching a glass of water. A decade earlier, Joseph Anderson had asked John why he never married. Joseph was taking the census, and the absence of any other white person on Peach Creek puzzled him. John fumbled for an answer, eventually insisting that no one would ever marry him "but for his property." Others smiled. Even then, "it was known by all on the plantation that Sobrina was his wife," and that "she had no other man and he no other woman."[64]

The State's Case: A Kept Woman

The children's case was not the first lawsuit attempting to get to the bottom of the proper heirs to John's estate. No one can die with that much property and not have persons with a common name or even a casual connection apply for its riches. Mildred Ann Wygall and Richard Clark were the first to file in 1867. They said they were John's sister and brother from Virginia. They claimed their parents brought them and their other two siblings, including John, to Alabama, where they stayed for a few years until all but John, Mildred Ann, and Richard died. John Wygall, from Virginia, then came down to Alabama, married Mildred Ann, and brought her and Richard, who suffered from a "weak mind," back to Virginia. Their brother John, they said, made his way to Texas. (Later allegations had their parents stopping over in South Carolina, where, it was claimed, John was born, to square his birthplace with the record.)[65]

By 1870, Richard had died, and his sister Mildred Ann passed away within the year. Mildred Ann's son and John's reputed nephew, Joseph Wygall, was substituted as the named plaintiff in the action, along with Joseph's brothers and sisters. Over the next few years the case grew in procedural complications, as other individuals, contesting Wygall's claim as well as asserting superior ones, descended on the courthouse, seeking to intervene. The case was initially filed in Wharton County, but it was quickly transferred to Fort Bend County on the motion of the plaintiffs on grounds of "prejudice against all persons claiming to be the heirs of John C. Clark." The plaintiffs, they said, "cannot have a fair and impartial trial." In 1868, however, the case was sent back to Wharton, only to be returned to Fort Bend in 1871. During May of that same year, the state legislature got involved, ordering through a special act that the case be tried in the state capital in Travis County. Local newspapers entertained their readers with updates and comments, with no shortage of jabs at the claimants, including how many of them suddenly took up residence in the state in an effort to establish their bona fides. "It used to be thought that the Smiths and Joneses were the most numerous families," the *Dallas Herald* joked, "but Clarks have in this case indicated their equal claim to number."[66]

Gray Franks, the children's lawyer, had little interest in diluting the children's claim in the muddy waters of the Wygall case. He knew, as did any lawyer, that under the laws of intestacy the possessions of a person dying without a will passed first to his spouse and, if no spouse, then to his children. Anyone else—brothers, sisters, nephews—took nothing. When he filed suit in Wharton County in March 1871, he ignored the other suits and simply asserted the rights of the children, now that Sobrina had passed away. The Wygalls sought to intervene, but the court rejected their motion, presumably on the grounds that the children, if lawful heirs, had priority over everyone and took all. The soundness of the decision was never appealed, but Wygall's lawyer later suggested that it was all part of a diabolical scheme rather than a decision based on the law. He went so far as to suggest Franks orchestrated the entire maneuver based on his legislative connections.[67]

The children's case was not without its own procedural snarls. As the parties readied for trial in August, the State moved for a continuance. The State maintained that, if the facts as alleged in the petition were true, and John and Sobrina were husband and wife, then any property acquired during the marriage passed first to her. If she had any other children—and there was no doubt she did, before John purchased her—they would have to be included as plaintiffs. They had as much right to what was now Sobrina's estate as did Lourinda, Nancy, and Bishop (although the separate property acquired before the marriage was subject to different rules). The legal skirmish provided for a short delay, and the case was rescheduled for December, when Judge William Burkhart circled back on his way through the county.[68]

Those listening to the testimony of Franks's witnesses could hardly have been surprised with their answers. After hearing their descriptions about life on Peach Creek, the conclusion was inevitable.

"Clark and Sobrina lived together as man and wife until their deaths."[69]

"John C. Clark treated Sobrina as a wife and lived together as such all the time I knew them."[70]

"[John] treated her exactly like a man does his wife."[71]

"Clark and Sobrina lived together as man and wife from the time I first knew them."[72]

"[Clark and Sobrina] continued to live together as husband and wife until Clark's death."[73]

It was a radical position to take, the sort of position that slavery's ideologues dismissed as absurd, and one the State would challenge. "Never heard a man acknowledge a negro for a wife," one of its witnesses testified, summing up the State's theory in a single note. The difficulty for the State was that its position was not as crisp as it would have liked. White Texans did not approve, and they passed laws to prevent it, but even the occasional example was enough to disprove the notion that interracial relationships of a meaningful sort could not happen. Up in Burleson County, in the central part of the state, William Oldham tried to keep his thirty-year relationship with Phillis Oldham a secret. But anyone with more than a passing familiarity with the family knew what was going on. "He was never married, but he had a nigger woman, Aunt Phyllis she was called, that he had some children by," one of Oldham's former slaves recalled many years later. "She was half white. I remember her and him and five of their sons." Up in Kaufman County, east of Dallas, residents clucked their tongues over Augustus Catchings's relationship with Sally Catchings, his former slave. When he announced that she was his "lawful wife," neighbors dismissed him as odd, yet the more honest among them knew he was not the only one. Rumors of marriages falling apart because of illicit relationships between white men and black women were not uncommon. And in towns like Austin, residents had grown so outraged at seeing "*white gentlemen* and black ladies trip it on 'the light fantastic toe'" that the editors of the *Austin, Texas State Gazette* felt the need to call out the practice in the pages of the newspaper. "The observer" to these unlicensed balls, the editors solemnly reported, "almost imagines himself in the land of *amalgamation, abolition meetings, and woman's rights conventions*."[74]

Still, the State hammered away at the children's case with a narrative that fit with the expectations of many. Stephen Heard, the son of William Heard, who purchased a portion of John's league in 1830, set the stage early when he drew a distinction between *having* children and *acknowledging* them. He knew, as did many in the neighborhood, that John had fathered children with Sobrina. But he was quick to point out that he "never knew Clark to recognize Bishop Nancy or Lourinda as his children."[75]

The testimony was bolstered by a handful of anecdotes from visitors. R. W. Smith once stayed ten days on Peach Creek, building cisterns for John. A bricklayer grateful for the opportunity to earn a few dollars, Smith had wandered in from elsewhere in the county. He said that Bishop was "under his control" during construction of the cisterns, and that he saw "no difference" in the treatment of either Bishop or his sisters. D. V. Myers agreed. John treated Bishop "as I would my servants," he said.[76]

Relegating the children to the status of slaves was nothing new. In Texas, as in the rest of the South, children followed the condition of their mothers, meaning that slave mothers gave birth only to slave children. To recognize the children as something else suggested more than most were willing to concede. The defense had no intention of allowing that aspect of the petitioner's case to go uncontested. "Never knew of Bishop or Lourinda calling him pa," Nelson Heard testified in response to a question. "Never saw [John] countenance [the girls] as daughters," J. P. Horton confirmed.[77]

The State commissioned two local district attorneys, S. G. Patton and Edward Collier, to represent it in the various suits the alleged heirs brought against John's estate. Collier had been a neighbor of John's beginning in 1853, living within a mile and a half of him until 1858. He then moved to neighboring Colorado County, where he entered into private practice with R. V. Cook. He was elected district attorney for the First Judicial District in 1860. The State undoubtedly reasoned that Collier's close connection to the county and to

John would be an asset. Collier said that he had dined with John on occasion and claimed that, although John kept to himself, he "was very conversational with me."[78]

The problem for Collier and his cocounsel, S. G. Patton, was that none of the State's witnesses claimed to know much about John. For a man who had so much, John hardly knew anyone, and hardly anyone knew him. It seemed that every time the defense tried to establish a witness's credibility to speak about John's personal life, the person confessed to being "not very intimate with him."[79]

"Clark received very little company," Joseph Anderson said. "When a man went there he had to attend to his business & leave instantly."[80]

Stephen Heard, who had lived within a few miles of John for thirty years, agreed. "It was pretty hard for any body to know much about him."[81]

Stephen's brother, Q. M. Heard, was not in the business of casting stones, but he did admit that John was a bit odd. "Clark did not act socially like other neighbors," he said.[82]

Despite their lack of personal knowledge, the defense witnesses refused to believe that John could have cared for Sobrina or that she might have cared for him.

How were they regarded in the community? defense counsel asked Stephen Heard.

"As far as I know they were regarded in the community as master and slave," he replied.

Did you not know they were living together since before the Runaway Scrape? Franks asked on cross, trying to shake him.

"It was generally understood in the neighborhood . . . that Clark was cohabitating [sic] with Sobrina," Stephen conceded. But "it was not understood that Sobrina was Clark's wife."[83]

The same question was posed to the attorney tasked with administering John's estate, Isaac Dennis. He considered it a challenge to his professional judgment. Although he knew about Sobrina and the children, he never assumed for a moment "that they were not slaves." He valued them at a hefty sum, and eventually had them sold.[84]

The witnesses for the defense provided comfort for those shaken by world in which African Americans were suddenly—and openly—defying all they understood and held dear. They knew that masters and their sons had taken black women for their use as often as they liked, or perhaps better stated, as often as they dared. But that did little to dampen the impression that these were dalliances to be tolerated rather than condoned.

How would you describe their relationship, S. G. Patton asked Edward Collier, who, despite his role as attorney, also served as a witness.

John "kept a negro woman Sobrina, as men frequently did in those days," Collier responded. But with a lawyer's understanding of what had to be proven, he was quick to add that "no one ever thought or was it reported that they were married or husband and wife."[85]

What was the general reputation of John Clark in the community? counsel for the State asked H. P. Cayce. Cayce was a familiar face around Wharton. Politically opposed to Gray Franks, like many of the defense witnesses, he was a former slaveholder, counting twelve slaves as part of his household in 1860.

"There was a report that Clark had a woman that he kept but [I] never heard her reported as his wife," he said. "He was always considered an old Bachelor."[86]

Relegating Sobrina to the role of a "kept" woman fit neatly with the views of the former slaveholders and their sympathizers that slaves in general and black women in particular lacked the ability to affect their lives or their surroundings. Indeed, the entire slave system was designed to strip them of all rights and deny them a will of their own. Black women were no more capable of influencing the feelings of a white man than they were in leaving the plantation without a pass or in selling vegetables on the market.

D. V. Myers's response was typical. "Never heard that Clark married Sobrina," he said.[87]

"Public sentiment was against it," Isaac Dennis confirmed.[88]

The Verdict

Gray Franks felt more comfortable about his case the longer the trial dragged on. As a small-time attorney from a small town, he was no match for the resources of the State. But his witnesses spoke with the type of authority that came from personal knowledge and a confidence in the truth of what they said. If neighbors did not witness John's commitment to his family, it was because John remained cautious, even as he withdrew. According to Bishop, he once told him that "people would talk about him if we called or treated him as a father in their presence," and for that reason they usually ate in the detached kitchen and slept elsewhere when others were around. This type of testimony put Edward Collier, for the State, in a difficult position. Despite his insistence that John had enough racial pride to maintain a clear wall between him and the woman he slept with, even he had to admit that "there might have been so far as I know a secret understanding between Clark and Sobrina."[89]

There is no doubt that John's relationship was the talk of the neighborhood. Not everyone knew about it, of course, but for those who did it was a source of consternation. Soon enough, people started to avoid visits to Peach Creek, "on account of him . . . keeping a negro woman." "Men who kept black women were not held in high esteem," Q. M. Heard, for the defense, observed. Clarisa and some of the other slaves turned those statements upside down, insisting that John's decision to have "but little to do with white people" had much to do with how things unfolded since the days of poking holes in the ground to plant corn. As time went by, John simply shared fewer of his neighbors' values, and the few conversations that took place seemed strained. They judged him, dismissing him as eccentric, and refused to "visit him on account of his having a negro wife." He minded less and less. By the end of his days, it was inevitable that he "placed himself on equality & footing with the blacks."[90]

Thirty years is a long time. That is how long John and Sobrina, according to their children, lived together, out on the grassy plains, as far in miles from their neighbors as they were in life. Clark knew "his neighbors did not think anything of him," but the older he got the more he lost interest and did not seem to care. He felt the same about his relatives who, for so long, "had treated him with silent contempt." He told Reason Byrne, who visited just before his death, that "he did not intend they should have any of his estate." He mentioned to Byrne, as well as to several others, that he intended to leave his property to his children. Albert Horton testified that John had even made a will, "and that Virgil Stewart had it & that his property was left to his children."[91]

No will was ever found, however, and few at the time could have guessed that the case would compete with Charles Dickens's story of *Jarndyce v. Jarndyce* for both length and complications because of it. Only a handful of people living off the plantation ever knew John, and even fewer knew of the fortune he had amassed. An obituary of sorts summed up his life two years after his death, highlighting a man who remained a mystery even to his closest neighbors: "He was a man of singular habits. He allowed no white person to stay immediately about him, and seemed to live entirely within and for himself, alone. . . . As his life was a blank, around his dying couch there were few mourners. . . . To live, to die and to be remembered, as John C. Clark lived, died and is remembered is a distinction which none may wish to emulate."[92]

Following his death in 1861, the court assigned Isaac Dennis and James Whitten to administer the estate. Along with over 8,700 acres of land, various personal property, farm equipment, livestock, and human chattel, the administrators listed Sobrina and John's children among his many assets. They were sold in February 1863 at public auction. The event drew "people from all parts of the State, who had come to divide out among themselves, the slaves and other property belonging to Clark's estate." Prices were high, with Bishop valued at $1,000, and his sisters—each assessed with a young child—valued at $1,200. Isaac Dennis overheard bystanders remark "that it was hard that a man's own son should be sold with his property."[93]

The jury assembled to decide, eight years later, if the money and residual estate that belonged to Bishop and his sisters was mostly, if not entirely, African American, reflecting the makeup of Wharton County and the impact of Reconstruction. Henry Fleming, the foreman, was a thirty-five-year-old farm laborer with a story no doubt typical of the other members of the jury. Ten years ago, at the time of John's death, he had been a slave. But now he was exercising the rights of a free man pursuing his own livelihood as well as casting ballots and serving on juries. Within a few years the federal government would abandon Texas, and the old Confederates and their sympathizers would systemically strip African Americans of their civil rights. But for now, in 1871, it felt like an entirely new world.[94]

The question before the jury was simple enough. It was the answer that provoked such a strong reaction. The trial judge instructed the jury on Franks's theory of a common-law marriage:

> In determining whether or not a marriage existed between said Clark and the said Sobrina you will take into consideration the manner in which the parties lived together—whether they cohabitated [sic] together observing chastity one to the other[,] whether they openly and publickly [sic] acknowledged and recognized each other as husband and wife and in their general intercourse treated each other as such[,] whether Sobrina's authority at their place or residence and over his property was such as to reasonably flow from the existence of the marriage[,] whether Clark recognized these Plffs as his children and treated them as such and all other matters and things calculated to establish the true relation of said Clark & Sobrina one to the other.

In a point that would become an issue on appeal, the judge added that Texas's original 1837 ban on interracial marriages would not prevent the jury from finding the existence of a common-law marriage if John and Sobrina began living together as husband and wife before the ban was in place. It took the State by surprise but was not without precedent. In a case decided two decades before, the Texas Supreme Court refused to declare invalid a marriage between a white man and his former slave that took place while Texas was still under Mexican rule. Citing Spanish law, which governed the parties at the time of marriage, the court held that "by marrying his slave he emancipates her." The holding had a curious impact on the case at bar. Not only did it suggest that Sobrina could have been John's wife, but it also meant that she (and her children) would have been free.[95]

Judge William Burkhart, who presided over the trial, was no friend of equality. He grew up in nearby Matagorda County in a home that counted slaves among its possessions. Aware of how things were, he made a point of instructing the jury that if John lived with Sobrina "as a concubine or kept-woman and not as a wife," they must find for the State. But in a move that disappointed defenders of the racial order, he also allowed for the circumstances of slavery in the finding of a common-law marriage. "The open and public acknowledgement and recognition of the marriage relation," he told the jurors, "need not be made at all times and under all circumstances if such recognition would endanger the personal safety of the parties." He added that "if the said Clark and Sobrina acknowledged the existence of the marriage relation as far as was consistent with their personal safety so to do—it is sufficient."[96]

By the time Henry Fleming and the other eleven jurors returned from their deliberations, the courtroom was once again abuzz. Judge Burkhart, known for his "strictness in the discharge of even the most intricate legal duties," called for quiet. He asked Fleming if the jury had reached a verdict. Standing tall, in a proud moment for this former slave, Fleming hitched his thumbs into his pants and replied that they had. None of the members were able to write, so Judge Burkhart asked him to announce it open court. The crowd held its breath. We the jury find, he said, that "John C. Clark and Sobrina were legally married in 1833 or 1834 and lived together as husband and wife until the death of John C. Clark."[97]

The children had just become some of the wealthiest people in Wharton County.

Postscript

Gray Franks, the children's lawyer, was shot to death on the streets of Wharton in the summer of 1874. His death came two and a half years after the jury returned a verdict in favor of his clients, and stood as a testament to the rough-and-tumble atmosphere that still pervaded this rural community. Franks was no innocent victim. Six months before, he had emptied both barrels of his shotgun into the shoulder of Isaac "Newt" Baughman, the sheriff of Wharton. Franks and Baughman had a long history. Both were radical Republicans with similar desires to incorporate the newly freed persons into the social and political economy. After Franks was elected to serve in the legislature, Baughman replaced him as the sheriff of Wharton. Baughman's tenure was spotty, having been accused by some of being corrupt. But in these matters, as was so often in the case during this tumultuous period, perspective tended to shape opinions. "His whole course of life," said one, offering insight into where the parties stood, "was studiously designed to stir up strife and confusion between the whites and blacks of the community."[98]

The dispute between Baughman and Franks had nothing to do with politics. It was far more mundane. Baughman had approached Franks's wife and made inappropriate remarks, either soliciting her to enter into a relationship or implying something about her sexual character. In a time-honored tradition, Franks confronted Baughman in the streets following the incident and shot him. The wound was not fatal, but the ordeal continued to fester in the minds of both men. The former associates could now barely stand each other. Six months later, in June 1874, one of Baughman's former deputies, a man named Lee Lacy, settled the score once and for all. When Franks ordered Lacy out of town, Lacy responded by shooting him dead.[99]

Franks's death had a profound impact on the lives of Lourinda, Nancy, and Bishop. Franks was, as Bishop said, "the only party to whom we looked for any protection in reference to our right in [our father's] Estate." There is a danger in giving too much credit to Franks in the outcome of the case, for surely he was not without fault. But at a time when he risked serious injury or even death by taking a case with such potential to upset the social and economic order, his contributions should not be minimized. Immediately after the jury's decision, the State filed its appeal. In the fast-track world unfamiliar to attorneys today, the Texas Supreme Court added the case to its docket in the same year, in 1872, and briefing took place in the spring. Franks built an appellate team with experienced cocounsel, Alfred B. Peticolas and W. P. Hamblin. The State was represented by William Alexander, its attorney general, and the private firm of Robards & Blackburn.[100]

At the time of the appeal, the Texas Supreme Court, like the state as a whole, was undergoing a major transformation. Following his election as governor in the fall of 1869, Edmund J. Davis, the radical Republican, immediately reconstituted the court to reflect the new order. He appointed three new members under the authority of the new constitution, Lemuel D. Evans as chief justice, and Wesley Ogden and Moses B. Walker as associate justices. A moderate, Chief Justice Evans was relatively uncontroversial. But the other two justices engendered the undying ire of conservative critics of the Davis administration and Congressional Reconstruction. Wesley Ogden was a staunch Republican who hailed from New York. Moses Walker came from Ohio, having served as a colonel in the Union army and moved to Texas in 1868 under the authority of the military. He was disparaged as a carpetbagger by those he ruled against. Among friendly audiences, however, he was considered "a lawyer of ability" and reportedly "possessed some literary talent," a skill too often overlooked in the stilted world of writing briefs and judicial opinions.[101]

Justice Walker wrote the decision in the Clark case. In an opinion that sent reverberations across the entire state, he upheld the jury's finding that Lourinda, Nancy, and Bishop were John's legitimate heirs. Defenders of the old order shook their heads in disbelief and dignified the decision with uncharacteristic silence. For a case that had captured the attention of so many, for an event that had packed the courtroom for days in Wharton, the court's decision simply disappeared into the other news of the day, better to be ignored than to be discussed and highlighted. In its opinion, the court rejected the State's argument that the facts did not support a finding that John and Sobrina treated each other as husband and wife. This part of the opinion should not have come as a surprise to the lawyers representing the State, even though they argued vigorously to overturn the verdict on factual grounds. "Even at this day," the State argued, "when it is hoped the world has grown wiser and better, it would seem a violent presumption to suppose that a man of Anglo-American birth and education would marry a woman of African descent, at that time his slave, his chattel. We may stigmatize this aversion of one race for the other unreasonable, without good sense, mere prejudice, yet all must admit that the fact of this aversion really exists in the minds of most all white men to such an extent that the idea of intermarriage of the races is wholly repulsive, even at this day." But as the attorneys well knew, on appeal, courts are loath to interfere with the factual findings of a jury, simply because juries are in the best position to judge the credibility of witnesses and resolve conflicts in the testimony.[102]

The State was far more disappointed in the court's legal analysis. Getting past the factual question of how John and Sobrina viewed themselves, the court upheld the finding that the marriage was lawful on two separate grounds. The first was that the parties were married before Texas outlawed interracial marriages, reaffirming the idea that what took place under Mexican rule was governed by Spanish law. "No law subsequently passed," it held, "could have divorced them or dissolved the marriage without the consent of at least one of the parties." The second relied on a new provision to the Texas Constitution of 1869 that legitimized all marriages between people who, "by the law of bondage, were precluded from the rights of matrimony." In a ruling that reflected Republican ideals, the court held that the provision applied not just to slaves trying to marry each other but also whites trying to marry blacks. Under either rationale, said the court on April 21, 1873, the facts supported the finding of a marriage, and the law made it legitimate.[103]

The case was sent back to Wharton for final disposition. On August 5, 1873, the district court ordered that the "judgment be in all things observed and enforced." Bishop and his wife Rosetta, Nancy and her husband Joseph Townsend, and Lourinda and her husband Pleasant Ballard shook hands with their lawyer and embraced one another, convinced that their long ordeal was over. In truth, it was only beginning.[104]

~

Gray Franks's death the following summer was by no means the only setback suffered by the children in their effort to become wealthy landowners in Wharton. But it certainly left them without a legal representative interested in acting on their behalf. The complications began two months after Franks died. For reasons that can only be explained by their lack of sophistication, in August 1874, the children entered into an agreement with Tilson Barden, a onetime legal partner of Franks. The agreement stipulated that the children would sell all but a few hundred acres of John's Peach Creek plantation, including most of the upper plantation and all of the lower plantation, totaling 3,296 acres, in exchange for $15,000. It was virtually a steal. Indeed, during the administration of John's estate a decade before, the same property was valued at $146,000. Whether the children understood at the time what they were giving up is unknown. But, as a skilled attorney with access to records, Barden certainly knew. He did his best to convince them that the deal inured to their benefit. Cash in hand, he likely told them, was better than an investment in property.[105]

The family soon came to regret their decision. Later that fall, Jackson Rust, another attorney, approached them in an effort to settle Franks's attorney fees, an amount that, thus far, had gone unpaid. Rust was serving as the administrator of Franks's estate. He greeted the news that Barden had convinced them to sell most of the property for incredibly low prices with a heavy sigh. Not only, he informed them, did Barden cheat them in the deal, but he also cheated Franks out of his fee. Rust quickly drew up some papers to formalize an agreement to make him the family's attorney, simultaneously taking steps to "revoke annul and make void all other powers of attorneys given by [the family] to any one and especially the power of attorney or agreement given to one T C Barden." In a companion document, Rust drafted a deed in which the family conveyed to Franks's estate roughly one-third of the property from John's upper plantation as payment for Franks's services. This arrangement, unlike the one with Barden, was not unfair. A one-third contingency fee was a standard amount to be paid in cases of this sort. The contract left each sibling with several hundred acres.¹⁰⁶

The legal morass created by competing deeds was never formally resolved. Barden registered his deeds and took possession of at least some of the property, giving him rights under a first-to-file and perhaps a first-to-occupy rationale. More importantly, the confusion over who owned what was only heightened in subsequent years, as others tried to bilk the family out of what was left. John Clark's purported relatives were still in the state, and they had no intention of giving up their claims, despite the Texas Supreme Court's decision upholding the verdict declaring John's children to be his legitimate heirs. In 1877, a person named Warren Clark and a host of his relatives instituted an action in Wharton County trying to overturn the judgment, naming Franks's estate as one of the defendants and arguing that the verdict was the result of collusion and fraud. Warren alleged that Franks concocted the entire scheme, drawing on his knowledge of John Clark's past and availing "himself of his extensive acquaintances with the colored people of Wharton County." Warren said that Franks procured the help of Bishop and his sisters, "enticing them into a conspiracy and fraudulent plot, confederating with them that if they would hold themselves out for and claim to be the children and heirs of John C. Clark begotten by him in lawful wedlock upon the body of their mother Sobrina Clark who was a woman of color and the former slave of the said Clark, they would secure all of the Clark estate." A confluence of fortuitous factors perfected the scheme, according to Warren. "The pleadings made by and on behalf of the so-called Treasurer were clumsily and inartistically drawn," Warren alleged, providing evidence that "the cause was for the State not pressed with vigor or spirit." Nor did it help "that the trial was had [*sic*, for "held"] at a time of high political excitement when industrious efforts were being made to poison the minds of the black people and sway them against the whites." Sparing no one, Warren also went after the jury in language that reflected the ideologies of those unable to accept a new order. "The cause was tried," he said, "before a jury of ignorant black people who were totally incompetent for so grave a task."¹⁰⁷

Meanwhile, Joseph Wygall and his relatives (all unrelated to Warren Clark and his family) continued to press their cause in court. Facing the daunting task of explaining why they never appealed the district court's denial of their motion to intervene in 1871, the Wygalls simply chose to ignore it. "[We] were not parties to the suit of Bishop Clark et al," they said, and as such were "not bound by it." Like Warren Clark, the Wygalls also seized on the notion of fraud, unable to comprehend how anyone could find that John and Sobrina were married. They took their allegations even further than Warren, insisting that Franks actually went back into the jury room and handed the jury a pre-written verdict. "They being all negroes and unable to write," the allegation went, the jury could not know what was on the paper. Yet they "handed in the same as their verdict." Adding to the conspiracy, the Wygalls further alleged that "much of the testimony introduced . . . was procured by bribery and was false and untrue," and that the record in front of the supreme court "was not truly copied or made out & the same was false."[108]

With both suits pending in the lower courts, Bishop and his family had rightfully grown concerned. They were suspicious of those who purported to act in their interests, and they were unsure of a legal system that, more and more, seemed uninterested in protecting the rights of people of color. When Warren Clark approached them and asked them to put their mark—their "X"—on a deed surrendering all rights to their land in consideration for his promise to give them one hundred acres apiece if he was ultimately successful in his suit, they knew it was not a fair deal. But under the circumstances they viewed it as their best option. They may have been right. The following year, Joseph Wygall successfully prosecuted his suit in Travis County and received a judgment declaring the Wygalls "the true heirs of John C. Clark, deceased, and entitled to his estate."[109]

The State appealed the *Wygall* decision to the Texas Supreme Court, making it the third time the case had gone up that high. In a decision that should have surprised no one, the court reversed the judgment on the grounds that it was in conflict with its previous decision in *Honey v. Clark*, and that the verdict in the children's case still stood "unreversed and in full force." But the court's tone indicated just how far the ground had shifted since the days when Justice Walker sat on the bench. In an opinion far more sympathetic to the Wygalls than to Bishop and his family, the court credited the allegations of fraud and the accusations that the jury was unable to render a just verdict. "It seems to have been their misfortune that they were not permitted to intervene in that suit," it said about the Wygalls, "and if the facts are true as asserted by them, it is, indeed, a sad commentary upon the history of the times during which that proceeding was pending."[110]

∼

In the last two decades of the nineteenth century, Wharton County remained what it had always been: a small agricultural community, further away in lifestyle and general outlook than it was in miles from the fast-growing city of

Houston. A majority of the residents were African American, and most of them continued to work the land as sharecroppers with little to their name. Whites from the county, though outnumbered, regained control of the engines of government in the same manner that they had throughout the state, and some of the storied families who came long before still owned vast stretches of land.[111]

After the court's 1879 decision in the *Wygall* case, despite the favorable outcome, the lives of Bishop and the others only seemed to worsen. With others claiming the land adverse to the family, either through deed or imagined right, and with the State apparently holding onto other assets while the cases worked their way through the courts, "it is said that a small pittance only ever reached the hands" of the family. Paging through the deed books, one can see the frustration—the desperation—of a family promised a comfortable living only to have it slowly and systematically stripped away from them. Land sold, land seized for failure to pay taxes. As late as 1907, claimants were still inquiring about the case, insisting that they—not the children—were the rightful heirs to the "Texas Millionaire."[112]

Even the Texas Supreme Court's holding in which it broadly recognized the rights of interracial families proved as fleeting as the verdict. After the former Confederates regained control of the governor's office, they also regained control over the judicial system, and they used the opportunity to roll back some of the progressive decisions of the Reconstruction-era court. Their opening to criticize their former colleagues came in a case handed down during the contested election of November 1873 between the conservative Richard Coke and the incumbent Edmund Davis. At issue was the placement of a semicolon in a constitutional provision governing voting. Called on to interpret the provision, the court concluded that it required four days of voting, not just the one that was allowed. The effect of the ruling meant that the election, which Coke had won, was void. Given its political significance, however, those seeking to redeem Texas from the hands of the "black Republicans" used it to their advantage, derisively referring to the case as the Semicolon Decision and the court that decided it as the Semicolon Court. Oran Roberts, who took over as chief justice after Davis conceded, and later served as governor, political historian, and law professor, helped turn generations of lawyers against the court. "So odious has [the decision] been in the estimation of the bar of the State," Roberts intoned, "that no Texas lawyer likes to cite any case from the volumes of the Supreme Court reports which contain the decisions of the court that delivered that opinion, and their cases are, as it were, tabooed by the common consent of the legal profession."[113]

Roberts took to heart his own remarks. He joined a decision in 1874 and wrote the opinion in a case in 1878 rejecting claims similar to the one brought by Bishop and his sisters. The first was brought by Mary Clements and the second by Phillis Oldham, both black women claiming to have had long and meaningful relationships with white men. Roberts, like Joseph Wygall, Warren Clark, and the witnesses for the defense, had trouble imagining a world beyond black and white. An ardent secessionist, he owned slaves before the Civil War and never lost his zeal for racist dogma. The *Clements* decision overruled *Honey v. Clark*, finding that it was "not the letter of the Constitution, nor . . . its intention, to confer on any parties, white or black, whose intercourse was illegal and immoral, the rights and benefits of lawful marriage." The *Oldham* decision reaffirmed the previous holding, conclusively rejecting the idea that persons of different races could be husband and wife.[114]

Annie Lee Williams, who wrote a history of Wharton County in the 1960s, notes that, sometime after the verdict in 1871, persons angry with the idea of wealth coming to the family stormed the home on Peach Creek and set fire to it, burning alive two persons and shooting at those who attempted to escape. Unfortunately, Williams did not provide any sources for her claim, and none were found to substantiate it. The story may have been just that—a story that started somewhere and was passed along until people just assumed it was true. Even if things did not unfold in the manner suggested, however, the story has value as a metaphor for the family's experience over the next several years and decades. Lourinda, the oldest daughter, passed away before most of the troubles began. She died in 1873 or 1874, leaving her husband, Pleasant, and several children behind. Nancy lived into the late 1880s or early 1890s, still sharecropping with her husband, Joseph, in Fort Bend County. Bishop was the only one of his siblings to witness the new century. His final years, like the final years for all of them, were difficult. He frequently found himself in court or the subject of legal action, never to his advantage. In 1901, his wife of over thirty years, Rosetta, divorced him, their marriage undoubtedly strained by their financial difficulties and the dreams of what might have been. Bishop, then in his seventies, died a few years later. Like his sisters, he passed away the same as he entered this world. With nothing.[115]

CHAPTER TWO

Slave Resistance and Class Conflict in the Redlands

Charles Brady shot Miles on the last day of March 1854. The bad blood between them had likely been brewing since Charles started overseeing on the Price plantation in San Augustine County in January of that year. Miles was considered a prime field hand, thirty-three years old and worth, in the slaveholder's world, about $1,000. Yet Miles was also strong willed, which, from the overseer's perspective, made him difficult to manage, notwithstanding his value. In shooting him, Charles had the immediate goal of reaffirming his control over the plantation. But the act also tied into the larger narrative of white supremacy. The doctrine had been ingrained into Charles's being over the course of his life. He had learned to view himself as superior to every person of color, no matter the circumstance, and the violence he used to bring Miles down was simply an assertion of what he saw as his natural right. The problem for Charles was that, when he filled Miles's back with shot, his version of the world bumped into a different one. The Price family had lost a productive slave, and they had no intention of letting the matter alone.[1]

Temperance "Tempe" Price had been running the plantation ever since her husband, Elijah, passed away two years earlier, in 1852. She wasted little time in discharging Charles from her employ, releasing him immediately after she learned of the incident. Charles was a man of little means and few opportunities, however, and he was counting on the $300 salary that he was to earn overseeing for the year. He filed suit against Tempe soon after, insisting in his petition that he was wrongfully terminated and entitled to the contract price. Tempe responded with her own claim, not only denying Charles's core assertions but also demanding that Charles pay her for the loss in value of her slave, still alive but unable to carry out the tasks of plowing and cotton picking.[2]

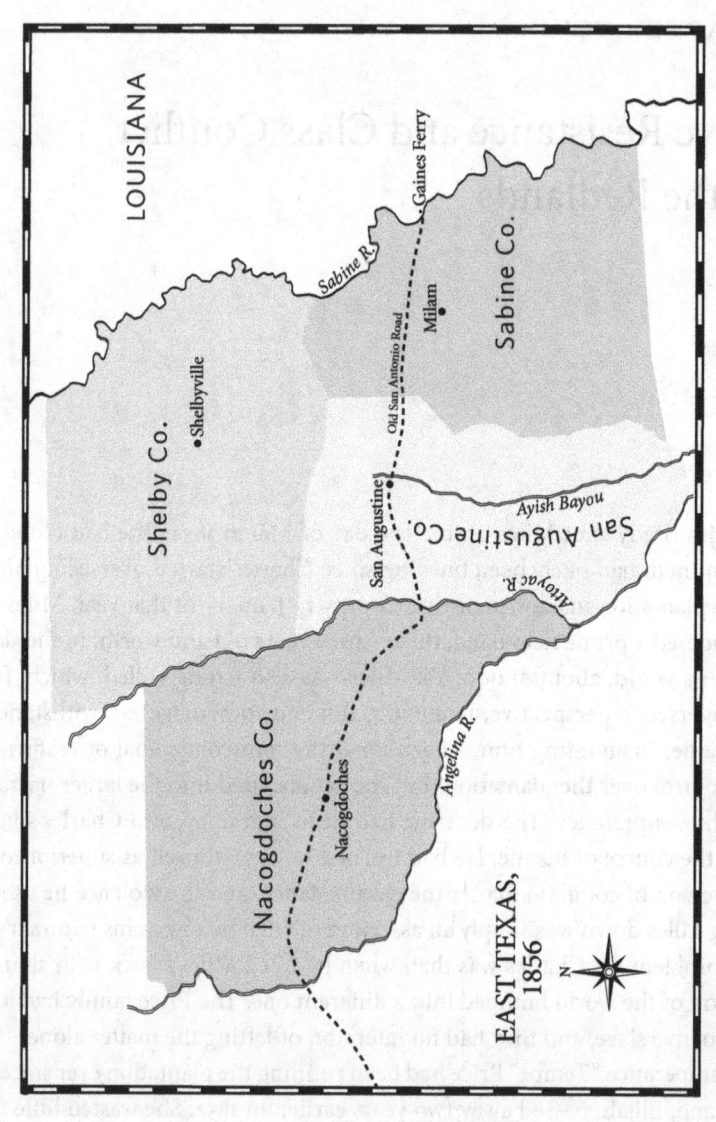

The case came to trial in San Augustine County Court in October 1856. Tempe Price and her family, who counted themselves among the county's elite, hired San Augustine's most famous resident, James Pinckney Henderson, the first governor of the new state of Texas, to represent them. Henderson built his case against Charles in the roundabout way familiar to antebellum lawyers in disputes involving slaves. Unable to call Miles or any of the hands under the rules of evidence, he relied on whites familiar with the parties, even if they did not witness the events. The picture these witnesses painted of Charles was not a positive one. They said he was a reckless overseer with a hot temper. These same witnesses described Miles as a reliable hand and a trusted servant, someone who had been a member of the Price "family" for years.[3]

This picture contrasted sharply from the one offered by Charles. Through his lawyer H. M. Kinsey, Charles told a story of a hardworking overseer and a "worthless" and "dangerous negro." Charles recounted how, a week before the shooting, Miles had encouraged another slave to disobey him and then attacked Charles before running off. When Miles came back, Charles demanded that Miles play the role of the obedient servant, issuing an order that Miles would ignore. From Charles's perspective, Miles had undermined his authority with his recent displays, and anyone with knowledge of the matter surely understood that loss of authority on a slave plantation meant resistance, rebellion, and even death. Charles swore that he had to shoot Miles "in defense of [his] life."[4]

The jury assembled to decide the case of *Brady v. Price* in October 1856 could have easily lost themselves in the back-and-forth between overseer and planter, weighing the testimony of the witnesses while trying to reconstruct the events that led to the shooting. But anyone who thought deeply about the matter would have been troubled by more than the conflicting testimony. For them, at issue were competing ideas about race, class, and slavery, suddenly and violently rammed headlong into each other. This was not a case simply about whom to believe. It was about opposing visions of an ideal world, one that pitted a slaveholder's economic interests and a belief in slavery's benevolence against an overseer's claim to racial superiority. Even more remarkable is that this heady debate was not being held in the halls of the legislature, by political men charting the course of the country. This debate was happening in a rugged East Texas courtroom, between whites of different classes, because Miles—a person defined by the law as property—had defied the role assigned to him. It was a class conflict, experienced through race, with observers to the trial receiving a firsthand look at an emerging Texas town struggling to reconcile the ideologies of slavery with the realities of daily life.

Gone to Texas

Miles had likely been owned by the Price family for most, if not all, of his life. He was born around 1821, probably in North Carolina. That much can be gleaned from the testimony of Albert and Benjamin Price, the two eldest boys of Elijah and Tempe. Albert and Benjamin were younger than Miles— Albert was about three and Benjamin about five years younger—but both had been born in North Carolina, and both remembered Miles from as far back as they could "recollect anything." Albert and Benjamin also remembered Miles's parents, although the family did not own them, at least at the time of the trial. The scene of a gut-wrenching separation of parents and child, played out countless times on the steps of a courthouse or an auction block, did not make it into any of the official records. But the frequency with which it occurred, combined with the knowledge that his parents were not around, makes it all but certain that it shaped Miles's life.[5]

Miles was about nine years old when the Price family left North Carolina for Alabama, around 1830. At such a young age, he had no idea what motivated the family to sell their land and look to the west. But it is likely that Elijah, about thirty-nine at the time and the patriarch of the family, left for the same reason many others did. Elijah came from an established North Carolina family. As a man of means, he saw opportunities to leverage his wealth in the abundant lands of the west, where cotton was king. With their own land in the Carolinas wearing out, the family decided to sell their farm and head down to Alabama, eventually making their way to Sumter County, on the state's western edge. There, Elijah planted cotton and quickly emerged as one of the region's leading citizens. Like many men of his station, with wealth, power, and prestige, Elijah had political aspirations, and locals elected him the first representative from the newly organized county in 1832. His obituary reports that he was never much of an orator, but he did impress the other members of the legislature, and "many important measures were advocated by him, and passed with his assistance."[6]

After a decade in Alabama, the Price family again looked to the west, this time to Texas. By now, Texas was a republic, having defeated Mexico in the Texas War for Independence in 1835–36. The area was still very much a primitive frontier, but the vast stretches of inexpensive and mineral-rich land also meant that ambitious settlers with money to invest could grow their fortunes at a rate that surpassed most anywhere in the South, including Alabama. "Here you can have more real good land than you can cultivate, without money and without price," insisted the editor of the San Augustine newspaper, in East

Texas, where the Prices would eventually settle. "If you are industrious, your labor will be repaid by ample harvests." By this time, the Prices had thirty-two human beings among their possessions, and they had heard how San Augustine had "a soil and a climate peculiarly adapted to the labor of negroes." Here, the San Augustine paper insisted, "more than double can be realized by the culture of our great staple, compared with what he is making by the same labor in a more northern latitude." It was a promise too good to pass up. In the winter of 1840–41, Elijah and Tempe decided to sell their Alabama farm and head for the Texas frontier.[7]

By the time Elijah and Tempe made their journey, they had six children. In addition to their two sons, Albert and Benjamin, aged sixteen and fourteen, they had four daughters. Cornelia was about fifteen, born the year after Albert, in 1825. And Mary was thirteen, born the year after Benjamin, in 1827. The other two girls were a lot younger. Susan was about four and Temperance was an infant. Miles, in contrast to the growing children, was about nineteen, considered to be in the prime of his life. Healthy and strong, his arms and body possessed the sinewy strength of someone who spent his waking hours engaged in manual labor. His back was not yet broken. That would come, to be sure, if he kept at it long enough, as it would for so many people of color forced to stoop in the dirt for years on end. "We woke up at four o'clock and worked from sunup to sundown," Wash Ingram, a Texas slave, said. A field hand's only break was a short one over lunch, along with Sundays and the occasional holiday, if they were lucky. The daily toil was exhausting. "When we comes in at night, we has to go right to bed," Adeline Marshall reported. Faltering was not an option. Anyone who failed to do what was required could count on a whipping that brought blisters and blood.[8]

The journey from Alabama to Texas was long. It amounted to four hundred miles or so. Miles, along with the other hands, likely walked the entire distance on foot, adding their numbers to what is known as the Second Middle Passage—the forced migration of roughly a million enslaved persons during the first half of the nineteenth century to developing lands in the Lower South, Louisiana, and Texas. It was a brutal time. Miles and the other hands were likely tied together, ragged and forlorn, while the Price boys and a trusted servant or two rode on horseback, herding restless cattle and cajoling stubborn hogs. Nothing in the record indicates that the Prices were as cruel to their slaves as some. Ben Simpson remembered how, on a similar journey from Georgia to Texas, his mother collapsed from exhaustion, only to be shot by her owner and left for dead. Still, the road was difficult. Often sojourns like this took place during the winter months, after the fall harvest and before the spring planting. Tired, cold, and hungry, they traveled at a staggeringly slow pace, covering about ten or fifteen miles a day, wading through streams and pushing the wagons when they got bogged down in the swamps of Louisiana. Along the way, Elijah likely conferred with other heads of household, stopping briefly to taste the soil or talk of things to come. Miles and the others did what they could to keep up, plodding on, "aimless, hopeless, thoughtless, more indifferent than the oxen to all about them."[9]

As they approached Texas from the east, Miles and the other slaves felt as anxious, if not more so, than the members of the Price family. Gone were the familiar surroundings, and with them the growing understanding that, whatever family and friends had been left behind, they would probably never be seen again. They crossed the Sabine River at Gaines Ferry on the Old San Antonio Road, a wagon trail that served as the primary route from East Texas into the interior. Thousands had traveled the road in the past twenty or so years, following its path to Nacogdoches and then on down to the Brazos and Colorado Rivers, before reaching San Antonio. Along the way, some caught feeder roads to Goliad or, later, Austin, after the latter was named the permanent capital in 1839. At the time, many of the roads through the country were better described as cattle paths. Travelers contended with fallen trees and unmarked routes, happy to call any day that they did not get lost or turned around a success.[10]

Once in Texas, the Price party covered another twenty-five miles before crossing Sabine County into San Augustine County. The two counties had been created in the first session of the Republic of Texas Congress, back in 1837. Sabine County bordered the river, while San Augustine County lay just to the west. The topography of both was similar to what they had just seen in Louisiana. The Price wagons bumped along over gentle hills, avoiding the muck and mire in the low areas as best they could. Belts of pine forests, intermixed with oaks and other hardwoods, were all around them. The party kept to the main road, as the region was thick with underbrush, making travel on anything but a cleared trail all but impossible.[11]

As Miles walked along, taking in his surroundings, his attention gradually turned to the heavy clay soil that stuck to his bare feet and anything else that touched the ground. The farther he got from the river, the more he noticed that the soil was stained a brownish red. If he had asked around, as Elijah did, Miles would have learned that its peculiar color came from an iron oxide in the earth. The color was so noticeable that some of the early residents identified the region by its most prominent trait, and they soon started calling it the Redlands. Elijah had heard about it on his travels, and he knew the region was extremely fertile, blessed with seasonal rain and the runoff from the many creeks and rivers zigzagging across the countryside. It seemed the perfect place for Elijah and Tempe, now fifty and thirty-five years old, respectively, to settle their growing household and plant the family's roots.[12]

The Gateway of Texas

The area that became San Augustine first attracted Anglo-American settlers even before Mexico had opened the region for settlement. Following in the fine tradition of other adventurers, a handful of families trickled over the Sabine River at the start of the century and built cabins in the woods. They did not own their property in the sense that they held a lawful deed, but it hardly mattered. They cleared a few acres for planting and lived off the land as generations before them had done. In 1825, when Mexico offered an *empresario* contract to Haden Edwards in order to boost the population of East Texas, there were already more than a dozen families scattered about who called the area their home. The old settlers, however, along with a few Mexican families who had moved to the region long ago, quickly found themselves at odds with the new *empresario*. In fulfilling his role, Edwards gave preference to the rights and views of those he brought in, rather than those who were already there, demanding that the first settlers and the Mexican nationals produce titles to their land. Those who could not were subject to high fees, and their diminished influence meant that their complaints fell on deaf ears. Local matters soon turned national, after Edwards certified and supported his son-in-law in a contested election, despite mandates coming from Mexican officials. Within the year, Mexico had seen enough. It nullified his contract. Soon after, Edwards declared a revolution, creating the Republic of Fredonia, which he claimed stretched from the Sabine River to the Rio Grande.[13]

The revolution was destined to fail. Stephen F. Austin, who was far more politically adept than Edwards, reportedly referred to Edwards and his rebels as a "small party of infatuated madmen." Mexico called out the military to put down the uprising, and the threat of certain death helped discourage all but the most resolute. The rebels soon fled to Louisiana, and the revolution collapsed before it began. Notwithstanding its inglorious end, however, Edwards's decision to ignore the law and go about things his own way provides insight into the nature of the country and many of those who immigrated to the region. They did not all fit the profile, to be sure, but in the early days East Texas was known as a place for the rougher sort, the type of settler who discarded the niceties of a more organized society in favor of a lifestyle where he could be left alone. Many were outsiders. A few were outlaws. Dressed in homespun and wide-brimmed hats, they grew and shot what they ate, splitting logs and putting up fences as much to keep livestock in as to keep others out. They often went days or weeks without seeing others, and when conflicts arose, they resolved them in much the same way they provided for their families—with a gun.[14]

The Regulator and Moderator War provides a glimpse into the attitudes of some of the early settlers to the region. The war occurred in Shelby County, just to the north of San Augustine County. The bloody feud lasted for several years, until 1844, as men on both sides openly flaunted the law, threatened government officials, and left the area in shambles. The war traced its origins to Charles Jackson's unsuccessful bid for the Texas legislature in 1839. Jackson, a fugitive from Louisiana, blamed his loss on the Shelby County land commissioners and their friends. Shelby County had long been the scene of a thriving business in fraudulent land certificates, ostensibly issued by the republic for military service or to encourage immigration. In the fallout from the election, Jackson publicly accused the commissioners of issuing forged and stolen titles, and he punctuated his argument by killing an unarmed resident who disagreed with him.[15]

Jackson was placed under arrest and indicted for murder. While awaiting trial, the sheriff, evidently a friend, released Jackson from custody. Jackson and his supporters then hid out in the woods and organized themselves into an armed group, calling themselves the Shelby Guards before adopting the moniker the Regulators. They said their purpose was to maintain order and "expel from their county, all persons of suspicious or bad character." Another group, concerned that the Regulators had taken the law into their own hands, formed themselves into an opposing faction. Armed to the hilt, they called themselves the Moderators. The county subsequently descended into a civil war, with public officials struggling to maintain control over a dangerous population. "It is painful to us," reported the San Augustine paper in September 1841, "to have so repeatedly to notice the conduct of those who call themselves Regulators. It argues the inability of the judicial authorities of the country, to enforce the laws. It is certainly a wretched state of affairs, when a man's life liberty and property are at the will of an infuriated mob." Over the next several years, more than fifty people were killed and countless others were bullied into submission. Order was not restored until 1844, when President Sam Houston brought out the militia and personally called for calm. Jackson, who was at the root of the feud, never suffered any consequences for shooting his opponent. At his trial, the judge left the courtroom and the prosecutor refused to introduce any witnesses. Jackson was found not guilty on the grounds of self-defense.[16]

In hindsight, it is unfair to taint an entire region as lawless based on the actions of an undetermined number of vigilantes. It might be true that East Texas had its share of rough-and-tumble residents, maybe more than most, but it was also a place where respectable families came in search of cheap land and the promises of a new beginning. "Among the early settlers of this county were some of the noblest men to be found," remembered Alexander Horton, who was fourteen when his family moved to San Augustine in 1824. "They were generous, kind, honest and brave." Within a short while, early residents got down to the business of organizing themselves into a community. They elected a sheriff and appointed an *alcalde*, who acted as a judge in all civil and criminal matters. Soon after, they marked off the boundaries of the commercial and political center of a town—which they also called San Augustine. The town was located on the east side of the Ayish Bayou on the Old San Antonio Road, chosen because of its accessibility to other places and because of the availability of a fresh water supply. The town's position on the main road through the Redlands played to its advantage. At the time there were only three main entries into Texas. Two were by water, into Galveston or Matagorda. The one by land came through San Augustine, and with the population ever growing, it soon became known as "the gateway of Texas."[17]

The law-abiding people who settled in the county gradually outpaced those who came looking for trouble. One associate wrote to Elijah Price in 1844, remarking that he "was happy to learn . . . you were better satisfied with your country than you had been at first." Elijah's brother-in-law added that he, too, was pleased to hear that "your country had become completely civilised [*sic*]," noting the good news "that you had not had any shootings in a long time." Many of those who helped contribute to the county were farmers or planters or others who drew their subsistence from the land. There were also a considerable number of merchants, lawyers, and professional men, many of whom took leading roles in Texas affairs. People like Texas Supreme Court justice Royall T. Wheeler, future justice and governor Oran M. Roberts, and Governor J. Pinckney Henderson all counted San Augustine as their home. Refusing to accept the position that frontier life equated with an uncivilized one, they chopped down trees, planted crops, and "established"—as one early historian of the area called it—"a little commonwealth in the wildern[e]ss." A sense of what mattered can be found in the institutions they created. In addition to conducting the business of government, they built two schools and established six churches. The first school was San Augustine University, chartered by the Republic of Texas in 1837. The second was Wesleyan College, built by the Methodist Church in 1842. Industrious men of the town also collaborated to start a newspaper—the politically influential *Red-Lander*, which Elijah's son, Benjamin, would eventually own.[18]

For certain, San Augustine was not for everyone. Frederick Olmsted, in his travels through the area in the 1850s, commented that the dozen or so buildings centered around a muddy public square "made no very charming impression as we entered, nor did we find any striking improvement on longer acquaintance." But for many others, San Augustine provided a civilizing element in an otherwise rugged and remote environment, becoming, as one said, "the Athens of the State." The editor of the *Red-Lander* echoed these sentiments when he insisted, in an effort to encourage more settlers, that the "county of San Augustine occupies the most enviable position in point of morals of any county in the Republic."[19]

Narratives of Slavery

When the Price family arrived in San Augustine County in 1841 the enslaved population stood at almost a thousand, making it the third-most populous slaveholding region behind only Brazoria County (1,665 slaves) in Austin's original colony and Red River County (1,789 slaves) in the northeast corner of the state. By 1850, the enslaved population had topped fifteen hundred, to go along with over two thousand white settlers, arriving daily, it seemed, following statehood in 1845. Though not a majority, as they were in six counties, the sheer number of people in bondage in San Augustine illustrates the importance slavery played in the development of the region. In 1860, roughly 37 percent of the total number of white families in the county owned at least one human being, higher than the state average (25 percent). Enslavers, moreover, put their property to all manner of use, depending on them to help them turn a profit and build for the future. Twenty-four families owned enough people—twenty or more—that historians would call them planters, including the Prices. Most owned fewer than five but hoped to acquire more.[20]

Early observers of the state insisted that Texans practiced a milder form of slavery than elsewhere in the South. The claim was a specious one to make, but it was seized on by subsequent generations and repeated often enough that some today, unfortunately, consider it to be true.[21] The people who fought so hard for freedom in 1835–36, however, never intended the system to be a weaker form of slavery. As soon as they gained independence from Mexico,

Texans declared in their 1836 constitution that all persons of color who were previously held as slaves were now legally slaves for life, and that the legislature could not force any slaveholder to free his slaves nor pass any law prohibiting immigrants from bringing their slaves into the republic. Subsequent laws and court rulings built on these basic ideas, ensuring that blacks were deprived of their most basic rights.[22] The law permitted slaves to be bought and sold, devised by deed or will, and hired out on terms set by the owners.[23] The law also allowed enslavers, and by extension slave hirers, to use any form of punishment on their slaves short of "maliciously" dismembering or depriving them of life.[24] The law also forbade slaves from using "insulting or abusive language" to a white person, and it mandated execution for such crimes as insurrection, poisoning, arson, burglary, murder, rape or attempted rape of a white woman, and assaulting a white person with intent to kill.[25] Statutes also prohibited slaves from carrying guns or gathering suspiciously in groups of three or more, and they made it a crime to buy liquor or trade in any goods without written permission of their owners.[26] The legislature also set up rules and regulations for slave patrols and gave to every white person the right to whip a slave found off the plantation or engaged in "turbulent conduct."[27] Texas law, in short, left no room for doubt: "The right of the master to the obedience and submission of his slave, in all lawful things, is perfect."[28]

The men and women charged with implementing and enforcing the daily routine of slavery also ensured that the system practiced in Texas matched the system practiced elsewhere. Court records reveal the truly horrendous nature of slavery. In 1841, the year that the Price party rumbled into San Augustine, Judge William Anderson, a local resident, beat his slave Nancy to death. The autopsy report described, in clinical detail, the depth of abuse. Nancy's head was "bruised so much . . . that note could not be taken of all [the bruises]." Anderson also beat her back, yanked her shoulder out of its socket, and caused bleeding into her brain. In the same year, Elisha Ellison, also of San Augustine, severely whipped Nancy, the slave of local resident Philip Sublett, for some infraction. He then sank his knife into her side, nearly killing her. Over in Harris County, near the developing town of Houston, William Wilson unleashed a beating so severe on a slave named Nat—he whipped him six hundred times with a gutta-percha strap—that Nat died.[29]

Former slaves from Texas recalled abuses so shocking that even persons with the most hardened sensibilities would recoil. William Moore's owner was a "fitty man for meanness." Taking out his "big bullwhip," he staked anyone committing an infraction to the ground and then had another slave "hold his head down with his mouth in the dirt." He then whipped him "till the blood run out and red up the ground." Van Moore recalled how his owner once dug a hole for a pregnant woman's belly, and then laid her down and tied her "so she could not squirm around any." Andy Anderson testified to the psychological toll these punishments inflicted. He recalled being whipped every half hour for four hours after the firewood cart he was pushing broke down. He lay in his bunk for two days, "getting over [the whipping] in the body but not the heart." Ben Simpson said his owner branded him as he would an animal, fed him raw meat and green corn, and forced him to sleep naked on the bare ground with a chain around his neck. Susan Merritt, as a young girl, had to walk barefoot through a bed of coals after her mistress blamed her for letting some young chickens flounder into a fire. Mintie Maria Miller's owner sold her from her mother to satisfy a debt, and the prospective buyer forced open her mouth to inspect her teeth.[30]

In the master language of slavery, told from the perspective of slave owners like the Prices, incidents like these were not supposed to happen. Texans labored mightily to convince outsiders—and themselves—that slavery was a benevolent system and a blessing to both races. In that perspective, far from being overworked and abused, slaves benefitted from the life their owners gave them. "It is notorious here that the Slaves, are a careless happy race," reported one local newspaper, "enjoying life far more than their masters, who have the nominal supremacy, but carry all the burthens of life, of which the slave carries none that do not end with the day's labor." Others built on this common theme, insisting that slaves were content with their condition. "Our negro is a slack, fatsided fellow," reported another paper. "He loves to eat and to laugh, and give him his belly full, and he is as happy as a prince." To be sure, Texas slave owners recognized that punishment was inevitable, but only in the sense that an unruly child might be disciplined. "Whipping is an institution here, of course, but resorted to with reluctance." To the extent that others went further, the problem was the individual or the circumstance, never the system. Judge C. A. Frazer of Upshur County penned an article extolling the good fortune of those "permitted to the condition of slaves." They "are afforded the blessings of family relations—never disturbed, with few exceptions; only when the vicissitudes of the master's fortunes compel it—and at all times so far as my observation extends," he insisted, "afforded with more means of intellectual and moral culture than ever has been, or ever can be furnished by the combined efforts of the civilized world in their native lands." Another commentator assumed he closed the matter when he assured his readers that whippings, although "passionate," were never "willingly cruel," and that the "guarantee for the safety of the black man in the south is that endemic good nature and sympathy of the Southern heart."[31]

The efforts of Texas slave owners to portray themselves and their system as benevolent were not especially unique or innovative. Like other areas of the South, Texans were stung by abolitionist criticism that slavery was an immoral institution, and they joined with other proslavery advocates in extolling slavery's virtues. "Take our slave population, compare it with the free laborers at the North, and the most rigid investigation will only show so far as the *'hog and hominy'* goes, and the *'ease of mind and body,'* that the negro is best off." Leading Texans studied up on their history, searched through the Bible, and concluded that slavery "is right in every light in which it can be contemplated." An editorial in the Galveston paper summed it up in 1856: "We confess we have always thought the South ought to place Slavery, properly regulated, on the broad ground of its being in accordance with every page of the revealed will of God, and in perfect harmony with natural laws and universal experience, (as in no age of the world has it ever ceased to exist,) and on the ground of its mutual blessings to both races."[32]

The paternalist ethos, however, was not the only justification for slavery. Texas's long history as a borderland meant that the image of the aristocratic planter and his family, fashionably dressed and living comfortably in a grand home, was better suited for another place and another time. Olmsted's observations along his East Texas route reveal that, even among some of the more successful, life for most Texans was hard fought. Outside San Augustine, Olmsted and his party visited a plantation for sale. "It was described in the hand-bills as having a fine house. We found it a cabin without windows." Under such conditions, the justifications for slavery had to be bent and shaped to address a more rugged existence, one in which three-quarters of white Texans did not own slaves and half of those who did owned fewer than five. These individuals cared little for talk of slavery's benevolence and were far more interested in what the institution could provide for them.[33]

Crafting language to appeal to the backwoods farmer rather than the slaveholding elite, many Texans sought to position slavery as a necessary corollary to freedom and the democratic ideal. Senator Thomas Rusk, who partnered with Governor Henderson, the Price family lawyer, in a law practice, gave voice to this notion during a debate over the Kansas-Nebraska Act: "You cry out for the freedom of the negro, and you abridge the freedom of the white man." The view had widespread appeal, removing the barriers of class to make all whites equal. "No such thing as a 'lower class' can exist where a servile negro population constitutes an element of society," insisted the *Austin, Texas State Gazette*. "The very existence of slavery keeps alive in the breast of every white citizen a jealous passion for liberty." These same proponents insisted that slaveholding should be the goal of "every thrifty man." Purchasing slaves was a sound economic investment, "not for political popularity or power, but for the domestic convenience and mental improvement of the many." Such views led to inevitable talk of reopening the slave trade or otherwise incentivizing slave ownership by bringing costs down. Slaveholding was not for the elite but for the hardy and industrious, the family who built a sturdy home and carved a plot of land out of the immense wilderness of East Texas. "We care nothing for the Slavery as an abstraction," insisted one, "but we desire the practicality; the increase of our productions; the increase of the comforts and wealth of the population; and if slavery, or slave labor, or Negro Apprentice labor ministers to this, why that is what we want." Indeed, so important was the institution to the freedom of the white race that the Galveston paper insisted that it was "the duty of the South to attach her people, one and all[,] to the institution of Slavery."[34]

A Day in the Life

Elijah and Tempe eventually settled their family on 1,476 acres of land ten miles west of the town of San Augustine. Elijah purchased the land from George Teal, and it lay on a portion of Samuel Steddham's original headright. Anxious to begin, Elijah quickly put his hands to work logging, burning, clearing, and fencing their surroundings. Sleeping in tents at first, they gradually built a small community, complete with a home for the Prices and slave cabins down the road. It was like a "small town," said Andy Anderson, who grew up in Texas, describing the plantation on which he lived. "Everything we uses am made right there." Elijah had enough slaves that he insisted some have special skills to use on the plantation. A tanner made shoes, and a blacksmith banged out plows and hoes and other metal goods. Some of the women cooked meals, sheared the wool from sheep, and made clothes. Miles and the others spent their days in the fields, turning up the soil, planting seeds, and tending to the lifeblood of the plantation.[35]

Former slaves from Texas provide insight into the life Miles led. As with everyone, it was a life dictated by the realities of the frontier. Miles and the others lived in one-room shacks made of pine logs with dirt floors and a few crude pieces of furniture. They built their beds right into the wall by making an "auger hole in [the] side of the house and put[ting] in pieces of wood to make the bed frame." The men and women stretched deerskin over the frame and then used whatever was handy—straw, moss, cornhusks, cotton—to make a mattress. Chinks in the cabin walls were both a blessing and a curse. In the summer, they allowed the air to drift through, bringing temporary relief from the stifling heat, thick with humidity. In the winter, they had to be stuffed with cotton or cornhusks for warmth.[36]

Miles's diet was sparse. He survived mainly on pork and corn, all from the plantation, supplemented with milk and butter from the cows. Miles and the others used hollowed-out sticks for spoons, scooping helpings out of a trough before some of the field hands grabbed their share with hands dirty from the day's work. Occasionally someone brought back a squirrel or a possum or a skunk or other wild game, which they roasted on the fire. If Elijah was feeling particularly generous, he may have allowed the hands a few vegetables in the summer. Even if not, some mother or grandmother may have tried to supplement their meager diet with special treats. Charlotte Beverly remembered when her aunt would "smash up [cinnamon] with butter and pour sweet milk and flour in it" to make cinnamon bread. Not everyone was so lucky. Sarah Ashley never had enough to eat on the farm her owners ran, so the slaves "keeps stealin' stuff." They had to. "Dey give us de peck of meal to last de week and two, three pound bacon in chunk. Us never have flour or sugar, jus' cornmeal and de meat and 'taters." In order to avoid detection, they kept a "big box under de fireplace, where dey kep' all de pig and chickens what dey steal, down in the salt." Whippings invariably followed when the thefts were discovered.[37]

There were a number of children on the Price plantation, but it is not known whether Elijah and Tempe encouraged marriage or they simply put "men and women together like horses or cattle," as they did on Josephine Howard's plantation. Savvy owners like the Prices understood the value of a self-reproducing labor force. When he went to buy slaves, Elijah always had his eye out for a good "breeder," as a smart purchase now would inevitably mean more slaves in the future. You are a "portly gal and Rufus am de portly man," the wife of one owner said to Rose Williams, when, at just sixteen years old, she was placed in a cabin with a burly man she hardly knew. "De massa" wants you two "to bring forth portly children." The records never say whether Miles had a wife. If he did, her companionship may have provided Elijah and Tempe with an additional benefit, as her presence may have prevented him from permanently running away, even after his dispute with Charles.[38]

Like other properties in the area, the Price plantation was devoted to growing cotton for the market. Miles and the other slaves had grown used to the unrelenting season, planting the seeds as early as March, thinning the crop over the spring and summer, and harvesting throughout the fall. "Among the productions which may be regarded as naturally adapted to the soil of Texas, and which now forms a chief and important article of commerce, cotton stands pre-eminent," said an article in *DeBow's Review*. Cotton was considered "the great crop of Texas, and the source of much of its wealth and power." Agricultural reports indicate that Texas as a whole produced over 57,000 bales of cotton in 1850, rivaling some of the older cotton-growing states, with much of it equaling "in length and fineness the Sea Island cotton" of Georgia. San Augustine produced 1,020 of these bales, ranking it high among the counties of East Texas, even if not as high as some of the counties along the Gulf.[39]

Elijah oversaw his plantation for several years. Throughout his fifties, he would saddle his horse every morning and ride around the plantation, surveying the fields and drawing satisfaction from seeing his profits, literally, grow in front of his eyes. Like other men of his station, it did not bother him that he was witnessing, as the former slave Harriet Jacobs once said, "the results of labor performed by men and women who were unpaid, miserably clothed, and half famished." He credited his success to his own hard work and business acumen. By 1848, he had done well enough to move his family to a hundred-acre homestead on the outskirts of town, leaving his plantation in the hands of others. One of the main reasons for the move was to provide his children with easier access to the local school. By this time, Elijah and Tempe had added four more children to their family—Virginia, Elizabeth, Elijah, and Archillas. An educated man, Elijah appreciated the opportunities afforded by the schools in town, and he insisted that his children be exposed at a young age to the fundamentals of good citizenship—spelling, reading, penmanship, grammar, arithmetic, and geography—so they could continue to represent the family's interests in years to come.[40]

As they prepared for the move, Elijah met with Stephen Blount, a successful merchant in town. The two agreed to start a cotton business in which they would buy cotton locally and sell it in New Orleans. This proved to be another smart decision for the Price family. With new settlers arriving daily, people were turning up the soil and planting crops, and the firm of Blount & Price capitalized on the changing landscape to help support a comfortable lifestyle for the owners. A sense of the importance of cotton to the economic development of the county can be found in the significant increase in the number of bales produced. In 1860, San Augustine produced 31,342 bales, roughly 30,000 more than in 1850. It was the most of any county in the state.[41]

Though the family now lived in town, Elijah still depended on crops grown on his plantation. Managing it from afar, he left the vast majority of his slaves, including Miles, to work the fields. In 1850, the thirty-odd enslaved men and women produced six bales of cotton and harvested 4,500 bushels of corn. During the same year, they also planted and grew Irish potatoes, and produced two hundred pounds of butter from the fifteen or so milch cows that Elijah owned. Elijah also owned steers—not as many as some of the large stock raisers in other parts of the state, but, with fifty head in 1850, he made a tidy profit from their annual sale. He also owned sheep from which Miles and the others produced seventy-five pounds of wool, together with horses, oxen, mules, and two hundred pigs.[42]

By the time of his death in 1852, at the age of sixty-one, Elijah had earned a place as one of San Augustine's "most esteemed citizens." Land, property, honor—these were the things by which white Texans judged success, and against that standard Elijah impressed many. Civic-minded, he was educated, enterprising, and well-to-do. But perhaps the single-most important indicator of his standing was the number of his slaves. In a society that measured success by counting slaves, Elijah ranked among the elite in the county. "We want more Slaves—we *need* them," thundered one editorial, providing dramatic insight into the importance of slave ownership to the people of Texas. Slave labor provided the "true element of social wealth and happiness." In 1852, when Elijah died, the Price family owned thirty-eight people, which made them one of the larger slaveholding families in the county. It was a number, moreover, that would only continue to grow over the decade, as the benefits of a labor force that naturally reproduced came to fruition. With each addition came a new name—like Henry, Jacob, Wiley, Peter, Mariah, or Penny—and the Prices worked them to become one of the wealthiest and most admired families in the area.[43]

Charles

Court week in antebellum Texas was always popular. It was a time for men and women to come together, catch up on old news, and share thoughts about topics big and small. The conversations were always lively, helped along by corn whiskey and home brews. They discussed politics and the pending cases, with never any shortage of opinions about either. Residents of the county had been holding court ever since the 1820s, first at the homes of the *alcaldes* and later in the old Mexican customhouse. In 1854, two years before Charles Brady and Tempe Price's case went to trial, locals put the last brick in the new courthouse, a sturdy two-story structure that was the pride of the town. The courtroom was on the second floor, and the halls regularly rang out with the eloquence of members of the local bar.[44]

The day of the trial between Charles and Tempe in October 1856 likely had a hum of activity louder than usual. The stakes this day were matched only by the intrigue. Pitted against the esteemed Price family was an overseer, a member of a group that played a critical—if much criticized—role in southern slavery. Overseers in Texas, as elsewhere, tended to fit a typical pattern. Often single, they rarely owned land or other significant personal property. Many were younger men, and often from the South, as the business of demanding production from a workforce who cared little for the result took a special constitution. Some owners, like Charles William Tait, a large Colorado County planter, insisted that his overseers "attempt to govern by reason in the first instance," never punishing "a negro when in a passion" and always giving orders "in a mild tone." But most probably had little time for such benevolent niceties, instead resorting to the lash and other physical punishments at the first sign of trouble. Unsurprisingly, former slaves from Texas minced few words when describing their overseers. Richard Caruthers said they referred to their overseer as Devil Hill, because his temper was born of the devil himself.[45]

Charles Brady was no exception. Rugged and individualistic, he brought forth images of some of the earliest settlers to the region, the ones with dreams of living off the land and owning their own farms. He was from North Carolina, like the Prices. But for Charles, at least, the promises of opportunity had proven elusive. In 1850, he was overseeing on the McNeill place in San Augustine. At the time, he was twenty-six and single. He did not own any land then, nor would he when he worked for the Prices. In fact, the only things he ever owned were a few cattle and a couple of horses, which he probably found roaming wild or received as payment for services.[46]

By 1853, Charles had left the McNeill farm and was overseeing George Teal's plantation, the same man who had sold Elijah his property. George Teal, like the Prices, was a wealthy farmer with land and substantial holdings. In 1850, he counted 44 slaves among his many possessions, and his plantation produced 54 bales of cotton and 2,250 bushels of corn. The relationship between George and Charles was probably never very good. Owners and overseers had a complex and often troubled relationship. Both were dependent on one another—the one for a salary and the other to maintain discipline—but both often wanted little to do with the other. Owners like George Teal constantly faulted their overseers, chastising them for their temperament and dismissing their tactics as overly aggressive and often unnecessary. "A mild expostulation is better than a fierce rebuke, a deliberate warning more effective than a hasty threat," counseled *DeBow's Review*, in an article about overseers and how they should govern. It was a convenient position for owners to take. Whether unconscious or deliberate, shifting the blame to overseers for the ills of slavery offered them the ability to present themselves as humane persons who cared about the individuals they owned, while at the same time growing their profits. If their slaves suffered, well, it was the overseers' fault, not the owners'.[47]

The tensions between owner and overseer were on display on George Teal's plantation in November 1853. At that time, in a telling illustration of things to come, George and Charles got into a heated disagreement over Charles's management of the plantation. The details are not known. Evidently, Charles had taken one of George's horses, and somehow the horse died. George subsequently fired Charles, blaming him for the death of the horse and insisting that Charles did not have permission to ride it. George also refused to pay Charles any of his salary, withholding it as compensation for the value of the horse.[48]

Two months later, in January 1854, Tempe hired Charles to oversee the Price plantation. Tempe likely knew about the dispute between Charles and George. After all, the families occupied similar positions, and word of good and bad overseers circulated among plantation owners in the same timeless manner information has always been exchanged. The dispute was evidently not enough to prevent Tempe from hiring Charles. For the last three or four years, Tempe's son, Albert, had been managing the farm. Once he left to become a planter in his own right, the family needed someone with experience to take over, even if he came with a questionable past. Under the contract, Charles was to receive $300 in exchange for ensuring the plantation remained productive. Charles would have thirty-eight men and women at his disposal, including Miles. It was a lot for one person to handle. But Charles, in the typical fashion of a professional overseer, dismissed concerns that he might have difficulty managing either them or the property. He might have been the only white person on the plantation, but, with a double-barrel shotgun in hand, he felt confident that his word was law.[49]

Charles's lawyer, H. M. Kinsey, later played off this theme of Charles being a firm yet committed overseer, determined to maintain control over a difficult and sometimes unruly labor force. Kinsey himself was not a slaveholder or a farmer or even a southerner—he was from Pennsylvania. But like any lawyer worth his salt he appreciated a good story and understood the importance of having the jury identify with his client. In 1850, Kinsey had been one of fifteen lawyers in town. He had a modest practice, grinding out a living in a way familiar to attorneys of every generation. With a few papers stuffed into his saddlebags, Kinsey rode circuit, picking up cases here and there as the "Old Fifth" District Court rotated between counties. He lodged in the Huston Hotel in San Augustine, and it was here that Charles approached him in the spring or summer of 1854, after Tempe let him go.⁵⁰

At the time, Charles was in a bad spot. He had nothing to show for his time overseeing the Teal plantation the year before, and he was now without a source of livelihood for 1854. As Kinsey listened to Charles recount the events of the past year, he came to the conclusion that the George Teal affair, rather than the Price one, was the more promising. At the Prices, Charles had shot a slave, and although the law defined both slaves and horses as personal property, Kinsey had to be conscious of how far he could push the theory. The Texas Supreme Court had recently upheld a homicide conviction of a white man for killing a slave—something not possible for killing a horse—on the grounds that slaves were to be "treated as *persons*, in the contemplation" of the criminal law. The court later expounded on the logic. "The interest of the master, as well as the dictates of humanity, require that [slaves] be within the protection of the law, and so they have ever been considered in this State." With this in mind, Kinsey convinced Charles to sue George first, insisting in the petition that Charles had every right to use George's horse and that the death was an accident. The strategy paid off. During the spring term of 1855, when the case went to trial, the jury awarded Charles $225 in damages.⁵¹

Buoyed by the success, and perhaps prodded by financial needs, Kinsey agreed to represent Charles in his suit against Tempe that following fall term. The allegations in the petition were simple and much as before: Charles had been hired to oversee the plantation for the year; he had been wrongfully discharged; and he was entitled to his wages plus damages. He asked for $500. For reasons that have long been lost, the original petition was misplaced or overlooked for a year. Kinsey refiled the same in the October term of 1856, scratching out the allegations in a hand that likely frustrated the court then as much as it does a reader today.⁵²

Kinsey's approach from the outset was to make this a case about Miles—he was a "worthless, malicious ... wicked and dangerous negro." The day Charles shot Miles was not their first encounter. The Monday before, while they were in the barnyard, Charles told another slave to take a yoke of oxen out to the fields. Miles immediately stepped forward and interfered with the order, insisting that the oxen were not to be worked. The reason Miles interfered is not stated. Miles may have seen this moment as an opportunity to damage Charles's standing with the Prices. If Miles disliked or hated Charles—a not unlikely scenario—he could have been expressing concern over the owner's property in an effort to turn the Prices against him. It was a common strategy. Enslaved individuals understood that an owner sometimes took the side of the slave, if only because, as Eugene Genovese put it, "overseers came and went; the slaves remained." Then again, Miles may have interfered simply because he knew more about farming than Charles. By taking over the management of the livestock, it offered him an opportunity to let Charles, for whom he likely had utter contempt, know where they both stood.[53]

Either way, Charles's frustration must have been palpable. He was the overseer, the only white person on the plantation. Yet here was a slave, someone who was supposed to be humble and obedient in all things, challenging his authority. The two exchanged a few more words before Charles picked up a piece of wood—a fence rail—and swung it at Miles. Miles was too quick on his feet, however, and Charles delivered only a glancing blow.[54]

Charles later insisted that, had he gotten "a fair lick at him," he would have "knocked him down."[55]

But Miles was too healthy, too strong. He grabbed Charles and wrestled him to the ground. Silence soon began to descend over the yard, as Miles wrapped his hands around Charles's neck and started to squeeze the life out of him.[56]

Some of the other nearby slaves, sensing the seriousness of the moment, grabbed Miles and pulled him off. Charles struggled to his feet, but by then Miles was gone.[57]

Miles stayed away a week, hiding out in the woods, waiting for tempers to cool. When he came back the following Monday, he went out into the fields and started plowing. Charles was irate. He grabbed his double-barreled shotgun, charged up to the fields, and confronted Miles at the end of the row Miles was plowing. Charles told him to stop but, in a move that should have surprised no one, Miles simply turned the corner and started up the next row, trailing his horse. Charles followed him for a handful of steps until they met up with another slave—maybe it was John or Ben or Philip—plowing the adjoining row in the opposite direction. Charles ordered the other person to take a hold of Miles's horse, but he refused. By this time, Charles's anger may have been turning to fear, as he began to wonder whether his white skin, which in his mind had entitled him to certain privileges, was now going to be his death. Miles and another man were staring him down, and others no doubt were close by.[58]

When Miles dropped his plowlines and began to run, Charles brought his shotgun to his shoulder and fired, emptying both barrels. Charles had previously loaded it with squirrel shot rather than buck shot because, he said, he only wanted to wound him, to restore order, not to kill him. Still, Charles hit him both times, penetrating a thick shirt to fill Miles's back and thighs as well as his head. Miles struggled forward another fifty yards, but Charles caught up to him. When he did, Miles pulled out a knife in desperation. Charles then drew his own and ordered Miles to put his away. This time, with blood dripping down his back and staining his shirt, Miles did as he was told.[59]

Keeping Miles in front of him, Charles had Miles start walking back toward the house. Charles stopped briefly to reload his shotgun, putting "in such a load as, if it had hit the Negro Miles, would have stopped him from ever running again." As Charles reloaded, Miles kept walking, creating considerable space between them. As they neared the house, Miles saw his chance, "skipped around the corncrib and ran away."[60]

Tempe

Tempe Price was born in North Carolina in 1804. She was the daughter of Ichabod and Susan Thomas, who were neighbors of the Prices in Edgecombe County. Edgecombe County was a thriving inland port at the time. Successful families, including the Prices and Thomases, engaged in farming and trade. In 1821, when she was seventeen years old, Tempe married Elijah, who was thirty at the time. She went on to bear ten children over the next three decades, as they moved from North Carolina to Alabama to Texas. In San Augustine, she and Elijah were among the first to join the Episcopal church there, which "Mrs. James Pinckney Henderson"—the wife of the lawyer who would represent her—"had labored so tirelessly to establish." In 1852, when Elijah died, Tempe was forty-eight years old and suddenly facing the difficult task of not just dictating the moral compass of the family but also overseeing its future economic success.[61]

Charles's lawyer, H. M. Kinsey, had nothing against Tempe. Whatever clients think about the parties on the other side, good lawyers are trained to stay focused on the merits, developing the arguments that best help the person they represent. Kinsey's case against Tempe depended on him keeping the jury focused on Miles's character. Playing up the image of the rebellious Nat Turner—the enslaved man who led a bloody insurrection across the Virginia countryside in 1831, striking fear in the hearts and minds of countless whites throughout the South—Kinsey hoped the jury would see that Miles's conduct in the yard and in the field demonstrated that he was far from the loyal servant, trusted to hold the keys or pull a wagon loaded with cotton to town. His "general reputation," said Samuel Colten, a witness for the plaintiff, "was that he was a disobedient, wicked & malicious negro."[62]

Kinsey knew what he was doing. Despite his northern roots, he knew that southerners in general and Texans in particular were comfortable talking about slaves as if they were bereft of moral agency or individual characteristics. He knew that it was far easier for whites to deny the humanity of people of color if they could be reduced to a stereotype: the good or bad slave, obedient or rebellious. Under Kinsey's version, Miles fell in the latter category and was not to be trifled with. I "shot him and would do it again," announced Charles, during a heated conversation he had with Tempe after the incident. Miles had flaunted his authority, had urged other slaves to disobey, had run away, and had threatened him with violence. The next step was outright rebellion.[63]

Governor J. Pinckney Henderson, the Prices' lawyer, told a far different story. Henderson's strategy did not involve disputing any of the major events. The difference in approach, in both style and substance, came in the focus. Where plaintiff's witnesses saw a "disobedient" slave, defendant's witnesses "never had any difficulty"; where one side saw a "malicious negro," the other side saw an "able hand." Through Henderson's deft questioning, the story shifted from a bad slave to a reckless and incompetent overseer. This was a man who had shunned the advice and refused the help of others. He had tried to run the plantation on his own and had lost control. Miles was not to be blamed. Under the Prices, Miles had been "a stout healthy man," a reliable servant "able to do as much work as any other hand." No one ever "had any difficulty in managing or controlling" him. If, under Charles, Miles became unruly and stopped following orders, the fault lay with the person who let him become that way.[64]

Henderson was cut from a far different cloth than Kinsey, and the methodical method by which he built his case only reminded those present of the differences between the two. An early settler of East Texas, Henderson was a soldier, statesman, and elite lawyer. Standing tall and erect, with rather severe features, Henderson impressed upon others that he was a man of intelligence and honor. In 1841, he started one of the most successful law practices in the state. His partner was Thomas Rusk, who, in addition to serving honorably in the Texas Revolution, had been chief justice of the Republic of Texas Supreme Court and would later become a U.S. senator. Four years later Henderson was elected the first governor of the state of Texas. After one term—he declined to run a second time—he returned to San Augustine to practice law. His wealth far surpassed most everyone in the area, with real estate estimated at $30,000 in 1850. In contrast to the simple cabins in which most residents of the area lived, Henderson built an impressive two-and-a-half-story house on the southern border of town, modeled after the plantation homes of the Old South. He was a grandee, in every sense of the word.[65]

J. Pinckney Henderson. Courtesy of the State Preservation Board, Austin, Texas

Henderson's physical presence in the courtroom must have served as a striking metaphor, reminding those present of the difference in worldviews of the two parties. Dressed in a tailored suit, with his hair combed neatly to the side, Henderson represented the benevolent side of slavery. This was the side of slavery that talked about servants—they preferred that term rather than "slave"—as if they were members of the family, with no "truer friends than the southern master." "If any sane man were asked what it is that would be best for these negroes," ran a common refrain, "he would say put them under the discipline and care of someone whose duty and interest it would be to train them to usefulness, and to care for them." Henderson played on this theme the further he got into his questioning. Miles scratched and crawled his way ten miles from the plantation to Tempe's home in town, Henderson suggested, not because Miles was near death and had nowhere to turn, but because he knew Tempe would take care of him like the Prices had always done. Watching from counsel's table, Tempe nodded her head in agreement. She called for the doctor, she told herself, because she was a humane owner, concerned about Miles's health, not because she was in danger of losing $1,000 worth of property as easily as if someone had come into her home and taken it from her dresser drawer.[66]

Henderson knew how to work a jury. He called on Albert and Benjamin to gather history on Miles. He also called on the treating physician, Dr. J. J. Roberts, to hear how much Miles had been damaged. Charles had put between "15 and 25 shot holes in him," firing from a distance of twenty to thirty yards. By the time the doctor examined him, Miles was running a high fever and was having trouble breathing. The doctor listened to his lungs and could hear fluid. He could not be sure whether the shot had penetrated the lungs, but there was no doubt, in his professional opinion, that Miles had grown sick as a result of the incident. Six months later when Dr. Roberts saw Miles again, he was exhibiting all "the physical signs of tuberculosis in his lungs." The doctor continued to treat him and Miles "improved very much," but Albert said that he had remained "sickly" and was "unable to do regular work." Benjamin said that, after the shooting, Miles could do "nothing but small jobs about the house—such as he could sit down and do." He had been "laid up" most of the time.[67]

Henderson's presentation of the case was designed to impress the jury that Tempe's decision to countersue Charles for $1,500 was not just about money. This was a culture steeped in honor, and "a man without honor," said the *Marshall, Texas Republican*, "is a dead body, from which every one turns with disgust." Charles had shot a member of their family, and the Prices could no more let this go than if it had been one of the daughters. "There are three things for which a southerner will quickly draw his knife," the *Galveston Weekly News* reported, "call him a liar, insult a female, or abuse his nigger." The benevolent side of slavery had picture-perfect representation.[68]

As Henderson finished questioning his last witness, gathering his notes before sitting down next to Tempe, the jury's attention shifted to Kinsey as he called two more witnesses to the stand. Kinsey, with trousers worn by the saddle, stood in sharp contrast to the well-dressed Henderson, highlighting their different views of the case. Disregarding the image of slavery's benevolence, Kinsey's case was all about the democratic appeal of the institution. It was a version of slavery that depended on race, not benevolence, exploiting notions of black inferiority and white superiority. "There is a *natural* inferiority in the negro slave," said an article published in the *Galveston Weekly News* around the time of the trial, "which gives dignity, and a mutually recognized equality to the white superior race, to whom they are subservient." Charles had lived his life according to this ideal. The shotgun he carried, the whippings he administered, the patrols on which he served—they all reinforced the notion that, when it came to race, things would break in his favor.[69]

Kinsey hoped his version of slavery resonated with residents of San Augustine. He had some reason for optimism. Some of the people following the trial were backwoods farmers fitting the old mold of the Regulators and Moderators. They were the type of people who bought into the notion that, when Miles challenged Charles's authority and refused to obey, it was an affront not just to Charles but to the entire white race. These men worked their fields without the benefit of slave labor. They chopped wood to build their own cabins and split rails to construct their own fences. They may have dreamed of owning slaves, but they did not respect the delicate hands of the planter elite. This was the frontier. In their minds, there were no distinctions among classes. Whether owner or overseer, they were entitled to certain privileges based on the color of their skin, including the right to demand respect from those who had a darker hue. The *Austin, Texas State Gazette* summed up their sentiments well. "All white citizens in the same circumstances," it insisted, "are entitled to equal civil and political rights, without regard to any difference of fortune or station."[70]

Miles

The twelve men asked to reach a verdict in *Brady v. Price* must have appreciated that this case took place in October. It was a pleasant time of the year. Westerly breezes, rustling the leaves of the oaks and pecans, helped bring the temperature down to tolerable levels and provided welcome relief from the stifling heat of the summer. October was also an important month for harvesting cotton, as the jury well knew. The fifteen hundred slaves in the county did the bulk of the labor, backs bent from years of stooping over and hands hardened by the sharp edges of the cotton bolls, but in a county so focused on cotton, the harvest invariably touched most everyone. In the courtroom, as the breeze drifted through the open windows, the sounds of the harvest would have been hard to escape—the rattle of a wagon filled with cotton on the rutted roads, the muffled negotiations of buyers and sellers haggling over a price.

The voices of those not present helped drive home the point that this was no ordinary case. The distant sounds of cotton commerce, like the appearance of counsel, signaled to the jurors that more was at issue than an isolated dispute between parties. They were debating the very essence of slavery—what it was and what it should look like. Miles could no longer participate in the harvest. Was Charles to be congratulated or was he to be punished? Did he rightly shoot a slave who had challenged white authority, or did he unnecessarily interfere with the property interests of the slaveholding class? Digging even deeper, for anyone looking around the courtroom filled with lawyers and jurors and clients and spectators—all white—the perceptive among them must have realized that they were hashing out and reconfiguring the boundaries of slavery because of the actions and perspective of a person they had repeatedly sought to contain and control. In the confines of the San Augustine courtroom, without saying a single word, Miles had successfully pitted owner against overseer, benevolence against democracy, white against white.

Miles's refusal to play the part of the obedient servant was part of a larger theme showing how the formal law of race was hardly reflective of the everyday experience of race and slavery. In the homes of owners and in the halls of the Texas legislature, slaves were made subordinate in all things, stripped of basic rights if not humanity itself. But each time Texans learned of a slave resisting or rebelling, they had to come to terms with the practical realities of persons with a will of their own. Anyone who read the newspaper knew that running away was common, with frantic owners placing ads offering handsome rewards for the return of their valuable property. The nature of the Texas frontier, with its vast, rugged stretches of under- and less-populated regions, helped increase its occurrence. Many only stayed away a week, like Miles did, hiding in the woods. Others sought to escape permanently, running not to the North but south to Mexico. By the time Miles ran away from Charles, the problem, in the minds of white Texans, had reached epic proportions. Mexicans were "placing themselves on an equality with the slave," intoned the editor of the *Austin, Texas State Gazette*, causing them to "stir up among our servants a spirit of insubordination." Texans subsequently convened a conference in Gonzales County to address the "hundreds" that were fleeing south. "The escape of our slaves into Mexico by the help of Mexicans and otherwise," the promoters warned, "has become a matter of magnitude, and of sufficient importance to demand some decided action on the part of the people of Western Texas."[71]

Texans appreciated the infectiousness of resistance and rebellion, given their own history at the Alamo and San Jacinto. As they well understood, when one rose up, others were bound to follow. Yet it must have felt to some that the harder they pushed, the more their slaves pushed back. With a curt, "I spects you does sir," a slave named John ran from Henry Hedgepeth after Henry threatened to whip him for taking down a fence rail. In the subsequent search, no one could find John, with everyone assuming he drowned in the river. The fact that he was an "expert swimmer," and very well could have found his way to freedom, was seemingly lost on his pursuers.[72]

The newspapers and law reports helped sensationalize each act of resistance. Readers of the *Austin, Texas State Gazette*, for example, learned how one runaway, after William and Matilda Baker tied him up in their house, found a butcher knife, cut himself loose, and stabbed them to death. Others read about a man and a woman who chopped up their owner with an ax and then burned the body in an effort to avoid detection. The story of Jake likely caught the eye of people in San Augustine. He was caught plotting to poison the family that enslaved him in nearby Nacogdoches. The *Clarksville Northern Standard* similarly frightened its readers with a story about two slaves of William Gaffeney, who "without a moment's warning," knocked him off his horse and beat him to death with a club. In the same county, readers learned of a runaway who beat his captor over the head with a sledgehammer after the captor foolishly forced him to help him fashion his own leg irons. The *Austin, Texas State Gazette*, popular throughout the state, had only this to say. "Negroes murdering white people in Texas is becoming painfully frequent."[73]

Individual acts of violence inevitably led to fears of insurrection. In October 1835, as the first shots were being fired in the Texas War for Independence, residents of Madison County were "in a state of considerable agitation and excitement," convinced of "a black and bloody conspiracy." A few years later, in Nacogdoches, talk of insurrection surfaced after several slaves were holding dances and "seen at all hours of night, coming in and going out of town." In 1856, the month before jurors heard testimony of how Miles talked back to Charles, they read about how slaves in Colorado County, before escaping to Mexico, had designs to murder all the inhabitants of the county, "with the exception of the young ladies who were to be taken captives and made the wives of the diabolical murderers of their parents and friends." Residents found evidence lurking under every bush, with every greeting, imagining the entire slave population to be in on the plan. "To carry out their hellish purposes," the reports claimed, slaves "organized into companies of various sizes, had adopted secret signs and pass-words, sworn never to divulge the plot under the penalty of death, and had elected captains and subordinate officers to command the respective companies."[74]

Put another way, it seems that, no matter how determined the whites of Texas were, the people they tried to control and hold down never went quietly, and the trial between Tempe and Charles, owner and overseer, brought this fact home and made it real. As much as the law sought to remove the will of slaves, to force them into utter submission and deny their humanity, in reality it was slaves that were making law and shaping the debate. Agency, perspective, participation—these were all things that white society tried to deny the slave. But Miles's conduct made clear that this goal was impossible to achieve. The laws and ideals of slavery had been made vulnerable by his refusal to obey.[75]

The Verdict

Judge Archibald Hicks, who presided over the case between Tempe and Charles, would surely have liked to avoid the difficult matters that occupied his court. The job of judging was tough enough. Along with the lawyers, judges also spent months away from home during their "annual migration," traveling with attorneys to hold court in counties assigned to them. Judge Hicks, who resided in Shelbyville, had been on the road since March, hearing cases in Sabine, Shelby, Jasper, Newton, Angelina, and Nacogdoches, in addition to San Augustine. His calendar of cases would likely take him into December before he could return to his home.[76]

The men who made up the jury reflected a broad swath of San Augustine. They were an eclectic group that gave Tempe and her lawyer reason for optimism even as Kinsey wove a story that made his client out to be one of them. To be sure, the jurors were not all members of Tempe's standing. In fact, of the nine jurors who can be positively identified, three did not even own their own land. But most probably agreed that Kinsey had the tougher charge. In the years since the first settlers carved their homesteads out of the woods, the population of San Augustine had grown to the point where it was no longer considered a borderland. With civilization came formalization, and with it a certain respect for the institutions of power, including a slaveholding power. Indeed, it was one thing to speak in platitudes about how all whites shared a common identity. It was another to convince the jurors of San Augustine in 1856 to vote that view into practice.[77]

Of the nine identifiable jurors, one of the more prominent was William Shaw, the assessor and collector of taxes for the county. Shaw was thirty-eight years old at the time of the trial. Originally from Kentucky, he had been a resident of Texas since at least 1842, when his oldest child was born. Shaw conducted the federal census in 1850, and as such had occasion to meet everyone in the county, including the Prices and Charles. His political responsibilities had served him well. Not only did he know about the lives and economic standing of all the residents, but he also understood that, in Texas as elsewhere, the relative worth of a man and the position he held was often tied to his economic success. On that score, Shaw had the right to include himself among the better-off, and, consequently, the better connected. In 1850 he owned real property worth an estimated $1,200. His fellow jurors elected him the foreman.[78]

Sitting next to Shaw in the jury box was O. H. P. Bodine. Bodine was one of four farmers on the jury. Thirty-five at the time of the trial, he had been living in Texas for a dozen years or more. Bodine owned his own farm, and while it was nowhere near the size of the Price plantation—he told Shaw it was worth $200 when the latter took the census—the fact that he called it his own meant that he could count himself among the successful. Living at Bodine's home in 1850 was Thomas Thompson, a young farmhand who helped Bodine in the days before his sons were old enough to participate in the harvest. Bodine was from Louisiana, and like his younger brother who lived nearby, was no doubt a strong supporter of slavery, hoping one day to join the ranks of the slaveholding class.[79]

Burwell Eaves was also a farmer who owned his own land. At fifty-eight, he was the oldest member of the jury. Eaves had come to Texas sometime before the Texas Revolution, offering him a unique perspective to go along with the wisdom of age. Eaves's wife had passed away before the 1850 census, but Eaves was not alone. A number of children, and perhaps grandchildren, lived on the family homestead. Like Bodine's farm, Eaves's property was not worth as much as the Prices'—he told Shaw it was worth $300 in 1850—but its small value belies the importance it played in the family's life and its future outlook.[80]

The other two farmers on the jury did not own their own land. Thomas Norwood was twenty-one at the time of the trial and the youngest member of the jury. He grew up in a large family that moved to Texas from North Carolina. The other farmer was John Henry. Henry was forty-five with a wife and several young children. Neither family had much to its name. Still, Norwood and Henry were able to claim something that Charles Brady could not, and it may have been enough to set them apart: both men worked for themselves. They grew their own crops and tended to their own livestock, taking pride in knowing that they could provide for their families as they built a better life for their children.[81]

Of the remaining four jurors who can be identified today, three practiced a trade. James Higgins was one of several carpenters in town. His skill was always in need, with the area continuing to expand as new immigrants moved into the county. He was thirty-five and married. He did not list any real property in the 1850 census, which meant he rented the home where he and his wife lived.[82]

Adam Smith was a wagonmaker from Germany. His decision to adopt an English-sounding name, as well as his decision to take up residence in San Augustine rather than in the broad, fragmented belt across the south central part of the state where most Germans settled, provides some insight into Smith's mind-set. Abandoning his native culture, he embraced the southern spirit and all it entailed. He married a woman from Alabama sixteen years his junior. He was a homesteader, with land and surrounding property worth a comfortable $1,000.[83]

J. T. Childers was a saddler from Virginia. He was thirty-eight at the time of the trial, with a wife and several children. Childers was doing well for himself. His property was worth $1,200, and he employed a tanner in his shop and trained two apprentices. In 1850 he also owned four slaves, all of them female. One was an adult and the other three ranged in age from one to eleven.[84]

The ninth member of the jury hailed from the Prices' economic and social status. He was a young man named Moses Broocks, and he was the son of Travis G. Broocks, an early settler of San Augustine and a well-respected resident. Travis had long been active in politics and the development of the county. He was a wealthy merchant and farmer with land worth $11,500 in 1850 and the owner of almost forty slaves in 1860. He was also an officer in the San Augustine militia, helping to put down the Regulator and Moderator War in 1844. Moses was a child at the time his father helped restore order to the neighboring county, but the event likely made a strong impression on him. "General" Broocks, along with others of his standing, made clear that people who took the law into their own hands constituted serious threats to a civilized society. Elijah and Tempe held the same view, and it should come as no surprise that the Prices and the Broocks knew each other well. Travis and Elijah were both members of the Masonic fraternity, and as town patrons they helped lead the area's annual July 4th celebration in 1851. "Under the management of Genl. T. G. Broocks, and Cols. Blount and Davis," the *Red-Lander* reported with great satisfaction, the morning of the festivities consisted of a well-organized parade and several inspiring speeches. Capped off by the reading of the Declaration of Independence, "the immense crowd moved on to the grove at Col Price's spring, where a sumptuous dinner was prepared, and one which was amply sufficient for all who were in attendance." When the trial between Tempe and Charles started in 1856, Moses was twenty-three and striking out on his own, no doubt hoping to follow in the footsteps of the generation before him to become one of San Augustine's leading citizens.[85]

The three remaining jurors are difficult to identify. The scribble of the clerk recording the names of two of them makes it impossible to conclusively identify those two. Another member, George Taylor, cannot be definitely found in the local records. Texas law did not require jurors at the time to be property owners, so there is no guarantee that the remaining three, much like Thomas Norwood and John Henry, owned their own land or counted much else among their possessions. Odds are, however, they resembled the other members of the jury in the sense that they either owned land or worked it themselves. Serving on juries was like voting. It was a privilege, an honor, extended to those who were thought capable of having a say in local affairs. It did not, in other words, include the type of people that Kinsey might have wanted, those who preferred their isolated existence and resented people like the Prices.[86]

When Judge Hicks sat down to instruct the jury, he made no mention of slavery's ideology. He never talked about the democratic ideal or the benevolence of the system. Instead, he kept the jury focused on the practical question of whether Charles's use of force was justified or excessive. An "overseer has the right to exact obedience to his lawful commands," he told them, "and to use such restriction, coercion, and chastisement as is necessary to make the slave obedient to his orders not extending to life or limb." He then added a proviso, which J. Pinckney Henderson had argued to be included. "But," he said, "[he] has no right to inflict serious bodily harm endangering life for mere disobedience to his order. The right to life and limb is an inherent right existing by the laws of nature & which the law of the land does not pretend to take from the slave."[87]

It is, perhaps, hard to know what the result might have been if the person shooting Miles had been his owner rather than an overseer. Like other states, Texans built protections in their laws to set limits on the mistreatment of slaves, making it against the law for anyone, including an owner, to "unreasonably abuse or cruelly treat a slave." But the "humanity" white Texans liked to celebrate as justification for these laws was probably less about protecting slaves than it was about guarding their own property rights and easing their own troubled conscience. After all, no one seemed much interested in the humanity of slaves on the public auction block. They sold them according "to strengt' and muscles," remembered Stearlin Arnwine, from nearby Rusk, in East Texas. "They was stripped to de wais'. I seed the women and little chillum cryin' and beggin' not to be separated, but it didn' do no good. They had to go." Writing protections for enslaved persons into the law, however, served the type of legitimizing purpose Eugene Genovese made current in his discussion about the hegemonic function of the law, allowing people from Texas to invoke the rights of a slave when circumstances "merited" it. It just so happened that this most often occurred when the person inflicting the harm was a third party, not an owner. In such a case, liability, whether civil or criminal or both, was likely to follow, with courts holding up their commitment to the rights of the enslaved as justification.[88]

Perhaps it is not surprising, then, as San Augustine County transitioned from a borderland society to a civilized one, that the jury in the case of an owner versus an overseer returned a verdict in favor of the owner, in the sum of $516.67. The amount is unusual and, we can only assume, reflected the intense negotiation and compromise that takes place among jurors. Tempe had asked for more—$1,500—but even the most favorable testimony had Miles—a dead Miles—worth only $1,000. Since he was still among the living, and capable of limited work, the jury must have concluded that he still had some value. Perhaps the jury also subtracted a reasonable amount of wages for the time Charles worked for Tempe, from January through March. Whatever its motivations, and however it came to its calculations, in finding in favor of Tempe the jury made clear that, even in the backwoods of Texas, there were limits to how far non-slaveholders could act out the privileges of whiteness, if it meant interfering with the rights of slaveholders. A poor overseer, tolerated but hardly admired, probably never had a chance. Race, it seems, had surfaced in the form of a class conflict, and Charles came out the loser.[89]

Postscript

Four years after the jury resolved the question of slavery in Tempe's favor, it was again thrown into question. Beginning in July 1860, a wave of fires swept across Dallas, Denton, and other communities in North Texas. Suspicion fell immediately on slaves and northern agitators, and soon the entire state was engulfed in wild tales of elaborate conspiracies. It was a startling contradiction to the benevolent story of slavery, which had played out to perfection in the San Augustine courtroom. "All experience hath shown that while an inferior being, the negro is indisputably adapted by nature, to the condition of servitude to the white man, yielding to him willing obedience and affection," reported the House of Representatives Committee on Slaves and Slavery, in what may have sufficed for J. Pinckney Henderson's closing argument. He is "enjoying a degree of health unequalled by any other servile class in any portion of the world; multiplying in a ratio unknown to most other races and conditions; and in that condition attaining a higher civilization and religious development, and enjoying more of the blessings of life than in any other state in which he has ever existed, in ancient or modern times." Yet, for some reason that was suddenly lost on those espousing this view, these same slaves were now trying to overthrow their owners in armed and violent rebellion.[90]

Charles Pryor of the *Dallas Herald* helped inflame the story of a slave rebellion, which began inconspicuously enough on a Sunday in July 1860, when a fire started outside a store in Dallas. Within hours, the fire spread to neighboring establishments, consuming two hotels, the printing building of the *Herald*, and several other buildings. During that same blistering day, in which temperatures topped "106 degrees F., in the shade" with "a high South-west wind blowing," another fire started in nearby Denton. It burned down several buildings before spreading to one that contained twenty-five kegs of gunpowder. Within a few moments the kegs "exploded with tremendous force, scattering fragments of the buildings and goods in every direction." Reports of the incident said that "pieces of burning timber, fragments of chains and casting were scattered for hundreds of yards, penetrating the buildings on the other side of the square, and setting several of them on fire, and it was only by the utmost exertions of the few people that happened to be in town that the remaining business portion of our thriving village was saved." This, it turned out, was only the beginning. Over the next several days and weeks, other fires started in several neighboring counties seemingly without explanation, burning down multiple businesses, residences, and stores.[91]

Looking back, it is hard to know whether the curiously large number of fires in the summer of 1860 were deliberately set or simply the inevitable result of a hot, dry summer in Texas. Dr. Pryor of the *Dallas Herald*, however, concluded that it could only be part of a "deep laid scheme of villainy to devastate the whole of Northern Texas." Through a series of articles republished throughout the state, Pryor played on the suppressed fears of a slaveholding population, as he kept them apprised of the scope of the "diabolical plot." Using the opportunity to drag down the North as well as invoke the same images Kinsey used to describe Miles, Pryor found evidence of rebellion in every suspicious glance. "Each county has a special Superintendent, a white man," he warned, "and each county is laid off into districts under the supervision of a white man, who controls the action of the negroes in that district." Plans, he said, involved setting fire to the homes of "our most prominent citizens," who "were to be assassinated when they make their escape." It was Texas's version of Nat Turner's rebellion, with warnings that shook the foundations of the entire state. "Arms have been discovered in possession of the negroes, and the whole plot revealed for a general insurrection and civil war at the August election. I write in haste; we sleep upon our arms; and the whole county is deeply excited."[92]

~

When H. M. Kinsey appealed the verdict in *Brady v. Price*, he was short on the type of hyperbole that found its way into Dr. Pryor's reports. There were no references to a "deep laid scheme of villainy," no warnings that this was the "day set for putting the white people to the fire and sword." It was for the better. The justices of the Texas Supreme Court were no more inclined to side with Charles than any other member of the prominent classes. Like J. Pinckney Henderson, who argued the case on Tempe's behalf, all of them were substantial property owners and established citizens, with slaves and personal holdings expected of men of their position. They dismissed Kinsey's argument that Charles "was justified in shooting the slave with small shot, when other means had failed to reduce him to obedience" in a short opinion. "The charge of the [district] Court was undoubtedly correct," it said, and Charles "had no right to shoot [Miles] down for the purpose of stopping him when retreating against his orders." This was not self-defense but a "wrongful act, for the consequence of which he was responsible to the owner of the slave." The Texas Supreme Court, as it had done many times before, had embraced the benevolent story of slavery, ruling against the democratic ideals of a landless overseer.[93]

Charles did not have the money to pay Tempe for Miles. If he had, the irony would not have been lost on anyone. If Charles had been able to afford Miles, if he had enough money to pay for another human being, he likely would never have found himself in this position to begin with. The difficult reality for Charles was that he had spent his entire life positioning himself on a rung one step higher than every person of color. Yet now a person of color was bringing him down to a spot where even most whites wanted little to do with him. Poor, isolated, and without a role to play, Charles found his world turned upside down. He drifted deeper into the woods and out of historical memory.

If Charles ever reemerged, it likely would not have been until after the Civil War. By that time his version of slavery—the one that emphasized white superiority and black inferiority—had squeezed out the one about benevolence in the minds of most white Texans. In the postbellum years, with people of color demanding to be equal participants in the American experience, whites found solidarity in their skin color as they struggled to hold blacks down. East Texas in particular was a dangerous place to be. The infamous lynching of Henry Smith in 1893 in Paris, Texas, where hordes of whites gathered to watch a black man die, was a scene too often repeated in this part of the state, including as recently as 1998, when three white men dragged James Byrd to death behind their car in Jasper. After the Civil War, and as the century came to a close, poor and disenfranchised whites had finally found themselves on a winning side, as class distinctions melted in the face of a race war.[94]

As for Tempe, after she recovered what she could from Charles, she sued to recover the rest of the verdict in a separate garnishment action against Louis Greer, alleging that Louis owed Charles money. It turned out that she was wrong, and Louis did not owe Charles money. The writ was dismissed. Tempe died two years later, in 1859, at the age of fifty-five, apparently without having recovered the whole of the judgment but with the satisfaction of knowing that she had helped her family secure a place of prominence in San Augustine. Benjamin took over the *Red-Lander*, while Albert owned a large plantation. The other eight children were successful in their own right. The Prices were a family who, by East Texas standards, lived a comfortable and prominent life. Profiled by the *San Augustine Tribune* in 1994, they were remembered as having left "quite a legacy for San Augustine, East Texas, and the state itself!"[95]

Miles's story is the hardest to recover. There is no telling what surname he adopted after the Civil War, making him impossible to trace in the census. No death certificate identifies him, nor any memorial. At the time of the verdict he was about thirty-five years old, hampered by whatever injury or illness had sapped his strength. When Tempe died in 1859, he was listed along with the other slaves in the estate. The administrators did not think him worth much. He was valued at $300, and whether someone purchased him, or whether one of the family members kept him, is not known. He likely knew about the small notation next to his name in the estate record, the one that said he was "diseased." The term, however, was probably a better descriptor of what was happening around him. Miles had exposed the fiction on which the formal law of slavery rested. Texans had built their institution on the notion that slaves were merely extensions of their owner's will. They were human beings without personhood; they were property without rights. But Miles refused to accept his assignment. Like others, he rose up and fought back. When he did, he forced an emerging East Texas town into a class conflict over what slavery meant. Even as residents came to an agreement, signaling where their society was headed, it would not be the end of the matter. Out there on the county roads of rural Texas, along the riverbeds and behind the barns, life was too messy and too unstable. As quickly as white Texans worked out their questions about slavery and race, enslaved men and women resisted and rebelled, and threw it back open for debate.[96]

CHAPTER THREE

A Free Family of Color on the Borderland

The shotgun blast shattered the still air. It was May 25, 1856, and Samuel Deputy was on a flatboat drifting down the Sabine River on his way home. The serene setting, five miles below the emerging town of Madison (later called Orange) in Orange County, belied the simmering tension just below the surface. Like the river itself, life among the pine forests and marshy wetlands was moving rapidly. Connections built and secured over a generation were being tested and pushed to their limits, as new settlers flowed into the area with their own ideas about how the county should be governed. Deputy was among the new cast of characters, having arrived in the county a few years before, with few allegiances beyond a commitment to the southern way of life.[1]

The first blast did not kill Deputy, nor did several more. As he lay dying in the boat, Deputy's assailant ended his life by smashing his skull into a bloody pulp with the butt of his gun. The author of this brutal message was Sam Ashworth, part of a clan of free people of color, most of them related, that had complicated the storyline of this remote section of Southeast Texas since before the Texas Revolution. The reason for the murder stemmed from a growing dispute between the old and the new. Not long before, the aptly named Deputy—he was also a onetime deputy sheriff of Orange County—had accused one of Sam's cousins, Clark, of stealing a hog. The charge was likely fabricated, or at least a mistake. The wealthy Ashworth clan owned both land and livestock, and the idea that they would purposely steal someone else's hog seemed out of character. The district court thought the charge merited an investigation, however, and it bound him over for a trial.[2]

Sam posted his cousin's bond. Soon after, bearing witness to the Texas wild, Sam challenged Deputy to a gunfight in the streets of Madison in an effort to

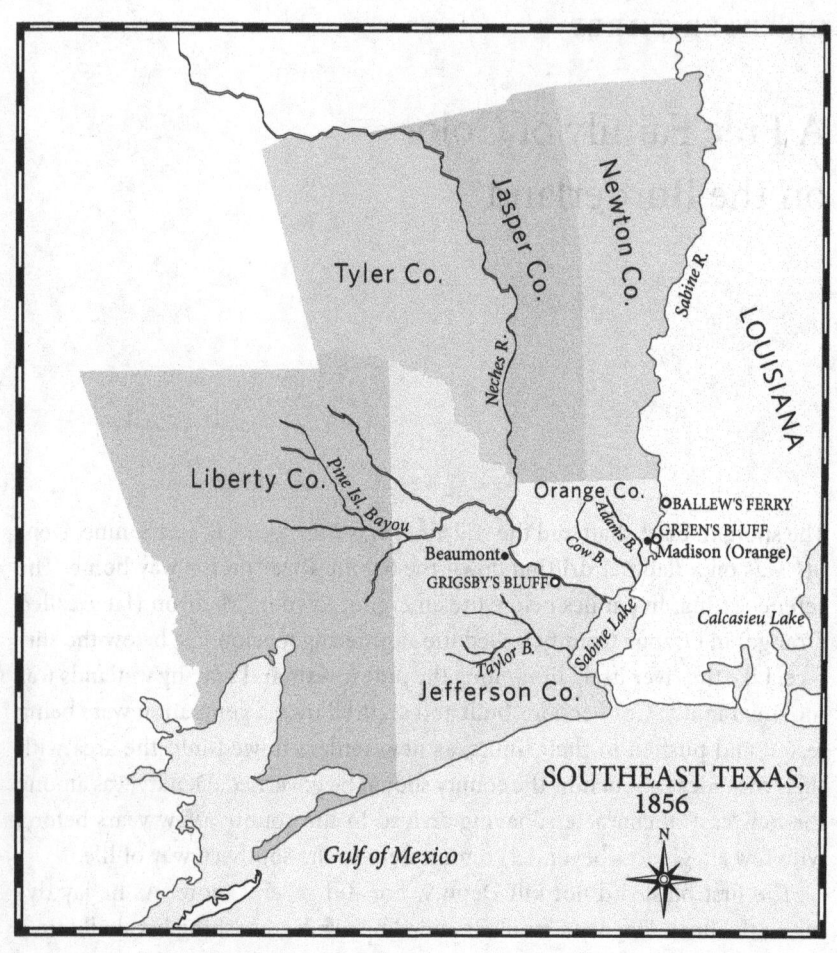

restore the family's name. With a crowd gathering, Deputy sidestepped the old-fashioned duel, choosing instead to go back to court and obtain another warrant, this time under a "statute providing against abusive language from negroes." Humiliated, Sam was brought before the same court as his cousin, and in short order it found him guilty and ordered a painful and degrading sentence of thirty lashes on a bare back.[3]

Perhaps if Sam had suffered the public reminder of his place, things might have turned out differently. Chances are, however, another spark would have started the fire that engulfed the region over the summer months to come. Things had begun to break against the Ashworths in recent years, as new arrivals pushed back against an ambiguous social and racial order created by the largest community of free people of color in Texas. They sought to harden the lines in Orange at the same time the rest of the state was tightening the boundaries between slavery and freedom. They found the Ashworths to be a troubling anomaly, and Texas laws and ideologies supported them in their views.[4]

But in a strange twist to the expected narrative, the community of Orange did not unite against the Ashworths. Some of the reports even suggested that the sheriff was on their side, having earlier helped Sam escape without a public whipping and then refusing to extend much effort in finding him and his two accomplices once the calls for their arrest were issued. The county soon descended into an all-out war, with the positions standing in for a much broader theme. Tucked in among the pines and winding bayous, with land, slaves, and white spouses, a free family of color had managed to embroil a Texas community in a violent confrontation over the meaning of race.[5]

The Redbones of Louisiana

Over in Big Woods, Louisiana, between the Calcasieu and Sabine Rivers, life was promising. James Ashworth had moved his family there in the first decade of the nineteenth century. Like so many others, the Ashworths left their corner of the world with hopes for a better future. They were stock raisers, most recently from the Pendleton District in South Carolina. The Pendleton District had once provided the Ashworths with a secure environment. It had long been remote, occupied primarily by Cherokee Indians. It was tucked away in the northwest corner of the state, far from the plantations along the South Carolina coast and the commercial center of Charleston. The Ashworths and a handful of other families with a common background, like the Perkins, the Dials, the Sweats, and the Goins, lived an isolated existence among the hills and hollows, letting their cattle graze in the native forests covered in peavine. As white residents of the low country slowly immigrated to the area in search of their own opportunities, however, the Ashworths found their way of life increasingly threatened. The new settlers brought with them notions about how to organize a society, which were often at odds with the frontier mentality of the Ashworths and the families that lived near them. Concerned that they would no longer be welcomed, the Ashworths and their neighbors decided to move on. As populations pushed west, bringing civilization, they pushed west too, past where most were willing to go.[6]

The family journeyed for months, following the worn-down paths of early explorers. They had heard that some families who shared a similar background had crossed the Blue Ridge Mountains into Tennessee and Kentucky. But the Ashworths and the Perkins and the others with them angled farther south, into Louisiana, before crossing into the Neutral Ground, a disputed area between Spain and the United States. The region took its name after President Thomas Jefferson negotiated the Louisiana Purchase with France and claimed that the province extended to the Rio Grande. His Spanish counterparts disagreed, maintaining that the Red River established the western boundary. With tensions high, the two sides avoided war only by drawing a line in the sand and agreeing to stay where the others were not. Spain promised not to cross the Sabine, and the United States agreed to stay east of the Calcasieu River and the Arroyo Hondo. The area was thus technically off-limits to settlers, whether from Spain or the United States, but these legalities did little to discourage the adventurous. Roustabouts and criminals, as well as frontier folk like the Ashworths, found the region too tempting to let alone. Sneaking across the river and squatting on undeveloped land, they built simple cabins out of rough-hewn logs and relished the distance between themselves and others.[7]

The area they settled eventually became St. Landry's Parish and then Calcasieu Parish, years after the border dispute was resolved in the United States' favor. The area was not for the pampered or those with weak constitutions. Alligators, hidden in holes, reached up with angry jaws to grab unsuspecting travelers. Mosquitoes buzzed incessantly during the warmer months, and stagnant pools were festering with snakes. But later reports also confirm the advantages the Ashworths sought. The Calcasieu was "a superb and solemn river, two hundred and thirty yards across and forty-five feet deep." It emptied into Calcasieu Lake, on the Gulf, and remained navigable for miles into the backcountry. Abundant rainfall and frequent flooding also meant that the land was relatively rich, requiring, a later source said, "but little labor to cultivate it successfully." Dotted among the pines and oaks were fruit trees, including peach, plum, and fig, providing welcome additions to the diet of those who settled there. Long-legged birds, "apparently on friendly terms with all the reptiles," positioned themselves in the swamps and creeks, and every spring migratory birds returned to "chant their melodious carols" from above.[8]

The Ashworths found much to like about the area. The "immense moist plain, bearing alternate tracts of grass and pine," provided the type of terrain the stock-raising family had sought since leaving South Carolina. Few inhabitants also meant their cattle, horses, and sheep could roam freely and undisturbed. But more important for them and the families who came with them, the undeveloped nature of the region meant they could set down roots past the lines of where most people cared. The Ashworths were part of a much larger network of distinct and identifiable families that had been living on the borderland of race for as long as anyone could remember. Back in the woods of Virginia and the Carolinas, and over in Tennessee and Kentucky, groups of people of ambiguous ancestry lived close to one another, mingling with whites but keeping to themselves when they could. Their white neighbors often gave them unusual names to reflect their mysterious backgrounds—the Melungeons, the Brass Ankles, the Croatans (now Lumbees), and the Turks. Their skin was swarthy, their eyes and hair dark brown or black. They possessed the kind of looks that kept the curious guessing about who they were. Some of the families invented tales about their own origins, in what was, no doubt, a transparent attempt to distance themselves from an African past. Some said they descended from the Portuguese-Spanish captain Juan Pardo's sixteenth-century expedition. Others preferred to tie their descent to Carthaginian or Phoenician seamen. Still others maintained they descended from survivors of the Lost Colony at Roanoke Island who married Native American women. All were fanciful tales and it is unlikely that many took them seriously. What mattered in the minds of most of the people who met them was that the families were not fully white, possessing a bit of European, African, and Native American, in quantities that no one seemed to know.[9]

When the Ashworths reached the Louisiana frontier, they circled their wagons around the families who had come with them. There were other free people of color in the area. Louisiana in general and New Orleans in particular had long been a haven for light-skinned blacks, many of them freed generations ago by wealthy French planters who had taken up with black women before there were laws against it. But the Ashworths and the other families, initially at least, kept a respectable distance, unsure of the language and culture of those who had adopted the surnames of their French fathers and grandfathers. The Ashworths, the Perkins, the Dials, and the Bunches staked out homes near one another and far from others, building a Baptist church where they could worship apart from the Catholics who settled there before them. They were close-knit and intimately connected—"clannish" in many ways, leading modern-day anthropologists and demographers to refer to them and the other groups scattered about the country as "tri-racial isolates." The handful of others who trickled across the Calcasieu and into their lives often did so with the understanding that some official policies would have to be set aside. Those who settled near them were adventurers, too, and out here the offer to help build a new roof or a kindly greeting—"Sit up, stranger, take some fry!"—often mattered far more than the rules of race. The white settlers took to calling the Ashworths and their neighbors Redbones, a term with an origin as mysterious as the people.[10]

~

William stood on the east bank of the Sabine, gazing across its expanse into Texas. He was one of nine children of James Ashworth and Keziah Dial, just a young boy when his parents started the long journey to Louisiana at the start of the century, but now, in 1831, a man of thirty-eight with his own wife and family. The Sabine was an impressive river. Like the Calcasieu, it emptied into its own lake before meeting up with the Gulf. Down here, where William stood, it was deep and powerful, with a remarkably strong flow. William had to be careful crossing it. It was easy for a person to become caught up in its current, and even easier for the cattle he planned to bring. Twelve years ago, in 1819, the Spanish and U.S. governments agreed to establish this part of the river as the border between Louisiana and Texas, and ten years ago the first of Austin's Old Three Hundred had crossed it, miles upstream, on their way to the Brazos. William had been across before, exploring the other side on his horse, considering whether its vast expanse might provide a suitable place to settle his family and his growing herds.[11]

William was the third son of James and Keziah. He had two older brothers, James and Jesse. His three younger brothers were Moses, Aaron, and Abner. William also had three sisters; Mary (whom they sometimes called Polly) was older than he, and Elizabeth and Sarah were younger. Like those before them, most of William's siblings intermarried with families with whom they had a long connection—two older brothers and a sister married members of the Perkins family, and two younger brothers married daughters of Drury Bunch. His sister Elizabeth married a member of the Nelson clan, another familiar name in the history of triracial isolates.[12]

William was the first of his siblings to venture outside the narrow kinship ties that bound the old families together, taking as his spouse a woman from the neighborhood rather than a cousin. Her name was Delaide Gallier, and her family story deviated little from the Ashworths, except in the color of skin. Like everyone in Big Woods, the Galliers were a hardscrabble lot. Women as well as men smoked pipes and chewed snuff, tanned cowhides, and gutted pigs. The family lived within a few miles of the Ashworths, and it was inevitable that they found things in common. They built their home out of the same pine logs, they trapped and hunted in the same woods, and they relied on the same resources to survive the hot summers and blustery winters. Looking back, for those unschooled in the ways of the frontier, hearing of interracial relationships of the type between William and Delaide confounds expectations. But in all likelihood, in this case as in so many others, the fact that she was white and he was not was dismissed as far less important than the ability to sustain a livelihood and provide for a family.[13]

On that score the Ashworths were in a better position than most. By the time William and Delaide, who was roughly ten years his junior, began living together, the family had herds of cattle and horses grazing along the plains. Their relative wealth brought a modicum of status, and the web of kinship provided security against encroachment. For over twenty-five years, the Ashworth clan had worked with others to make this "thinly settled" region a habitable slice of wilderness. Travelers passing through were not always impressed. Frederick Olmsted took note of the "vulgar obscenities" that seemed to pepper the most benign conversations, and he commented disparagingly on how residents "entertained one another with stories of fights and horse-trades." But what made the area undesirable to some was also what made it attractive to the Ashworths. The benefits of knowing this was a place where persons of like mind could be left alone, close to one another yet far removed from the opinions of others, was just what the family sought.[14]

In Louisiana, William and Delaide's marriage was never formalized, at least in the sense that they paid the filing fee and obtained a marriage certificate. That would have to wait several more years, until the end of the 1830s. The informal nature of their relationship, however, should not be interpreted as a lack of commitment. By the time they started talking seriously about moving across the Sabine into Texas, William and Delaide had five children, expanding the family's presence in the community and causing some to question the wisdom of the venture. With pine knots burning in fireplaces, cousins asked about starting over, about building cabins and planting crops in unfamiliar territory. But William assured them that the move was worth it, drawing on some of the same reasoning that motivated earlier immigrants.

Land was cheap and plentiful, with even more space than they had now. The soil was fertile, washed over with sediment from the Sabine. There were also two navigable bayous, "forming," a later source described, "two of the most beautiful natural canals that can well be imagined." And the Neches River, which flowed down from the northeast into Lake Sabine, ensured that, no matter where they were, they could readily navigate the marshy terrain and build for the future.[15]

The question of Texas being part of Mexico came up. The Ashworths and their neighbors were not a literate group, so what they knew had been learned from people coming and going. Those on their way out of Texas often spoke of the hardships, of the deprivations that accompany any effort to venture where there are few others. But William, at least, identified with the spirit of those on their way in. What he liked most about the idea was the freedom that Texas signified, and not just freedom in the sense that some white migrants emphasized. But freedom in the sense that there were no laws placing special burdens on people like him. Even in Louisiana, where free people of color had managed to create a caste of their own, they still often found themselves treated more like black slaves than white citizens. The law denied them access to the ballot box and certain professions, and they could expect a whipping rather than a fine when they violated the rules.[16]

Mexico, in contrast, did not place any special restrictions on free people of color. According to the law, they were simply Anglo-Americans, entitled to the same rights and benefits as others. William Goins (sometimes spelled Goyens or Goings), whose extended family migrated to Louisiana with the Ashworths, came over early because of it. He crossed the Sabine with some of the first settlers, perhaps as early as 1820, quickly earning a reputation in his home near Nacogdoches as a "very respectable coloured man." Lewis B. Jones was another of a handful of free people of color to venture over in the years before the Texas Revolution. He settled in Austin's colony in 1826.[17]

The perception that Mexico was a place that welcomed all comers, regardless of race, also inspired the likes of Benjamin Lundy. Lundy was a northern abolitionist who had lived in the same Missouri town as Moses and Stephen F. Austin when they formulated their colonization plans. Aware of their efforts as well as Mexico's antislavery stance, Lundy came to imagine Texas as an ideal place for free people of color. He was convinced that, freed of oppressive laws and the biases of others, black families would prosper and thrive, dispelling the commonly held notion that people of color were incapable of making it on their own. Texas was, he said, a "fine region where the rigors of winter are unknown, and where man, without distinction of color or condition, is looked upon as the being that Diety made him—*free and independent.*"[18]

Lundy proposed to secure a land grant to settle four hundred families of color on the Texas frontier. He took his first trip in 1832 and followed it up with two more, venturing deep into the Texas territory to explore its possibilities. Limited resources meant that he walked most of the time, allowing himself the luxury of a pony—procured by William Goins, whom he met and got to know—only on his final trip. A man of remarkable resilience, Lundy encountered numerous hardships and countless indignities. Settlers looked on him with suspicion, and Mexican officials provided conflicting and sometimes disappointing views of the project. One of Lundy's main stumbling blocks was a decree issued by the Mexican government on April 6, 1830. At that time, Mexican officials, growing concerned that Texans were refusing to give up their allegiances to the United States, decided to cut off further immigration of Anglo-Americans into the territory. The law, evaded by some, posed significant problems for Lundy, given the scale of his project. He found himself trying to convince officials of the merits of his proposal, negotiating terms and asking for exceptions. Even in the dark days, however, he remained optimistic. He continued to believe that Texas would "*present an asylum for hundreds of thousands of our oppressed colored people*," and he pursued his project with the type of dogged determination only a man convinced of a higher purpose could. Only after Mexico lost the territory in the Texas Revolution did Lundy give up his dream of a homeland for free people of color. By that time, he knew that the soul of Texas had been lost to the slaveholding interests.[19]

William's plans, of course, were far less ambitious than Lundy's. For him, the 1830 decree that had served as such a major stumbling block for Lundy was a nuisance, but nothing more. To be sure, under the law, a settler on government land was better defined as a squatter, unable to obtain a land title. But William came from a long line of individuals unconcerned about such details. His own father had ignored a similar prohibition twenty-five years ago when he crossed the Calcasieu and ventured into the Neutral Ground. William rationalized his move as no different. As he saw it, thousands of acres of land lay undeveloped on the other side of the Sabine, all for the taking. The decision had been made. In the spring of 1831, William and Delaide and their five children packed their belongings and headed toward the Sabine.[20]

Into Texas

William and Delaide approached the Sabine River from the saturated ground of Calcasieu. The children were too young to be of much help with the cattle, so William's brothers helped herd them through the bottoms. The muck and mire took its toll. By the time they made it to the river's edge, they were already exhausted, with the hardest part still to come. They needed to get across. William went first, guiding his horse into the turbid water. Behind him the others tried to keep the cattle contained, urging them forward with whoops and hollers. Once in the water, the drove struggled against the current, slowly swimming their way to the opposite shore. One of William's brothers tried to keep the herd facing upstream, or at least not downstream, lest they lose the greater part even before they set foot on dry land.[21]

On the other side, after gathering the herd, William and his family followed the Neches River for several miles. William had already familiarized himself with the area and where others had settled. Up on Green's Bluff, Bob Johnson and his wife had built a cabin six or seven years ago. Green's Bluff was on an elevated landing on the Sabine, where the river gently curved. Years later residents would insist that it was "one of the handsomest locations imaginable," and they built the town of Madison on its spot. Nearby, members of the Jett family, the Garners, and the Harmons set down roots. About twelve miles due west, on the Cow Bayou, George A. Pattillo and his family cleared a small plot of land about a year before William arrived. Pattillo was a wealthy landowner who would come to play an important role in the county as a political leader and judge. Across the Cow Bayou was the home of Claiborne West, another influential settler who would add his signature to the Texas Declaration of Independence. Below Pattillo were the Dysons. The family had ventured over from the same part of Louisiana as the Ashworths, providing a recognizable face and a testament of character. Along the Neches, the homes of Gilbert and William Stephenson, as well as a handful of others, dotted the banks.[22]

William and Delaide kept to the east side of the Neches. After the Texas War for Independence, the area on both sides of the river became Jefferson County, and in 1852 the part where William and Delaide lived became Orange County. When they arrived, however, it was simply a marshy wilderness, not unlike what they had left behind in Louisiana. Belts of pine forests were the most dominant feature, interrupted here and there by small plains of coarse grasses. The terrain was gently undulating, and low elevation meant that the area was frequently flooded by the rivers and bayous, making overland travel all but impossible during heavy rains. There were no such things as roads. William and his family picked their way along cattle paths, avoiding the fallen timbers and dense undergrowth as best they could. There were no large plantations at the time. The handful of settlers, spread out and tucked away in the woods, were subsistence farmers and cattle grazers.[23]

William and Delaide settled near the small community growing up around

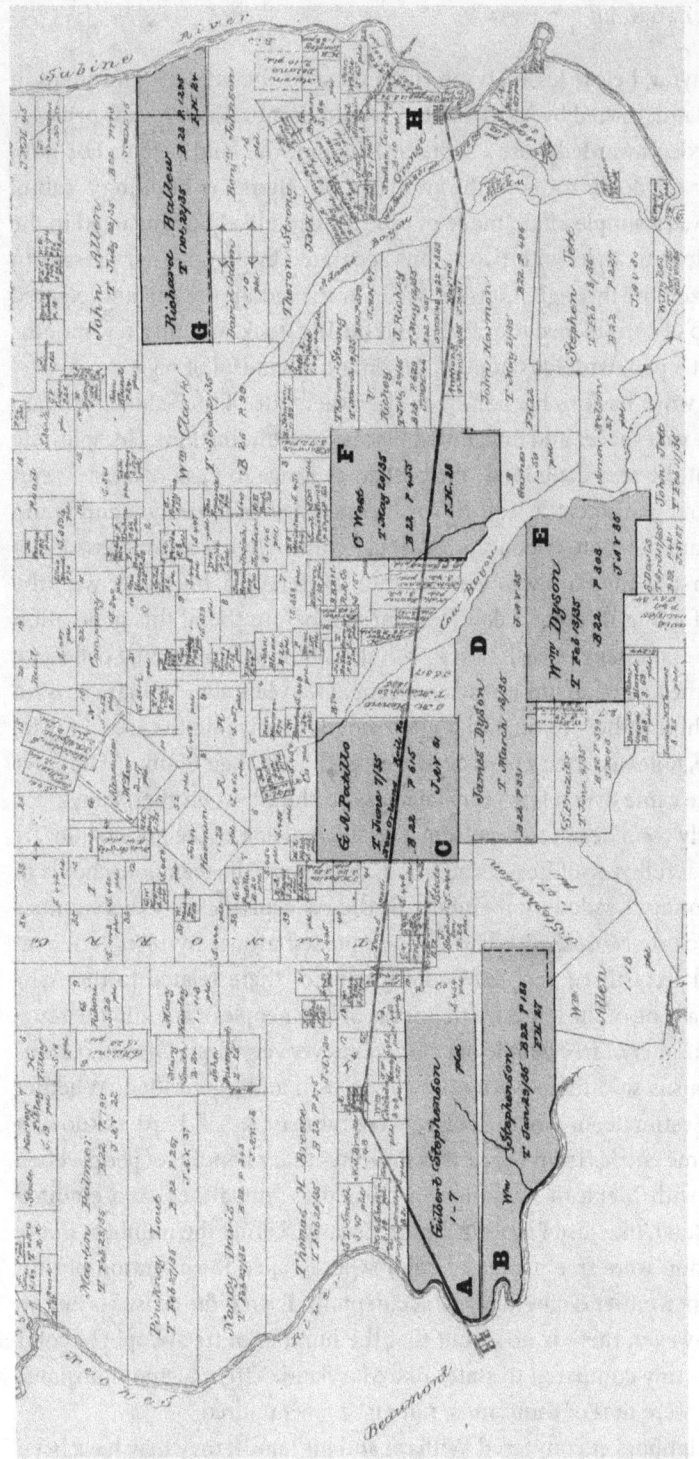

Orange County. Landholdings: A. Gilbert Stephenson; B. William Stephenson; C. G. A. Patillo; D. James Dyson; E. William Dyson; F. Claiborne West; G. Richard Ballew; H. Town of Madison (later Orange). Map of Orange County, Texas, 1880, no. 748, Archives and Records Program, Texas General Land Office, Austin the Cow Bayou, below Jesse Dyson. Like most of the land around them, it was public land, owned by Mexico. They would eventually pay a fair price for it, after Mexico awarded Jesse's brother, William, the land patent. For now, they simply set down roots in the tradition of others: by building a cabin. The home was a simple affair, made of pine logs and likely constructed in the Louisiana dogtrot style, with two rooms separated by an open-air passage to let the breeze flow through. Outside William turned up the soil and planted his first crop of corn to feed the family and the livestock. Within a few months he also built a pen, with logs of pine, to contain a handful of pigs.[24]

Sending word back to his family on the other side of the Sabine, William spoke of the vast spaces and unclaimed places surrounding him. He rightfully bragged that the area contained "the best stock range in Eastern Texas," with wild herds of Spanish cattle waiting for the industrious to contain and brand them. William meant to encourage others to come. He was an ambassador of sorts, the first of the family to venture into the territory but never with the intention of going it alone. Like their parents before them, this generation preferred the company of each other, with their numbers providing collective strength in the face of an unknown landscape. Two years after William crossed the Sabine, his brother Aaron, in 1833, moved his family into the area. In 1834, Abner came, followed a year later by Moses, each with their family.[25] His older brother Jesse came over a few years later, as did the eldest brother, James.[26]

The family soon began to represent a sizable portion of the population. By 1846, the first full year of Texas statehood, there were thirteen households in Jefferson County headed by members of the Ashworth clan. (This number does not include Moses, who had already passed away.) By 1850, Jefferson County had sixty-three people of color, many of them related to the Ashworths. It was one of the largest settlements of free people of color in the state, where the number of free people of color was never very large. Official records from the census said there were only 397 in 1850 and 355 in 1860. Whether this is a fair estimate, or whether there were more or less, is hard to know. A review of some entries from the census indicates that a handful of people born in Mexico, with Mexican surnames, are listed as "mulattoes" and counted toward the total, like José Flores in Bexar County. Tilting the numbers in the other direction were free people of color who escaped the attention of officials altogether, either deliberately or accidentally. Even if the census is just an estimate, however, there is no doubt that the number of free people of color in Texas was tiny compared to states like Maryland, Virginia, and Louisiana, where there were tens of thousands, not just a few hundred.[27]

When neighbors encountered William and his family, they may have been distrustful at first. But any misgivings soon gave way to practical realities, and racial questions drifted into the background, just as they had in Louisiana. This was a frontier society, where people lived "in isolated cabins, hold[ing] little intercourse with one another, and almost none with the outside world." Members stressed individual worth and the common good, and the Ashworths were a family who held the same values they did. They brought their cattle and established their homes, urged on by a shared desire to make this a livable corner of the world.[28]

The family's contributions created good will among those who knew them. Influential men, like William Hardin, a well-known lawyer, politician, and land speculator, embraced having them as neighbors. In 1834, when Mexico lifted its ban on immigration, he supported William's application for a government land grant. He insisted in William's character certificate that William was "a man of good moral and industrious habits." Claiborne West, a neighbor and political leader on the Cow Bayou, said the same about Aaron. Abner had John Stewart, the commissioner for the precinct at Cow Bayou, provide similar testimony on his behalf.[29]

The title applications were never finished, however, likely stalled as a result of the growing conflict with Mexico. But they stand as an early testament to the impact the Ashworths made in the few short years they lived in Texas. Years later, people talked about them as having a "reputation for great hospitality, keeping open house for all who call." Always willing to do their part, they helped their neighbors whenever asked, shingling a new roof or clearing a new path to the river. In the springtime, they pooled their cattle with other ranchers and made the long journey to New Orleans together. They were gone for weeks on end, dependent on each other for the basic needs of life. Out here, it was hard for people not to know them, and hard for people not to respect them, even if their skin was tinged a bit darker and their history a bit more unknown. Out here, in the unsettled region of Southeast Texas, the family had found a home.[30]

Revolution

In October 1835, William started on his way to San Antonio de Bexar, a dusty journey of roughly three hundred miles. With him was his captain, David Garner, one of the first residents of the county, together with other volunteers from the area. The small group of ragtag men, outfitted in homespun and an assortment of guns, had taken up arms after news of the war against Mexico started trickling in. At the beginning of the month, Samuel McCulloch Jr., a free man of color, was shot during the siege of Goliad, an early skirmish in the developing conflict. The wound was not fatal. But it allowed McCulloch—a black man long forgotten in most histories of Texas—the honor of being "the first whose blood was shed in the War for Independence." William, hearing of the action along the border, was inspired to commit to the cause, agreeing with the patriotic sentiment of his neighbors that Texas should be free and independent. Leaving his wife and children, he saddled his horse and followed the cry of "On to Bexar."[31]

By the time Garner's volunteers reached the outskirts of San Antonio, they found several hundred soldiers restless and bored. Mexican forces, having secured the town, were holed up inside, and disagreements about whether and when to attack created confusion. Some fell ill, others drank, while each side waited for reinforcements and additional artillery. As the month of November dragged on, William was among those eager for engagement. The opportunity came at the end of the month, when a scout rode into camp with a report of a hundred Mexican soldiers in a large packtrain headed toward San Antonio. A rumor quickly spread that the horsemen were carrying silver as payment for the garrisoned soldiers. Led by Jim Bowie, the notorious hothead and soon-to-be hero of the Alamo, William and the other volunteers attacked the Mexican column, only to discover it was carrying grass, not silver, for the hungry horses in the town.[32]

The "grass fight" broke the spirit of many of the volunteers, including William. Cold and hungry, he was among several hundred who started back home in December. On their return, friends and family greeted the volunteers with handshakes and slaps on the back, grateful for their service even if the war was yet to be won. Captain Garner spoke highly of his men, about their bravery and resolve, and awarded everyone, including William, an honorable discharge. Few around Beaumont questioned why William and his family supported the war effort. Having established themselves as contributing members of the community it was only natural that they would join forces against Mexico. For the Ashworths, the war was never about race, or even about slavery. It was about freedom. They resented Mexico's attempt to assert more control over Texas as much as their neighbors. They disliked the high import duties imposed by the government, with the ban on immigration, which had thus far only worked against them, adding to their frustration. They liked the idea of Texans controlling their own affairs, and with the support of their neighbors, they assumed that they would continue to play a role in local matters. William's commitment was such that, even after fighting was over, he signed up when Captain B. J. Harper called for additional volunteers in the summer to help escort Mexican troops back to Mexico. Past his prime at the age of forty-three, this time he outfitted and paid for a substitute. His brother Aaron did, as well, a telling sign of how the family as a whole felt about the matter.[33]

Other free people of color shared their sentiments. Far from opposing the war, the handful of free people of color who lived in Texas at the time fought for their adopted land. William Goins, well connected and prosperous, became an Indian agent for General Houston, using his language skills to act as an interpreter in the negotiations with the Cherokees in order to prevent Mexico from staging a rear attack. James Richardson joined a unit of Velasco volunteers under the command of Captain Thomas Bell. Henry Bird served for three months in the spring of 1836 before he was honorably discharged. Robert Thompson, recognizing that wars cannot be won solely through numbers, "furnished a valuable mare and rifle gun for the use of the army of Texas."[34]

If asked (and they were), most people around Cow Bayou would have spoken highly of the Ashworths. These "free men of colour," they said, were "peaceable and respectable citizens." They "contributed generously to the advancement of the Revolution, that glorious struggle which resulted in bursting the fetters of tyranny and which has elevated Texas to a star in the seal of nations." This hard-earned praise illustrated how interconnected the Ashworths had become in the political and social economy. They had staked their livelihoods here. They built homes and cleared land for planting, they brought their cattle and participated in the local commerce. Small wonder that they sided with their neighbors in the dispute with Mexico. They had always, as William Goins liked to say, "identified with the feelings and interests of the Anglo-American population."[35]

A Most Obnoxious and Dangerous Population

In light of their contributions and close connections, the Ashworths might be forgiven if, at the close of the revolution, they failed to realize that their future in Texas was much in doubt. Several months before, in the fall of 1835, local residents had started meeting in the cabins around Beaumont, prompted by the news that the northern abolitionist Benjamin Lundy was trying to settle four hundred families of color on the Texas frontier. No one knew yet what the future held, but these individuals wanted to make certain it did not include an assault on their racial sensibilities. Styling themselves as a "Committee of Safety," they decided that the time for action was now. Opting for hysterics over specifics, and forgetting about their neighbors the Ashworths, they wrote to the provisional government demanding that the Texas General Council act quickly to protect residents from free people of color and their "repeated acts of wantonness and cruelty too tedious to mention at this time."³⁶

The General Council (the temporary legislative body, operating between November 14, 1835, and March 1, 1836) took the threat seriously. Lundy had already left the country, and the war had yet to be won, but neither prevented it from acting. "The residence of such free negroes and mulattoes among us," it summarily concluded in January 1836, "would prove an evil difficult to be remedied should it once be tolerated." Irony was not part of the discussion. No one mentioned the Ashworths or their kin, or talked about the contributions of William Goins or Samuel McCulloch Jr. Texans had taken up arms, at least in part, for the right to own people of color, not to have them live next door. Men stood up, banged their hands on tables, and ranted about how "free negroes in a slave State [are] a great nuisance," constituting "a most obnoxious and dangerous population."³⁷

Pressed for details, white Texans drew on the same virulent racism to condemn freedom for people of color that allowed them to reduce blacks to property. Free people of color are a "miserable, starved, degraded race, owing partly to their own wretched idleness, and partly to that scorn for the negro which has ever existed on the part of the white race," said one editorial. Whites simply could not imagine interacting with people of color on terms that recognized that they had the same basic rights as whites had, like freedom of movement, the right to pursue a livelihood, and the right to own property. Their natural state—ordained by God as well as the laws of every southern state—was to serve the white population. The only thing free people of color did in a slave society was foment discontent in the minds of those still in bonds. "With most free negroes," warned the editor of the *Austin, Texas State Gazette*, "their abodes are places for slaves to lounge at. They are always the associates of the slave; they trade with them and aid them frequently in thefts, conspiracies and other outrages."³⁸

With such dim prospects and such strong potential for danger, in January 1836 the General Council agreed with the Beaumont committee's warnings that action had to be taken. "The infusion of dissatisfaction, and disobedience into the brain of the honest and contented slave, by vagabond free negroes," it said, "cannot be too promptly guarded against." With high hopes of an independent nation, the General Council passed an ordinance prohibiting "any free negro or mulatto to come within the limits of Texas." The ordinance was prospective only, and did not apply to the Ashworths or those who had already arrived. But it reflected the growing sense that, when Texans were shouting for freedom and independence from Mexico, free people of color were not part of the community they hoped to build.[39]

As is often the case, the disdain and distrust white Texans felt for free people of color was based on perceptions rather than on actual experience. There were simply so few of them, spread across hundreds of miles and in different locales, that most whites never had contact with them. It was instead the *idea* of free persons, of what they *might* do or the message they *might* send, that drove people to act. "The negroes, when free," the *Marshall, Texas Republican* intoned, unconcerned about examples or proof, "sometimes get idle and dissipated; and their offspring generally are more objectionable than the original stock. Besides[,] they increase very rapidly."[40]

The ideology was hardly supported by the unassuming lives of most free people of color in Texas. Some of them lived in the emerging towns and cities, working as washers, milkmaids, or on the docks. Others found work as cooks and day laborers. A few practiced a skilled trade, including barbers, blacksmiths, carpenters, and wagoners. Others had success in farming or ranching. In Jackson County, between the Colorado and Brazos Rivers, Samuel McCulloch Jr., who was the first person wounded at Goliad, owned a cattle ranch. Nearby, the Reynolds family also owned cattle. Juan Baptiste Maturin had a league of land—4,428 acres—in Nacogdoches County, where he made "valuable improvements" and supported a large family. In the same county, William Goins built a sizable estate, including over 12,000 acres of land and almost $12,000 in personal property.[41]

The difficulty encountered by the Ashworths and others like them, however, was that a nation's laws are often built on ideas, not local experience. Residents may have told them not to worry, that no one meant to lump them in with the unruly and dangerous free black population that had infected their imaginations. But over at Washington-on-the-Brazos, those distinctions were not being made. A group of prominent men had gathered there at the start of March 1836 to draft the Texas Declaration of Independence and a constitution for the new republic. Debating consequences, jotting down notes, no one paused to make exceptions. The consensus was that free people of color were a threat and that the authors of the January 1836 ordinance had got it right. Building off their original position, the drafters of the March constitution prohibited the future immigration of free people of color into the republic and then took the additional step of forcing those already in Texas to leave. "No free person of African descent, either in whole or in part," they wrote, "shall be permitted to reside permanently in the republic, without consent of congress."[42]

Life on the Neches

The odds that William Ashworth ever met Greenberry Logan are low. The two were among hundreds of men camped outside of San Antonio in November 1835 at the start of the war, but, belonging to different groups of volunteers, their interactions were likely limited. Greenberry and William were a lot alike, however. Both were free men of color and both were fighting for their adopted land. Following the grass fight in November, Greenberry was one of a handful who stayed long enough to follow "old" Ben Milam into San Antonio, helping to take the town briefly in the beginning of December, before it fell again in March. He had a bullet in his right arm to prove he was there.[43]

After voters approved the constitution in September 1836, including the provision banning free people of color from the republic, news of it slowly drifted down the Brazos to the settlement of Brazoria, where Greenberry was living. He was a blacksmith by trade, but he had not been able to use his arm since his injury, and was now running a boardinghouse with his wife, Caroline. He wrote to the Texas Congress in March 1837 detailing his service and explaining his hope that after the "patriotism evinced by him in fighting for the liberty of his adopted country, and his willingness to shed his blood in a cause so glorious, he might be allowed the privilege of spending the remainder of his days in quiet and peace." A group of local residents signed his petition, including Stephen F. Austin's cousin Henry, "who has known Mr. Logan five years and has seen him conduct himself as a first rate citizen."[44]

Members of the first congress in the Republic of Texas never responded directly to Greenberry. But they ultimately granted him the relief he sought, altering in June 1837 the constitution's original position by granting to all free people of color "who were residing within the republic of Texas at the date of the declaration of Independence" the right to stay. The decision in no way undermined feelings toward free people of color, at least as they were viewed in the abstract. The ban on immigration remained in effect, and in the next legislative session members enacted stringent provisions against those who were here. Following in the steps of other southern states, Texans grouped free people of color with slaves when they outlined crimes worthy of capital punishment, including murder and the rape or attempted rape of a white woman. They made it a crime for any person of color, slave or free, to insult a white person. They also threatened free people of color with slavery if they encouraged people held in bondage to rebel or escape. The decision to lift the ban on people already living here, however, at least conveyed a sense that their loyalty to the republic was worth something.[45]

Back in the area around the Neches River, the Ashworths continued about their business, not knowing much about the shifting legal terrain for people of color. They had always focused on the here and now, far more concerned about day-to-day concerns than the rules of a distant government. Around their home people left them alone, as everyone adjusted to life under the republic. The first congress established the region as Jefferson County, embracing both sides of the Neches, and local leaders soon gathered under shade trees to conduct the business of moving forward. They elected the Ashworths' neighbor, William Stephenson, as sheriff and appointed Claiborne West, who signed the Texas Declaration of Independence, as their local representative. The following legislative session, the people elected Joseph Grigsby to represent them. Grigsby lived close to the Ashworths, on what everybody referred to as Grigsby's Bluff. His plantation on the Neches, worked by more than twenty slaves, was the first large cotton plantation in the area. He also owned the first horse-drawn cotton gin, and he built a landing on the river that served as a shipping point for bales of cotton and other goods. Grigsby eventually acquired over ten thousand acres on his way to becoming the wealthiest man in Jefferson County.[46]

Across the river from the Ashworths, the town of Beaumont was taking shape. With land donated by Grigsby and Nancy Tevis, people knew it would be a place "of considerable importance," and the name—which means "beautiful mountain"—struck the editors of the *Telegraph and Texas Register* as "very appropriate." In 1838, residents moved the county seat there, and in the same year Christian Hillebrandt and others obtained a charter to operate the Neches Steam Milling Company within its boundaries. Timber, more than cotton and as much as cattle, would come to play an important role in the development of the region. Pine, oak, and other hardwoods grew in abundance, and entrepreneurs recognized that there was money to be made from the county's largest resource. Within a decade, residents were producing enough cut lumber and shingles to export, and by the 1850s the region was one of the top producers in the state.[47]

The business of exporting was made possible by an extensive system of waterways in Jefferson County. Long before the railroads cut their way through the area, the rivers and bayous provided the primary mode of transportation, for both goods and people. As quickly as they came, early settlers lashed together pine logs to make primitive flatboats. These cumbersome crafts were guided with an assortment of rudders, poles, and paddles, but they nonetheless provided a sturdy platform to float timber and cotton and other products down to Lake Sabine, where they could be loaded onto ships bound for

Galveston or New Orleans. In the 1840s, settlers welcomed the arrival of the steamboat, watching it chug up the river with a belch of black smoke and a promise of opportunity.[48]

William capitalized on the role of the water in the lives of the early settlers. Even before the war he had been operating a ferry across the river from his land—locals called it Ashworth's old field—to Beaumont. After the county was formed, the county court granted him an exclusive license in 1838 to keep it going. William's ferry was not unlike others. Patterned after the flatboats plying the rivers, it had the appearance of a small barge. Travelers descended the banks and scrambled aboard, grateful to place several coins in the hands of the operator, especially after spending several hours waiting in the hot, soggy breath of the bottoms. Jefferson County Court set out a detailed pricing scheme. William received two dollars for every man and his horse that he ferried, and five dollars for a cart and a team of horses.[49]

The Ashworths' contributions to local life were of the sort that kept them in good favor. To be sure, their status was never on par with the rest of their neighbors. When the Jefferson County Court first met in 1837, for example, it left the large family off the rolls of eligible jurors, an indelible sign that, as free people of color, they could not participate in one of the most important privileges of whiteness. But as long as they did their part, the community kept their promises. They were wealthy citizens, at least by the standard of the frontier. In 1840, William owned 520 head of cattle, making him the third-largest rancher in the county, behind only future cattle baron Christian Hillebrandt, who owned 775, and David Burell, who owned 627. Other family members mingled their cattle near William's, adding to the impression that they were a family of considerable standing. They branded their cattle with hot irons, usually on the left hip, often with variations on the letter *A*—some "tumbling" or "lazy" (in cattle-speak), others with short curves or strokes to make it "running." Aaron, Margaret, Alfred, and Keziah were among the first in the county to register their brands, with the marks captured in the neat hand of the clerk on April 25, 1837.[50]

After the family was excepted from the general ban on free people of color, they continued to see their standing, if not their acceptance, improve. They were as eager as anyone to see the area develop. Ineligible to serve as jurors, they were also ineligible to vote. But this did not prevent them from participating in local discussions and adding their voices to the direction of the county. When talk of road building took place, they agreed to help with a portion leading from Beaumont to Richard Ballew's ferry, just above the future site of the town of Madison. It was hard work, but it was work worth doing, as

George Stephenson and David Harmon, two of William's earliest neighbors, recognized. They had been assigned to the same portion of the road as William, along with the likes of Joshua Ashworth, Elisha Thomas, Aaron Nelson, Jesse Chavis, and Moses Nelson—all of whom were free people of color and most of whom were kin. In 1838 William and Delaide also took a step that was as much an indication of how they viewed themselves as it was a testament of how they were viewed by others. They paid their fee to the county clerk and received a marriage certificate, and with it official recognition that their family was legitimate. No one bothered to object that, as an interracial couple, the marriage was against the law, just as no one objected when William's younger brother Abner married Delaide's sister, Rosalie.[51]

The Ashworth Act

If life ticked along at an uneventful pace around Beaumont and the Cow Bayou, things were playing out far differently in the halls of the capitol in 1840. Three years earlier, the Texas Congress had been persuaded that the original constitution's ban on all free people of color worked an injustice on those who had come before the Texas Declaration of Independence and who fought on behalf of the republic. But three years is a long time, and as memories of the war faded so too did the memories of the contributions of people like William Ashworth, Samuel McCulloch Jr., Greenberry Logan, and William Goins. Those who never knew them lumped them together with other free people of color, and they once again looked like anomalies in the racial order. The cry that "all blacks be slaves" was hard to resist, and fears that free people of color would beget more free people of color only hastened the conclusion that they did not belong.

The Ashworths' neighbor, Joseph Grigsby, was not a member of the Texas Congress when it sat down to reconsider the status of free people of color. After serving in the second and third legislatures, he was back at home, having either lost or declined to serve in the fourth session. Whether he would have taken a stand on his own initiative is hard to know. But one thing is certain. With no one there to urge restraint, with no one there to remind congress of the contributions of people like the Ashworths, the battle over free people of color in the republic was lost before it began. In February 1840, with Texas moving steadily toward a slave society, congress came to the consensus that the drafters of the original 1836 constitution had got it right. Reiterating the long-standing prohibition on free people of color immigrating into the state, the Texas Congress passed a new law with the additional provision that all free blacks "who are now in this Republic" must leave by the first of January 1842 unless they obtained express permission to stay from the legislature. The penalty for disobedience, moreover, was severe. The person, formerly free, would be subjected to fines and, if unable to pay, sold to the highest bidder as a slave for life.[52]

Never ones to scour the papers for news of current events, the Ashworths and their kin learned that they were no longer welcome in the Republic of Texas in the same manner they acquired other information—through word of mouth. Residents far more connected to the mechanics of government climbed aboard William's ferry on their way to Beaumont, or spotted Abner or Aaron or one of the many relatives tending to cattle, and delivered them the news. Every time it was raised, however, it seemed that it was followed up with a statement that it was a grave injustice. Residents had no problem with the law in the abstract. Free people of color, they all thought, were a "positive nuisance," and the best course was simply to eliminate them from the republic. But in their minds the Ashworths and their kin were different. They knew them. They saw how the family embraced many of their same ideals. When residents of Jefferson County spoke to Joseph Grigsby about serving in the next legislature, therefore, many insisted that the law had gone too far. The act, they said, "will operate oppressively" on "peaceable and respectable" citizens that had lived here since "before the declaration of independence."[53]

The residents who supported the Ashworths were propertied men, they were successful men, and they were men who could vote. They reelected Grigsby to the House of Representatives in the fall, in part, no doubt, because he promised to address the impact of the 1840 act on the family. Meeting on the muddy roads in the new town of Beaumont, they spoke passionately about the need to take an active role in carving out an exception to the law. Grigsby's hand would be strengthened, they all thought, if the legislature knew the Ashworths had the support of their community. Taking out a pen, they scribbled out a petition on behalf of "Joshua Ashworth, Aaron Ashworth, David Ashworth & William Ashworth," representing that they were "free men of colour and citizens of said county." The petition was bold. In it, friends and neighbors urged the legislature to "pass an act for their relief exempting them from the operation of said law and granting them the privilege of living in this Republic." Others signed a separate petition on behalf of just William and Abner, stating that the 1840 act would "operate oppressively and grievously upon them the said Ashworths by forcing them from the Country whose battles they have fought and whose independence they assisted in achieving."[54]

It was a remarkable stance, made more so by the individuals who signed the petition. Old neighbors like the Stephensons, John Harmon, and Richard Ballew, together with Captain David Garner and other individuals who had lived or fought alongside the family, added their names to the documents. These were people who had repeatedly said to themselves and each other that the Ashworths did not pose the type of threat so often tossed around when conversations turned to free people of color. Far from it. "They have ever been peaceable respectable and useful citizens," they said. In all, forty-seven residents added their name to the first petition, and seventy-two signed the second.[55]

Joseph Grigsby agreed to take the petitions back to Austin when the legislature convened its fifth session. He presented them in November 1840, and the matter was promptly referred to a special committee of three, of which Grigsby was appointed chair. The committee issued a report the next day that many agreed struck the appropriate tone.

> The Select Committee, to whom was referred the several petitions from a number of the citizens of the County of Jefferson, praying the action of the Congress in behalf of certain free persons of color, residing in said county, have had the same under consideration, and upon a close examination of the subject referred to them, they find the following to be the facts as set forth in said petitions:—That the free persons of color, petitioned for, have resided in that county for several years; some of them were there even before the Declaration of Independence and have contributed towards its achievement, both by personal services, and by their substance, generously bestowed without fee or reward; that they have at all times conducted themselves well, and are men of good credit wherever they are known, having been at all times punctual to their engagements, upright in their dealings, and peaceable in their dispositions. And, although your Committee are well satisfied that, as a general rule, it is not the true policy of this country to encourage the introduction of this description of persons among us, nor even to allow them to remain, yet your Committee believe that the persons, set forth in the petitions which they have had under their consideration are, and should be, an exception to that rule; and we, therefore recommend to the House the passage of a bill for their relief, which they beg leave to introduce.[56]

Grigsby's report carried considerable weight. He was, after all, a distinguished servant of the republic, boasting more land and money in 1840 than most would see in a lifetime. At almost seventy years old, he moved slowly and spoke deliberately, adding a sense of down-home wisdom to the things he said. He was no radical, he was a slaveholder, and yet he had no hesitation recommending that these individuals be rewarded for their service and be allowed to stay. As more petitions from other free people of color arrived, including ones from William Goins, John and Charity Bird, Patsy, Fanny McFarland, Allen Dimery, Diana Leonard, James Richardson, Robert Thompson, Joseph Tate, the children of David and Sophia Towns, and Elisha Thomas, each was added to the file and corroborated Grigsby's assessment that action should be taken. The following Tuesday, the House passed a bill "for the relief of certain free persons of color" from the general ban. Two weeks later, on November 23, 1840, the bill passed the Texas Senate.[57]

President Mirabeau Lamar signed the bill into law on December 12, 1840. As laws often are, this one was given a shorthand name, and people started calling it the Ashworth Act in honor of the family that prompted it. The law would have a lasting impact, as the final version extended its scope to include not just the Ashworths but all free people of color who arrived prior to the Texas Declaration of Independence: "Be it enacted ... That William Ashworth, Abner Ashworth, David Ashworth, Aaron Ashworth, Elisha Thomas, and all free persons of color, together with their families, who were residing in Texas on the day of the declaration of independence, are, and shall be exempt from the operation and provisions of an act of Congress, entitled 'An Act concerning Free Persons of Color,' ... and that the above named persons, with their families, are hereby granted permission to remain in the republic." The law, in other words, gave to the Ashworths and all free people of color who had come to Texas before March 1836 the absolute right to remain, "anything in the laws of the country to the contrary notwithstanding."[58]

The Ashworths greeted the news of the change in the law with expected relief. The anxious prospect of having to pack their belongings and abandon the life they had made had weighed on them for months, years even. The family had never lost their connections to Louisiana. Several cousins and other distant relatives still lived over there, and William and his brothers frequently combined their cattle with them on drives to New Orleans every spring. But the connections they maintained in Calcasieu say little about the significance of being allowed to stay in Texas, the place where the family had put down roots in an effort to expand their wealth and establish a life. The notion that we are owed something for our efforts is nothing new, and the Ashworths, as much as others, felt they had a rightful claim to all that they had built.[59]

Those unfamiliar with the story of the family might have thought it a strange thing to have a man like Joseph Grigsby speaking on their behalf. Yet his commitment to their cause is proof of how deeply entrenched they had become in the life of Jefferson County. Their neighbors spoke about them as "people of mixed blood." But they were quick to add, in language that says more about the family's position than their color, that they were "nearly white." They shared mutual goals and aspirations, and, like people everywhere, the scattered households around the Neches appreciated all they had to offer. "I think they get along exceedingly well & peaceably," it was once said about them, "considering all of [their] drawbacks."[60]

Perhaps there is no better evidence of how deeply entrenched the family had become in the shared values of Jefferson County than their participation in the slave economy. Like their white neighbors, the Ashworths looked on slavery as a positive good, necessary for the development of the region and a testament of a person's standing in the community. Even before the passage of the Ashworth Act in 1840, in which residents of Jefferson County testified to the family's strength of character, members of the Ashworth clan counted slaves among their personal possessions. Joshua paid taxes on one in 1837. William owned slaves at least as early as 1838, putting his "negroes" to work building the road to Richard Ballew's ferry. In the 1840 census of the republic, Abner is listed as the owner of one, Aaron four, and William four. Six years later, after Texas joined the Union, Aaron and Abner both owned five. William owned two. In 1850, the first year Texas was included in the U.S. census, Aaron owned six, William four, Abner three, and Joshua one. James, who by this time had made his way to Angelina County farther west, owned one slave. Jesse, officially residing in Calcasieu Parish, though he kept cattle in Texas, owned nine slaves. By 1853, William had six and Aaron had five. By 1860, Jesse owned twelve.[61]

An article published in the *Austin Southern Intelligencer* lamented how free people of color "become, in some cases, the enslavers of their race." In some places, these "enslavers" were the husbands, wives, or parents of the persons they owned because it was the only means of keeping their spouses and children safe and close, given growing restrictions on emancipations and the ability of newly freed people to live in slave states. But whatever the motives of others might have been, with the Ashworths slave ownership was about embracing the southern ideal. Acquisition of property, in whatever form, was as much a characteristic of the South as it was the North, particularly on the frontier, where the rigid rules of the aristocracy and who could be a member gave way to more fluid boundaries. Owning slaves was like owning land. It signaled to others that a person came from wealth and was deserving of status. It was also a very lucrative investment. In a bad year, a crop could be destroyed, but the demand for slaves kept rising. With the Ashworths, slave ownership did even more, demonstrating to everyone who knew them what the free black Peter Allen once mused, "All [their] interests sympathies and feelings" were with the Republic of Texas.[62]

Even in later days, as the population expanded and people were less likely to know one another personally, residents knew of the Ashworths as a wealthy slaveholding family. A traveler happening into a local conversation would invariably hear about them. One story, told to Olmsted in the 1850s, was about "a negro of the neighborhood, who had been sold to a free negro, and who refused to live with him, saying he wouldn't be a servant to a nigger." It was a clear reference to the Ashworths, the most prominent free family of color in the area. "We inquired about the free negroes of whom they were speaking, and were told that there were a number in the county, all mulattoes, who had come from Louisiana." The group Olmsted encountered "all agreed" that the enslaved person "was right" to insist that he be sold. In such minds, the Ashworths had upset their core ideas about race and status, and the only way to correct the off-kilter world where the family owned slaves and they did not was to strip them of their property. As resentful as they were, however, it may have been the people they enslaved who despised the family the most. It did not matter if the rumors were true that the Ashworths were "kind to [their] negroes." In the end they treated them like animals, as a fourteen-year-old boy found out when Luke Ashworth traded one hundred cattle for the right to call him his own.[63]

Buying and selling slaves was something all the family members engaged in throughout the period. William sold one of his slaves, Lucy, with her two-year-old infant, to Richard Ballew in 1839. A month later, evidently in need of a strong hand to help clear the fields and tend the cattle, William used the money to purchase "a certain negro boy slave named Thorton about seventeen or eighteen years old" from John Williams. Later, in 1853, William received the hefty sum of $1,500 for a proven "breeder," a twenty-four-year-old woman, and her three children. The following year William's wife, Delaide, sold another woman and her thirteen-month-old child for $900.[64]

Abner was also very active in buying and selling slaves. In 1843, he affixed his mark to a sale involving a twenty-eight-year-old named Socalo, warranting him to be in "sound mind and in good helth [sic]." Three years later Abner recorded his purchase of a twenty-two-year-old slave named Moses. A few months later he bought another slave, this one a thirteen-year-old boy. In 1853, Abner purchased a twenty-eight-year-old woman named Devine and her fourteen-month-old daughter, Elouisa, for $1,000. In 1858, interested in ensuring the financial future of his children, Abner gifted this same girl, now about seven, to his daughter Sidney Jane. To his other daughter, Lydia Ann, he gifted a nine-year-old girl named Clementeen, "together with the increase of said negroes to each of them generally." Abner gave to his son, Phillipe (or Phillipaugh), a six-year-old boy named Jeff. The following year Abner and his wife, Rosalie, "for and in consideration of the love and affection" they had for their children, gifted two more slaves in their early twenties, Lewis and Jack, to be held jointly by all three Ashworth children.[65]

In the end, it cannot be known for certain how the Ashworths rationalized owning others based on their race when they themselves shared a similar background. If they had ever been enslaved, it would have been generations ago. But now, decades if not centuries later, they evidently viewed slaveholding as simply another method of increasing their economic wealth and social standing. The Ashworths had no interest in challenging the system. As upwardly striving individuals, their principal desire was to acquire property and provide for their families. As a result, they were far more interested in distancing themselves from the slaves now living in Texas than in finding common ground with them. As Olmsted's recollections suggest, this may have struck both their neighbors and their slaves as tragically ironic. But for the Ashworths, who had long ago tied their identities to their white neighbors, owning slaves was simply a matter of course.

Good and Worthy Members

Life along the Neches in the weeks and months following the passage of the Ashworth Act matched the inevitable flow of the river. Still very much a rugged region, with humid summers, soggy ground, and ferocious mosquitoes, it nonetheless attracted a steady stream of new immigrants. The timber industry helped turn the area into a place where people could find work, and soon enough the population grew to 1,121 free persons and 178 slaves by 1846. Of those who came, some had money to buy land—not much, perhaps, but enough to plant a few subsistence crops or graze a handful of cattle. The region was not considered a "paradise" by any stretch of the imagination. But, as a *DeBow's Review* article once said about Texas as a whole, "it is a country where the poor man can easily obtain land, and when he has it he can always turn it to good account in the support of his family."[66]

The Ashworths came to the area for the same reason many other immigrants came. Like others, land brought them here, but their attempts to lawfully acquire it, at least early on, proved elusive. Squatting on publicly owned land at first, their bid to obtain a Mexican land grant fell apart with the Texas

Revolution. After the war, they filed another application, this time with the newly created General Land Office, whose business was "to superintend, execute and perform all acts and things touching or respecting the public lands of the republic of Texas." Like Mexico before it, the republic promised one league and one labor, or roughly 4,605 acres, to all heads of families living in Texas before the revolution. It was a generous reward for the earliest settlers, and at a cost to each recipient of only a few dollars per acre, it provided unique opportunities to expand and grow. William and his brothers, Aaron and Abner, together with the heirs of his brother Moses, filed their applications soon after the creation of the county.[67]

The Ashworths' neighbor, Joseph Grigsby, served as a member of the three-person local board to address the applications of those from Jefferson County. The Ashworth siblings swore an oath that they satisfied all the requirements for the grant and paid the required five-dollar fee. In the spring of 1838, Grigsby and the other members of the board approved their applications and issued each a certificate, the first step in the land grant process. It was evidently a matter of course. After all, by this time, family members had been living along the Neches for a number of years. They had fought in the Texas War for Independence, built roads, and ferried hundreds. There was no dispute as to who they were, how long they had been here, or what they had contributed. During the same spring, the board approved the applications of a number of their neighbors, including other free people of color who had immigrated with the Ashworths and who had settled in the county. They included Aaron Nelson, John Willis, Hiram Bunch, Elijah Thomas, Jeremiah Going, Elisha Thomas, Henry Bird, and John Bird.[68]

Perhaps if the rest of the republic had not been caught up in a real estate quagmire, things would have turned out differently. But when property boundaries are determined by notches in trees, conflict is inevitable. Squatters contended with deed holders, while others filed false claims or forged preexisting grants. The complexity of the matter prompted the creation of traveling boards of land commissioners (not to be confused with local boards), under the authority of the General Land Office, whose sole purpose was to root out problematic claims. Traveling to the various counties, the three board members climbed off their horses and reviewed the books to make sure government land did not fall into the wrong hands. When the board reached Jefferson County, it issued a ruling that everyone should have expected but no one saw coming. It overturned the certificates issued to the Ashworths and their kin because they were "coloured persons" prohibited by the constitution from acquiring government land. Asked to explain, they said that, under the terms of the constitution, headrights were limited to "citizens," a term that excluded "Africans, the descendants of Africans, and Indians."[69]

When the traveling land board rejected the Ashworths' land certificates, the family's response was to turn to the same community that had supported them in previous battles with the legislature. Neighbors turned out to petition that the Ashworths were "good and worthy members of the community," suffering from "great and embarrassing inconveniences" as a result of being "people of colour." In the petition they submitted to congress, they reminded the legislature that these "individuals have uniformly discharged the duty of good and patriotic citizenship both during the contest with Mexico for our independence ... and since that time." As before, the view was expressed by many. Seventy-odd residents of Jefferson County said "that they view with strong feelings of sympathy the situation of these worthy families," acknowledging that "had there been no taint of blood in their veins" they would be entitled to headrights like the rest of them. They urged the legislature to pass a special law for the Ashworths' benefit or, at the very least, allow them to hold land either as "aliens or by lease for a long term of years." Adding strength to the petition were the signatures of all three members of the local board of land commissioners, including Joseph Grigsby, just below the scrawls of all three members of the traveling land board who had denied their applications in the first place.[70]

The petition took some time before it was introduced to the House, but it finally was, on December 10, 1842, roughly two years after the passage of the Ashworth Act. Two years is a long time to live in the sort of legal limbo occupied by the family. But as in other instances in which life along the river operated under a different set of rules than those of a far-off government, after they were allowed to remain in the republic the family did not stray far from the life they had lived before. They continued to occupy the land they had lived on for almost a decade, grazing their cattle and horses and participating in the local commerce. William continued to operate his ferry, while cousins and nephews and nieces trickled in and out from across the river in Calcasieu.[71]

When the petition was finally introduced, it was immediately referred to the Committee on the State of the Republic. The committee reported back several days later, referring to the Ashworths and the other petitioners as "good, orderly, industrious persons." After confirming the facts in the petition, and careful not to avow "any partiality for this description of the population," the committee did what the Ashworths had hoped. It recommended the passage of a bill requiring the General Land Office to issue patents on the certificates issued by the Jefferson County board. In quick succession, things fell into place. By the middle of January 1843, the bill had passed both chambers of congress and President Sam Houston had signed the bill into law. Before the winter was out, in a statement that was as remarkable for what it said about the times as it said about the family, the Ashworths had become wealthy landowners in a country that had sought to exclude people of color. The act, by its terms, directed the Commissioner of the General Land Office "to issue patents ... to William Ashworth, Abner Ashworth, Aaron Ashworth, the heirs of Moses Ashworth, deceased, Henry Bird, John Bird, and Aaron Nelson."[72]

~

William was proud of his clock. It was one of his few luxuries of note when he first arrived in Texas. He took it down from its spot near the chimney every evening, winding it with slow, deliberate turns. It was made of wood and brass, with a glass door, the type found in the homes of city dwellers and the more prominent. William never failed to show it to the handful of visitors who stopped over, whether neighbors or travelers passing through. A few remarked that it was a curious item to have out here in the middle of the woods. But all agreed it was a fine specimen and worthy of high praise.[73]

With their land grants secured and their residence assured, the Ashworths spent the next decade growing their wealth and, with it, their position in their community. Between them, the entire Ashworth clan would come to own thousands of acres in multiple counties, as they bought, sold, and leveraged land to their advantage. This included not just William and his brothers. All told, at least seventeen families bearing the Ashworth name owned real property in Jefferson County, later Orange County. Much of it was undeveloped land used for grazing cattle, but they also cleared plots to grow corn, beans, peas, and potatoes to feed their families and their livestock. William's brother Abner was the only one who developed enough land to make a profit. He grew rice for the market, producing 900 pounds in 1850. Several also owned town lots, which they held for investment purposes.[74]

The 1840s was a promising decade for the Ashworths. By the time it was over, the family had emerged as some of the wealthiest people in Jefferson County. William's brother Aaron was the county's largest rancher, with a herd numbering 2,570 head. Abner was the next largest in the family, with 975. William owned 900, Joshua 550, and David and Aaron Jr. 170 each. Following years of driving their cattle overland along a hazardous route to New Orleans, they were among several who welcomed the arrival of the steamship to the region. They slaughtered the beeves and sold the hides as well as the meat downriver, investing the money they earned in more land and more cattle.

It was hard for anyone not to know them or be impressed with their wealth. Roughly forty Ashworths grazed their cattle in Jefferson, each diligently registering their brands with the county clerk.[75]

In a sign of the times, the Ashworths embraced their status with all the expectations of people of their standing. They quietly accepted that they were not full citizens—they never were allowed to serve as jurors, for example, or exercise other civic responsibilities of whiteness—but their significant presence in the fabric of Jefferson County led to assumptions that they were entitled to all they earned. In 1845, William fended off a lawsuit brought by Nancy Hutchinson and her husband to strip him of his ferry license, relying on the courts to protect his rights just like anyone else. After getting the case dismissed, he obtained, together with costs, a promise from Nancy that "she will no further prosecute this suit." William's brother Aaron also sought to build on the family's presence by employing a private tutor named John Woods for his four children, Sam, Nancy, Sublett, and William. His decision to hire a private tutor, rather than send them to one of the local schools, was probably because the school was open only to white children. Still, insisting that his children be educated signaled that the family meant to stay and be counted, embracing the view that an educated population is a prosperous one.[76]

On the Frontier's Edge

Built on the site of Green's Bluff, at "a most beautiful crescent curve," the town of Madison (now Orange) in Orange County was situated on the banks of the Sabine twelve miles from its mouth. Those that lived near it thought it "a very pretty town." It was cooled by the breezes from Lake Sabine, and residents, conscious of the stagnant heat of the bottoms, bragged of "the benefit of the balmy air." Madison was the county seat of Orange, which had been cut loose from Jefferson in 1852, using as its boundaries the Neches on the west and the Sabine on the east. The county had gone from only a handful of settlers in the 1830s to 1,524 free persons and 392 slaves by 1860 (Jefferson County had a comparable population of 1,995), providing a striking reminder of the growth and industry of Southeast Texas. The town of Madison boasted 429 residents, serving a community that drew livelihood from timber, cattle, cotton, shipping, and all the hubbub that accompanied them.[77]

Throughout the 1850s, as the population grew and the frontier began to disappear, the Ashworths found themselves increasingly marginalized. They had always been anomalies in the social script, but they had been able to rely on kinship and patronage ties to navigate a path that allowed them to play a role in the community even if they were not full members. Recent arrivals, however, far from being impressed with the family's history, resented them for exposing the lie of slavery's ideology. They embraced a world where whiteness meant freedom and blackness meant slavery, a position that was only magnified as the sectional tensions mounted. "The basis of Southern prosperity," thundered one editorial in 1854, "is in African Slave labor." The Ashworths created confusion, and those unfamiliar with their contributions wanted to push them out.[78]

The family was slow to recognize the change in circumstance. No one came to their cabins with loaded pistols, at least not yet. But the signs that things were beginning to break against them could be found in little things, like the time William and his son Henderson were charged with playing cards and assessed a ten-dollar fine. Gambling was a crime, to be sure, but not a very significant one, and not one commonly enforced on the frontier.[79] Some accusations were more serious. People counted their herds and concluded that they must be up to no good. They accused them of stealing cattle and other livestock, an easy claim to make and a difficult one to disprove.[80] Even William, the patriarch of the family who had built roads and ferried hundreds, did not escape the accusations of others.[81] Some, like Joseph Dark, simply took the family's property without fear of consequence. One afternoon he rode his horse onto William's ranch and took a thousand cattle, replacing William's brand with his own. He said he took the cattle as payment on a note, and then he filed suit against William for money outstanding. There does not appear to have been much merit to the case. William countersued for $6,000, later amended to $10,000, for the price of the cattle. He lost at the trial court, in a telling sign of where things were going, but he successfully appealed the judgment to the Texas Supreme Court.[82]

J. P. Barnes similarly sought to exploit the Ashworths' increasingly precarious situation. In 1853 he got into an argument with William's brother Abner. Barnes had been going around telling people that Abner, in conduct hardly befitting a man of his position, got drunk one day and fell into a grave while digging it. Hearing of the assault on his reputation, Abner charged up the road and demanded that Barnes tell him who started the story, bursting out that "if it was a woman [who said it, then] she was a damned whorish liar." Barnes took a step back before taking two forward, threatening through gritted teeth and clenched fists to sue Abner for slander on the grounds that it was his wife who had told him the story, and Abner had just defamed her with the most vile accusation. Barnes demanded compensation, and pressured Abner to give him two thousand dollars, payable in three notes, one for one thousand and two for five hundred, in consideration for not pursuing the matter in court.[83]

It was an outrageous gambit, and perhaps the issue would have died on its own, except Barnes later gave the thousand-dollar note to Christian Hillebrandt, the wealthy rancher and longtime community member, to pay off his own debt. Hillebrandt, stuck holding the paper, sued Abner when he refused to pay it. By this time Abner had come to his senses, convinced that Barnes had played on his race to bilk him of thousands. As he stated in his answer, the fact that he "was of African descent by common report was used to excite his fears that should a suit be instituted against him by said Barnes a white man he would be stripped of his property." The defense worked. The jury found in Abner's favor, concluding that the note was obtained by fraud and without consideration.[84]

But perhaps the most telling illustration of the shifting ground on which the Ashworths stood was the repeated efforts to stop them from marrying into local white families, disrupting their connections and isolating them further. They were all "good-for-nothing people," insisted one observer to Olmsted when talking about the whites who intermarried with the family, and claimed, in partial truth, that "they [the families] couldn't live in Texas after it; all went over into Louisiana." The sentiment against interracial marriage was shared by local prosecutors, especially against the younger generation. William and Abner and their spouses Delaide and Rosalie were left alone. But the grand jury in 1845 indicted Sillistia Gallier—Delaide and Rosalie's relative—for "marrying a colored woman" when he married Margarette Ashworth. Two years later, after being forced to continue the case because the defendant refused to appear, the prosecutor agreed to dismiss the charges, but only if the couple "go hence without [delay] from the county." Sillistia and Margarette took the threat seriously. They moved back to Calcasieu, where they raised a family of six children.[85]

William's son Henderson—who was later involved in the shooting of Samuel Deputy—was also indicted for living with his white wife, Letitia Stewart. The first charge was adultery, handed down in the spring of 1847. The charge was dismissed the following term, however, because adultery wrongly implied that the two were married to others.[86] The prosecutor quickly remedied the mistake, bringing the more fitting charge of fornication in the same term, the accusation implying that they were having sexual relations without being married. This time the grand jury was persuaded. It issued the following bill in legalese typical of the time: "That Henderson Ashworth, being a free person of color, of African descent, laborer, and Lititia [sic] Stewart, late of said county, *spinstress*, on the first day of April, and on divers other days and times thereafter, and before the finding this bill, to wit, in the county aforesaid, did then and there live together in fornication, contrary to the statute."[87]

In the 1848 fall term, Henderson's case went to trial, and he defended on the ground that he and Letitia were married, making the charge of fornication as inappropriate as adultery. The jury rejected the argument, however, refusing to legally recognize a marriage between a white person and a person of color, regardless of whether they identified themselves as husband and wife. Henderson was found guilty by a jury and assessed a fine of $100.[88]

It was more than Henderson was willing to pay, especially as the charge was meant to convey a larger message of inequality. The older generation urged restraint, but they too were nonplussed, including some of the old friends and neighbors who stood by William and his brothers and remembered what they had done. Captain David Garner, William's commander in the Texas Revolution, personally put up $500 as security to allow Henderson to appeal to the Texas Supreme Court. Henderson fared no better there, however. Shoddy legal work meant that the court had no statement of facts or bill of exceptions to consider, and from the verdict and the judgment, the court could discern no legal error. The marriage was against the law, and thus living together under such circumstances fully justified the verdict.[89]

It was a difficult judgment to enforce, however. Henderson and Letitia repeatedly failed to appear in court to pay the fine, evidently maintaining their home in Texas but slipping across the border to Louisiana whenever court was in session. The sheriff of Orange County eventually grew frustrated with their blatant disregard of the law. He arrested Letitia and brought her to the Beaumont jail in Jefferson in February 1855. She paid a bond of $150 and promised to appear in court the next month, but she was nowhere to be found when her case was called. Meanwhile, the district attorney filed another indictment against Henderson and Letitia in Orange County, but these efforts met with no better success.[90]

It was a test of wills, with local officials demanding that the Ashworths adhere to the rules of race and the Ashworths equally steadfast in their refusal. Aaron's daughter, Keziah, and her husband, Willis Goodman, engaged in a decade-long battle with the prosecutors of Jefferson and Orange, with the case eventually going to trial and the jury finding Willis guilty of fornication with "a free woman of color." After avoiding their court dates with the same finesse as their cousins, they later moved back to Calcasieu to escape the harassment.[91] Martha, another daughter of Aaron's, married Jacob Pender, and they were indicted for their offense.⁹² Three of William's children, Emily, Clark, and Nancy, were also charged, along with either a cousin or a sibling named Sarah.⁹³ Their white spouses may have been "good-for-nothing" in the minds of some. But better to break the connection and disrupt the unions than allow a free family of color to expand their reach into local life through marriage and intimate ties. With the population growing, and the frontier closing, the Ashworths' ability to live on the borderlands of race had grown vulnerable.⁹⁴

The Disturbances of Orange County

When Aaron's son, Sam, blasted a hole in Samuel Deputy in the summer of 1856, the family's fate was probably already decided. In a storyline that, by this time, had become all too common, the dispute began when Deputy accused Clark, one of William's sons and Sam's cousin, of butchering one of his hogs. As in the other cases, there is no telling whether the assertion was true, although the large number of hogs owned by the family—the value of Clark's brother Henderson's hogs alone was $600 in 1855—casts some doubt on its validity. This is not to say that no one had taken Deputy's property. Reports from the time indicate that hogs and other livestock roaming the countryside commonly found their way into a new owner's hands. But Deputy's decision to accuse an Ashworth is hardly surprising, and it was not without precedent. Said one contemporary, who obviously thought little of the Ashworths and their sympathizers: None of them "were ever known to labor as honest men do for a living, yet always managed so as to have a full share of the good things of this life."⁹⁵

More troubling for Sam, however, was the humiliation he suffered in the streets of Madison. After securing his cousin's release by providing security on a bond, Sam armed himself with a double-barreled gun and, with his friend William Blake, challenged Deputy to a fight on the outskirts of town. Deputy refused, however, and instead had Sam arrested under a statute "providing against abusive language from negroes." Sam was surely in a rage. In a culture steeped in notions of honor, Deputy had insulted his family's reputation by accusing them publicly of being thieves. But even worse: his refusal to fight Sam sent the decisive message that Deputy—who had once served as a witness against William in a suit over money—viewed the Ashworths as his inferiors. Duels, as everyone knew, were fought between equals, not between individuals of different classes. Arresting Sam and charging him with insulting a white person made this point as clear as it could be. It meant that, no matter how much land and cattle the Ashworths owned, they were still beneath every white. In the ensuing trial, Billy Smith testified "that he considered the said Sam Ashworth to be of mixed blood or, a mulatto." Apparently, most understood the underlying meaning, and the justice of the peace agreed. He sentenced Sam to thirty lashes on his bare back.[96]

Following the conviction, Sam was committed to the custody of the sheriff, E. C. Glover, who would carry out the punishment. What followed, however, remained in dispute. Some said he escaped; others insisted that Glover, sympathetic to the Ashworths, let him go. Regardless, Sam soon made his way to Henderson's house, where he obtained guns, clothes, and a skiff. Meeting up with Jack Bunch, another cousin of mixed-race descent, the two quietly maneuvered the flatboat along the Cow Bayou to Shell Bank, seven or eight miles below Madison on the Sabine. When Deputy showed up in his own boat, together with A. C. Merriman, Sam "commenced shooting, and continued his fire until he had discharged both double-barrel guns, and three loads from his revolver." As Deputy lay clinging to the boat, Sam smashed in his head with the butt of his gun. Merriman, who stood white as a ghost, was left unharmed.[97]

When news of the murder spread, residents quickly fell into two groups, reviving the old names of the Moderators and Regulators of East Texas fame. The Moderators accused the sheriff of failing to take the necessary action to apprehend Sam and the others. The eight-man posse he formed, they said, consisted "mostly of his own sort, special friends and associates of the murderer," who delayed their efforts in order to give the Ashworths "ample time to carry their threats into execution and make good their escape." Sheriff Glover, unwilling to accompany the posse, appointed another old friend of the family, Joshua Harmon, as his deputy. Mr. Harmon and his posse allegedly spent several days and nights scouring the countryside, looking for Clark, Sam, Henderson, and Jack Bunch. They failed to find them, however, and one resident insisted it was because some "of our depraved citizens were acting as spies for the parties sought," singling out Sheriff Glover, among others.[98]

On their return to Madison, the "friends of law and order" formed a vigilante committee some sixty strong, dredging up the old name Committee of Safety. Like their predecessor in 1835, this one similarly came to believe that the problem was not with any one individual but with the entire free community of color. They "resolved that all the free persons of color should leave the county" immediately, and backed up their threat with force of arms. As an added measure, the committee also ordered all the Ashworth supporters, including the sheriff, to leave as well.[99]

Olmsted learned about the "disturbances in Orange County" as he made his way through the area a couple of years later. His recollections, combined with current newspaper articles, indicate that the county descended into a minor civil war—"a guerrilla of skirmishes and murders"—throughout the summer of 1856. The Moderators were heavily armed, with double-barreled shotguns and a "general assortment of 'Colt's jewelry.'" But the Ashworths and their friends did not go quietly. Olmsted reported that they "formed an organized band, and defied the Committee." At first, they tried to take the offensive, planning an attack on the committee in the town of Madison on June 15, 1856. A mail rider from Louisiana tipped off the committee, however, and that afternoon Jack Cross of the Moderators got into an argument with Burwell Alexander and shot him in the neck. Dr. Mairs, who was on the side of the Ashworths, started to attend to his wounded friend. In so doing, he "so enraged Cross that he shot [Dr. Mairs] dead in the street."[100]

Soon after, there "ensued a series of assassinations, burnings of houses and saw-mills, and open fights." One former resident remembered that things had gotten so bad that "people were afraid to sleep in their beds or light their candles at night." Following the murders of Alexander and Mairs, the Moderators took to the countryside and demanded "that every man, capable of bearing arms, should join them, or quit the county on pain of death." They assailed people like the longtime resident Hugh Ochiltree, "a quiet and most respectable citizen, living at Green's Bluff." They also drove off a large number of the Ashworths' cattle and took several of their horses. The fighting culminated when twenty-eight committee members, "well armed and mounted," led a surprise attack on the house of Joel Brandon. There they found the sheriff concealed under a bed and arrested him. Nearby, in another house, they found Jack Moore, with an assortment of counterfeit bills and fake land certificates. In defending himself, Moore was shot dead. Sheriff Glover was taken a few miles into the open prairies, where he asserted that he would neither leave the county nor be taken back to town as a prisoner. The committee, "all of one mind, discharged their duty" and shot him dead as well.[101]

By the end of the summer, with the death of the sheriff and some of their supporters, a number of the Ashworths conceded the fight and moved back to Calcasieu Parish for their own safety. An account from the *Galveston News* reported as much with apparent satisfaction. "The chief portion of the disreputable residents have left the county," it noted, while "others are in prison and a few have suffered the extreme penalty of the lynch code." Sam's uncle Abner, perhaps wondering if he could ever come back to Texas, began selling off some of his land on Adams Bayou soon after. As he noted in one deed to Charlton Midkiff in August, he was "being compeled [sic] by the disturbances in [the] County in the month of June and July A.D. 1856 to remove myself & said children beyond the limits of said County."[102]

Later that fall, Sam Ashworth and Jack Bunch were indicted for murder. The indictments were probably not hard to obtain. On the grand jury was John Merriman, presumably a relative of A. C. Merriman, who had been on the boat when Deputy was shot. Following the indictments, Sam eluded the authorities for over two years, until the fall of 1858, when Sheriff William Poff of Hopkins County in North Texas captured him 450 miles away. Sam was going by the name Mr. Harris and was said to be "a fast young man, fond of cards and race horses." The sheriff promptly brought him to Orange County, where residents surrounded the jail and threatened to lynch him. Before they could administer their special form of justice, however, he escaped. For the next several years, his whereabouts remained unknown, with one former resident convinced that he had made his way to Indian country. At the start of the Civil War—in a startling testament to where his sentiments still lay—he reportedly joined the Confederate army and was killed at the Battle of Shiloh.[103]

Jack Bunch met a different fate. Caught a few months after the shooting heading west in the town of Columbus in Colorado County, he was transported back to Orange. After the case was transferred to Jefferson County on the motion of the defendant, he was convicted and sentenced to be hanged. At eleven o'clock in the morning of November 21, 1856, Jack descended from the third story of the courthouse, where he had been confined, and approached the crowd of people who had come to watch him die. He gave them a smart, "God d——n it, gentlemen, how do you all do?" as he headed to the rear of the courthouse. As he did, he told both friends and foes to "keep out of bad company" and that "loose companions had brought him to the gallows." He then ascended the ladder, making "a general request to the crowd to see that his remains were decently cared for, and did not fall into the hands of the doctors." The executioners then pulled the ladder out from underneath him. "Persons present say he died with scarce a struggle; he had been hanging scarcely a minute when his eyes closed, and the pulse soon ceased to beat."[104]

A month after the murder, in July 1856, authorities caught Henderson along with Mart Stewart and William Blake, the man who confronted Deputy on the streets of Madison with Sam. The judge found that there was insufficient evidence to hold any of them for murder, however, and let them go. While Mart and William were "safely escorted out of town," Henderson barely made it out. Residents handcuffed him and placed a rope around his neck, threatening to hang him from a tree. At that point, he started "bidding high for his life," and offered "one man as high as twenty-five Spanish mares to save him." "The citizens were divided as to what disposition they should make of him," however, and eventually let him go. Later that fall, when the district court came to town, he was indicted for being an accessory to murder. With no interest in standing trial, he remained a fugitive until he was caught with his cousin Sam in Hopkins County in 1858. After the sheriff brought him back, angry residents took him from the jail and whipped him a hundred times. After that, he either escaped or was let go, with neither the approval or consent of the court. Long gone, his case remained on the docket, with the court continuing it every term in which his case was called. Eventually, in the spring term of 1867, following his death from unknown causes, his case was dismissed. The notation in the minute books—"Abated by death of [the defendant]"—was a striking reminder of how much life had changed in recent years. An article published after the long, hot summer of 1856 captured it best. The "white folks," it said, "have triumphed at last."[105]

Postscript

Charles James McDonald Furman, who lived from 1863 until 1904, was fascinated with history. The native South Carolinian was a bit of an eccentric, the great-grandson of the Reverend Richard Furman, the person after whom Furman University is named. Among his other pursuits, McDonald Furman took an interest in the old mixed-race families that used to live in South Carolina. He collected newspaper clippings and wrote letters to people in an effort to gather information on their background. Although he never wrote a book or an article of any length, his research has provided a helpful avenue for those seeking additional information about the people who used to live there, including those who shared a possible ethnic connection.[106]

One of the letters McDonald Furman received was from A. Rigmaiden, the treasurer of Calcasieu Parish, Louisiana, in 1893. "I suppose you know the kind of people who are called red bones," Rigmaiden started out, in response to an inquiry from McDonald Furman. "The oldest ones came from SC many years ago. There are a great many of them in this Parish . . . & a good many in Texas too." Listing the "principal & oldest families," he named the Ashworths first, followed by the Goins, the Perkins, the Sweats, and the Dials, among others. "They are neither white nor black as well as I can find out," he said, later adding that "they are not looked on as being negroes, Indians nor white people." Noting that the families had long occupied the borderlands of race, Rigmaiden confirmed that they still seemed to prefer the company of each other. "These people keep pretty well together & marry amongst themselves mostly." The self-imposed isolation came as old news to those who knew them. Black people had "no use or love for them & they don't like the negroes any better," Rigmaiden said. In 1893, with the state of Louisiana among those convinced that even "one drop" of African blood tainted the entire line, they also were not welcome in the white community, at least among the respectable class of Louisiana. "Occasionally a white man or woman marries among them but if they do it is generally a low class of white people. It is . . . very unpleasant to live about these people for this reason."[107]

Following the events of 1856, the family's standing in Orange and Jefferson Counties continued to suffer. After the violence died down, a few Ashworths who fled to Louisiana crossed back over the Sabine into Texas to join the one or two who had never left. The tax records reveal, however, that it was only those families of the older generations, those who had proved their worth and earned enough respect from the early settlers to continue to live in a country now openly hostile to free people of color. In 1857 and 1858, William was there, as were Sam's father, Aaron, and a family member named Luke. In 1859, Sam's uncle Abner came back. But none seemed able to regain their footing, struggling to retain their former positions of wealth and prominence. Aaron, once the largest stock raiser in the county, had only twenty cattle left in 1860. He died two years later, in 1862. Abner died in 1860. At the time of his death, he no longer had any property left in Orange County, since he had sold it all. His white wife, Rosalie, remained, but without any land her existence was increasingly tenuous. The 1860 census indicates that she still owned four slaves. But her right to claim other people as property would end in five years, further divesting the family of its wealth.[108]

The final years of William's life followed a similar path. He, along with Luke and a man named William Smith, was forced to borrow $1,365 in October 1856, shortly after the fateful summer. A year later, he still had not paid all of it back, was subsequently sued by the holders of the note, and found liable. During the same year, to help pay off the debt, he started selling his land. In May 1857, he sold two town lots to the wealthy merchant Hugh Ochiltree. Four months later, he sold nine hundred acres of his vast estate on Cow Bayou to Moise LaBleu, including the homestead where he and Delaide lived. This same deed reserved only 211 acres "known as the Luke Ashworth place," where Luke, who owned no more property of his own, still resided. By December, William had transferred sole ownership of Luke's place to Delaide, keeping only two hundred acres of another plot of land as his own. He likely crafted the arrangement to thwart creditors. The previous year, with William struggling to make ends meet, the sheriff seized some of his cattle and auctioned them off to the highest bidder. A few years later, in 1860, Delaide filed a document in the clerk's office detailing what she called her separate property, in what was surely another attempt to hide William's assets. Among Delaide's possessions were items undoubtedly acquired during the marriage, including a hundred head of cattle, twenty hogs, a mule, a horse, a mare and colt, most of the household furniture, and the family's four slaves. The community property William and Delaide listed consisted of little else beyond the clock he used to proudly display, along with another that he had acquired along the way.[109]

In the end, it seems that, although the events of 1856 may have provided the ultimate spark, the era of the Ashworths' ability to live between freedom and slavery, black and white, had come to an end. For years they had successfully straddled the lines of both status and color, allowed to remain and even supported by some because of their contributions and their good name. After Sam killed Deputy, however, and the county split into warring factions, their good name suffered and never fully recovered. By 1860, the number of free people of color living in both Jefferson and Orange had dwindled to thirty-one, down from a high of sixty-three. William, the former cattle baron, had conceded his role as a leading citizen and was now working as a laborer, likely in the sawmills. He died in 1864, four years after his brother Abner and two years after his brother Aaron, the last of the Ashworth patriarchs of Southeast Texas.[110]

~

Race is a curious concept. People are often convinced they know what it is, with the typical explanation based solely on appearance or some reference to a biological trait, such as the hair, the nose, or the shape of the foot. The view dates back centuries, with courts adding a layer of legal respectability to the notion that one race can easily be differentiated from another. "The distinguishing characteristics of the different species of the human race are so visibly marked," insisted the Virginia Supreme Court in an early case on the matter, "that those species may be readily discriminated from each other by mere inspection only. This, at least, is emphatically true in relation to the negroes, to the *Indians* of *North America*, and the *European* white people." In the midst of such clear-cut distinctions, the Ashworths, just like every person of mixed-race descent, were an anomaly. They muddied the waters, never falling neatly into one category or the other. People had to guess who they were and where they were from, suspicious of their skin, their hair, and their insular ways.[111]

People like the Ashworths and the countless others of ambiguous ancestry are the reason scholars of race reject the biological approach to the subject, emphasizing instead the notion that race is a social construct. Society—not biology—determines who belongs to what race and why. Things such as a person's reputation in the community, the people with whom she associates, and how she acts or "performs" race, often work alongside appearance and legal definitions to shape a person's racial identity. On that score, it does no good, as a handful of descendants have done, to insist that the Ashworths and other triracial isolate families have been wrongly linked to an African past. For decades—no, for as long as anyone can remember—society treated them as people of color, calling them "free negroes," "mulattoes," and "people of mixed blood." Even Abner himself swore under oath that he was "of African descent."[112]

The fascinating aspect of the antebellum Ashworths of Southeast Texas, and those family members in Calcasieu Parish, Louisiana, is that they managed to carve out a middle ground in a loosely populated territory, in the process shining a vivid light on the area and the period. Despite the black-and-white world that existed on paper, William and his generation lived comfortably and successfully, never challenging their racial designation yet defying all it signified. White people embraced them and came to their defense. Neighbors thanked them for their contributions and welcomed them into their community. Rigmaiden, in his letter to McDonald Furman, insisted that "these people are as good citizens as any."[113]

In Louisiana, the family followed a different trajectory than in Texas. Members of the Ashworth clan can be found in the census records of Calcasieu Parish in the second half of the nineteenth century, along with their neighbors the Goins and the Perkins and others, listed as "mulattoes" and of moderate standing. To be sure, given Louisiana's tradition of recognizing mixed-race persons as a separate and distinct caste, they were never fully integrated into either the black or white world, but it was likely a mutual decision on all sides. Rigmaiden said that "they (the white people) don't put themselves on equality, socially, with any other people except white people," and black Americans, many of whom were former slaves, did not embrace them either. But the Ashworths and their kin managed on their own. They owned property, farmed, and participated in local life despite the perceived "drawbacks" of their race.[114]

In Texas, the descendants of William and his siblings charted an alternate course. They were no longer significant property owners, and records show that some of them struggled to make a living. In the early 1880s, William's wife, Delaide, then in her seventies, applied for a veteran donation land certificate for William's service in the Texas Revolution. She acknowledged that she had no land and was living on William's war pension of $150 a year. Twenty years later, the massive Spindletop oil field was discovered in Jefferson County, bringing unbelievable wealth to many. Having long ago sold their property, however, the Ashworths were not among the fortunate.[115]

During this time, in an interesting twist, some family members achieved a different goal. Mindful of the increasing significance of race on the Texas side of the Sabine, especially after the events of the 1856 and the Civil War, descendants of William and his siblings began to drift between the color line. In Louisiana, there was comfort in numbers, with family members continuing to intermarry and reinforcing their social and economic positions. In Texas, people were pushed out and forced to adapt, as the lines of race were made sharper in the decades before the century drew to a close. The middle ground had eroded. The place occupied by William and his siblings and their family before them was gone. In the postbellum world, a person was either black or white, with the law defining anyone with a known drop of an African past as black. The Ashworths who remained—and the generations that followed them—decided to chart a new course. They hid their past, and they became white.[116]

Appendix

Putting together the Ashworth family tree has been a great puzzle, requiring several sources to reach simple conclusions. The names of the nine Ashworth children can be found in the will of Abner Ashworth, filed in 1851 in the Jefferson County Courthouse. From there, the names of the children's parents—James Ashworth and Keziah Dial—can be learned from the marriage records in Louisiana, where the names of the bride's and groom's parents were also listed. The 1850 census records indicate the approximate ages of five of the male siblings in 1850, with the four eldest having been born in South Carolina and the youngest in Louisiana: James, aged sixty-one (b. 1789); Jesse, aged sixty (b. 1790); William, aged fifty-seven (b. 1793); Aaron, aged forty-seven (b. 1803); and Abner, aged forty-one (b. 1809).[117]

The final brother—Moses—died about twelve years before the 1850 census, making his precise age difficult to determine. The 1830 census, which only provides a date range of persons in the household, indicates that he was between twenty-four and thirty-six years of age, meaning that he was born between 1794 and 1806. He likely fell between William and Aaron.[118]

There were also three sisters. Abner's will refers to one sister as Mary Perkins, and marriage records indicate that "Polly" Ashworth, the daughter of James Ashworth and Keziah Dial, married George Perkins in 1810. This is likely the same person, as Polly is a common nickname for Mary. "Mary" Perkins, moreover, subsequently appears with George Perkins in the 1850 census records from Calcasieu Parish. She is listed as fifty-eight years old, meaning she was born in 1792, and from South Carolina. Abner's will also references another sister, Elizabeth Nelson. No definitive marriage records or census records were found providing insight into her background. The third sister, Sarah, died in 1843 of unreported causes. Her estate records indicate that she was never "lawfully married." She left behind three minor heirs.[119]

CHAPTER FOUR

Lawyers and Slaves on Galveston Island

In the spring of 1857, Mark M. Potter of Galveston, Texas, asked his colleague, William Pitt Ballinger, to help represent a new client in an intriguing case. At issue was the validity of the will of David Webster, an unusual man of uncommon wealth. David was a northerner by birth and a ship's carpenter by trade, but he had made a considerable fortune speculating in land and other ventures, first in Florida and later in Texas. By the time he died in 1856, he owned several town lots in Galveston and over five thousand acres in various counties in other parts of the state. He also owned several slaves, firmly establishing him as one of the island's more prominent residents. What made the case intriguing, however, had less to do with what he did in life than what he did in death, for in his will he emancipated a woman he owned and left her almost all of his property. Her name—and the attorneys' new client—was Betsy Webster.[1]

This was not the type of case that outsiders would expect either attorney to take. Mark Potter was a respected member of the Texas legislature, said to be "a man of great weight of character, of unblemished moral worth, of marked ability, and of well matured statesmanship." A committed Democrat, like most Texans he embraced the slave system with vigor, casting votes to further entrench the system while also counting slaves among his many possessions. William Pitt Ballinger was also among the island's leading citizens. By the time he took Betsy's case, at the age of thirty-two, he was already considered one of the best attorneys in the state. Active in politics, his name was regularly mentioned at the highest levels and for the highest offices. As with Potter, slaves attended to his and to his family's needs, and he talked about

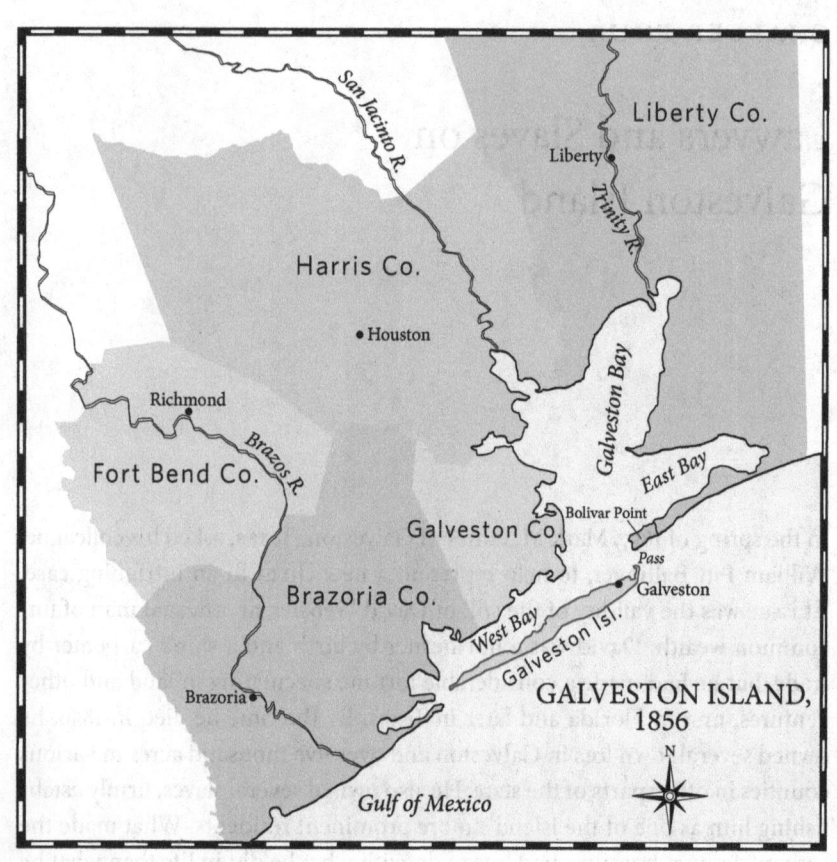

the institution as being an uplifting experience for blacks and one that they should appreciate rather than rebel against.²

Taking on Betsy's case was thus a curious decision as well as one fraught with personal and professional risks for both attorneys. These were men who placed a heavy emphasis on their reputation and moral worth. They followed, as other individuals of their station did, a code of honor that frowned on activities that diminished their public standing. By taking on Betsy's case, however, they set themselves up for criticism. It had long been the policy of the state to limit the number of free people of color within its borders, and owners who freed slaves were discussed as "the worst enemies of slavery." With the country spiraling toward a Civil War, moreover, battle lines were becoming even more pronounced. It was thought that the only place for people of color, whether ordained by the natural order or justified by humanity concerns, was in a state of slavery. Representing a woman who sought to be free exposed both attorneys to charges of disloyalty and not being sound on the state's most sacred institution.³

Further complicating matters was Betsy herself. Outsiders pondering why Ballinger and Potter took the case likely did not give her much thought. After all, as an African American woman who had spent her entire life as someone's slave, she never had a legally recognized personality. White people dismissed her as they had dismissed all enslaved people, ignoring the part she played in shaping her destiny by writing her out of the storyline. To these outsiders, this was a case about policy makers and property rights, not about slaves. It was a case about the rules they set, not about the rules she broke. By the time David died, however, Betsy had demonstrated that she was adept at managing relationships and getting what she needed. If the attorneys took the case, and if they were to successfully represent her, perhaps it had as much to do with Betsy as it did with them.

The dispute over David Webster's will and the property that went with it occupied the courts, on and off, for almost three decades. The legal issues were complex, and the policy implications were significant. A person might be forgiven for losing track of winners and losers, as the success or failure of the case could not be measured in simple terms. Following its tangled trail into accusations of fraud and deception, however, as well as pleas for what is just and fair, affords an opportunity to examine a relationship between lawyers and slaves that, like the case itself, defies easy answers. Indeed, after four trips to the Texas Supreme Court, about only one thing is certain. Understanding Betsy's experience with slavery, freedom, and the law is best appreciated by venturing down to Galveston, walking the streets, and reconstructing the lives of the people who played a part in the making of her story.⁴

David Webster

When David Webster arrived in Galveston in 1846 or 1847, many already considered it a treasure. Although twenty-seven miles long, the barrier island off the Gulf Coast ranged in width between only 1½ and 3 miles. It was a burgeoning port of entry into the state, 50 miles southeast of Houston, with a harbor in the Galveston Bay that many thought "superior to any other on the Gulf between Pensacola and Vera Cruz." There was roughly twelve feet of water on the bar, and although more than one captain grounded his ship on the approach, the island was "easily come-at-able to the initiated." The city of Galveston sprang up at the eastern end of the island. Its population was variously estimated at between four and nine thousand, easily making it the largest town in the new state of Texas.⁵

Anyone arriving from the sea during this time would have been impressed with the city's visual splendors. Travelers gazed on a series of whitewashed homes, many of them exhibiting "a fine architectural taste." Beautiful oleanders, in every imaginable color, decorated the gardens and lined the streets. In the 1840s, when David arrived, Galveston had come a long way since the days when the famed pirate Jean Lafitte built a home on the island and preyed on Spanish shipping. "The society appears to be as good as is to be found in any town of a like population," one visitor from the time said, adding that "there is more than an average quantum of intelligence, and some decided talent." The *Galveston News*, edited by Willard Richardson, began circulation in the early 1840s and would become a major voice in Texas affairs over the next several decades. Three other important newspapers also operated in the city during the period. Hamilton Stuart published the *Civilian*, and Ferdinand Flake, a German immigrant, published *Die Union* in his native tongue and, for English speakers, the *Bulletin*.⁶

David immigrated to Galveston after he "lost heavily" speculating in land in Florida. Taking risks had always been part of David's nature, reflective of both an independent and adventurous spirit. More than thirty years before, when he was just a teenager, he had left his home in New England—people thought he was from Vermont or Maine—and made his way down to the emerging port of Mobile on the Gulf. He was no more than eighteen, likely sailing down on an oceangoing vessel from Boston. It was an experience that shaped the rest of his life. Never again would he live far from the sea, drawn to the activity of the docks and the spectacle of its inhabitants. In Mobile, he plied his trade as a ship's carpenter, giving him an intimate look at the hustle and bustle that took place whenever a ship arrived or sailed out to sea. Harbors were exciting places to be, and even as he grew older David never lost his zeal for the energy of the wharves or the mysteries of the sea. In the parlor of his home in Galveston, he kept a telescope, ready to spot vessels sailing into port.[7]

David lived in Mobile for about a decade, leaving in the late 1820s to pursue opportunities in the infant town of Apalachicola in the Florida Territory. Lying at the mouth of the Apalachicola River on the Gulf, the town bore a striking resemblance to how Mobile looked when David first arrived, at least in terms of its size and future outlook. Mobile had grown from an undeveloped outpost on the Mobile River to a town of over three thousand inhabitants in 1830, as planters from the cotton district of the Lower Mississippi Valley, newly arrived from Virginia and the Carolinas, required a port to ship and receive products and supplies. David sensed that Apalachicola, 250 miles to the east on the Florida Panhandle, would play a similar role for western Georgia and eastern Alabama. His speculations proved prescient. Commerce in the region grew rapidly over the ensuing decade, as immigrants to the territory sought to profit in the trade of the soft, fluffy fiber and all its attendant business. In 1835, merchants shipped forty thousand bales of cotton out of the Apalachicola harbor.[8]

To an entrepreneur like David, however, who immigrated to the area to build his fortune, the town lost its luster just as it seemed to be making its mark. The reason had to do with an 1835 U.S. Supreme Court decision. At issue was the ownership of over 1.25 million acres of land in the middle of Florida, embracing, at the western edge, Apalachicola and its access to the Gulf. In its opinion, the Court held that the land belonged to the Apalachicola Land Company, under deeds acquired from the Creek and Seminole Indians decades ago. The decision meant that David and anyone with an eye on the future and the capital to invest had lost their ability to buy public land at cheap prices and develop it for a profit. A dozen of them decided to branch out and build a rival town thirty miles to the northwest, on a bay on the Gulf that was outside the company's claim.[9]

In hindsight the decision was a poor one, and David would lose much of his fortune over the next several years developing the project. But these were ambitious individuals, certain that they could divert cotton's commerce to the competitor town, which they christened St. Joseph. It would take a considerable investment, the largest of which involved devising an efficient route from the Apalachicola River to the bay. David and the others scouted out Lake

Wimico as the starting point. The lake drained into the river and, with some dredging, would get them to within eight miles of the proposed town. The rest of the distance could be covered by either a canal or railroad. Additional money would be needed to establish the town, fronting wharves and other necessary facilities. It was a considerable undertaking but, as investors have to, David believed in its merits and feasibility. He served on the board of directors of the company that oversaw the project, the aptly named Lake Wimico & St. Joseph Canal and Railroad Company.[10]

The project was not an immediate bust. In the first few years, the two towns competed for supremacy, and it was anyone's guess as to which would emerge the victor. David "was probably worth more" at that time "than at any other period of his life." He borrowed heavily and bought over eighty slaves to add to his real-estate investments, using those he purchased to help widen the channel, build the wharves, and grade the railroad line. By the start of the 1840s, however, it was clear that St. Joseph did not have the political power or the financial backing to replace Apalachicola as the primary commercial port. As if to signal the end of the competition, in the summer of 1841, yellow fever swept through and devastated the town. David survived the epidemic, attending to his neighbors and his life the best he could, but by this time he had lost just about everything. Approaching fifty years of age, he was ready for a new start. He hoped Galveston would provide it.[11]

Betsy Webster

The black population in Galveston in 1850, four years after Betsy Webster's arrival, was larger than might be expected for a city largely devoid of agricultural pursuits. There were 708 people of color, which was roughly 20 percent of the total population. Most of them worked in the homes, hotels, restaurants, shops, and saloons, and on the wharves. A slave's experience in the city was different from that in the country, but different should not be mistaken for better. Slaves in the city suffered through the same indignities, the same abuses of power, as those on farms and plantations. A forty-five-year-old woman named Lucy was driven mad by her situation and murdered her new purchaser, Maria Dougherty, in the hotel where the purchase took place by stabbing her in the head. Lucy had been "dissatisfied with her new mistress," but rather than examining the events leading to the homicide, the *Galveston Civilian* focused on the "bad conduct of the slave," describing her as a "most ill-favored looking wretch." She was put to death.[12]

Still, it was not uncommon for some slaves to take life in the city over the monotony of field labor. Many of Galveston's slaves were known "to find their own jobs, earn their own wages, rent their own dwellings, and manage their own time." The increased independence led naturally to more involvement in the social and economic life of Galveston, often with the portion of the white population that worked in similar jobs, and generally to the chagrin of the city's leaders. The *Galveston News* reported on one meeting held "at the request of the Mayor" to discuss "the necessity for more stringent regulations touching our slave population." Too many of them were forgetting their place, shopping at stores, holding dances without permission, and going about their affairs, sometimes after dark. Concerned citizens at the meeting "agreed, almost unanimously, in recommending the passage of an ordinance prohibiting those having the control of slaves from giving them a pass or permit to hire their own time for a longer period than a week at a time, and another ordinance, making it an offense of the owners or those having the management of slaves, to allow them to live in houses separate and apart from themselves."[13]

By 1857, the city followed through on the recommendations and passed several regulations to supplement state laws restricting the rights of black people. Many were directed at the market. City leaders sought to prevent the sale of merchandise or the leasing of property to slaves without their master's permission. Liquor was singled out. Restrictions were also placed on the ability of slaves to hire their own time or "to go at large and trade as a free person." Blacks, whether slave or free, were prohibited from owning guns, knives, "or other offensive weapon," playing cards, or "going at large in the streets of the city" at night. A person of color who gave a "seditious speech" or attempted to "strike any white person" was punished with up to thirty-nine lashes on a bare back. Many of these ordinances also addressed the conduct of whites who associated with blacks. Penalties were assessed for those who permitted "a negro ball," served them alcohol, or sold them goods. Although never fully successful, the laws nonetheless provided a powerful enforcement tool to match an ideology that drew bright lines between white and black.[14]

Betsy came to Galveston as a member of her owner David's household. She had belonged to him since 1830 if not before, and was the only person he did not sell or turn over to creditors after his financial collapse in St. Joseph. When she stepped off the boat at the Galveston harbor in 1846, her entire life packed into a bundle, anyone asking her how old she was would have been greeted with a shrug. On her deathbed, in 1880, she told people she was a hundred years old. Ten years earlier, she said she was seventy-six. This kind of past was typical of people born into slavery. With no one interested in keeping records, what they knew of themselves had been passed on by word of mouth and maintained by memory. Betsy knew she was from Mississippi, but as for a birthdate, it was anyone's guess.[15]

Betsy was a bright woman. She did not know how to read or write, and years after David died, despite reports that "she was trying to learn," she was still signing her name with an "X." But people who knew her sensed that she had a sharp mind—"close and particular"—and was savvy about the ways of the world. David's old acquaintances credited her as much as David with his successes. She "assisted in making much of his property if she was not the origin of it," Mary Hopkins, a neighbor from Florida, said. Marcia Paschal agreed. She said that Betsy, through "her labor and economy and advice," was responsible for "the first rise to [David's] Independence."[16]

Some who knew David and Betsy suspected that there was more to the decades-old relationship than master and servant. One ventured that "the connection between them was for a great number of years of the most intimate character." Galveston, as might be expected of a port town in a frontier state, had its share of gambling and bawdy houses frequented by men and women of both races. But the popularity of these underground haunts did little to shift public opinion on the matter. A sense of the disgust that members of the respectable classes felt toward race mixing was expressed after three free women of color converted a stable into a house of prostitution. Insisting that the details were "too loathsome to appear in print," the editor of the *Bulletin* informed his readers only that it was "one of the vilest dens imaginable." The three madams were charged with keeping a "disorderly house" and sentenced to ten days in jail. The *Bulletin* expressed its gratitude for the prompt action, encouraging the mayor, with subtle reference to the large number of similar establishments, to "not stop until every one of these dens are broken up."[17]

David and Betsy were never open about the full extent of their relationship, at least not with the general public. They never did what George and Mary Clements did. After the Civil War, George secured a note by executing a deed of trust on his home in the city of Galveston. After he failed to satisfy its conditions, Mary, "a mulatto woman" who called "herself his wife," made herself a party and tried to prevent creditors from seizing the family's home. In open court, the couple "showed that they had resided on the premises together for several years," and argued that the deed was invalid because Mary, as his wife, had not participated. David might have guessed at the result—the couple lost because the court refused to recognize an interracial marriage—and perhaps the opprobrium encountered by the family was enough to keep David quiet. But even those who preferred to describe Betsy as a "faithful servant" admitted that David never married or, as far as they knew, courted anyone, either.

He had spent his entire adult life with Betsy. She seemed to be the only one that mattered.[18]

Betsy helped David regain his footing in Galveston and recover from his devastating losses in Florida. Land speculators could hardly find a better place to start over than Texas. Government land was still being offered for cheap, and persons with an understanding of the market could always find underpriced land at a sheriff's sale, sold to the highest bidder. Over the course of ten years, through a series of smart financial moves, David acquired over five thousand acres of farmland. With an investor's zeal, he bought property all over the state: two separate tracts of 640 acres each on the Bosque River, 640 acres on the Trinity River near Houston, 320 acres on the Cow Bayou in Fall County, nearly 1,000 acres on the Paluxy River, and one-third of a league (1,476 acres) on Blue Creek in Wharton County.[19]

David also bought several town lots in Galveston. Galveston had been laid out on a grid in the late 1830s, with the streets running at right angles. Those running parallel to the bay and the Gulf were labeled in alphabetical order, starting with Avenue A at the wharf. The intersecting roads were labeled numerically, starting with 1st Street at the eastern tip of the island. Over time, some of the lettered avenues were renamed. Avenue B became Strand, Avenue E became Post Office, and Avenue J became Broadway. The island's beaches were on the opposite side of the harbor, facing the Gulf, accessible through the numbered streets. David owned lots in both the business and residential sections of town. A block off Galveston Bay on the harbor, he owned part of a lot on Strand Avenue, between the corners of 24th and 25th Streets. He owned seven lots between 28th and 29th Streets, on Avenue I, just off Broadway. A dozen blocks east, he owned twelve lots between 15th and 16th Streets, some facing Avenue I and others facing Avenue H.[20]

David's property provided considerable income. All told, including both the farmland and the town lots, the properties were worth about $10,000, and he rented out most of them while holding on to others to sell off later. His home, where he lived with Betsy, was on the corner of Avenue I and 15th Street. Like others in the neighborhood, it was done up in "comfort and taste—a white cottage embowered amid flowers and orange trees." It had high ceilings, large windows, and broad veranda doors, "all designed to permit the greatest possible ventilation." Inside the home, visitors took note of the rug on the floor, the well-furnished dining room, the clock on the mantle, and the various knickknacks and accoutrements of a successful man from the city. A few may have noticed that there was only one bed in the house. They simply had enough decorum not to ask who slept in it.[21]

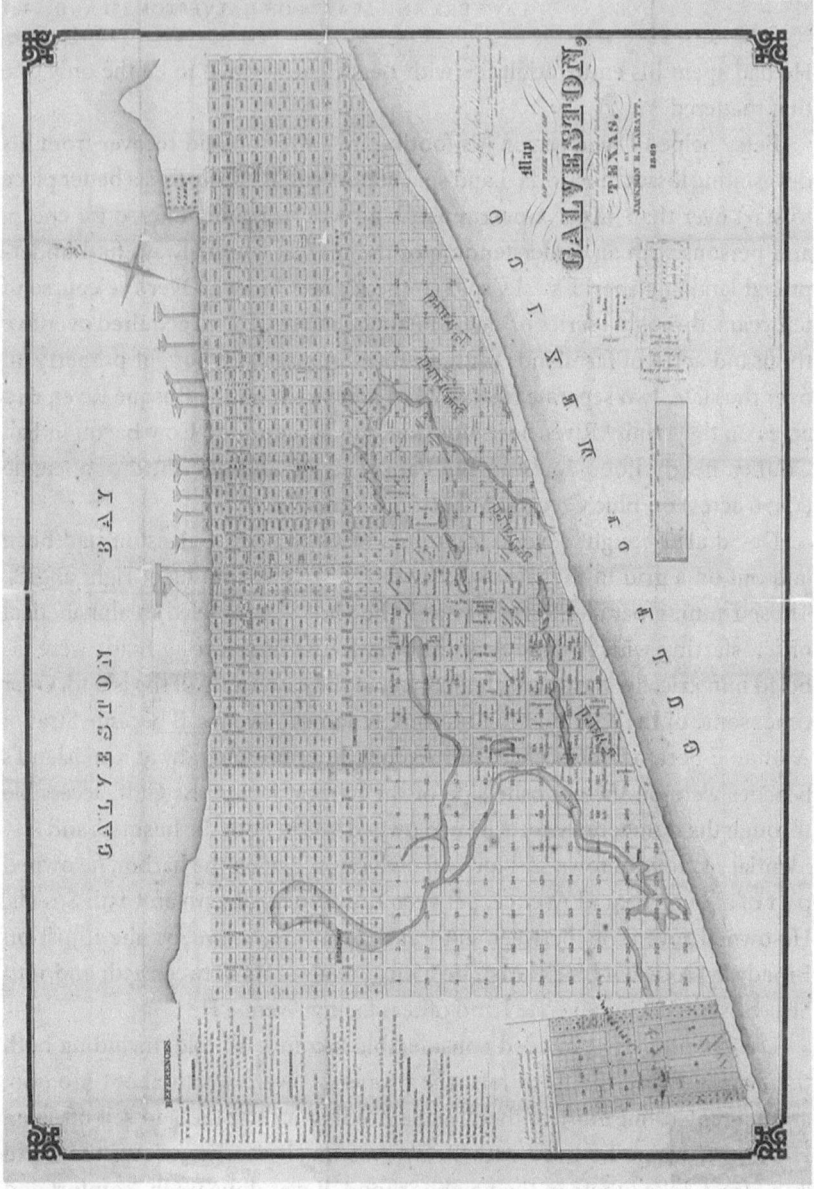

City of Galveston. Courtesy of the Texas State Library and Archives Commission

Mark M. Potter

In the March 30, 1858, edition of the *Civilian*, William Pitt Ballinger, one of the attorneys who would represent Betsy, greeted the close of the theater season "with pleasure." "During the last three months," Ballinger wrote, using "B." as his byline, "the performances at this resort have been a libel upon the town and an insult to the intelligence of the people." Continuing with the legal metaphors, Ballinger insisted that a grand jury sitting in the boxes "would be unfit to perform their whole duty" if they did not find "a true bill against the whole concern as a nuisance." The year certainly had not been a good one for those with advanced tastes. "The only *legitimate drama* that we have had," Ballinger wrote, "was Donnetti's *acting* monkeys, and they were bad enough, God knows. When will the people of Texas learn to frown upon these clap-trap clowns, and cease patronizing every humbug announced in flaming hand bills."[22]

Galveston was home to the state's busiest harbor before the Civil War. In the twelve months between August 1, 1856, and July 31, 1857, a total of 201 sailing vessels of varying sizes—ships, barks, brigs, and schooners—put into port, along with 149 steamships. The river steamers brought cotton from Southeast Texas to the city, where the state's chief export was loaded onto deep-water ships bound for New Orleans, New York, Boston, and Great Britain. The 1858 shipping season saw 200,000 bales of cotton compressed and shipped out of the Galveston port, about two-thirds of state's entire cotton production, on an average selling price of fifty dollars per bale. When the ships returned, they brought goods of every imaginable sort. Pianos were unloaded next to bags of seed; French wine and silver plates next to coffee, salt, and flour. Most of the necessaries of life were carried to the interior, up the rivers and bayous to settlements and small towns. The luxuries stayed in Galveston.[23]

Galveston's elite was a small but established group who enjoyed the opportunities afforded by the city's connection to other coasts. Members prided themselves on their worldly outlook and cosmopolitan tastes, recalling the aristocratic attitudes of some of the nation's older cities. Socially, they stood above the island's German population, as well as the large and transient group of clerks, traders, laborers, and sailors. They idealized themselves as benevolent paternalists to those beneath them, whether they were working-class whites or black slaves. Their conservative outlook was something they celebrated, oblivious to how their views might be considered by others. Ballinger's broadside to close out his theater review revealed as much about him and the views he had of the general population as it did about the performances. "We are emphatically a show-ridden people," he huffed, "and the dimes flow alike into the coffers of those who exhibit a monstrosity in the shape of a bearded woman, or the equally unnatural burlesque of the histr[i]onic art."²⁴

Many who counted themselves among the city's elite derived their income from the maritime enterprises—shipping, mercantile, and banking. Others were doctors, lawyers, politicians, and professional men. A few, like Robert Mills, owned large plantations elsewhere in the state but maintained a residence on the island, grateful for the ocean breezes in unbearably warm country. David's wealth and knowledge of business affairs assured that he had a place among them. He brought a developer's perspective to the conversation, drawing on his past experiences to help articulate a plan to grow the city. Discussions naturally centered around improvements to the harbor and port. But forward-looking city leaders also stressed the need to bring a railroad to the island city if it hoped to keep pace with its rival, Houston. It was a battle Galveston would eventually lose, a result of its inability to transition from a shipping port to an industrial center, but compounded by the hurricanes that hit and destroyed buildings and businesses every few years. When residents elected David to be one of the city's aldermen in 1853, a legislative post tasked with the responsibility of devising the rules and regulations of the city, people were still confident about the future.²⁵

The island's leaders were men who dominated public affairs, with many solidifying their positions through friendship and close connections. Discussions that started in government buildings and lawyers' offices often carried over to people's homes. Galveston's leading citizens, one early historian wrote, moved "in a rather closed circle, bound together by a custom of visiting and entertaining each other in the many fine houses set amidst the splendid oleanders and gardens in their small but wealthy city." David's home was well equipped for engaging others. Conversations drifted from the maps on the wall to the books on the shelves. From the demijohns of wine, David, or more likely Betsy, poured glasses for the guests, unless they preferred whiskey, also in constant supply. Dinner was served in the dining room, which Betsy oversaw. David owned four other slaves when he died—a young woman named Mary and her son Jim, an eleven-year-old named Harry, and a man named Washington—and while Washington was hired out, the others helped attend the guests and put on the event. Following dinner, the guests retired to the sitting room, where David and any others with musical talent ended the evening by playing guitar, flute, clarinet, and violin.²⁶

One of David's periodic guests was Mark M. Potter, who, along with William Pitt Ballinger, would represent Betsy in her efforts to be free. David and Mark Potter lived just down the street from each other, and their paths invariably crossed on regular occasion. Potter was born in Connecticut in 1819. Trained as a lawyer, he got his start in politics in 1847 as a member of the Texas House of Representatives in the second legislature. After his two-year term there he moved into city politics, serving as a city alderman in 1851, a post David held two years later. He subsequently returned to the state legislature, serving as state senator from 1853 until 1861, and returning to the House from 1861 until his untimely death in 1863 at the age of forty-four. "His influence in the halls of legislation has been second to that of no man in the State for quite a number of years," the *Houston Tri-Weekly Telegraph* reported following his death. The *Austin, Texas State Gazette* agreed. He "was one of the most influential members of that Body." He was respected by many, and his friends "were knit to him as with hooks of steel."[27]

David served with Potter on the Galveston Democratic County Committee. The county committee was formed following the Democratic State Convention in 1854, where Potter served as the Galveston delegate. Both men were committed to the ideals of the party. They were suspicious of federal power and a national bank, taking as their "political creed" a "form of government, springing from and upheld by the popular will." Critical to the platform was the party's insistence that "Congress has no power under the Constitution to interfere with or control the domestic institutions of the several States, and that such States are the sole and proper judges of everything appertaining to their own affairs, and prohibited by the Constitution." Potter, like David, was a slaveholder, and there were few "domestic institutions" more important to the Texas Democratic Party than slavery. Members resolved to "resist all attempts at renewing in Congress, or out of it, the agitation of the Slavery question, under whatever shape or color the attempt may be made."[28]

Potter's support of slavery was not limited to platitudes. The owner of close to a dozen slaves, he also provided both his name and his financial support to the Texas filibustering campaigns of the 1850s, privately funded efforts to establish slaveholding states in Cuba and Central America. They were ambitious projects. Dreaming of immense wealth from cotton planting in Texas, backers were convinced that reopening the slave trade was the only viable option to achieve it. They hoped to take over countries in the Caribbean to use as local trading stations for African slaves. The projects, a form of "private imperialism" if ever there was one, were taken seriously by prominent men in both Galveston and Houston, fading only after General Walker, the brash commander in charge of the Nicaragua expedition, was executed in 1860.[29]

Potter was the type of man to extol slavery, to boast of its benefits to both blacks and whites. He no doubt agreed with the position of the *Texas Alma-*

nac, published annually by Willard Richardson of the *Galveston News*. "Every citizen of the United States should be the warm friend, the unceasing advocate and the bold defender of the institution of African Slavery, as it exists in the Southern States of the Union." Potter's legislative record is filled with votes to advance the slave system. During his tenure, the state passed laws imposing tighter restrictions on slave movement, enhancing penalties for slave crimes, and limiting the abilities of whites to interact with enslaved men and women on the grounds that they might interfere with the owner's property. He would even go so far in the 1858 session as to vote in favor of a bill allowing free people of color to voluntarily enslave themselves. The bill, which became law, was based on the perverse proposition that, since blacks were better off as slaves, they should have the right to place themselves back in chains. At least on paper, Potter seemed like the last person to take an interest in Betsy's cause.[30]

The Will

David's death in the summer of 1856 was marked with little fanfare. The *Galveston News* published a one-sentence obituary: "Died . . . On the 8th inst. [of May], David Webster of this city, formerly a citizen of Florida." What started as routine, however, quickly became a topic of much local interest and excitement. For in his will, David made clear his intention to "manumit, emancipate and set free [his] negro woman, Betsy, and declare her to be entirely liberated from slavery, and entitled to all the rights and privileges of a free person with which it is in [his] power to vest in her." He thereafter bequeathed to her "all the real and personal and mixed estate belonging to [him] in the City of Galveston," including "all the houses, household furniture, effects and appurtenances appertaining to the same." Notably, and perhaps critically, David did not give the property to Betsy outright. Instead, he created a trust, to be administered by Jane Hardin (or Mrs. E. J. Hardin, using the initials of her husband) with directions to "dispos[e] of said property at the pleasure and request of said Betsy." Hardin, then living in Georgia, had been a friend and neighbor of David's when they both lived in Florida. As for the rest of his property, including farmland in the country, he left it to old friends, along with a handful of miscellaneous items and relief from debt.[31]

Those named as beneficiaries in the will—including (other than Betsy) John Ruau, Martin Hardin (the son of Jane, the trustee), Henry Martin, and Francis Whiting—were grateful for David's friendship and were anxious to see the will enforced. But others looked on the entire affair as scandalous if not subversive. Those who never asked about the relationship between David and Betsy, who never inquired about where Betsy slept, were now wondering aloud about the full extent of their commitment. It was certainly not the first time someone tried to free a favorite slave. But all except those who were blissfully ignorant or had something to hide realized that, in situations like this, there was often more to the promise of freedom than a reward for years of service. Such was the case when Spire Hagerty deeded a woman and her two children to his sister, for the purposes of setting them free, during a contentious divorce. The injured spouse insisted that her husband and the woman were having "adulterous intercourse," and that his efforts to convey her and their children were all part of a shell game designed to deprive her of her community property. David's actions in freeing Betsy raised similar questions. The people of Galveston shared the sentiments of other Texans when they lashed out against interracial relationships. Yet here was someone they had invited into their homes, and visited his, who had potentially cared deeply for a woman of color, and perhaps even regarded her as his wife.[32]

Even those who could put these concerns aside, dismissing them as small fissures in an otherwise well-organized society, nevertheless reacted negatively to the will. Texans had made clear their views toward manumission in their 1836 Constitution of the Republic of Texas. In the same breath that they prohibited free people of color from immigrating to the country, the drafters also made it illegal for slaveholders to emancipate slaves in the republic without congressional approval. The rationale was the same. "Free negroes in a slave State are a positive nuisance," the *Austin Southern Intelligencer* intoned. Their mere existence served as a constant reminder that they were competent and capable, challenging contemporary assumptions that blacks needed the civilizing hand of a white master. The editor of the Austin paper was having none of it. "Of all the enemies to the institution of slavery, those misadvised owners who, by their last wills manumit their slaves, are the worst.... Even if a man could doubt the moral right to hold his slave, he cannot doubt but that to manumit him adds ten-fold to his misery." As slaves, they were content and happy. As free people, "they relapse into savage barbarity," becoming public nuisances who plant the seeds of rebellion and escape into the minds of the other slaves.[33]

The case of Anthony Hays was the quintessential illustration of all that could go wrong if people like Betsy were allowed to go free. Anthony was a free person of color from Boston who came to Galveston and tried to hide a runaway aboard a brig bound for his home city. He was caught and convicted and subjected to a tongue-lashing from the local judge in front of a courtroom full of anxious spectators. "You have not only attempted to abduct the slave," the jurist opined, expressing the hidden fears of a white populace, "but you have inculcated into his mind the opinion that there is no crime committed by a slave who steals from a white man—that every thing in this country belongs to the slaves." Invoking the image of Nat Turner, by the time of the sentencing the judge had abandoned all reason in favor of complete hysteria. "One more step in your mad and fanatical career," he lectured, "and you would bring on a war between the races that would deluge this lovely land in blood, and result in the total extinction of one or the other." The people of Galveston had no interest in adding to the ranks of the free population. Anthony's fate was to be sold as slave to the highest bidder, and people thought Betsy should remain enslaved, as well.[34]

David's decision to leave her his house and all his possessions, together with all his ownership rights to the other town lots, only complicated matters further. It was bad enough that Betsy might be free. But to be a conspicuous owner of that much wealth—more than most would see in a lifetime—was tremendously problematic. To be sure, there were exceptions to every rule. But people in Galveston were likely unfamiliar with successful free families of color like the Ashworths in Jefferson and Orange Counties, those who had ingrained themselves in the social and economic fabric years ago. Virtually every person of color they encountered was a slave, denied by the laws and custom of the time of claiming any property as their own. The handful of those who were free—there were officially thirty in the city of Galveston in 1850—were quietly scratching out a living in the parts of the city that were hidden or ignored by many of the island's residents. Some had families—the Townsends, the Joneses, the Coopers, and the Greens—while others lived on their own. Whatever money they had, they kept buried in the yard or under lock and key. They risked much should a white person see their success.[35]

Betsy, however, was not of the mind to ponder the policy implications of the will. At close to sixty years old, all that mattered to her was her ability to live out the rest of her life on her own terms. She reportedly said on numerous occasions that she had no intention of leaving Galveston. Few could blame her. Her house was a beautiful place, "noted for the many flowers, fruit trees and shrubbery upon it." She had friends and companions and contacts in high places. She had no interest in starting over, even if that meant, according to Oscar Farish, the clerk of the court, remaining in Galveston as a nominal slave rather than somewhere else as free. "All her affections clung to this island home, where she had lived with her former master, sustaining, perhaps, relations to him not sanctioned by the law, but sanctified by all the sentiments of her nature."[36]

After David's death, Betsy took the will to Leslie Thompson, an attorney down the street who had known David from Florida. Thompson filed the will with the county court on May 15, 1856, requesting that the court assign Philip Tucker as the administrator. Within days, however, Henry Martin and Francis Whiting—two of the beneficiaries in the will—petitioned to replace Philip as administrators. They said David and Philip "were not on friendly terms" and that David "had a great dislike [of] said Tucker and would not willingly have allowed his estate to have been placed in his hands." The court agreed and promptly made the substitution. As for Thompson, it was clear that his legal relationship with Betsy would not last. Despite his agreement to file the will, he had no interest in the case. He frankly admitted that he thought that the devise of the property to Betsy "was utterly void." Plus, he thought Betsy "was very annoying," perhaps because she showed some self-determination and did not play the role of the humble and obedient servant. Thompson was the owner of twenty slaves in 1860, unused to the idea of a black person exercising her free choice. She "did not follow my directions," he said, dismissing everything about the case as inconsistent with what he knew about life.[37]

Following the appointment of Martin and Whiting as administrators, the county court ordered that the estate be appraised and debts paid. As the process dragged on through the summer and fall, news of David's death and his considerable estate drifted back to New York, where Martha Greenwood lived. Martha reached out to people in Galveston and told them that she was David's cousin and sole surviving heir. Unable to accept that David would leave most everything he owned to a slave, she filed suit in the district court in April 1857, challenging the will. In her petition, she asserted two substantive challenges. The first was that David was not of sound mind when he made the will. It was a common argument to make under such circumstances, and it reflected Martha's inability to accept David's dying wishes. As she saw it, his decision to leave his property to Betsy rather than his white relative, no matter how distant, was proof that he was suffering from a defect of the mind.[38]

The second ground was built on the first but was dressed up in accusations of fraud. Martha alleged that, because no competent white person would willingly turn over his estate to a slave, the will must have been the result of collusion between the administrators, who sought to control David's property through Betsy. In Betsy's world, both arguments were unfair and unreasonable. After all, she had spent a lifetime with David. She knew that David was not confused when he dictated the will and that the will was not the result of outsiders peddling a scam. But lawyers versed in the laws of slavery would have taken both arguments seriously. The second, in particular, would be difficult to overcome. Stripped of its accusatory tone, it rested on the basic premise of Texas law that free people of color were not welcome in the state. Any owner seeking to manumit his slave would either have to seek permission from the Texas legislature or arrange to have her transported to another part of the country, such as Ohio or New York. Not only did David fail to do either one, but he went a step further and provided a home for Betsy in the city of Galveston. This was against the law, and neither Betsy nor her administrators could rightfully claim control over the property.[39]

Once she learned of the suit, Betsy approached Thompson and asked him to defend the will in court. By this time, however, Thompson was no longer interested in representing a woman he felt was trying to upset the natural order of things. He turned her down even when she "offered to pay [him] as much as [he] would ask," showing him "gold pieces in a handkerchief" to demonstrate her good faith. But Betsy was not the type to give up. She insisted that she was entitled to her freedom and all the rights that accompanied it, and she was determined to prove that in court.[40]

After Thompson declined to represent her, Betsy turned to her neighbor, Mark Potter. The two had then been in contact about her rights under the will for almost a year, with Potter providing some informal advice since June 1856, a month after David's death. "Her affairs were much talked of and conflicting opinions were even presented to her," Martin Hardin reported of the time, and "consequently her mind was much disturbed and troubled." It was a complicated situation, to be sure. As they talked in more depth, Potter avoided the embarrassing details of Betsy's relationship with his old friend David and instead focused on the legal issues at play. Potter informed her that her chances of successfully defending the will were not high. The last time a case with similar issues reached the Texas Supreme Court, in a case called *Purvis v. Sherrod* in 1854, the court made clear that it was state policy to forbid owners from freeing their slaves within the state's territorial jurisdiction. Potter did not bring up his own views. Unlike Thompson, he kept to himself his fervid support of the slave system and his unswerving belief that slavery was the best of all conditions, saving them for discussions on another day and at another place. Right now, he was involved in concrete conversations about the wishes and desires of a friend with a woman he had come to know.[41]

William Pitt Ballinger

William Pitt Ballinger's professional résumé was one to be admired. He was born in 1825 in Kentucky, the asthmatic son of a county clerk. Unable to participate in the rigorous activities of other young men, he turned to books at a young age and acquired a lifelong love for learning. When he was eighteen, he moved to the balmy air of Galveston to read law under the tutelage of his uncle, James Love, a local attorney of considerable prominence. After passing the bar in 1847, and with his uncle's assistance, he went to work for the firm of Jones and Butler, "then the most extensive practitioners at the Galveston bar." There he gained experience drafting wills and writing deeds before developing an expertise in the complex area of Texas realty law. His skill and professional acumen soon caught the eye of those higher up. At the age of twenty-five, in 1850, he was appointed United States Attorney for the District of Texas, a position he filled for the next three years "with ability and distinction."[42]

Ballinger returned to private practice in 1853. After just a year with his prior firm, in 1854, he formed the partnership of Ballinger and Jack with his brother-in-law, Thomas Jack, who had just passed the bar. By now, Ballinger's reputation was firmly established. Business and political leaders sought his counsel on complex and delicate matters, and with each success his name only grew. One of his most difficult cases from the decade—for which he was uniformly admired—involved the "famous litigation" between the city and the Galveston Wharf Company. The dispute had its origins in the city's attempt to take over the possession and title to property located along the waterfront. In 1854, the Galveston Wharf Company, led by the city's founder, Michel Menard, had successfully consolidated the property into one corporation, giving the company a monopoly. Public officials sought to break the monopoly and take control of the property by claiming that the Galveston Wharf Company usurped public land. The company hired Ballinger as its counsel, and he countered the city's claims by maintaining that the land was part of the original grant given to Menard by the republic in 1838, and that he never relinquished title. Digging up old deeds and theorizing on the rights of property, Ballinger ultimately prevailed in litigation worth thousands, securing his reputation as one of the state's premier litigators.[43]

Like Potter, Ballinger did not appear, at least on paper, to be someone who would be interested in Betsy's case. He had long been a strong supporter of slavery and all it represented. To be sure, as the Civil War approached, Ballinger opposed talk of secession and aligned himself with the Union. But Ballinger's opposition to secession had nothing to do with his views on slavery; it was based instead on his firm belief in the rule of law. He viewed secession as "revolution." A committed Whig and later Democrat, he had no fondness for the Republican Party or President Lincoln. In public speeches as well as in his private diary, he made clear that he thought the federal government had no business meddling in the affairs of the states, especially on the slavery

William Pitt Ballinger. Courtesy of the Rosenberg Library, Galveston, Texas

question, and the Republican Party's designs, as he saw it, to violate state sovereignty were "dangerous & unconstitutional." But he believed that the answer to Republican overreach was "to be sought peacefully & within the Union & that the disruption of the Union without such efforts is treason to humanity." Ballinger's positions were not popular in Texas—"Those who will act with the Disunionists are a much larger majority than I supposed," he once said—but even his opponents respected his careful and deliberate arguments. "My line of duty," he maintained from the start, "is in a strict & diligent devotion to my profession."[44]

Once Texas voted to secede, Ballinger accepted with a lawyer's dispassion that his position was no longer tenable. Committed to his adopted state, he became a devoted Confederate and pledged his efforts to ensuring the success of the South. During the Civil War, political leaders counted on his "mild and congenial" disposition on a number of occasions. In 1861, they sent him to the capital of the Confederacy in Richmond, Virginia, to obtain a cannon for the defense of Galveston. The journey would have tried the patience of most anyone, with the frustrations of bureaucratic delays matched only by a lengthy return that sapped his strength. It exemplified the type of leadership, however, that earned him the respect of his peers. At the war's end, Governor Pendleton Murrah sent him to New Orleans as the representative of the civil authority to help negotiate the surrender of the state. Later, in 1875, he was one of the three representatives of Galveston County in the Texas Constitutional Convention, where he was regarded as "one of the ablest members."[45]

As active as he was in political affairs, Ballinger never sought public office. But "his eminent legal qualifications" were such that members of both parties "urged and recommended [him] as one capable of the highest judicial position in the gift of the people." Governor Edmund Davis, the Republican governor during Congressional Reconstruction, sought to appoint him to the Texas Supreme Court in 1871. Ballinger turned the offer down. Two years later, after the former Confederates regained power, Governor Richard Coke again offered him the position. Ballinger accepted the post long enough to assist with the reorganization of the court under the new administration. Then he resigned, citing personal and financial reasons. Four years later, in 1877, a wide swath of the Texas delegation put his name forward for an opening on the U.S. Supreme Court. He remained on President Rutherford B. Hayes's short list until he voluntarily withdrew his name from consideration.[46]

When Ballinger died in 1888, accolades poured in from across the state. He was "one of the most brilliant lights known to the history of the present age of jurisprudence in this state," said the *Galveston News*. William Ballinger "had no superior at the bar of Texas," said the *Fort Worth Gazette*. The *Waco Examiner* insisted that he "was widely known throughout the south for his pre-eminent abilities as a lawyer and scarcely a great case has come before the Texas courts in twenty years in which he has not appeared as one of the leading counsel." His biographer reports that Ballinger appeared before Texas Supreme Court at least 350 times, a feat that few if any from the time could match. Some of the high-stakes cases involved tort law and the railroad, after the "robber baron" Jay Gould acquired the Galveston, Houston & Henderson Railroad and hired Ballinger as counsel. But a testament to his abilities as a lawyer came through in some of the smaller cases, where he prepared just as diligently and advocated just as convincingly. "The imprint of his genius, as shown by Texas law reports wherein he appeared as counsel," the *Galveston News* reported, "will live after him as monuments to his brilliancy as a jurist and able pleader."[47]

Mark Potter was one of the many who knew William Ballinger professionally. In 1854, they partnered as cocounsel on a case before the Texas Supreme Court. During the same period, they appeared on the opposite side of the courtroom in the famous Wharf case, with Potter employed as one of the city's attorneys, along with Leslie Thompson. As leaders of the Galveston bar, they were often called on to educate the general public about topics of concern. The two debated the merits of remaining with the Union or seceding—"Potter took half way ground"—at a public meeting on the eve of the Civil War. As with others of wealth and standing on the island city, however, the connection between the two men was not limited to courts of law or the public square. They forged a friendship in the parlors of their homes. In 1863, while Potter lay ill with a fever and intestinal complaints, Ballinger visited him on his bedside, just days before he died.[48]

It was only natural, then, that Potter would turn to Ballinger in the spring of 1857 after Betsy approached him about defending the will in court. One gift of a good lawyer is an ability to recognize when matters are beyond his expertise. The difficult legal issues posed by Betsy's case called for someone with a keen understanding of property law and a nuanced appreciation of the state's policy on slaves and slavery. When Potter approached Ballinger, the latter accepted the invitation with enthusiasm, surprising some. "Potter told me today he wanted me to unite with him to defend the suit brought against Webster's will—to which I acceded—no contract yet—It is a GREAT CASE!" The agreement between them had Potter handling some of the more mundane aspects of the case—contacting witnesses and filing papers—with Ballinger developing the legal strategies and arguing in court. "My employment," Ballinger said, "had reference mainly to the defence [sic] of the suit, and to the legal questions involved in the will." Ballinger was never one to boast excessively about his skills. But those who knew him realized that Betsy, perhaps unwittingly, had just secured one of the best attorneys in the state.[49]

~

Years later, Ballinger testified that he did not know Betsy before she hired him. Yet he most assuredly knew David, and Betsy, in the observant way of a servant in the background, undoubtedly knew him. Ballinger and his wife, Hally, were known for their hospitality and constant entertaining. "The elegant Ballinger residence," the *News* reported, was the scene "of some of the most elegant social entertainments ever given in Galveston." Throughout his time in the city, David lived only a short walk from Ballinger, and the two crossed paths at social events and gatherings at each other's homes. Even after David's death, Betsy continued to see him about town. In the latter part of 1857, Ballinger moved about a mile away from her, building a new home on the corner of Avenue O at 29th Street. It was a handsome affair, a large, white two-story home set far back from the street and surrounded by shade trees. In the tradition of men of his standing, he gave his home a name, calling it the Oaks. Betsy walked by it often, if only to enjoy its beautiful gardens and grandiose displays of wealth. Occasionally she caught a glimpse of Ballinger walking between his home and his office on the Strand, near the courthouse. It made for a jaunt of about fifteen or twenty minutes, which he repeated two to three times a day.[50]

After Ballinger agreed to act as cocounsel on Betsy's case, the first order of business was to solidify their relationship in a contract. For strict adherents to the slave system, the idea itself may have seemed problematic (indeed, it would become an issue in subsequent litigation). After all, until the will was legally recognized, Betsy was a slave, and everybody knew that slaves were not able to enter into binding contracts. Even putting these technical concerns aside, how she might pay for their services was a very real issue. It is not known what happened to the gold pieces she offered Thompson. Perhaps she spent the money, or did not offer it, or it was not enough. Regardless, the focus of the fee arrangement was on the very property tied up in the dispute over the will. As they started to discuss options, Betsy proposed to Potter and Ballinger the only arrangement that made sense. She promised to pay them a portion of the estate if they successfully represented her.[51]

Potter and Ballinger agreed that this was a sensible approach, but they disagreed with Betsy on the amount. Betsy's original offer was generous. Knowing of the difficulty of the case, and the reluctance of people to undertake it, she offered to pay them half of the value of the estate. It was a considerable amount. The previous year, during the administration of the estate, David's property had been inventoried at near $21,000, meaning that the lawyers would have about $10,500 to split between them. At the time, Ballinger's yearly income was between $6,000 and $10,000, considerably more than a typical lawyer in Galveston. But even for him the fee was substantial, offering him a chance to increase his income by 50 percent or more. Ballinger and Potter, however, turned Betsy's offer down, in a move that might have surprised anyone unfamiliar with the ethics of the two men but, in hindsight, should have been expected. Half of the estate, they said, was too much. A typical contingency fee arrangement was one-third of the recovery, they explained to Betsy, and that is all they would accept from her.[52]

The decision to take less than what was offered—or, for that matter, to take the case at all—was notable considering what was at stake. The personal convictions of both men counseled against undertaking a case with such potential to disrupt the natural order of things. Ballinger's views on slavery were unsurprising for a man of wealth and prestige. They paralleled those of Potter and just about every white person who tried to convince themselves that they were moral beings despite participating in a immoral institution. Adopting the language of the benevolent paternalist, he spoke of slavery's "blessings— its 'ennobling' influences to use Mr. Mason's well considered expression." Jotting down his thoughts before he drifted off to sleep one night, he told himself that depriving someone of all her rights and her dignity "is far better for the slave. It is in fact the only relation that can exist where the African is in any considerable numbers, and it seems to me if the hand of Providence be visible in any thing in this world it is in the American slavery—necessary, I believe, in the first place to the development of this country—'elevating' to the African race & promising their redemption hereafter."[53]

Convinced of the moral value of slavery, Ballinger saw little irony in his decision to own human beings. He owned six slaves at the time of Betsy's suit, in varying ages and sexes to attend to different responsibilities around the home. When he went to purchase a slave, he approached the transaction as he might the purchase of an ox or a horse. "Went . . . to look at negroes [and saw] a very good looking black girl of 15—well grown was priced to me at 1225," he wrote on one occasion. "Wd have bo't her if I had had the money." At the time, Ballinger was in the market for a new personal servant for his wife, Hally, whose standards were no less demanding than her husband's. One woman was being offered for sale for $1,800, a high price to pay but thought worth it for the skills she reportedly possessed. "Hally took her out home to try her & seems to like her." Things fell apart after two weeks, however, as Hally came to the conclusion that her potential purchase was "an untruthful negro." After the sale fell through, Ballinger and his wife continued to look at several others, though "they always have some fault," he wrote. Hally did like one—"She liked her face"—but the problem was that she was "only between 14 & 15 and is in a family way." With a lawyer's skill for negotiation, Ballinger turned her pregnancy to his advantage, bringing the seller down from $1,200 to $1,050. "The girls name is Agnes," he reported after finalizing the sale. "Hally thinks she will like her. I hope very much she will prove a good & useful servt. Hally has been wanting to get a girl a long time."[54]

Like most slaveholders convinced of the righteousness of the system, Ballinger believed that blacks who resented being enslaved suffered from personal defects and were troublesome rebels. Never did he use the occasion for serious reflection. When his own slave, Dave, stole money and valuables, together with powder caps, matches, and a "pair of Derringer pistols," Ballinger framed the issue in terms of disobedience. Dave breached Ballinger's trust (as well as his trunk), and the fact that he also ran away, perhaps "with a view of seeing his mother," did little to dissuade him of his view. He vowed to "send him to the penitentiary to be worked and treated as a convict." Either that, or he would sell him "to the country where he will not be likely to return here." Ballinger's only regret was that Dave would be worth little. "I should tell all the facts, & I don't see what any one would want a burglar so daring & skillful on his premises for. Besides, he wouldn't stay." In the end, he opted for placing him in jail, after he had him "thoroughly whipped."[55]

In light of his personal experience living under Ballinger's hand, someone like Dave may have questioned why his owner would agree to represent Betsy. It was easy for Dave to see the incongruity of on the one hand insisting that blacks were better off as slaves but then on the other hand helping Betsy to obtain her freedom. Some whites around town felt the same. People often opt for simple answers over complex ones, and decisions like David's to free Betsy, and Ballinger and Potter's decision to help her, are easier to understand if they can be reduced to black and white. "The man who by his last solemn act manumits his slaves," the fiery editor of the *Austin Southern Intelligencer* paper fumed, "thereby records his dying judgment against the institution." There was no middle ground. Either a person supported slavery, and did all he could to further it, or he opposed it, and risked being tarred and feathered, imprisoned for seditious acts, or worse. The owner who frees his slave "does a great wrong to the manumitted negroes, whose condition he makes worse; and to society, upon which he throws a useless and dangerous population," the Austin editor concluded.[56]

Residents of Galveston—at least those who did not know the attorneys or the parties—made clear that they disapproved of Ballinger and Potter representing Betsy. In their minds, this case was never just a dispute about the ability of a man to dispose of his property as he saw fit. It was a case that called into question their entire way of life. Ballinger's uncle and mentor, James Love, was concerned when he learned of Ballinger's involvement in the case. He warned his nephew that many residents would react "most strongly against your defending of a negress." Love encouraged his nephew to drop the suit out of fear to both his person and his professional reputation. "Many of your friends & associates will believe you have betrayed your Southern principles," he wrote, "& that you are no longer to be considered sound on the subject of slavery. You will be accused of all manner of wrongdoing & your honour and integrity as a gentleman will be assailed. May Providence help you in this present affair."[57]

Ballinger was acutely aware of the difficulties posed by the case, both in terms of its merits and its social implications. "It was almost the general professional opinion that she was *not* entitled to her freedom or property," he would later recall, and "to maintain the contrary, required one to face the prejudices of this entire community." Others remembered how the case animated the population. "I think the validity of Webster's will was a good deal discussed," said A. H. Cleveland. From the back alleys to the parlors of the homes, people who liked to pontificate on the state of their society had little good to say about Betsy or the attorneys who represented her. "There was talk of her not being entitled to her freedom and being put back into slavery," Cleveland reported.[58]

Yet, as common as the view might have been, it was not held by everyone. Betsy's time in the community had earned her a place among a small cadre of individuals. Jane Hardin, the trustee, wrote to Potter that she was "perfectly willing and determined to do all in my power to forward the happiness of Betsy and that she may rightfully retain the property her master clearly designed be hers." Among those who knew her, Betsy was well liked and trusted, hardly fitting the image of the idle free person that inhabited the imaginations of so many. People stressed her "sensible" nature, insisting she "was a quiet peaceable inoffensive person." A group of them even got together to petition the Texas legislature for her freedom. This happened on July 1, 1856, roughly two months after David died and shortly before the dispute over the legality of the will was challenged in court. Henry Martin and Francis Whiting signed it, along with the clerk Oscar Farish and twenty-some others. They "pray[ed] for the passage of a law allowing Betsy a free negro woman to remain in this State." Betsy, they said, "is quiet, orderly and respectful, and has ample means for support during her life, having been set free and provided for by the last will of her late owner David Webster deceased."[59]

Ballinger and Potter's decision to take the case thus was not reducible to a simple equation, any more than were the efforts of those who signed Betsy's petition. Neither the attorneys nor the petitioners ever doubted the ideology of slavery. But abstract principles have a way of losing their force when contradicted by daily events. "As far as I know the feelings towards Betsy have always been friendly and kind among those who knew her," an acquaintance testified. Ballinger and Potter dismissed the criticism of others because of a personal connection to Betsy and David. Others may have threatened them, and surely they fretted over the implications, but there is no evidence they ever considered withdrawing from the case. To the contrary, as Ballinger put it, they "took an active and zealous interest in it."[60]

The Lawsuit

Martha Greenwood, David's purported cousin, was represented in her suit by Ebenezer Allen of the firm Allen & Hale. Allen & Hale was a Galveston firm that Ballinger considered "of the first respectability and ability." Accordingly, he and Potter defended the case "in that view," always believing, he said, it "was a suit in good faith." Ebenezer Allen hailed from the same social and economic class as Ballinger and Potter. He served as attorney general under President Anson Jones of the Republic of Texas, and later under Governor Peter Hansbrough Bell. He subsequently built a highly successful practice in Galveston, where, among other pursuits, he was involved with the railroad. By 1860, he owned real estate worth $36,000. He also owned slaves.[61]

After reaching their fee agreement with Betsy, Ballinger and Potter met in Ballinger's office on the Strand to discuss the merits of Martha's suit. Neither one was of the type to take any of the arguments in Martha's petition lightly. They knew that her first claim—that David was not of sound mind when he made the will—was a difficult legal position to take, but they also knew that it was of the sort that made sense to the common person. Nobody in his right mind would turn over a fortune to a black woman, many people thought, especially one who had lived her life as a slave. David must have been confused—senile even—to have handed thousands of dollars of land and personal property over to Betsy.

To rebut the claim, Ballinger and Potter tracked down several witnesses who knew David and could testify that not only was he competent at the time he made his will, but that his intention to free Betsy and leave her all of his property had been in the making for years. H. R. Taylor was a boarder in David's home when he lived in Apalachicola, Florida, years ago. He said that, from what he knew of David and Betsy, he would "have been surprised if [David] had pursued any other course toward his servant Betsy than that adopted by him" in the will. Taylor went on to say that he could not, "for a moment doubt that if [David] had had any anticipation of the difficulties in regard to the settlement and disposition of his estate, according to his wishes, he would have taken such legal measures as would have at once put a stop to them." Robert Meyers, who knew David from 1834 until he left for Galveston in 1846, had a similar impression. He "always supposed as did all the neighborhood that in case of [David's] death, the negro woman, Betsy, would be set free and get his property." Meyers may have been more honest than most. He was the one who frankly admitted that Betsy and David had always been "intimate." But he apparently spoke for the neighborhood when he said that "had [David] not have set her free at his death giving her also most of his property, it would have been to me conclusive evidence that his mind was unsound and weakened at the time of making his will."[62]

Others who saw David in the days before his death confirmed what these witnesses thought, insisting that he was lucid and fully capable of disposing of his property. Nancy Thomson said he was "perfectly sane." Another said he had known David since 1822 or 1823, and when he saw him on his sickbed, he "conversed with him . . . and thought him sane." Betsy personally contacted another witness and asked him if he "thought that Mr. Webster [was] in his proper senses or not when [he] had seen him." This witness—his signature is illegible—responded in a letter to Potter that he was "perfectly satisfied that he was as much as ever he had been since [the witness had] known him."[63]

It may have been true, as H. R. Taylor remarked in an oblique reference to David's close relationship to Betsy, that "Mr. Webster was a man possessing much eccentricity of character." But eccentricity is not the same thing as incompetency, and Ballinger and Potter were correct in assuming that courts were loath to interfere with personal decisions about how to dispose of one's property absent strong proof of a mental defect. State supreme courts in several jurisdictions, including Texas, had even upheld this right when, like here, a slave owner had freed a slave woman or the child he had with her and left her all his property. The decisions had nothing to do with sympathies for the enslaved; rather, they were about upholding property rights. The rationale was succinctly stated by the Texas Supreme Court in an emancipation case shortly after Texas became a state. "We believe that the right of property connects with it the right of relinquishing that property."[64]

With enough evidence to feel comfortable that the first claim would fail, Ballinger turned to the more difficult accusation in Martha's suit. It was the one that relied on the assumptions that free people of color were not welcome in Texas and that any effort to emancipate a slave had to provide for her removal to a free state. Around town, it was this argument that led to much "discussion and doubt among the lawyers as to the validity of the bequest to her in Webster's will," as most lawyers and policy makers knew about the Texas Supreme Court decision in *Purvis v. Sherrod*, the case Potter had in mind when Betsy first approached him. *Purvis* involved an owner who manumitted three slaves in his will, including a woman, her son, and the testator's own son. In order to provide for their well-being, the dying man and father stated in his will that the three beneficiaries "be settled near" his sister in Texas, giving them sufficient funds to set up a comfortable life. As in Betsy's case, however, it did not take long before disappointed relations challenged the testator's wishes, insisting that Texas law and policy prohibited emancipation within the state.[65]

The Texas Supreme Court agreed with the challengers, in a case that required a few leaps of logic but was nonetheless celebrated by many on the grounds that it came to the right result. In reaching its conclusion, the court acknowledged that there was nothing in the 1845 constitution, adopted after

Texas became a state, to prohibit "the natural right of the owner to dispose of his [slave] property as he pleased." Unwilling to close the matter on these grounds, however, it concluded that the framers of the 1845 constitution must have had the 1836 Constitution of the Republic of Texas in mind when they ratified this one. Under that constitution, no slaveholder was "allowed to emancipate his or her slave or slaves without the consent of Congress, unless he shall send his or her slave or slaves without the limits of the Republic." Seizing on the language, the court in *Purvis* reasoned that, although this "organic law was superseded by the Constitution of [1845]," it nonetheless should be "referred to, not only to show the true meaning of the [1845] Constitution . . . but also the policy of the restrictions on emancipation."[66]

Having so held, the court nonetheless created a way out from underneath its ruling. While a will that emancipated a slave in the state would be invalid, if a person wishing to free his slave provided that the manumission take place outside of Texas, that wish would be upheld. "A bequest of freedom," the court said, "not to take effect until the slave is removed beyond the territorial limits of such State, is nevertheless a valid bequest." In this way, the court skirted the issue of interfering with a person's natural right to dispose of his property, while also furthering the state's policy of limiting the number of free people of color within its borders. The court's fine-tuning of its holding benefitted the testator in *Purvis*. In that case, the testator had enough foresight to provide in his will that, if the state of Texas or any of his relations objected to the freeing of his slaves, his sister would have "full power to send them to a free State, or to Liberia, as she and the three negroes may agree."[67]

Ballinger thought *Purvis* had been wrongly decided, and he made clear that he was prepared to take Betsy's case up to the Texas Supreme Court to press his position. His argument was premised on the notion that the court "went too far in giving effect to the former Constitution." In his view, when the people ratified the Texas Constitution of 1845, the provision under the constitution of the Republic of Texas prohibiting owners from freeing their slaves in the state absent congressional permission should have been "entirely obliterated." Ballinger accepted that "the question as to the policy of the State with respect to permitting free negroes to remain in the State or compel them to leave it" was a good one. But it "was an entirely different and subsequent question" than the one at issue here. As it stood, under the 1845 state constitution, there was "no law of the State to prevent the owner from emancipating his slaves." Betsy was thus entitled to her freedom, as the will was valid.[68]

However, even if he failed to convince the court to reverse itself, Ballinger believed that he could fit Betsy's case into the exception carved out in *Purvis*.

As he freely acknowledged, *Purvis* required that, for a valid devise of freedom, owners had to provide "for the extradition of the slave from the State," and a will which did not contain such a provision would not be upheld. But, he maintained, if the will contained such a provision, "it vested the right to freedom," and the "question of removal became a question between the court and the trustee, or a question for the State to enforce its policy of removal." Ballinger was confident David's will met this basic requirement. A basic hypothetical illustrated his point:

> Suppose David Webster had manumitted Betsy and willed to Mrs. Hardin $1000 to remove her to Ohio? Suppose the administrators had paid over to Mrs. Hardin the $1000, to carry out this will; but instead of removing her to Ohio, Mrs. Hardin had pocketed the money, and left Betsy penniless and shiftless on our streets. Would any court have said that on this ground she continued, or again became a slave? No court ever did, or could have said so. Her status of slavery ceased by the will, her title to her freedom was perfect. The question of her extradition would have been one for the State.[69]

In Ballinger's view, David's will was thus no different from the will in *Purvis*. Like that one, David's will was "consistent with [Betsy's] removal," and as such her "right was fixed and perfect." Ballinger conceded that the will did not include a specific provision for extradition. Yet it did contain the catch-all phrase that the trustee be "herein empowered to carry out the true intent of this will." Ballinger argued that this provision was sufficient. "Here was a devise of freedom to Betsy," he said, "and of ample property and powers to her trustee to consummate it in accordance with law." It may have been true that Betsy had not left Texas, but "her removal was considered with this will and would be ordered . . . whenever the question arose." It became "a condition subsequent, not precedent."[70]

As Ballinger explained his litigation strategy to Potter, the friend and associate knew he made the right choice when he brought the star of the Galveston bar on board. In the manner of a great lawyer, Ballinger had a way of reducing complex material down to a line of thought that seemed obvious in its logic. Of course the court had been wrong in *Purvis*, and, even if not, of course David's will fell within its exception. It was a sound legal argument, and one Ballinger thought he could win. But, again, while good lawyers develop strong arguments in response to specific claims, great lawyers counter with new and unexpected arguments. In this case, Ballinger and Potter countered Martha's claim that she was entitled to David's estate by questioning whether she even had standing to make it. Betsy likely spurred the talk. In all the years she had known David, she told them, she never once heard him mention a cousin named Martha Greenwood or, for that matter, anyone else. Maybe this person was not David's cousin at all. Maybe she was simply an interloper seeking to capitalize on a lonely man's death.

Ballinger and Potter pursued the factual inquiry with as much vigor as the legal theories. They knew, as everyone did back then, that births and marriages were not always recorded, and even when they were, the records were often lost or destroyed. Proof of a familial connection in this case, like in most others, likely would fall on witnesses. H. R. Taylor, the boarder who lived in David's home in Apalachicola, confirmed what Betsy had said. He stated that he "never heard [David] say anything relating to family connecxions [sic], and [he was] not aware that there was anyone claiming any relationship to him." Robert Meyers, David's friend from St. Joseph's, agreed. He said that he "never heard him say that he had any relations." John Ruau was also from Apalachicola and he had known David since 1831. He said he had "no recollection of [David] mentioning any relative of his [that was] living."[71]

Other friends and associates of David testified to the same. Marcia Paschal, Mary Hopkins, and Thomas Duval were siblings who had known David in Florida. Marcia said she knew David "intimately." He lived next door to her and her husband, Dr. William Price, in St. Joseph, and he visited them weekly, if not daily. Marcia testified that David informed her "that he did not know of his having a relative living in the world." Even more, Marcia said that "on one occasion [David] said that if he had knowledge of having relations he would leave them nothing—not one cent." Her sister Mary Hopkins said she had known David for twenty years. She could not recall if he ever told her the name of his parents. She also testified that David had informed her "that he had no near relatives living." Their brother Thomas Duval had known David in both Florida and Texas. According to Thomas, David "had no relations living that he knew of."[72]

Ballinger and Potter had found a winning argument, as simple as it was. Martha's attorney, Ebenezer Allen, might have dismissed it as a nettlesome concern in the beginning, but as the evidence challenging the relationship mounted he began to realize that his case was in danger of falling apart. He wrote a letter to Martha and requested a continuance from the court so that Martha could reply with "the names and residences of her witnesses together with an abstract of what she could prove." Whether the letter never reached her, as Allen suggested, or whether she simply decided not to pursue the action any longer, is not known. Regardless, the district court denied the continuance and on July 3, 1858, dismissed Martha's case. Betsy had won.[73]

Freedom

During the Civil War, Galveston was upended. Union forces took the city in October 1862, following the decision of General Paul Herbert to abandon its defenses. William Ballinger, who had moved his family to Waco at the start of the war, called it a "bleak day in our history," his frustration reaching a boiling point over military men treating his island home so dismissively. Five of the eight cannons he had secured in his journey to Richmond had been sent to Houston rather than Galveston, as Confederate officials decided to make their stand in the Bayou City rather than Ballinger's hometown. Federal troops would not hold the city for long, however. In the early morning hours of January 1, 1863, having recently taken command of the District of Texas, Confederate general John B. Magruder staged an attack on both land and sea and retook the island. Even so, life was hardly normal for most of the city's residents. Many had left before the city fell, following General Herbert's orders to vacate the island. Those who stayed or returned found the city a shell of its former self. A Union blockade meant that the city's shipping industry had ground to a near halt, with the bulk of cotton exports shifting to a route from Brownsville to Bagdad, a Mexican coastal town on the Rio Grande. Sometimes it felt as if the only ones on the island were the poor and the destitute, or those with nowhere else to go. Betsy Webster was among them.[74]

Ballinger later testified that he and Potter "were greatly relieved when the suit was dismissed." To put it mildly, the "questions were difficult and doubtful," and a "strong opinion existed that the will was not valid." Yet, following the dismissal, there was no one else to contest its terms, and the probate court subsequently enforced it to the letter.[75]

Ballinger credited Potter with handling most of the details in the probate court. There were the standard controversies with the administrators, with some hints that they may have tried to cheat Betsy out of some of her property, but Potter "held them to strict account." During August 1858, shortly after the dismissal of Martha's case, the administrators presented their final tally to the court. In addition to the usual expenses, the administrators asked for reimbursement for the upkeep of David's slaves. Notably, these were part of David's personal estate, and under the terms of the will they would revert to Betsy. Perhaps to avoid the thorny issue of a free person of color owning slaves, the administrators, with the permission of the court, sold Mary and Jim for the sum of $1,200. They attempted to sell Harry, as well; however, their efforts were unsuccessful. Apparently Harry, despite being only eleven years old, displayed a spirited disposition that potential owners found troubling—

he "frequently ran away . . . without reason or assignable cause." During the final accounting, Harry appeared as a line in the cash account, bringing over $100 for a period of hire. Washington also appeared in the final accounting with a list of his expenses and wages, suggesting that he practiced a trade and worked in a shop or for another. Whether his special skills explain why they never tried to sell him is unknown. But both he and Harry would become part of Betsy's property in the final decree.[76]

Martha Greenwood's lawyer, Ebenezer Allen, made a last-ditch effort to stop the distribution of the estate, but the probate court showed little interest in hearing from him. Allen ultimately withdrew his objections after he failed to present any new evidence. In the final decree, issued during the November term in 1858, Martin B. Hardin, under the terms of the will, received the bulk of David's real property on the mainland of Texas, including property on the Paluxy River, the Bosque River, the Trinity River, and the Cow Bayou in Fall County. David's land in Wharton County, which was never mentioned in the will, was put up for sale to cover the cost of administration. Apart from that, the court awarded Betsy what was promised to her by David. This included all of his real estate in Galveston, together with the "houses, household furniture, effects and appurtenances," as well as "all the rents, profits, and emoluments and debts accruing to the same." In addition, she inherited his choses in action and "all the other notes and accounts due and owing." Finally, in a remarkable summation, the court awarded her all the residual "personal property of every kind and description, which were owned by said Webster in the city of Galveston at the time of his death."[77]

There is nothing in the record that describes Betsy's reaction to the court's order. There are no scribbles in the margins to indicate that she leapt to her feet when she learned of her freedom or, perhaps alternatively, collapsed in a heap on the floor. But only those lacking an imagination can fail to appreciate what this day meant. A woman in her sixties who, until this moment, did not even possess a last name now found herself the owner of the most precious right of all—the ability to chart her own destiny. "Everybody went wild," Felix Haywood said, when freedom came to him at the end of the war. "We all felt like heroes, and nobody had made us that way but ourselves. We was free. Just like that, we was free."[78]

Betsy took to her freedom and her newfound status in characteristic stride. She had always been a "very industrious careful sensible person," and now that she was free she had every intention of playing an active role in managing her own affairs. Looking back, people who knew her were hardly surprised. Oscar Farish, the clerk of the court, recalled one story that exemplifies how she would conduct her life following her freedom. Right after David's death, Jane Hardin, the trustee of Betsy's property, arrived in Galveston to attend to the will. Betsy, however, "was very anxious to get rid of her." She was concerned that "she would have to support Mrs. Hardin and her family if she stayed here and she did not intend to do it." Even back then, Betsy had every intention "to 'boss' herself." She therefore took it upon herself to not only encourage Hardin to go back to Georgia, but also to learn everything she could about her case. As Farish put it, she came to his office "a great deal," prompting him to think that Betsy "knew all about Webster's estate and her own finances and property as well as any white person could."[79]

After the probate court awarded Betsy her property, in a manner consistent with her knowledge of local affairs, she promptly began to take steps to lessen her impact on the community. She knew better than anyone the "consequence of a colored woman coming into possession of so much property." After talking over the matter with Mark Potter, she agreed that "her best policy was to convert most of her property which was then considered bearing a high price into money and that she hold the money rather than manage property." Soon after, she began to sell "the greater part if not all of her real estate." She sold lots to Dietrich Wilhelm, John Danagh, and Jacob Kichoe in the spring of 1859, pocketing over $3,200 in the process. She also sold several lots on her block to John Corbett and placed the title to her homestead in his name, as well.[80]

Corbett was someone whom Betsy had come to trust. The two had known each other for several years. He lived a block away from her and after David's death began acting as her "agent or guardian." The decision to place the title to her homestead in his name was something that everyone at the time seemed to believe was the right thing to do, including Potter. The two recorded a deed in which Betsy purported to sell him her homestead in exchange for $4,500. No money exchanged hands, however, and no sale took place. "The deed was only given," explained Farish, who recorded the deed, "in order that Corbett should hold the property for her benefit." Soon after, Betsy entered into a different contract with Corbett for several more lots on the same block as her home. These were undeveloped lots, at the time growing wild and covered in banana plants. Corbett paid $2,800 for the property, which John Jones testified was more than fair-market value. Sydney Fontaine, who was a law student in Potter's office at the time, was present when the parties signed the contract in Potter's office. Corbett "counted out the money on the table in gold & silver & some bills." Betsy took it and "put it in a handkerchief on the table, a white one on the inside, a gingham head kerchief on the outside." She "tied it up and seemed pleased." She had a right to be. Following the various deals and land sales, she had over $6,000, which she had buried in the backyard of her home.⁸¹

Betsy continued to live comfortably, if sparingly, off her inheritance in the short time between the court's order and the outbreak of the Civil War. Proud of her garden, with its oleanders and fruit trees, she kept it up the best her crooked hands and aging back allowed. She maintained cordial relations with her neighbors, associating with them as well as the people of color, both slave and free, she encountered in the streets and in the market. Still, even after the settlement of the estate, Ballinger and Potter continued to fret about Betsy's status and the implications of a free woman of color of notorious wealth. Their concerns were not without justification. Soon after the final distribution, Colonel Malcolm Graham, the state attorney general, was in the Galveston County courthouse rummaging through the files. Despite the order of the probate court, he "spoke of proceedings for [Betsy's] property and enslavement on behalf of the State." Apparently, he never pursued the matter. But this did not stop Potter and Ballinger from continuing to raise with Betsy the possibility of moving out of the state for her own security. She "positively refused to leave Galveston," however, causing Potter to contemplate introducing the earlier petition for her freedom—still languishing in the files of the state legislature—to settle the matter once and for all.⁸²

The petition was never introduced, and no explanation was ever given. Perhaps it was because the Civil War broke out soon after, and few around town felt the need to bother with an old woman. "Betsy has held her freedom and property like any other free person, without interference from any person so far as I know," A. H. Cleveland said. Betsy's abilities to negotiate the lines of race and slavery had served her well, and they would continue to do so during the war. In 1863, soon after the battle of Galveston, Confederate general Magruder issued an order "that all free negroes should be removed from the Island." The captain in charge of enforcing the order found only three, one of whom was Betsy. The provost marshal came to her defense, however, telling the captain that Betsy "was a quiet peaceable inoffensive person and very useful in case of yellow fever." It was a familiar refrain. Betsy "was never abused or treated with indignity," Oscar Farish said, at least among those who knew her. Connected and competent, Betsy "bore the very best character." The captain conveyed this assessment to General Magruder, "and the order was not enforced against her."⁸³

When Potter died in 1863, shortly after Magruder retook the city from the Union forces, no one invited Betsy to his funeral. It was probably just as well.

The two operated in separate worlds. One was a prominent resident of the city and a popular member of the state legislature. The other kept mainly to herself. Yet the divide between them was not as large as the official policies or even their own statements might suggest. They had still nodded to one another when they passed on the street and exchanged the type of pleasantries that were common among those who knew each other. Always resourceful and fiercely independent, Betsy had known what she wanted, and she found two attorneys who agreed to speak on her behalf. To this day, people struggle with the irony of two slaveholders advocating for the freedom of a slave. Yet the key is probably simpler than we might think. Long convinced of her humanity and the rights established by the will, Potter and Ballinger got to know Betsy on a personal level, ultimately viewing themselves as "her champion and her friend."[84]

Postscript

The end of the Civil War brought many things to the people of Texas, particularly people of color—the end of slavery, the beginnings of freedom. Galveston slowly came back to life, regaining its footing after Union troops pulled out of the Gulf and people moved back into their homes. But the end of the war did not bring peace to Betsy. Now that she was in her seventies, most still described her as being "of sound mind" and knowledgeable about her rights and interests. But her age was starting to take its toll. Her daily walks to the market were slower, and her eyesight was declining. She began to rely more on Thomas Baker, a "mulatto" whom she employed as her gardener and later "adopted" as her son. She also began to believe, rightly or wrongly, that people were trying to cheat her out of her property.[85]

Betsy found a voice (and some encouragement) for her concerns from a man named Jesse Stancel. Stancel was a lawyer who had lived in Austin until the fighting broke out, advertising himself as someone who "will attend faithfully to all business entrusted to his care." As the war approached, Stancel left the city and joined the Union army, "being one of those whose opinion did not coincide with the revolutionaries." He served as a lieutenant colonel, earning a reputation in the eyes of those who knew him as "an estimable and honorable gentlemen." He was the nephew of the provisional governor Alexander Jackson Hamilton, someone he looked up to and admired for his willingness to denounce slavery and the slaveholders he believed were subverting democracy. Colonel Stancel was a "good speaker and hard student." He moved to Galveston in September 1865, joining his brother's law office on Post Office Street, near Tremont Avenue, not far from the harbor.[86]

Stancel was never of the stature of William Ballinger or Mark Potter or many of the other estimable attorneys in the city prior to the Civil War. But he earned his keep in the short time he was there, maintaining a modest practice and a modest income. He was the kind of person who may have drifted off into obscurity, if he had not decided to break the law rather than uphold it.

In the 1870s, Stancel became one of the most notorious con artists in the state, and by decade's end he was locked up in the penitentiary. He was serving time for forgery in what the *Galveston News* dubbed the Great Texas Land Theft. Stancel had been honing his particular form of art for several years. After becoming the register in bankruptcy court in Galveston, he was indicted for "extorting illegal fees in a large number of cases." He evaded punishment, however, only to be indicted again in Kerr County in 1876 for "passing a forged instrument of writing as true." He was convicted but had his conviction reversed in the Texas Supreme Court because the indictment failed to charge him with "knowingly" passing as true the forged instrument, a key element of the crime. The court's decision earned him only a short reprieve, however, as prosecutors in several other counties were lining up to bring cases against him and his associates. As he sat awaiting trial for one of them, the *Galveston News* reminded its readers of some of their former resident's exploits, stating that he "now stands charged with one of the most stupendous land swindles ever heard of." In 1880, he was convicted and sentenced to two years and nine months in prison, earning the dubious recognition in the supreme court as being a "professional forger."[87]

Betsy of course had no knowledge of Stancel's future wrongdoings, and at the time he proposed to help her she had little reason to believe that he had anything but the best of intentions. She expressed to him her concerns about her property in the fall of 1865, trusting the man who had fought against the slave interests during the war and now professed to have her best interests at heart. After reviewing David's will and the records on file, and discussing the events surrounding the litigation, Stancel seized on two transactions that took place at the conclusion of the case. The first involved her former attorneys, William Pitt Ballinger and Mark Potter. The other transaction involved John Corbett, Betsy's neighbor, to whom she sold several lots on the same block as her home.

~

The final matter of Betsy paying her attorneys' fees was uneventful at the time. Just after the final decree, on January 6, 1859, Ballinger and Potter visited Betsy's home to settle the fee. John Corbett and another man, "acting as her friends," were present, as well. The group discussed the value of Betsy's estate under the will, estimating it to be $21,000, and agreed under the terms of the contract that Ballinger and Potter were entitled to one-third, or $7,000. As payment, Betsy assigned to them a debt owed to the estate worth $3,700, seven lots on a block in Galveston with an estimated value of $3,150, and $150 in cash. Shortly after, Potter and Ballinger negotiated a sale of the lots to Dr. Thomas Heard. Betsy, in conjunction with her trustee, Jane Hardin, then conveyed the property to Heard for the negotiated amount.[88]

Stancel minced few words the more he discussed the matter with his new client. As he saw it, the payment of attorney fees and subsequent sale of the property was "a base fraud and forgery, perpetrated against [Betsy] by certain parties . . . for the purposes of fraudulently swindling her out of her just, lawful and equitable rights and property." Convincing her to file suit during the next session of the district court, Stancel scribbled out the petition on February 7, 1866. In making his case, Stancel relied on legal arguments that were in direct opposition to Betsy's interests at the time Ballinger and Potter represented her. Citing *Purvis v. Sherrod*, the very case Ballinger labored to challenge and distinguish, Stancel insisted that Betsy had never been lawfully freed under the terms of the will because she had never been "removed beyond the limits of the State." As such, she remained a slave (and had always been a slave, despite what everyone thought), and at best "had only an equitable interest" in the estate. Conveniently, with the Civil War over, Stancel argued that Betsy was now free and entitled to everything promised to her in the will. But any transactions that took place prior to this point, including the one at issue, were null and void. Betsy was a slave and "was incapable of contracting or giving her assent to any contract whatever."[89]

It is hard to know whether the lawsuit was more of Betsy's making or Stancel's. One thing is certain, however: Stancel never gave Betsy much credit, talking about her in court papers and private conversations in ways that others did not. He referred to her as "an ignorant negro" who "could not know anything about the value of property." He also stood to gain handsomely should her suit be successful. He took Potter and Ballinger to task for their one-third contingency agreement; yet he negotiated a contract that would pay him "one half of whatever may be recovered." He may not have been trying to con her, as he would do to others when he sold them fraudulent deeds, but he did press a case that many lawyers would deem frivolous, in both law and equity. At least that is what the courts thought. It took several years for the case to come to trial. But when it did, in January 1869, the trial judge found in favor of Potter and Ballinger, and dismissed the case.[90]

The following year, in *Webster v. Heard*, the Texas Supreme Court affirmed.

In its opinion, the court made clear it was not impressed with Jesse Stancel's arguments. As it saw the matter, "a court of competent jurisdiction decreed the will valid, and thereby decreed Betsy a free woman." For counsel to now suggest otherwise, after Betsy had lived for many years as free in the quiet enjoyment of her home, was disingenuous and a misapplication of the law. "As the judgment or decree of this court has never been set aside, reversed or appealed from, but remains and ever has been in full force, virtue, and effect," the court said, "it thereby follows that from and after the time that this judgment or decree took effect, Betsy was a free woman." As such, the court concluded, Betsy in 1859 "was just as free to make a contract conveying her property . . . as she was on the day she instituted this suit." The payment to her attorneys was thus valid, including the property sold to Dr. Heard.[91]

Having resolved the case in favor of the defendants, the court leveled an uncharacteristic parting shot at the attorney who brought the case. Ballinger and Potter's reputations had been on trial, and as everyone knew, the reputation of men of their standing was "of more value" than any monetary judgment that might have been assessed against them. Potter had been dead for several years. But Chief Justice Amos Morrill, a Unionist who fled Texas during the war, was no more interested in seeing Potter's name impugned than he was seeing Ballinger's.

> The charges of fraud against her attorneys by the plaintiff have as little foundation to stand upon in the minds of those well acquainted with them, as the facts disclosed in the record. When we take into consideration what the laws then required, and more especially what public opinion was, relative to making slaves free, and placing them pecuniarily in a position superior to that of a majority of those born free and belonging to a different and dominant race, we are led to believe that a person of less legal ability and tact, of less influence in regulating and controlling public opinion, of less legal, political and moral standing in the community than her counsel, could have saved for her either the property or freedom devised.[92]

Notwithstanding the inglorious end to the case, Betsy's complaints that people she entrusted had not always treated her fairly may not have been solely the ramblings of an old woman or the trumped-up charges of a shady lawyer. "Betsy was very suspicious people would cheat her," Oscar Farish, the county clerk said. Having grown up a slave, it was a small wonder. If anything, her suspicion was the result of being "very smart," as only a fool would place complete trust in those who had formerly robbed others of their humanity. Betsy had initially transferred title in her home to John Corbett in an effort to hide her assets from those who might object. The two, however, eventually had a falling-out. Corbett insisted it was Betsy's fault. "She made the trouble," he said, though, in a telling sign of his perspective, he also admitted that he "had her arrested for insult." In 1861, in a sign of things to come, Betsy filed a deed in which she put title to her homestead in Oscar Farish's name instead of Corbett's, stating in the document that the prior conveyance to Corbett had been "without consideration." Four years later, after talking with Jesse Stancel, Betsy had it in her mind that the entire business with Corbett had been a sham. Stancel notified General Edgar Gregory of the Freedman's Bureau of what he knew, and the two evicted Corbett from the property "with force and arms" in November 1865. Three months later, on February 7, 1866, on the same day he filed the petition against Potter and Ballinger, Stancel filed suit against Corbett.[93]

The theory behind the suit against Corbett evolved from the time of the first petition to the filing of the second amended one. Seizing on his favorite words—words that would eventually be spoken against him—Stancel first insisted that the contract was a "base fraud and forgery" because Betsy "never bargained or sold" the lots to Corbett. The argument was specious, however. He said that Betsy "never had any knowledge of" the contract with Corbett until Stancel found it in the clerk's office and called her attention to it. It was the rookie argument of someone unfamiliar with the history of the case or the population of the island. Too many people knew about Betsy, and too many had witnessed her negotiate the contract herself and sign it in the presence of others. In his amended petitions, Stancel therefore shifted back to the argument he used against Potter and Ballinger, maintaining that Betsy never was properly freed by David's will and hence, as a slave, could not contract to sell her property. For good measure, he dragged the attorneys back into the case against Corbett, insisting that it was all "part and parcel of a scheme . . . to cheat and defraud plaintiff out of the entire property bequeathed to her" under David's will.[94]

The jury rejected the argument here, just as it did in the case against Potter and Ballinger. But in a ruling that surprised many, the Texas Supreme Court in *Webster v. Corbett* overturned its prior decision in *Webster v. Heard*, decided less than a year previous, concluding that "when the deed was made, Betsy Webster was a slave and could not make a deed." The court in *Corbett* held, in other words, that the will of David Webster did not free Betsy, and that for the several years everyone thought she was free, she was in fact a slave. Lawyers who believed in the consistency of the law and the power of precedent—that prior judgments should be followed absent a grave error or injustice—had a hard time explaining the court's rationale. After all, the lower court had declared Betsy free, and the court in *Heard* had upheld that finding. To suggest now that the decision was erroneous, and that she was never free, was troubling.[95]

Stepping back, however, anyone familiar with the members of the court at the time quickly understood what it was trying to accomplish. This court, later known as the Semicolon Court, was different from the one that decided the case against Potter and Ballinger. Republican governor Edmund J. Davis had just appointed three new members, including Moses Walker, who wrote the opinion here and would also write the opinion in *Honey v. Clark*, discussed in chapter 1. Trying to right the wrongs of the past, under the facts of the case, Justice Walker's opinion did not tarnish the credibility of the two attorneys, Potter and Ballinger, or anyone else. It merely held that, as a slave who was unable to contract, Betsy was legally entitled to the lots. There was no fraud; there was no forgery. To the extent that Corbett appeared to come out the loser, the court had a solution to that as well. It ruled that "equity" demanded that Betsy refund Corbett his purchase money before she was entitled to a reconveyance of the property. The court thus seemed to be dressing up an end it deemed just in the language of the law. Betsy had a choice. She could have her property back, if she was willing to pay for it.[96]

The last ten years of Betsy's life did not bring her relief from her troubles. Inching into her eighties, if anything, matters seemed to only get worse, at least in her mind. She does not appear to have ever regained the lots she sold to Corbett, perhaps unable to come up with the money to repay him along with the fee of one-half of the value of the property recovered that Jesse Stancel would demand. Even more unfortunate, the house she had lived in for more than twenty years, the beautiful home surrounded by flowers and orange trees, was sold from underneath her in 1876 by someone she had loved. Seven years earlier, in 1869, Betsy deeded the lots that made up her homestead to Thomas Baker, her "mulatto" gardener, in consideration for his "love and affection" and for taking care of her. According to Betsy, Baker did not hold up his end of the bargain. He "ill-treated her after she executed the deed, by keeping her confined on the premises in suit, in not allowing others to have access to her, and in not attending to her bodily wants." Others, of course, had very different recollections. The purchaser, George Mann, said that Baker's treatment of her "was kind and considerate." Baker maintained the place and paid the taxes. When he went to sell, moreover, Baker insisted that the lots containing Betsy's house be leased back to him until Betsy died, "stating that as she had given them to him, he would not move her from the lots."[97]

Betsy found out about the sale after Mann built a house on one of the lots, a year later. Mann offered to let Betsy continue to live in her home "as his tenant," presumably at no charge, but she refused, choosing instead to sue to stop the sale. In the end, what had made Betsy so remarkable, what had led to her finding and convincing two of the finest attorneys in the city to represent her, what had allowed her to negotiate the lines between freedom and slavery, would also work against her in the present suit. Her latest attorney—this one was named Wharton Branch—said that she was old and feeble and incompetent, and that she never understood anything about property or the deeds she signed. But no one in the community found the argument convincing. Betsy "was a woman of most excellent judgment." When she "desired us to act for her in any particular matter we acted accordingly, complying with Betsy's wishes." She was "sharp in a trade" and "competent to act for herself." She lost the case and the two appeals that followed.[98]

Betsy's story is an exceptional one. She grew up a slave and fought for her way to freedom, not by following the usual narrative and running away, but by using the courts to advance her cause and test her rights. She did not win every case, and even those she did win—even the victories—were made vulnerable by the precarious position on which she and other African Americans lived. But the courtroom provided her access to mechanisms of power that often eluded people of color. In the courtroom, Betsy helped shape the story of slavery and freedom in Galveston as much as anyone from the era. Her actions exposed a rift between the formal rules of slavery and everyday life, as she convinced two slaveholding attorneys to put their beliefs aside and advocate for her freedom. She died on May 24, 1880. A plaque commemorates the location of William Pitt Ballinger's estate. As of this writing, there is no historical marker for Betsy.[99]

CONCLUSION

Telling Stories of Slavery and Freedom

Ann—the young woman sketched in the introduction—was seventeen years old when twelve white men sat down to deliberate for the second time whether she was black or white, slave or free. Three years earlier, in March 1856, a jury in Limestone County had arrived at an unanimous conclusion. Ann, they said, was a "free white girl" who had been wrongly enslaved by a Choctaw Indian named George Gaines. The jury had brushed aside George's efforts to trace Ann's lineage back to an enslaved woman living on a Missouri farm. They could see with their own eyes what the doctor said during his time on the witness stand. Scrubbed clean, Ann had none of the "distinguishing characteristics of the negro," and as such could not be a slave. One hundred and forty miles away, however, three justices on the Texas Supreme Court saw the case differently. Examining the record rather than the girl, they found the evidence "clear and unequivocal" that Ann descended from an enslaved woman. The court sent the case back for another trial.[1]

George passed away in September 1856, after the appeal but long before the case could be retried. The administrator of his estate took over as the plaintiff, and the case dragged on through delays and multiple continuances until April 1859. George's estate successfully moved to have the venue transferred to neighboring McLennan County, where, according to the *Texas Almanac*, the town of Waco was emerging as "an important inland city, the centre of travel, and, beyond a doubt, the great traveled thoroughfare of Texas." The lawyer of George's estate felt the odds of a victory in Waco were higher than they were in Limestone County. There were more slave owners in the county, with 40 percent of families counting at least one human being as part of their household, and twenty-seven plantation owners with twenty or more enslaved persons.

Right before the trial was set to begin, the lawyer amended George's original petition to insist that "the girl Ann is reasonably worth and is of the value of the sum of two thousand dollars." He insisted further that George and his estate had been injured in the sum of "twenty dollars per month" since William Thomas "unlawfully" took possession of Ann back in the summer of 1855.[2]

As the residents of the surrounding area gathered once again to hear the intriguing case of what Ann was, they unwittingly encountered a side of slavery few openly discussed and most chose to ignore. Perhaps spurred on by the Texas Supreme Court's emphasis on descent, the lawyer for George's estate dug deep into Ann's early life in order to prove that she was a slave, born of a slave mother. Ann was born in Mary Vanlandingham's kitchen on November 6, 1842. Mary was the daughter of Joseph Hawkins, and the fourteen or fifteen slaves Joseph owned on his Missouri farm, including Ann, "were all the children or grandchildren of his slave Nancy, except one man named John, and they were all of a copper color." Each of the witnesses avoided saying who impregnated Nancy to create these "copper"-colored individuals. But their refusal to directly implicate Joseph as the father of at least some of the children was lost on only a few. Nancy's daughter (and Ann's mother) Sarah "was a yellow girl—a bright mulatto probably ¼ to ½ of the African race," said Dr. Samuel Rhodes. "Her father was probably a white man or a mulatto." Still, Mary and her husband, Louis, deflected any questions away from their father as the likely culprit. Sarah was "a bright mulatto" and "she had some white blood in her," Mary's husband said, but then, inexplicably, changed course. "[I think] her father must have been a negro." The testimony was reflective of southern culture as a whole and recalled the comments of Mary Chesnut, an insightful woman who revealed much about the twisted world of the southern plantation in her personal diary. "God forgive us," she wrote, "but ours is a *monstrous* system and wrong and iniquity. Perhaps the rest of the world is as bad—this *only* I see. Like the patriarchs of old our men live all in one house with their wives and their concubines, and the mulattos one sees in every family exactly resemble the white children—and every lady tells you who is the father of all the mulatto children in everybody's household, but those in her own she seems to think drop from the clouds, or pretends so to think."[3]

The deeper the lawyer for George's estate dug into the background of Ann, the uglier the story became. "Sarah was a shade lighter than a common mulatto and Ann at her birth was a still lighter color than her mother Sarah," said Mary's husband, Louis, who was present at the birth. In fact, had he not known her mother, Louis "could not have told that the girl Ann was of the negro race." Mary confirmed her husband's testimony. "Ann had blue eyes &

black hair, very curly and was sometimes mistaken for a white girl." Like her husband, she confessed not to know who Ann's father was, though she did admit that "her mother, Sarah, said he was a white man." Dr. Rhodes delivered Ann. He "supposed [her] to be ⅛ to ¼ African blood" and also presumed that "the father of Ann was a white man." None of the witnesses thus far felt the need to identify who he was, however, with Mary's husband going so far as to suggest that it was pointless to try. "Sarah the mother of Ann had connexion with different men both white and black," he said, playing on the myth that black women were naturally lascivious and cared nothing for monogamous relationships. It mattered little that Sarah was only seventeen when she had Ann. In the minds of whites, people of color were possessed of lustful and uncontrollable desires, even at a young age. The ruse worked until Mary's brother Strother Hawkins took the stand. Strother inherited Ann from their father, Joseph. Ignoring decorum, he blurted out what the rest of the family had tried to keep secret. Ann's father was Mary's brother-in-law, who had raped Sarah just like their father Joseph had raped Nancy.[4]

In 1859, in a courtroom full of people capable of stripping others of their humanity, the acts of Mary's father and her brother-in-law were not crimes. Indeed, the reason the lawyer for George's estate uncovered the family's secrets was not to gather indictments or even sully the family's name. It was to prove that Ann was a slave. Dr. Strother testified that he delivered Ann from "the body of Sarah," making Ann a slave just like her mother. The defense's only counter on cross-examination was to suggest that Ann might have been switched at birth, like something straight out of Mark Twain's novel *Pudd'nhead Wilson*. It is hard to imagine that many took the suggestion seriously. Sarah had given birth to Ann on a cabin floor on a Missouri farm. Aside from a few small children, no one else was there except the doctor, Mary, and her husband. The lawyer for the estate must have felt like he built an impenetrable case, with the laws of slavery demanding a result too clear for argument.[5]

Good trial lawyers know, however, that the courtroom is made up of more than just laws. There were real people sitting in the jury box and in the galleys. As it did before, in its case in chief, the defense played to the people's instincts, urging them to reject the plaintiff's evidence in favor of their common sense. They knew race when they saw it. The defense called only two witnesses. The first was a doctor who testified that "he did not see in Ann any evidence of the negro" and, moreover, "that he did not think she was the descendant of a negro." The second was the woman who housed Ann for two years while her case was awaiting trial. She swore that Ann's appearance had not been altered, and that "she had not dyed her hair." The case, in other words, unfolded in much the same way as the first. It was a trial of race against status, with the evidence designed to answer the simplest of questions: Was this young woman white or was she a slave? On the eve of the Civil War, with white Texans clambering for clarity over who could be a slave and who could be free, the answer could not be both. Too much was riding on the simple equation between blackness and slavery, whiteness and freedom. With Ann on full display, the jury in Waco reached the same conclusion that their neighbors to the east had reached three years earlier. "We the Jury find," they said, "the girl Ann to be free and not a slave."[6]

The second trial of *Gaines v. Thomas* provides a fitting end to a narrative about locally made law and the experiences of everyday people. Ending where it began, this book has sought to capture the stories of individuals regularly overlooked in most histories of Texas during this period. Delving into the intimate details of their lives, finding out who they were and what mattered to them, helps illustrate that daily life was filled with complexities and contradictions. Laws and bright-line rules tell only part of the story. The real action happens when we journey down to the local courthouse, uncovering the stories of men and women who pushed back and rebelled and parted ways with the ideals of their society. By looking at their actions and responses, by thinking about their goals and legal strategies, and by listening to their testimony and verdicts, we step closer to understanding what life was really like for most people. The answers are sometimes surprising, sometimes not. But there can be no doubt that such a process adds texture to the story, as we come to realize that these individuals played a far greater role in shaping the history of Texas than we have previously imagined.

Ann's story is no exception. Following the second trial, in which she was once again declared free because she looked white, the lawyer for George's estate appealed the verdict to the Texas Supreme Court. The court reached its decision during its 1862 term, and its exasperation with the ongoing saga was evident. This was "not a case of conflicting evidence, where the verdict should not be disturbed," it concluded in a terse opinion. Quite the opposite. The verdict in favor of Ann's freedom was simply "not supported by the evidence." In the minds of the men who made up the court, Ann's appearance had nothing to do with her status. She was a slave, born of a slave mother, and the rights of property trumped the sentiment of a group of residents of Central Texas. It reversed the jury's verdict and remanded the case for a third trial.[7]

From there the trail ends. It is possible that the parties reached a settlement, or perhaps the estate simply decided not to pursue the case in light of more pressing matters. Texans, after all, were in the throes of the Civil War, and many had likely lost interest in the slave who looked white. At any rate, there was never another trial, making it difficult to know what ultimately happened to Ann. She had been twenty when she learned (for the second time) that the Texas Supreme Court had stripped her of her freedom, and she was twenty-three when Texas surrendered to Union forces and slavery ended. But, without subsequent records, her life becomes difficult to track. To be sure, her life had been filled with tragedy and sorrow. She was born after her mother was raped. Six years later, the son of the man who had raped her grandmother took her from her mother and brought her to Texas. From there, she was sold—twice—first to Joseph Cox and then to George Gaines. Scared and alone, she then bounced around like a pawn in a game, with the law treating her as property despite her humanity. After the war ended, it is a small wonder that she disappeared. She had no interest in being found.[8]

In the short time we knew her, however, Ann's imprint on slavery and freedom in Texas was profound. Even the Texas Supreme Court saw it. Ann's case "cannot fail to give rise to some grave reflections on the law as it now is," the court observed in its first opinion. Referencing the Texas statute that defined a "mulatto" to be anyone with ⅛ or more African blood, it remarked, somewhat in shock, that Ann was "the last degree prohibited by law from giving evidence against a white person." It then carried its logic to the final extreme, with frightening consequences for defenders of the social order. "Her child, if by a white man, would be a competent witness against a white person, but following the status of its mother, it would be a slave, and it would so descend, ad infinitum, so long as the descent from a slave mother could be traced, though the blood be of the smallest possible amount." Nonetheless, the court felt powerless to take action. It thought the only body that could correct the schism created by the current law was the legislature. In truth, the jury that would decide Ann's case three years later would reshape the law on its own, as it did during the first trial and as local communities were regularly doing in cases involving similar issues. Texas during this period was no place for rigid rules. Out here, on the rough-and-tumble frontier, life was far more fluid, bending and adjusting as the old met the new.[9]

In much the same manner as Ann, the persons involved in each of the stories presented in this book impacted the history of race, slavery, and freedom in Texas in significant and important ways. John and Sobrina added complexity and nuance to questions of interracial relationships; Miles demonstrated how one act of resistance could expose the fault lines in the ideology of slavery; the Ashworths upended common assumptions about free people of color on the borderland; and Betsy showed through resourcefulness and determination how a person of color could utilize the courts to pursue justice long denied. The memory of their names pales in comparison to people like Stephen F. Austin, Sam Houston, and Jim Bowie, and their cases barely register against events like the Alamo and the debate over secession. But their stories are as important, if not more so, in understanding the everyday life of slavery and freedom in Texas.

NOTES

ABBREVIATIONS

CAH	Dolph Briscoe Center for American History, University of Texas, Austin, Tex.
ETRC	East Texas Research Center, Stephen F. Austin University, Nacogdoches, Tex.
GCC	Galveston County Courthouse, Galveston, Tex.
GLO	Texas General Land Office, Austin, Tex.
JCC	Jefferson County Courthouse, Beaumont, Tex.
MCC	McLennan County Courthouse, Waco, Tex.
OCC	Orange County Courthouse, Orange, Tex.
Reminiscences 1	J. H. Kuykendall, "Reminiscences of Early Texans." *Quart. of the Texas State Hist. Assoc.* 6, no. 3 (1903): 236–53.
Reminiscences 2	J. H. Kuykendall, "Reminiscences of Early Texans." *Quart. of the Texas State Hist. Assoc.* 6, no. 4 (1903): 311–30.
Reminiscences 3	J. H. Kuykendall, "Reminiscences of Early Texans," *Quart. of the Texas State Hist. Assoc.* 7, no. 1 (1903): 51–52.
RL	Rosenberg Library, Galveston, Tex.
SCL	South Caroliniana Library, University of South Carolina, Columbia, S.C.
SHLRC	Sam Houston Regional Library and Research Center, Liberty, Tex.
SLPC	St. Landry Parish Courthouse, Opelousas, La.
THL	Tyrrell Historical Library, Beaumont, Tex.
TSLAC	Texas State Library and Archives Commission, Austin, Tex.
WCC	Wharton County Courthouse, Wharton, Tex.
WCCA	Wharton County Courthouse Annex, Wharton, Tex.
WCHM	Wharton County Historical Museum, Wharton, Tex.

INTRODUCTION. White Slaves and Ownership Rights in Central Texas

1. Walter, *History of Limestone County*, 24–37. A helpful comparison of wealth, including slaveholding, in the different regions of Texas in the antebellum era can be found in Randolph B. Campbell and Richard G. Lowe, *Wealth and Power*. Limestone County falls in region 3, the more sparsely settled and less developed area in north-central Texas, where the number of non-slaveholders far exceeded the number of slaveholders. Ibid., 16, 27–31. In Limestone, while 182 families owned at least one slave by 1860, only 6 families owned large plantations worked by twenty or more. U.S. Bureau of the Census, *Agriculture of the United States in 1860*, Texas: Slaveholders and Slaves, 241.

2. In 1860, 6 of the 182 slaveholding families in Limestone County owned roughly 25 percent of the total slave population. Of the remaining 176 slaveholding families, 62 percent owned fewer than five slaves. Roughly 70 percent of the total number of families in Limestone in 1860 did not own any slaves. U.S. Bureau of the Census, *Agriculture of the United States in 1860*, Texas: Slaveholders and Slaves, 241; U.S. Bureau of the Census, *Statistics of the United States*, Miscellaneous Statistics: Number of Families and Free Population, 1860, 349.

3. Petition, *Gaines v. Thomas*, no. 175, p. 1 (Tex. Dist. Ct., Limestone Cty., Aug. 1855) (identifying George Gaines as a citizen of the Choctaw Nation), McLennan County District Court Records, MCC; Walter, *History of Limestone County*, 29 (noting that the Springfield Road was the main road of travel from Houston to North Texas); Exley, *Frontier Blood*.

4. Petition, *Gaines v. Thomas*, no. 175, pp. 1–2; copy of bill of sale, ibid., 1; statement of facts, testimony of Strother M. Hawkins, ibid., 1–2; testimony of Solomon Hiatt, ibid., 3.

5. Answer of defs, *Gaines v. Thomas*, no. 175, p. 1; statement of facts, testimony of Dr. Slater, ibid., 5–6.

6. Jury verdict, transcript from Limestone County, *Gaines v. Thomas*, no. 426, p. 5 (Tex. Dist. Ct., McLennan Cty., Apr. 1857), McLennan County District Court Records, MCC; *Gaines v. Ann*, 17 Tex. 211, 215 (1856).

7. DeBow, "Texas," 642.

8. U.S. Bureau of the Census, *Population of the United States in 1860*, State of Texas, Table No. 2—Population by Color and Condition, 486; statement of facts, testimony of Strother M. Hawkins, *Gaines v. Thomas*, no. 175, pp. 1–2.

9. Campbell, *Empire for Slavery*, 1–9. Selected sources on Texas slavery published prior to Campbell's work appear in the bibliography.

10. Campbell, *Empire for Slavery*, 257.

11. Barr, *Black Texans*, 13–38; Torget, *Seeds of Empire*; Carroll, *Homesteads Ungovernable*; Baum, *Counterfeit Justice*; Crouch, *Dance of Freedom*; Crouch, *Freedmen's Bureau and Black Texans*; see also Glasrud, *African Americans in South Texas History*; Hales, *Southern Family*; Moneyhon, *Edmund J. Davis*; Silby, *Storm over Texas*.

12. Schoen, "Free Negro in the Republic," chapters 1–6; Muir, "Free Negro in Harris County," "Free Negro in Fort Bend County," "Free Negro in Jefferson and Orange Counties," and "Free Negro in Galveston County." For additional studies of free people of color in Texas, see Barr, *Black Texans*, 1–12; Woolfolk, *Free Negro in Texas*; Fisher, "Legal Status"; J. Marks, "Community Bonds"; Shelton, "On Empire's Shore"; Treat, "William Goyens"; Pratt, "Free Negro in Texas"; Prince, "William Goyens."

13. The most definitive work on free people of color is Berlin, *Slaves without Masters*. Texas, however, did not figure prominently in Berlin's study. For some of the notable book-length studies of free people of color that focus on specific states and regions, see Breen and Innes, *"Myne Owne Ground"*; Franklin, *Free Negro in North Carolina*; Fields, *Slavery and Freedom*; Mills, *Forgotten People*; Sterkx, *Free Negro in Ante-Bellum Louisiana*; Wikramanayake, *World in Shadow*.

14. J. Marks, "Community Bonds," 267–69. For examples of local histories of free families of color in areas other than Texas, see Ely, *Israel on the Appomattox*; M. Johnson

and Roark, *Black Masters*. Part of the difficulty in studying free people of color in Texas has been the lack of diaries or other comprehensive sources adding insight into their lives. For comparison, see Hodges, *Free Man of Color*; Hogan and Davis, *William Johnson's Natchez*; Lane, *Narrative of Lunsford Lane*.

15. Campbell, *Gone to Texas*, 239–67. For the estimate on the number of Confederate troops, an uncertain and disputed number, see ibid., 261. For a comparison of cotton production in 1860 in the various states, see U.S. Bureau of the Census, *Agriculture of the United States in 1860*, Recapitulation—1860, Agriculture, 184–85 (indicating that Texas was among the top five producers of cotton, behind Mississippi, Alabama, Louisiana, and Georgia).

16. Testimony of Abraham Kincheloe, transcript of trial, *Clark v. Honey*, no. 789, p. 73 (Tex. Dist. Ct., Wharton Cty., Dec. 1871), Supreme Court Records and Briefs, no. M6614, TSLAC.

17. Ross, *Great New Orleans Kidnapping Case*, 6. For additional examples, see McLaurin, *Celia*; A. Rothman, *Beyond Freedom's Reach*; J. Rothman, *Flush Times and Fever Dreams*; Sharfstein, *Invisible Line*; Scott and Hébrard, *Freedom Papers*.

18. For discussions about the strengths and weaknesses of utilizing statutes versus trial records in the study of history, as well as the importance of everyday experiences with the law, see Jordan, *White over Black*, 587–88; Gross, "Beyond Black and White"; W. Johnson, "Inconsistency, Contradiction, and Complete Confusion"; Wiecek, "Statutory Law," 279–80. On the hegemonic function of the law, echoed in the cases discussed in the book, see Genovese, *Roll, Jordan, Roll*, 25–49.

19. Texas State Library and Archives Commission, "Stolen Texas Supreme Court Records Cache."

CHAPTER 1. Sex, Race, and
Family on the Gulf Coast

1. Transcript of trial, *Clark v. Honey*, no. 789 (Tex. Dist. Ct., Wharton Cty., Dec. 1871), Supreme Court Records and Briefs, no. M6614, TSLAC; *In the Estate of John Clark*, Wharton County Probate Book A, 325 (Aug. 1861), WCCA; "Notice," *Columbia Democrat and Planter*, Oct. 22, 1861. The estate sale took place over several days beginning on February 3, 1863, and netted $450,147.55. *Report of the Sales of the Estate of J. C. Clark*, Wharton County Probate Book B, 257–64 (Feb. 1863), WCCA. Later that month the *Houston Tri-Weekly Telegraph* raved at the amount people paid for Clark's slaves, stating that it was "a remarkable sign of the times." Untitled, *Houston Tri-Weekly Telegraph*, Feb. 20, 1863. In 1867, the *Austin, Texas State Gazette* reported deposits totaling $329,069.49 from the estate sale into the state treasury. "Special Deposits," *Austin, Texas State Gazette*, Oct. 19, 1867.

2. Transcript of trial, *Wygall v. State*, no. 5021 (Tex. Dist. Ct., Travis Cty., Oct. 1878) (Virginia claimants), Supreme Court Records and Briefs, no. M8083, TSLAC; *Clark v. Barden*, no. 1059 (Tex. Dist. Ct., Wharton Cty., Dec. 1877) (Alabama claimants), Wharton County District Court Records, WCHM; letter from Thomas H. Bayliss to A. H. Pearce, Oct. 1, 1880 (Indiana claimants), Miscellaneous Papers, WCHM; letter from H. E. Valen-

tine to G. G. Kelley, Dec. 13, 1907 (Iowa claimants), Miscellaneous Papers, WCHM; "Estate without Known Heirs," *Dallas Herald*, Oct. 12, 1867; "The Deceased Texas Millionaire—Who Are the Heirs?," *Dallas Herald*, Feb. 18, 1871; "A Big Stake: How an Indiana Man Makes Out His Claims in the Estate of a Texas Millionaire," *San Marcos Free Press*, Feb. 22, 1879.

3. Petition, transcript of trial, *Clark v. Honey*, no. 789, pp. 1–8; *Gaines v. Ann*, 17 Tex. 211, 214 (1856) ("On the question of her condition of slavery, the doctrine is too well settled to require a reference to authority, that the offspring follows the condition of the mother.").

4. A. Williams, *History of Wharton County*, 164–67, 169–81, 187–93 (discussing newspapers, railroad, and schools); "Internal Improvements," *Houston Evening Telegraph*, May 23, 1870 (noting how grading had begun for railroad to Wharton).

5. A. Williams, *History of Wharton County*, 32–40 (history of courthouse).

6. 1860 U.S. Census, Wharton Cty., Tex., Schedule 1—Free Inhabitants, s.v. "J. C. Clark," accessed through Ancestry.com (listing John's birthplace and his birth year); testimony of Reason Byrne, transcript of trial, *Clark v. Honey*, no. 789, p. 65 (John said his "relations had treated him with silent contempt").

7. Testimony of Edward Collier, transcript of trial, *Clark v. Honey*, no. 789, p. 96 (stating that John was a "solitary" man).

8. "Important from Texas," *Illinois Gazette*, Nov. 17, 1821; Wortham, *History of Texas*, 1:125; testimony of Sharp Jackson, transcript of trial, *Clark v. Honey*, no. 789, p. 69 ("I came with Alexander Jackson to Texas and Clark came with us").

9. Wortham, *History of Texas*, 1:115–40; "Miscellaneous remarks," by J. H. K. in Kuykendall, "Reminiscences 3," 51–52.

10. A. Williams, *History of Wharton County*, 15–16; Wortham, *History of Texas*, 1:127; Yoakum, *History of Texas*, 1:223; recollections of Judge Thomas M. Duke in Kuykendall, "Reminiscences 1," 247–48; recollections of Abraham Alley in Kuykendall, "Reminiscences 3," 47–48.

11. Bugbee, "Old Three Hundred," 108–9; extracts from a biographical sketch of Capt. John Ingram in Kuykendall, "Reminiscences 2," 324–25.

12. A. Williams, *History of Wharton County*, 1–4, 41–51; Bugbee, "Old Three Hundred," 111. Wharton County was created in 1846, out of Matagorda, Jackson, and Colorado Counties. A. Williams, *History of Wharton County*, 29.

13. *Title to John C. Clark*, Colorado County Spanish Translations Deed Book A, 54–58 (July 16, 1824), CCC; Holly, *Texas*, 50 ("taste like the kernel of the peach stone"); Bugbee, "Old Three Hundred," 113–14; recollections of Capt. Gibson Kuykendall in Kuykendall, "Reminiscences 3," 29–30 ("Deer and turkies [sic] were abundant."); Wortham, *History of Texas*, 1:129.

14. Testimony of Reason Byrne, transcript of trial, *Clark v. Honey*, no. 789, pp. 61, 63, 64 (general description of cabin together with dates he visited); testimony of Clarisa Bird, ibid., 55 ("Mr. Clark at that time had a house with a plank floor."); testimony of H. P. Cayce, ibid., 84 ("House was a common rough log cabin might have had a loft . . . Log house cracks open but one room."); Olmsted, *Journey through Texas*, 76–77.

15. Recollections of Capt. Gibson Kuykendall in Kuykendall, "Reminiscences 3," 30; Wortham, *History of Texas*, 1:128–29 (talk of trading horse for corn).

16. A. Williams, *History of Wharton County*, 6, 293–94; recollections of Capt. Horatio Chriesman, son-in-law of William Kincheloe, in Kuykendall, "Reminiscences 1," 236–41; Barbara L. Young, "Kincheloe, William," *Handbook of Texas Online* (http://www.tshaonline.org/handbook/online/articles/fki14), accessed June 5, 2015, uploaded on June 15, 2010, published by the Texas State Historical Association.

17. Testimony of Clarisa Bird, transcript of trial, *Clark v. Honey*, no. 789, p. 55 ("Capt. Herd [sic] bought his land from Master."); testimony of Geo. W. Hooken, ibid., 93 ("miserly"). For a brief historical sketch of W. J. E. Heard, including when he arrived, see A. Williams, *History of Wharton County*, 294–97. The deed of sale between John Clark and W. J. E. Heard was not filed until June 5, 1838, after Texas became a republic and shortly after the formation of Colorado County, which included parts of Wharton. *Deed from John C. Clark to William J. E. Heard*, Colorado County Deed Book A, 258–59 (June 5, 1838), CCC. Family lore, however, along with comments from the trial record, indicates the sale took place years before the deed was filed. A. Williams, *History of Wharton County*, 295 ("'To the best of our knowledge, this land was bought in 1830 but not recorded until Colorado County was formed,' said George Northington III," one of the descendants). For a discussion of the cost of public lands in relation to Texas, see Campbell, *Gone to Texas*, 104 (public lands in United States sold for $1.25 an acre after 1820).

18. Campbell, *Empire for Slavery*, 13–16; "Colonisation Law of 1823, art. 30," in Gammel, *Laws of Texas*, 1:27, 30.

19. Instructions to Deputy in State Congress, June 4, 1824, in Barker, *Papers of Stephen F. Austin*, vol. 2, pt. 1, p. 809; Fehrenbach, *Lone Star*, 142 (noting that most of the original colonists came from one of the southern states); James Henry Hammond, "Letter to an English Abolitionist," in Faust, *Ideology of Slavery*, 170; "Letter from Judge Frazer," *Marshall, Texas Republican*, Dec. 8, 1860.

20. Stephen Austin to William Kincheloe, permit to settle, Oct. 16, 1821, in Barker, *Papers of Stephen F. Austin*, vol. 2, pt. 1, pp. 421–22 (offering 80 additional acres for every slave brought to the colony); Bertleth, "Jared Ellison Groce," 359; Bugbee, "Old Three Hundred," 113.

21. Barker, "African Slave Trade in Texas," 150 ("Indeed, under some name, negro slavery, it may be said, was absolutely essential to the development of Texas."); Austin to Governor Rafael Gonzales, Apr. 4, 1825, in Barker, *Papers of Stephen F. Austin*, vol. 2, pt. 2, pp. 1065–67; Padrón a la Colonia de Austin (1826), box 126, folder 2, Spanish Collection, Archives and Records Program, GLO. The decree prohibiting the slave trade, issued in July 1824, did not make clear whether it prohibited all importations of slaves, including by their owners, or just the importation of slaves for sale. Campbell, *Empire for Slavery*, 16–17.

22. "Constitution of the State of Coahuila and Texas, art. 13," in Gammel, *Laws of Texas*, 1:423, 424; Parker, *Trip*, 162. Ellis Bean, who proposed calling slaves "indentured servants" as early as 1826, described his plan this way: have the settlers "Gow in Presens of an Alcalde stating that this nigro cost you so much and when he Pays it by labor Don you have no charge against him he Discounts so much a month as any other hirid

Persons a small sum so that he will be the same to you as Before." Ellis H. Bean to Austin, July 5, 1826, in Barker, *Papers of Stephen F. Austin*, vol. 2, pt. 2, pp. 1368–69. Austin helped secure passage of this proposal in 1828. Campbell, *Empire for Slavery*, 21–23 (discussing the 1827 provision and the efforts to get around it).

23. Manuel Dublán and José Maria Lozano, eds., *Legislación mexicana ó colección completa de las disposiciones legislativas*, 2:239, cited in Howren, "Causes," 416; Yoakum, *History of Texas*, 1:254; Campbell, *Empire for Slavery*, 35–39; Lack, "Slavery and the Texas Revolution"; Stephen Austin to Mrs. Mary Austin Holley, Aug. 21, 1835, in Barker, *Papers of Stephen F. Austin*, 3:101–2.

24. Barker, "African Slave Trade in Texas," 145–49; Lack, "Slavery and the Texas Revolution," 186–87; McComb, *Galveston*, 35; D. Harris, "Reminiscences of Mrs. Dilue Harris I," 97–99.

25. Testimony of Edward Collier, transcript of trial, *Clark v. Honey*, no. 789, p. 97; testimony of Pleasant Ballard, ibid., 76; *In the Estate of John C. Clark*, Wharton County Probate Book B, 224–28, WCCA (Oct. 8, 1861); *Report of Sales of the Estate of J. C. Clark*, Wharton County Probate Book B, 257–64.

26. *In the Estate of John C. Clark*, Wharton County Probate Book B, 224; 1850 U.S. Census, Wharton Cty., Tex., Schedule 4—Production of Agriculture, s.v. "John C. Clark," accessed through Ancestry.com; 1860 U.S. Census, Wharton Cty., Tex., Schedule 4—Production of Agriculture, s.v. "J. C. Clark," accessed through Ancestry.com.

27. G. White, *1840 Census*, 26; 1850 U.S. Census, Wharton Cty., Tex., Schedule 2—Slave Inhabitants, s.v. "John C. Clark," accessed through Ancestry.com; 1860 U.S. Census, Wharton Cty., Tex., Schedule 2—Slave Inhabitants, s.v. "J. C. Clark," accessed through Ancestry.com; *Report of Sales of the Estate of J. C. Clark*, Wharton County Probate Book B, 257–64. In 1860 there were 76,781 families in Texas. Of those, 21,878 owned slaves, or 28.5 percent. U.S. Bureau of the Census, *Statistics of the United States*, Miscellaneous Statistics: Number of Families and Free Population, 1860, 349. Moreover, of the 21,878 slaveholding families, 11,342 (51.8 percent) owned fewer than five slaves, 16,292 (74.5 percent) owned fewer than ten, and 19,715 (90.1 percent) owned fewer than twenty. U.S. Bureau of the Census, *Agriculture of the United States in 1860*, Texas: Slaveholders and Slaves, 242. The numbers were similar to other states. Parish, *Slavery*, 26–27. In Wharton County the percentage of slave owners and the size of their holdings was higher than Texas's average. In 1860, there were 159 families in Wharton, and of these, 128 of them (80.5 percent) owned slaves. Among this group, 20.3 percent owned fewer than five slaves, 42.2 percent owned fewer than ten, and 64.1 percent owned fewer than twenty. U.S. Bureau of the Census, *Agriculture of the United States in 1860*, Texas: Slaveholders and Slaves, 242. Only John Clark and four others from Wharton owned more than 100 slaves. The other four were A. C. Horton, R. D. Sorrel, M. S. Stith, and David T. Stevens. 1860 U.S. Census, Wharton Cty., Tex., Schedule 2—Slave Inhabitants, s.v. "A. C. Horton," accessed through Ancestry.com; ibid., s.v. "R. D. Sorrel;" ibid., s.v. "M. S. Stith;" ibid., s.v. "David T. Stevens."

28. U.S. Bureau of the Census, *Agriculture of the United States in 1860*, Texas: Slaveholders and Slaves, 242 (indicating that only 54 out of 21,878 slaveholding families, or 0.2 percent, owned more than 100 slaves); Olmsted, *Journey through Texas*, 49–52; see

Oakes, *Ruling Race*, x–xiii (challenging assumption that slaveholders were unconcerned about profits and capitalism).

29. Testimony of Clarisa Bird, transcript of trial, *Clark v. Honey*, no. 789, pp. 50, 55–56; *In the Estate of John C. Clark*, Wharton County Probate Book B, 225 (listing "Clarissa" in the inventory with the notation "90 years of age").

30. Testimony of Clarisa Bird, transcript of trial, *Clark v. Honey*, no. 789, pp. 50–51 ("knew when he got Sobrina—but cannot state the date—four years after he got me—a number of years before the runaway scrape"); testimony of Sharp Jackson, ibid., 69 ("Got Sobrina three or four years before the runaway scrape"); testimony of James Montgomery, ibid., 58 (stating that Clark "had only two hands when he got Sobrina"); testimony of David Prophet, ibid., 70 (explaining that he knew Clark when he had only three slaves, "and Sobrina was one of them"); testimony of James Montgomery, ibid., 60 ("She belonged to Gilbert before he got her."); testimony of Stephen R. Herd, ibid., 81 (Gilbert "lived 6 or 8 miles from Clark's"); testimony of Reason Byrne, ibid., 61 (Sobrina was a "dark mulatto"). Sobrina was listed in the 1863 probate records as being sixty years old, meaning that she was born around 1803 and was likely in her late twenties when John bought her. *Report of the Sales of the Estate of J. C. Clark*, Wharton County Probate Book B, 257, 259. Sobrina's children before John were Dan, Louis, Sethe, and Jane. Testimony of Albert Horton, transcript of trial, *Clark v. Honey*, no. 789, p. 56. Preston Gilbert and his wife Sarah are listed among the Old Three Hundred. Bugbee, "Old Three Hundred," 112.

31. Jacobs, *Incidents*; Betty Powers, in Rawick, *American Slave*, vol. 5, pt. 3, pp. 190–92; Elvira Boles, in ibid., vol. 4, pt. 1, pp. 106–7; Rose Maddox, in ibid., vol. 7 (supp.), pt. 6, p. 2531. According to Catherine Clinton, "Consent would never be more than a minor factor in a society where slaveowners maintained despotic rule. The female slave, for example, could not give herself 'freely,' for she did not have herself to give: she already belonged to the master." Clinton, *Plantation Mistress*, 213.

32. Testimony of Clarisa Bird, transcript of trial, *Clark v. Honey*, no. 789, p. 51 ("his own woman"); testimony of Edward Collier, ibid., 96 ("solitary"); testimony of Clarisa Bird, ibid., 52 ("few women in the country"); testimony of Sharp Jackson, ibid., 70 ("keep out of the way"); testimony of Clarisa Bird, ibid., 53 ("first child was born about one year after").

33. U.S. Bureau of the Census, *Agriculture of the United States in 1860*, 140–51; "Our Coast Counties," *Houston Telegraph*, Feb. 24, 1870; Ivan, "Masters No More," 216–17 (Wharton contained "some of the largest cotton and sugar plantations in antebellum Texas"); U.S. Bureau of the Census, *Population of the United States in 1860*, State of Texas, Table No. 2—Population by Color and Condition, 486; U.S. Bureau of the Census, *Statistics of the Population of the United States*, Population by Counties—1790–1870, Table II.—State of Texas, 65–66; Crouch, "Spirit of Lawlessness"; Kosary, "Wantonly Maltreated"; "Letter from Wharton County," *Freedmen's Bureau Online* (http://www.freedmensbureau.com/texas/whartonletter.htm), accessed June 6, 2015 (reproduced letter from F. G. Franks to the editor of *Flakes Bulletin*, July 27, 1868).

34. "Our Coast Counties," *Houston Telegraph*, Feb. 24, 1870; *Texas Almanac for 1871*, 158. For an overview of the decline in production of agriculture following the Civil War, see Ivan, "Masters No More," 204.

35. "From Wharton," *Houston Daily Union*, Dec. 30, 1871 (noting sign that said "carpetbaggers" outside Franks's store); "Letter from Wharton," *Houston Union*, Aug. 17, 1869 (mentioning speech by Franks, among others, in support of Davis); "Our Next Legislature," *Houston Telegraph*, Jan. 13, 1870 (listing Franks as a new member of the House for 1870); "The Legislature," *Dallas Herald*, Nov. 23, 1872 (listing Franks as new member of Senate for 1872); "Francis Franks." Gray Franks is listed as ten years old under his father John Franks's household in 1850 in Monroe County, Mississippi. 1850 U.S. Census, Monroe Cty., Miss., Schedule 1—Free Inhabitants, s.v. "John Franks," accessed through Ancestry.com. John moved his family to Wharton sometime in the 1850s, and he is listed as living in the county in 1860. 1860 U.S. Census, Wharton Cty., Tex., Schedule 1—Free Inhabitants, s.v. "John Franks," accessed through Ancestry.com. John owned nineteen slaves in 1860. 1860 U.S. Census, Wharton Cty., Tex., Schedule 2—Slave Inhabitants, s.v. "John Franks," accessed through Ancestry.com.

36. "The Wharton Rebellion," *Houston Union*, Sept. 9, 1869 ("abused and cursed"); "Texas Legislature," *Houston Telegraph*, Feb. 24, 1870 (listing Franks's vote in favor of ratifying the 15th Amendment); "Letter from Wharton," *Houston Union*, Sept. 7, 1869 (describing mob); untitled, *Houston Telegraph*, Sept. 9, 1869 (same).

37. *Deed from Bishop Clark to Jackson Rust*, Wharton County Deed Book C, 51–52 (Dec. 1, 1874) (stating that parties entered into an agreement with F. G. Franks to represent them on Sept. 15, 1870), WCCA; petition, transcript of trial, *Clark v. Honey*, no. 789, p. 3 (indicating that Sobrina died around Dec. 25, 1869); testimony of I. M. Dennis, ibid., 91 ("black woman as his wife"); Memorials and Petitions to Congress, Petition of the Children of David and Sophia Towns (Oct. 1840) (petition located in William Goyens's folder), TSLAC; *Bonds v. Foster*, 36 Tex. 68, 68–70 (1871); *Smelser v. State*, 31 Tex. 95, 96 (1868). A growing number of scholars have detailed relationships between whites and blacks in the 19th century that defy traditional assumptions in favor of complexities and contractions. See, e.g., Cott, *Public Vows*, 41–47; Gordon-Reed, *Hemingses of Monticello*; Hodes, *White Women, Black Men*.

38. "An Act To legalise [sic] certain Marriages; to provide for the celebration of Marriages and for other purposes, sec. 9, 1837," in Gammel, *Laws of Texas*, 1:1087, 1294; "Unlawful Marriage," in ibid., 4:873, 1036–37; "Of Incest, Adultery and Fornication," in ibid., 4:873, 1037; Morgan, *American Slavery, American Freedom*, 327. For a comprehensive look at the bans on interracial marriages, see Pascoe, *What Comes Naturally*. The 1870 census records indicate that none of the children owned land and that only Bishop and Nancy owned any personal property, likely some livestock or farming equipment. 1870 U.S. Census, Wharton Cty., Tex., Schedule 1—Inhabitants, s.v. "Bishop Clark," accessed through Ancestry.com; ibid., s.v. "Pleasant Ballard;" ibid., Fort Bend Cty., Tex., Schedule 1—Inhabitants, s.v. "Joseph Towns" (surname spelled incorrectly in original).

39. Testimony of James Montgomery, transcript of trial, *Clark v. Honey*, no. 789, p. 60 (describing children); testimony of Clarisa Bird, ibid., 53 (discussing runaway scrape and stating "we all ran away on account of the Mexicans—We went as far as the Trinity"); testimony of James Montgomery, ibid., 58 (stating that he knew Clark "in the runaway and we camped together on Trinity"). Washington-on-the-Brazos was on the La Bahia Road, one of the main roads in and out of Texas. William Fairfax Gray, who was at the

NOTES TO CHAPTER ONE 189

convention at Washington, described how a "constant stream of women and children, and some men, with wagons, carts and pack mules are rushing across the Brazos night and day." Gray, *Diary of William Fairfax Gray*, 125. For an additional account of the Runaway Scrape, see D. Harris, "Reminiscences of Mrs. Dilue Harris II."

40. D. Harris, "Reminiscences of Mrs. Dilue Harris II," 168 (discussing celebratory mood following news of victory); "Constitution of the Republic of Texas of 1836, General Provisions, sec. 9," in Gammel, *Laws of Texas*, 1:1069, 1079.

41. Testimony of Clarisa Bird, transcript of trial, *Clark v. Honey*, no. 789, p. 53 (stating that they came back from the Runaway Scrape in time for "cropping").

42. Ibid., 51. The witnesses offered different accounts of the interior of the cabin. H. P. Cayce stated that he remembered the cabin having only one room and that it "might have had a loft." Testimony of H. P. Cayce, ibid., 84. David Prophet, on the other hand, said that "Sobrina & Clark had one room and the children another." Testimony of David Prophet, ibid., 71. Either way, as Abraham Kincheloe put it, "There was only one bed in the room and they slept in it." Testimony of Abraham Kincheloe, ibid., 72.

43. A. Williams, *History of Wharton County*, 32–34.

44. Testimony of Clarisa Bird, transcript of trial, *Clark v. Honey*, no. 789, p. 51.

45. The transcript of the trial is a narrative of the answers from witnesses. The questions during witness examination have been inferred from the nature, sequence, and context of the narrative record.

46. Ibid., 51–54.

47. Ibid.

48. James Green, in Rawick, *American Slave*, vol. 4, pt. 2, p. 88.

49. Testimony of James Montgomery, transcript of trial, *Clark v. Honey*, no. 789, p. 59.

50. Testimony of David Prophet, ibid., 70–71.

51. Testimony of Sharp Jackson, ibid., 69.

52. Testimony of Albert Horton, ibid., 56–58.

53. "General Laws of the Seventh Legislature of the State of Texas, tit. 4, chap. 1, art. 644," in Gammel, *Laws of Texas*, 4:873, 1114.

54. Testimony of Albert Horton, transcript of trial, *Clark v. Honey*, no. 789, 56–58.

55. Testimony of Abraham Kincheloe, ibid., 72.

56. Testimony of Pleasant Ballard, ibid., 74–75.

57. Testimony of James Montgomery, ibid., 60; testimony of David Prophet, ibid., 71–72; testimony of Pleasant Ballard, ibid., 76; testimony of Dan Owens, ibid., 78.

58. Campbell, *Empire for Slavery*, 141.

59. Testimony of David Prophet, transcript of trial, *Clark v. Honey*, no. 789, pp. 70–71; Carole E. Christian, "Washington-on-the-Brazos, TX," *Handbook of Texas Online* (http://www.tshaonline.org/handbook/online/articles/hvw10), accessed August 09, 2015, uploaded June 15, 2010.

60. Testimony of David Prophet, transcript of trial, *Clark v. Honey*, no. 789, pp. 70–71 (describing trip to Washington); testimony of Clarisa Bird, ibid., 54 ("The children i.e. the girls went off to Washington to school but they took sick and returned."); "Female Academy," *Washington American*, Aug. 11, 1857. John is listed as literate in the census returns. 1850 U.S. Census, Wharton Cty., Tex., Schedule 1—Free Inhabitants, s.v. "John C.

190 NOTES TO CHAPTER ONE

Clark," accessed through Ancestry.com. There were no schools in Wharton in 1850. U.S. Bureau of the Census, *Seventh Census of the United States*, Texas: Table VII—Colleges, Academies, Schools &c., 511.

61. Testimony of Clarisa Bird, transcript of trial, *Clark v. Honey*, no. 789, p. 52 ("dressed her better"); testimony of Abraham Kincheloe, ibid., 72 ("always treated her kindly"); testimony of Albert Horton, ibid., 57 ("dear"); testimony of Pleasant Ballard, ibid., 74 ("old woman" and "old man"); testimony of James Montgomery, ibid., 59 ("old man"). The references to the stores in Washington can be found in the advertisement section of *Washington American*, Aug. 11, 1857.

62. Testimony of Clarisa Bird, transcript of trial, *Clark v. Honey*, no. 789, p. 51 ("mistress of the plantation," "carried the keys," "gave orders"); testimony of Abraham Kincheloe, ibid., 72 ("charge of his keys & money"). For an engaging discussion of marital roles and identities in the nineteenth century, see Hartog, *Man and Wife in America*.

63. Testimony of Clarisa Bird, transcript of trial, *Clark v. Honey*, no. 789, pp. 53, 55; testimony of James Montgomery, ibid., 59 ("always took authority just like a white woman"); testimony of Abraham Kincheloe, ibid., 72 ("attended to everything on the place"); testimony of Reason Byrne, ibid., 63 ("acted as wives usually do"); testimony of Albert Horton, ibid., 57 ("has had me whipped"). For some of Olmsted's impressions of the wives he met, see Olmsted, *Journey through Texas*, 49–52, 209–10. For a detailed explanation of the increasing role of love in marriage, see Coontz, *Marriage, a History*.

64. Testimony of Clarisa Bird, transcript of trial, *Clark v. Honey*, no. 789, p. 52 ("Sobrina took care of him until his death and did all that could be done for him with the affection of a wife."); testimony of Pleasant Ballard, ibid., 75 ("Sobrina took care of Clark with Lourinda when he was sick."); testimony of David Prophet, ibid., 71 ("Sobrina and one of the children attended him when sick."); testimony of Joseph Anderson, ibid., 86 ("no woman would marry him but for his property"); testimony of Clarisa Bird, ibid., 54 ("Sobrina was his wife"); testimony of David Prophet, ibid., 70 ("no other woman").

65. Petition filed Feb. 5th, 1867, transcript of trial, *Wygall v. State*, no. 4232, pp. 1–7 (Tex. Dist. Ct., Travis Cty., Apr. 1880), Supreme Court Records and Briefs, no. M9774, TSLAC; statement of facts, ibid., pp. 43–44; statement of facts, transcript of trial, *Wygall v. State*, no. 5021, p. 69 (reference to John's birth in South Carolina).

66. Suggestion of death of Richard J. Clark, transcript of trial, *Wygall v. State*, no. 5021, p. 11; motion to make parties Plffs, ibid., 13; plaintiff's 1st supplemental petition, ibid., 15 (detailing procedural history); application for change of venue, transcript of trial, *Wygall v. State*, no. 3103, p. 2 (Tex. Dist. Ct., Fort Bend Cty., Mar. 1869), Supreme Court Records and Briefs, no. M5206, TSLAC; "An Act changing the venue of a certain suit hereinafter named," *General Laws of the Twelfth Legislature of the State of Texas*, chap. CV, in Gammel, *Laws of Texas*, 6:883, 1011 (moving case to Travis County); "The Deceased Texas Millionaire—Who Are The Heirs?," *Dallas Herald*, Feb. 18, 1871. For additional news coverage, see "District Court," *Brazos Signal*, Oct. 24, 1868 (discussing postponement in the "well-known cause of Wygall & Clark vs. the State Treasurer" and sarcastically noting that "only three new parties have intervened in said cause, at this Term, up to date"); "Intervenor," *Brazos Signal*, Nov. 7, 1868 (commenting that "there have been six or eight intervenors" in the "great Clark case"); untitled, *Houston Weekly*

Telegraph, Mar. 25, 1869 (updating readers on the Wygall suit and briefly explaining procedural history); "Senate," *Flake's Semi-Weekly Galveston Bulletin*, Mar. 8, 1871 (noting $1,000 had been appropriated to take evidence "in the escheated estate of J. C. Clark").

67. "An Act to regulate the descent and distributions of Intestates [*sic*] Estates," *Laws Passed by the Second Legislature of the State of Texas*, chap. 103, sec. 2, in Gammel, *Laws of Texas*, 3:1, 129; plaintiff's 1st supplemental petition, transcript of trial, *Wygall v. State*, no. 5021, pp. 14–17.

68. Application for continuance, transcript of trial, *Clark v. Honey*, no. 789, pp. 14–16. Clarisa Bird's testimony was taken in the August term. She died before the trial resumed in December, when it was read into the record. Testimony of Pleasant Ballard, W. P. Hamblin, and F. G. Franks, ibid., 50.

69. Testimony of Clarisa Bird, ibid., 52.

70. Testimony of Albert Horton, ibid., 56–57.

71. Testimony of James Montgomery, ibid., 58.

72. Testimony of Sharp Jackson, ibid., 69.

73. Testimony of David Prophet, ibid., 71.

74. Testimony of I. M. Dennis, ibid., 91; *Oldham v. McIver*, 49 Tex. 556 (1878); Auntie Thomas Jones, in Rawick, *American Slave*, vol. 4, pt. 2, p. 205; *Clements v. Crawford*, 42 Tex. 601 (1874); *Wilson v. Catchings*, 41 Tex. 587 (1874); "Patrol," *Austin, Texas State Gazette*, July 22, 1854. For divorce cases in the Texas Supreme Court involving allegations of interracial infidelity, see *Cartwright v. Cartwright*, 18 Tex. 626 (1857) and *Hagerty v. Harwell*, 16 Tex. 663 (1856).

75. Testimony of Stephen Herd, transcript of trial, *Clark v. Honey*, no. 789, p. 81.

76. Testimony of R. W. Smith, ibid., 87–88; 1860 U.S. Census, Wharton Cty., Tex., Schedule 1—Free Inhabitants, s.v. "R.W. Smith," accessed through Ancestry.com; testimony of D. V. Myers, transcript of trial, *Clark v. Honey*, no. 789, p. 90.

77. *Gaines v. Ann*, 17 Tex. 211, 214 (1856); testimony of Nelson Herd, transcript of trial, *Clark v. Honey*, no. 789, p. 89; testimony of J. P. Horton, ibid., 98.

78. Testimony of Edward Collier, transcript of trial, *Clark v. Honey*, no. 789, pp. 96–98. Collier cannot be located in the 1860 census. He was living in Colorado County by this time, however, because he was advertising his firm, Cook & Collier, in the Colorado *Citizen*. See, e.g., *Colorado Citizen*, June 16, 1860. The paper also announced his candidacy for district attorney, stating that he was from Colorado County. *Colorado Citizen*, June 2, 1860. The paper also announced his victory. *Colorado Citizen*, August 11, 1860. Edward Collier appears as a resident of the county in 1870. 1870 U.S. Census, Colorado Cty., Tex., Schedule 1—Inhabitants, s.v. "Edward Collier," accessed through Ancestry.com.

79. Testimony of H. P. Cayce, transcript of trial, *Clark v. Honey*, no. 789, p. 83.

80. Testimony of Joseph Anderson, ibid., 86.

81. Testimony of Stephen Herd, ibid., 80.

82. Testimony of Q. M. Herd, ibid., 83.

83. Testimony of Stephen Herd, ibid., 80, 82.

84. Testimony of I. M. Dennis, ibid., 91.

85. Testimony of Edward Collier, ibid., 97.

86. Testimony of H. P. Cayce, ibid., 84; 1860 U.S. Census, Wharton Cty., Tex., Sched-

ule 2—Slave Inhabitants, s.v. "H. P. Cayce," accessed through Ancestry.com. During the 1869 election, H. P. Cayce gave a Democratic speech in favor of Hamilton at a barbecue attended by Franks and other Republicans. "Letter from Wharton," *Houston Union*, Aug. 17, 1869.

87. Testimony of D. V. Myers, transcript of trial, *Clark v. Honey*, no. 789, p. 90.

88. Testimony of I. M. Dennis, ibid., 91.

89. Testimony of Bishop Clark, ibid., 78–79; testimony of Edward Collier, ibid., 97.

90. Testimony of Reason Byrne, ibid., 64 ("keeping a negro woman"); testimony of Q. M. Herd, ibid., 83 ("Men who kept black women"); testimony of Clarisa Bird, ibid., 54 ("but little to do with white people"); testimony of David Prophet, ibid., 70 ("having a negro wife"); testimony of Clarisa Bird, ibid., 54 ("equality & footing with the blacks").

91. Testimony of Sharp Jackson, ibid., 69 ("did not think any thing of him"); testimony of Reason Byrne, ibid., 65 ("silent contempt"); testimony of Albert Horton, ibid., 58 ("Virgil Steward had it"). For instances in which witnesses heard John talk about leaving his property to his children, see testimony of Clarisa Bird, ibid., 53; testimony of Reason Byrne, ibid., 65; testimony of Sharp Jackson, ibid., 69; testimony of Pleasant Ballard, ibid., 74.

92. Dickens, *Bleak House*; "A Visit," *Bellville Countryman*, Feb. 14, 1863.

93. *In the Estate of John C. Clark*, Wharton County Probate Book B, 224–28; *Report of Sales of the Estate of J. C. Clark*, Wharton County Probate Book B, 257–64; "A Visit," *Bellville Countryman*, Feb. 14, 1863; testimony of I. M. Dennis, transcript of trial, *Clark v. Honey*, no. 789, p. 79.

94. The only juror listed in the trial record is the foreman, Henry Fleming. Verdict and decree, transcript of trial, *Clark v. Honey*, no. 789, p. 112. The minute books, however, list thirty-eight men as members of the petit jury during the December term, and eleven of them would have served alongside Henry Fleming on the case. "List of Jury Served," Wharton County District Court Minute Book C, 76 (Feb. 1871), WCC. The poor handwriting of the clerk makes it difficult to identify all of them. Of the thirty-eight men listed, twenty have been positively identified and located in the 1870 census records. Those twenty are: George Bryant, Spencer Daniel, Gilbert Gathers, Albert Horton, Gabriel Augustin, Abram Hart, Nero Julius, Paul Evans, Manuel Louis, Billy Bryant, Giles Leafton, Warner Long, Joe Palmer, Alford Young, Isaac Hodges, Bob Bilerny, John Ricks, Harry Boon, Alford Fisher, and Henry Fleming. Alford Young is listed as "mulatto," and the rest are listed as black. See 1870 U.S. Census, Wharton Cty., Tex., Schedule 1—Inhabitants, s.v. "George Bryant," accessed through Ancestry.com; ibid., s.v. "Spencer Daniel;" ibid., s.v. "Gilbert Gathers;" ibid., s.v. "Albert Horton;" ibid., s.v. "Gabriel Augustin;" ibid., s.v. "Abram Hart;" ibid., s.v. "Nero Julius;" ibid., s.v. "Paul Evans;" ibid., s.v. "Manuel Louis;" ibid., s.v. "Billy Bryant;" ibid., s.v. "Giles Leafton;" ibid., s.v. "Warner Long;" ibid., s.v. "Joe Palmer;" ibid., s.v. "Alford Young;" ibid., s.v. "Isaac Hodges;" ibid., s.v. "Bob Bilerny;" ibid., s.v. "John Ricks;" ibid., s.v. "Harry Boon;" ibid., s.v. "Alford Fisher;" ibid., s.v. "Henry Fleming."

95. Charge of court, transcript of trial, *Clark v. Honey*, no. 789, pp. 103–4; *Guess v. Lubbock*, 5 Tex. 535, 549 (1851).

96. Charge of court, transcript of trial, *Clark v. Honey*, no. 789, pp. 101, 104–5. Wil-

liam Burkhart is listed in the 1870 census as a thirty-year-old lawyer, born in Pennsylvania. 1870 U.S. Census, Matagorda Cty., Tex., Schedule 1—Inhabitants, s.v. "William Burkhart," accessed through Ancestry.com. He appears in the 1860 census as a twenty-one-year-old lawyer under Catherine Burkhart's household. 1860 U.S. Census, Matagorda Cty., Tex., Schedule 1—Free Inhabitants, s.v. "Catherine Burkhart," accessed through Ancestry.com. In 1860, Catherine Burkhart is listed as the owner of three slaves, and George Burkhart, who lived next door, is listed as the owner of four slaves. Ibid., Schedule 2—Slave Inhabitants, s.v. "Catherine Burkhart"; ibid., s.v. "George Burkhart."

97. "From Wharton," *Houston Daily Union*, Dec. 30, 1871; verdict and decree, transcript of trial, *Clark v. Honey*, no. 789, p. 111.

98. Untitled, *Austin Weekly Democratic Statesman*, June 18, 1874; untitled, *Houston Daily Mercury*, Nov. 26, 1873; "Wharton County Outrage," *Colorado Citizen*, Mar. 11, 1875. (For digital reproduction, see "Isaac N. Baughman," *RootsWeb* (http://freepages.history.rootsweb.ancestry.com/~barrettbranches/sherriff/isaacnbaughman.html), accessed August 26, 2016.

99. Untitled, *Houston Daily Mercury*, Nov. 27, 1873; "Wharton County Outrage," *Colorado Citizen*, Mar. 11, 1875; "Journal of William F. S. Alexander, Fleetwood Plantation," Nov. 8, 1873, and June 12, 1874, entries. (For a digital reproduction, see "Journal of William F. S. Alexander," *RootsWeb* (http://freepages.history.rootsweb.ancestry.com/~barrettbranches/plantations/fleetwood/alexanderjournal.html), accessed August 26, 2016.

100. *Bishop Clark to J. Rust, Bill of Sales Power of Attorney*, Wharton County Deed Book B, 190–91 (Nov. 14, 1874), WCCA; assignments of error, transcript of trial, *Clark v. Honey*, no. 789, p. 122; *Honey v. Clark*, 37 Tex. 686 (1872), overruled by *Oldham v. McIver*, 49 Tex. 556 (1878), and *Clements v. Crawford*, 42 Tex. 601 (1875). The Texas Supreme Court file contains the original briefs.

101. Norvell, "Reconstruction Courts of Texas," 148, 158–62.

102. *Honey v. Clark*, 37 Tex. at 698.

103. Ibid., 706–9. The date the Texas Supreme Court issued its decision in *Honey v. Clark* is referenced in defendant's amended original answer and exhibits, transcript of trial, *Wygall v. State*, no. 5021, p. 43.

104. *Clark v. Honey*, no. 789, Wharton County District Court Minute Book C, 201 (Aug. 5, 1873), WCC.

105. *Deed of Bishop Clark et al to T. C. Barden*, Wharton County Deed Book C, 54–55 (Aug. 7, 1874) (conveying 1,491 acres of land from 2,391 acres in Clark league, "better known as John C. Clark's upper place of home plantation tract whereon he resided," for $5,000), WCCA; *Deed of Bishop Clark and others to T. C. Barden*, Wharton County Deed Book C, 55–56 (Aug. 7, 1874) (conveying 1,805 acres of land in the Huff league, "known as John C. Clark's lower plantation," for $10,000), WCCA. For the value of land at the time of the estate sale, see *Report of the Sales of the Estate of J. C. Clark*, Wharton County Probate Book B, 257 (valuing Clark league at $82,489.50 and Huff league at $64,077.50).

106. *Bishop Clark to J. Rust, Bill of Sales Power of Attorney*, Wharton County Deed Book B, 190–91; *Deed from Bishop Clark to Jackson Rust*, Wharton County Deed Book C, 51–55.

107. Petition, *Clark v. Barden*, no. 1059, p. 16 (suggesting that Barden registered his deeds and went into possession before the family revoked the August 1874 deeds). For the quotes from the petition, see ibid., 4, 5, 12, 11, 8.

108. Plaintiff's 1st supplemental petition, transcript of trial, *Wygall v. State*, no. 5021, pp. 14, 29.

109. *Deed from Bishop Clark to T. B. McClure Agent for W. H. Clark Heirs of John C. Clark*, Wharton County Deed Book C, 322–23 (Dec. 20, 1876), WCCA. Two years later, McClure, as attorney for Warren Clark, deeded the rights to the property to Warren's new attorney, George Dorman. See *Quit Claim Deed from Warren H. Clark to Wilson, Wamock & Dorman*, Wharton County Deed Book D, 328–29 (Nov. 27, 1878), WCCA. Pursuant to this agreement, Dorman eventually deeded 100 acres to Bishop Clark in February of 1886. See *Deed from George Dorman to Bishop Clark*, Wharton County Deed Book H, 47–48 (Feb. 8, 1886), WCCA. For the result in Joseph Wygall's case, see trial and judgment, transcript of trial, *Wygall v. State*, no. 5021, p. 55.

110. *State v. Wygall*, 51 Tex. 621, 632–33 (1879).

111. Ivan, "Masters No More," 200–26. For a discussion of the change in political power from a Republican government to a Democratic one, including the triumph of the Redeemers, see Moneyhon, *Texas after the Civil War*, 188–205.

112. *Wygall*, 51 Tex. at 629. The other two Texas Supreme Court decisions in the case were *State v. Wygall*, 46 Tex. 447 (1877), and *Wygall v. State*, 33 Tex. 328 (1870). For the 1907 claimants, see Letter from H. E. Valentine to G. G. Kelley, Dec. 13, 1907, Miscellaneous Papers, WCHM.

113. *Ex Parte Rodriguez*, 39 Tex. 706 (1873); Roberts, "Political, Legislative, and Judicial History," 2:209. For more on the "Semicolon Decision," see Ariens, *Lone Star Law*, 44–47; Norvell, "Reconstruction Courts of Texas," 149–53.

114. *Clements v. Crawford*, 42 Tex. 601, 604 (1874); *Oldham v. McIver*, 49 Tex. 556 (1878). Roberts owned eight slaves in 1860. 1860 U.S. Census, Smith Cty., Tex., Schedule 1—Free Inhabitants, s.v. "O. M. Roberts," accessed through Ancestry.com; ibid., Schedule 2—Slave Inhabitants, s.v. "O. M. Roberts."

115. A. Williams, *History of Wharton County*, 115. For a report of the divorce, see "Fifty-Fifth Civil District Court," *Houston Daily Post*, Feb. 12, 1901.

CHAPTER 2. Slave Resistance and
Class Conflict in the Redlands

1. Answer, *Brady v. Price*, no. 1132, p. 2 (Tex. Dist. Ct., San Augustine Cty., Oct. 1856), San Augustine County District Court Records, ETRC; Testimony of Benjamin F. Price, ibid., 12 (stating that Miles was worth $1,000); inventory of the property of the Estates of Elijah and T. Price, *Estate of Elijah and Tempe Price*, 7 (Tex. Cty. Ct., San Augustine Cty., May 1859) (listing Miles's age as 38 in 1859, meaning he was 33 in 1854), San Augustine County Probate Records, ETRC; cf. partition, ibid., 3 (Dec. 1859) (listing Miles's age as 44 in 1859, meaning he was 39 in 1854). The discrepancy in Miles's age is typical for enslaved persons, as slave owners rarely kept birth records.

2. "Obituary Notice," Nov. 23, 1852, William F. Price Collection, ETRC; petition, *Brady v. Price*, no. 1132, pp. 1–2; answer, ibid., 1–3.

3. See, e.g., testimony of Col. S. S. Davis, *Brady v. Price*, no. 1132, pp. 3–4.

4. Amended complaint, ibid., 1–2; testimony of Col. S. S. Davis, ibid., 1–3.

5. Inventory of the property of the Estates of Elijah and T Price, *Estate of Elijah and T Price*, 7; testimony of A. G. Price, *Brady v. Price*, no. 1132, p. 10 ("recollect anything"); testimony of Benjamin F. Price, ibid., 11–12 (same); ibid., 12 ("I knew the father & mother of the negro Miles—I have not seen them for about sixteen years."); 1850 U.S. Census, San Augustine Cty., Tex., Schedule 1—Free Inhabitants, s.v. "Benjamin Price," accessed through Ancestry.com (listing Benjamin's birthplace as North Carolina and his age as 24 in 1850, meaning he was born in 1826); ibid., s.v. "Albert G. Price" (listing Albert's age as 26 in 1850, meaning that he was born in 1824). In the 1850 census, Albert's birthplace is listed as Alabama. In the 1860 census, however, it is listed as North Carolina, the same as his younger brother. 1860 U.S. Census, San Augustine Cty., Tex., Schedule 1—Free Inhabitants, s.v. "Albert G. Price," accessed through Ancestry.com. The 1870 census also lists Albert's birthplace as North Carolina. 1870 U.S. Census, San Augustine Cty., Tex., Schedule 1—Inhabitants, s.v. "A. G. Price," accessed through Ancestry.com.

6. "Obituary Notice," Nov. 23, 1852; 1850 U.S. Census, San Augustine Cty., Tex., Schedule 1—Free Inhabitants, s.v. "Elijah Price," accessed through Ancestry.com; *The Last Will and Testament of Elijah Price*, Will Book No. 1, pp. 198–99 (North Carolina Sup. Ct., Martin Cty., Jan. 1, 1794) (detailing extensive property holdings), William F. Price Collection, ETRC; Harry Noble Jr., "Elija [sic] Price Refused to be Drafted as First State Representative," *San Augustine Tribune*, Nov. 24, 1994; Harry Noble, "Elijah Price Accumulated Fortunes and Friends," *San Augustine Tribune*, Dec. 1, 1994.

7. "Deplorable Case of Poverty," *San Augustine Red-Lander*, July 23, 1842; 1840 U.S. Census, Sumter Cty., Alabama, s.v. "Elijah Price," accessed through Ancestry.com; untitled, *San Augustine Red-Lander*, Oct. 7, 1841.

8. Wash Ingram, in Rawick, *American Slave*, vol. 4, pt. 2, p. 178; Adeline Marshall, in ibid., vol. 5, pt. 3, p. 46. The names and ages of the Price children can be determined through probate and census records. Elijah and Tempe ultimately had ten children: Albert, Cornelia (Sossaman), Benjamin, Mary (Davis), Susan (Smith), Temperance (McLaurin), Virginia, Elizabeth (Smith), Elijah, and Archelaus. Petition of Benj. F. Price, *Estate of Elijah and Tempe Price*, 1–2 (Nov. 1859). The 1850 census records indicate that six were born before the family moved to Texas. 1850 U.S. Census, San Augustine Cty., Tex., Schedule 1—Free Inhabitants, s.v. "Elijah Price," accessed through Ancestry.com (listing Benjamin, Susan, and Temperance as being born in North Carolina); ibid., s.v. "Charles Sossaman" (listing Cornelia); ibid., s.v. "Samuel S. Davis" (listing Mary); ibid., s.v. "Albert G. Price."

9. W. Johnson, *Soul by Soul*, 3–8; Josephine Howard, in Rawick, *American Slave*, vol. 4, pt. 2, p. 164; Ben Simpson, in ibid., vol. 5, pt. 4, p. 27; Olmsted, *Journey through Texas*, 54 (detailing impressions of immigrants and their slaves).

10. Crocket, *Two Centuries in East Texas*, 89; Olmsted, *Journey through Texas*, 58, 58n8 (Gaines's ferry).

11. "An Act to define the boundaries of the counties of San Augustine and Sabine," in Gammel, *Laws of Texas* 1:1343, 1394; "San Augustine," *Texas Almanac for 1858*, 83.

12. Olmsted, *Journey through Texas*, 59–60 ("The Red Land District").

13. Horton, "Life of A. Horton"; Campbell, *Gone to Texas*, 108–9.

14. Austin qtd. in Campbell, *Gone to Texas*, 109.

15. Ibid., 182; Paulsen, "Short History," 261–63.

16. Campbell, *Gone to Texas*, 182; Paulsen, "Short History," 261–63; untitled, *San Augustine Red-Lander*, Sept. 30, 1841.

17. Horton, "Life of A. Horton," 306; Crocket, *Two Centuries in East Texas*, 101–27; Shindler, "San Augustine," 41.

18. Letter from Jas. B. [illegible] to E. Price, Apr. 5, 1844, William F. Price Collection, ETRC; letter from Morrison Thomas to Elijah Price, March 31, 1844, William F. Price Collection, ETRC; Crocket, *Two Centuries in East Texas*, 101, 111, 112, 246; Shindler, "San Augustine," 42.

19. Olmsted, *Journey through Texas*, 60; Shindler, "San Augustine," 41; "San Augustine County," *San Augustine Red-Lander*, Oct. 21, 1841.

20. Campbell, *Empire for Slavery*, 57, map 2: Slave Population of Texas in 1840; U.S. Bureau of the Census, *Seventh Census of the United States*, Texas: Table I—Population by Counties, 503–4; U.S. Bureau of the Census, *Statistics of the United States*, Miscellaneous Statistics: Number of Families and Free Population, 1860, 349 (listing 391 families in San Augustine); U.S. Bureau of the Census, *Agriculture of the United States in 1860*, Texas: Slaveholders and Slaves, 241 (identifying 144 slaveholding families and the number of slaves each family held).

21. *DeBow's Review* printed an early report about the mildness of slavery in Texas. DeBow, "Texas," 637 ("There is a large black population in Texas, and though forever the property of their masters, and under the restraints of the law, they are invested with more liberty, and are less liable to abuse, than the slaves of the southern states generally"). Later generations made similar claims. See, e.g., Curlee, "Study of Texas Slave Plantations," 146 ("On the whole, the Texans managed their plantations with more humane consideration than was customary throughout the Old South, despite some slight evidence to the contrary").

22. "Constitution of the Republic of Texas of 1836, General Provisions, sec. 9," in Gammel, *Laws of Texas*, 1:1069, 1079. The constitution of 1845, ratified when Texas became a state, retained critical portions of the constitution of 1836, including the provisions prohibiting the legislature from forcing slaveholders to emancipate their slaves or from preventing immigrants from bringing their slaves with them. See "Constitution of the State of Texas of 1845, art. VIII, sec. 1," in Gammel, *Laws of Texas*, 2:1275, 1296. In 1858, the Texas Supreme Court summed up the laws of slavery this way: "The master has an absolute property in the faculties and services of the slave. The intelligence and the strength of the slave belong to the master, and may be put by him to any use, not contrary to the law." *Callihan's Ex'r v. Johnson*, 22 Tex. 596, 600 (1858).

23. Slaves' role as property—in sales, in deeds, in wills, in hiring, etc.—gave rise to a number of cases. For breach of warranty cases, see, e.g., *Doty v. Moore*, 16 Tex. 591 (1856); *Murphy's Administrators v. Crain*, 12 Tex. 297 (1854); *McKinney v. Fort*, 10 Tex. 220

(1853); *Ables v. Donley*, 8 Tex. 331 (1852). For disputes in deeds and wills, see, e.g., *Hunt v. White*, 24 Tex. 643 (1860); *Hillard v. Fratz*, 21 Tex. 192 (1858); *Hagerty v. Harwell*, 16 Tex. 663 (1856); *Purvis v. Sherrod, Ex'r*, 12 Tex. 140 (1854). For cases involving slave hirers, see, e.g., *Callihan's Ex'r v. Johnson*, 22 Tex. 596 (1858); *Echols, Adm'r, v. Dodd*, 20 Tex. 190 (1857); *Townsend v. Hill*, 18 Tex. 422 (1857); *Robinson v. Varnell*, 16 Tex. 382 (1856); *McGee v. Currie*, 4 Tex. 217 (1849); *Mims v. Mitchell*, 1 Tex. 443 (1846).

24. See "Constitution of the State of Texas of 1845, art. VIII, sec. 3," in Gammel, *Laws of Texas*, 2:1275, 1296. An 1858 statute codified what was undoubtedly the rule in practice, that an owner, except in extreme cases, had sole discretion to determine the type and extent of punishment. See "Rules Applicable to Offences against the Person When Committed by Slaves or Free Persons of Color," *General Laws of the Seventh Legislature of the State of Texas*, chap. 121, pt. 3, tit. 2, sec. 3 (1858), in Gammel, *Laws of Texas*, 4:873, 1059 ("A master, in the exercise of his right to perfect obedience on the part of the slave, may correct in moderation, and is the exclusive judge of the necessity of such correction").

25. See "An Act to Provide for the Punishment of Crimes and Misdemeanors Committed by Slaves and Free Persons of Color, secs. 1, 6 (1837)," in Gammel, *Laws of Texas*, 1:1343, 1385–86. The list of capital offenses remained relatively unchanged throughout slavery. Cf. "Of the Punishment of Slaves and Free Persons of Color," *General Laws of the Seventh Legislature of the State of Texas*, chap. 121, pt. 3, tit. 3, chap. 1 (1858), in Gammel, *Laws of Texas*, 4:873, 1060 (listing murder, insurrection, arson, rape of a white woman, robbery or a white person, assault with intent to rape, rob, or kill a white person, attempted rape of a white woman, and assaulting a white person with a deadly weapon).

26. On guns, see "An Act to prevent slaves from carrying guns or other dangerous weapons," *General Laws of the Sixth Legislature of the State of Texas*, chap. 152, secs. 1–2 (1856), in Gammel, *Laws of Texas*, 4:419, 499–500. On the number of slaves constituting an "insurrection," see "Exciting insurrection or insubordination," *General Laws of the Seventh Legislature of the State of Texas*, chap. 121, pt. 1, tit. 19, chap. 1 (1858), in ibid., 4:873, 1046–47. On trading with slaves, see "An Act Concerning Slaves," *Laws of the Republic of Texas Passed at the Session of the Fourth Congress* (1840), in ibid., 2:175, 345; "Trading with Slaves," *General Laws of the Seventh Legislature of the State of Texas*, chap. 121, pt. 1, tit. 19, chap. 7 (1858), in ibid., 4:873, 1048–49.

27. On slave patrols, see "An Act to provide for the appointment of Patrols and to prescribe their duties and powers," *Laws Passed by the First Legislature of the State of Texas* (1846), in Gammel, *Laws of Texas*, 2:1307, 1497–1501. On offenses justifying chastisement, see "Rules Applicable to Offences against the Person When Committed by Slaves or Free Persons of Color," *General Laws of the Seventh Legislature of the State of Texas*, chap. 121, pt. 3, tit. 2, sec. 9 (1858), in ibid., 4:873, 1059–60.

28. "Rules Applicable to Offences against the Person When Committed by Slaves or Free Persons of Color," *General Laws of the Seventh Legislature of the State of Texas*, chap. 121, pt. 3, tit. 2, sec. 1 (1858), in Gammel, *Laws of Texas*, 4:873, 1058.

29. Post mortem examination on the body of one negro woman—Nancy—the property of Wm Anderson, *Republic of Texas v. Anderson*, no. [not stated], pp. 1–3 (Rep. of Tex. Dist. Ct., San Augustine Cty., Dec. 1841), Ralph Smith Collection of San Augustine County Records, ETRC; indictment, *Republic of Texas v. Ellison*, no. [not stated], pp. 1–2

(Rep. of Tex. Dist. Ct., San Augustine Cty., March 1841), San Augustine County, Texas Records, ETRC; *Wilson v. State*, 29 Tex. 240 (1867).

30. William Moore, in Rawick, *American Slave*, vol. 5, pt. 3, pp. 133–34; Van Moore, in ibid., vol. 5, pt. 3, p. 130; Andy Anderson, in ibid., vol. 4, pt. 1, p. 15; Ben Simpson, in ibid., vol. 5, pt. 4, p. 28; Susan Merritt, in ibid., vol. 5, pt. 3, p. 78; Mintie Maria Miller, in ibid., vol. 5, pt. 3, p. 86.

31. "The Cloud in the Distance; and considerations connected therewith," *Clarksville Northern Standard*, Feb. 19, 1859; "Slave Labor," *Austin, Texas State Gazette*, Feb. 23, 1856; "The Condition of Southern Slaves," *Galveston Weekly News*, Aug. 9, 1859; "Letter from Judge Frazer," *Marshall, Texas Republican*, Dec. 8, 1860; "The Condition of Southern Slaves," *Galveston Weekly News*, Aug. 9, 1859.

32. "Slave Labor," *Austin, Texas State Gazette*, Feb. 23, 1856; "Letter from Judge Frazer," *Marshall, Texas Republican*, Dec. 8, 1860; "Is the Morality of Slavery a Question for Political Parties to Decide?," *Galveston Weekly News*, Oct. 14, 1856.

33. Olmsted, *Journey through Texas*, 60.

34. "Hon. T. J. Rusk on Slavery in the Territories," *Austin, Texas State Gazette*, Feb. 28, 1857; "Negro Slavery," *Austin, Texas State Gazette*, Apr. 14, 1860; "The Cloud in the Distance; and considerations connected therewith," *Clarksville Northern Standard*, Feb. 19, 1859; "Exemption of Slaves from Execution," *Galveston Weekly News*, Jan. 20, 1857.

35. *Deed from George Teal to Elijah Price*, San Augustine County Deed Book F, 309–10 (Mar. 20, 1844), ETRC; *Deed from George Teal and Samuel Stiddum to Elijah Price*, San Augustine County Deed Book F, 543–44 (Nov. 22, 1845), ETRC; Andy Anderson, in Rawick, *American Slave*, vol. 4, pt. 1, p. 14.

36. Charlotte Beverly, in Rawick, *American Slave*, vol. 4, pt. 1, p. 85. For additional descriptions of living conditions, see Harriet Barrett, in ibid., vol. 4, pt. 1, p. 49; William Byrd, in ibid., vol. 4, pt. 1, p. 182; Richard Caruthers, in ibid., vol. 4, pt. 1, p. 197; Adeline Cunningham, in ibid., vol. 4, pt. 1, p. 266; Olmsted, *Journey through Texas*, 59.

37. Charlotte Beverly, in Rawick, *American Slave*, vol. 4, pt. 1, p. 85; Sarah Ashley, in ibid., vol. 4, pt. 1, p. 35. For additional examples of diet and general living conditions, see John Barker, in ibid., vol. 4, pt. 1, p. 43; Wes Brady, in ibid., vol. 4, pt. 1, p. 133; Jeff Calhoun, in ibid., vol. 4, pt. 1, p. 188; Simp Campbell, in ibid., vol. 4, pt. 1, p. 191; Adeline Cunningham, in ibid., vol. 4, pt. 1, p. 267; Bill Homer, in ibid., vol. 4, pt. 2, p.153; Walter Rimm, in ibid., vol. 5, pt. 3, p. 247; Annie Row, in ibid., vol. 5, pt. 3, p. 258.

38. Josephine Howard, in Rawick, *American Slave*, vol. 4, pt. 2, p. 163; Rose Williams, in ibid., vol. 5, pt. 4, pp. 176–77. For discussions of slave marriages, see Jeff Calhoun, in ibid., vol. 4, pt. 1, p. 189; Jeptha Choice, in ibid., vol. 4, pt. 1, p. 218; Chris Franklin, in ibid., vol. 4, pt. 2, p. 57.

39. Debow, "Texas," 630–31; U.S. Bureau of the Census, *Seventh Census of the United States*, 517–18.

40. Jacobs, *Incidents*, 94; *Deed from John G. Brooke to Elijah Price*, San Augustine County Deed Book G, 345–46 (Oct. 9, 1848), ETRC; "Obituary Notice," Nov. 23, 1852 (Elijah "finally settled near the town of San Augustine, for the convenience of educating his children"). In his will, Elijah stressed the importance of education when he stated his "desire that each and every one of our children who may be unmarried at the time of my

NOTES TO CHAPTER TWO   199

death may be educated and maintained out of the profits and produce of my said estate." Will of Elijah Price, Nov. 14, 1852, William F. Price Collection, ETRC. The family home was located next to Wesleyan College. Harry Noble Jr., "Elija [sic] Price Refused to be Drafted as First State Representative," *San Augustine Tribune*, Nov. 24, 1994. A list of Elijah and Tempe's ten children appears in note 8. The ages of the four that were born after the move to Texas can be determined from census records. 1850 U.S. Census, San Augustine Cty., Tex., Schedule 1—Free Inhabitants, s.v. "Elijah Price," accessed through Ancestry.com (listing, in addition to the others, Virginia, Elizabeth, Elijah, and Archelaus).

41. Harry Noble Jr., "Elija [sic] Price Refused to be Drafted as First State Representative," *San Augustine Tribune*, Nov. 24, 1994; Crocket, *Two Centuries in East Texas*, 220; 1850 U.S. Census, San Augustine Cty., Tex., Schedule 1—Free Inhabitants, s.v. "Stephen W. Blount," accessed through Ancestry.com (identifying Blount as a merchant with real holdings worth $12,000); U.S. Bureau of the Census, *Seventh Census of the United States*, Texas: Table XI—Agriculture, 517–18; U.S. Bureau of the Census, *Agriculture of the United States in 1860*, State of Texas: Agriculture, 144–45.

42. 1850 U.S. Census, San Augustine Cty., Tex., Schedule 4—Production of Agriculture, s.v. "E Price."

43. "Obituary Notice," Nov. 23, 1852; "The Cloud in the Distance; and considerations connected therewith," *Clarksville Northern Standard*, Feb. 19, 1859; "Slave Labor," Austin, *Texas State Gazette*, Feb. 23, 1856; *Tax Assessment Rolls of San Augustine Cty., Tex., Made for the Year 1852*, s.v. "Elijah Price," San Augustine County Tax Rolls, ETRC; inventory of the property of the Estates of Elijah and T Price, *Estate of Elijah and Tempe Price*, 7 (containing names and ages of slaves).

44. Crocket, *Two Centuries in East Texas*, 101–2, 109–10, 254–67.

45. Plantation Rules of Charles William Tait, General Rules, ¶¶ 1, 3, 4, Charles William Tait Papers, CAH; Richard Caruthers, in Rawick, *American Slave*, vol. 4, pt. 1, p. 197.

46. 1850 U.S. Census, San Augustine Cty., Tex., Schedule 1—Free Inhabitants, s.v. "J. A. McNeill," accessed through Ancestry.com (listing Charles Brady as a member of household); 1850 U.S. Census, San Augustine Cty., Tex., Schedule 2—Slave Inhabitants, s.v. "J. A. McNeill," accessed through Ancestry.com; *Tax Assessment Rolls of San Augustine Cty., Tex., Made for the Years 1850, 1851, 1852, 1853, 1854, 1855, 1856*, s.v. "Charles Brady," San Augustine County Tax Rolls, ETRC.

47. 1850 U.S. Census, San Augustine Cty., Tex., Schedule 1—Free Inhabitants, s.v. "George Teal," accessed through Ancestry.com (real estate worth $5,000); ibid., Schedule 2—Slave Inhabitants, s.v. "Geo Teul" [sic]; ibid., Schedule 4—Production of Agriculture, s.v. "George Teal;" DeBow, "Overseers at the South," 278; Genovese, *Roll, Jordan, Roll*, 13–22.

48. Answer, *Brady v. Teal*, no. 1016, pp. 1–2 (Tex. Dist. Ct., San Augustine Cty., Oct. 1854), San Augustine County District Court Records, ETRC.

49. Testimony of A. G. Price, *Brady v. Price*, no. 1132, p. 10; testimony of Col. S. S. Davis, ibid., 1, 3–4.

50. 1850 U.S. Census, San Augustine Cty., Tex., Schedule 1—Free Inhabitants, s.v. "Almanzon Huston," accessed through Ancestry.com (listing H. M. Kinsey as resident of hotel).

51. *Chandler v. State*, 2 Tex. 305, 309 (1847); *Nix v. State*, 13 Tex. 575, 578 (1855); verdict, *Brady v. Teal*, no. 1016, p. 2.

52. Petition, *Brady v. Price*, no. 1132, pp. 1–3.

53. Amended complaint, *Brady v. Price*, no. 1132, p. 2; testimony of Col. S. S. Davis, ibid., 1, 4; testimony of David Earl, ibid., 5; see Genovese, *Roll, Jordan, Roll*, 17.

54. Testimony of Col. S. S. Davis, *Brady v. Price*, no. 1132, p. 2; testimony of David Earl, ibid., 5.

55. Testimony of Col. S. S. Davis, *Brady v. Price*, no. 1132, p. 2; testimony of David Earl, ibid., 5.

56. Testimony of Col. S. S. Davis, *Brady v. Price*, no. 1132, p. 2; testimony of David Earl, ibid., 5.

57. Testimony of Col. S. S. Davis, *Brady v. Price*, no. 1132, p. 2; testimony of David Earl, ibid., 5–6.

58. Testimony of Col. S. S. Davis, *Brady v. Price*, no. 1132, pp. 2–3; testimony of David Earl, ibid., 6. The probate records contain the names of the slaves, including John, Ben, and Philip. Inventory of the property of the Estates of Elijah and T Price, *Estate of Elijah and Tempe Price*, 7.

59. Testimony of Col. S. S. Davis, *Brady v. Price*, no. 1132, p. 3; testimony of David Earl, ibid., 6–7.

60. Testimony of Col. S. S. Davis, *Brady v. Price*, no. 1132, p. 3; testimony of David Earl, ibid., 7.

61. 1850 U.S. Census, San Augustine Cty., Tex., Schedule 1—Free Inhabitants, s.v. "Elijah Price," accessed through Ancestry.com (listing Temperance); Harry Noble Jr., "Elija [sic] Price Refused to be Drafted as First State Representative," *San Augustine Tribune*, Nov. 24, 1994.

62. Testimony of Samuel Colten, *Brady v. Price*, no. 1132, p. 14.

63. Gross, *Double Character*, 72–97; testimony of Col. S. S. Davis, *Brady v. Price*, no. 1132, p. 13.

64. Testimony of Samuel Colten, *Brady v. Price*, no. 1132, p. 14 ("disobedient," "malicious"); testimony of A. G. Price, ibid., 10 ("never had any difficulty," "able hand"); testimony of Col. S. S. Price, ibid., 3–4; testimony of David Earl, ibid., 7–8 ("stout healthy man," never "had any difficulty").

65. Crocket, *Two Centuries in East Texas*, 112–13, 235–37; 1850 U.S. Census, San Augustine Cty., Tex., Schedule 1—Free Inhabitants, s.v. "James P. Henderson," accessed through Ancestry.com.

66. "The Condition of Southern Slaves," *Galveston Weekly News*, Aug. 9, 1859; "What shall be done with the Captured Africans!," *San Antonio Herald*, Sept. 18, 1858.

67. Testimony of Dr. J. J. Roberts, *Brady v. Price*, no. 1132, pp. 8–9; testimony of A. G. Price, ibid., 10; testimony of Benjamin F. Price, ibid., 11–12.

68. Answer, *Brady v. Price*, no. 1132, p. 2; "On Honor," *Marshall, Texas Republican*, July 4, 1835; "The Condition of Southern Slaves," *Galveston Weekly News*, Aug. 9, 1859.

69. "Negro Slavery," *Galveston Weekly News*, Aug. 9, 1859.

70. Cheryl Harris, "Whiteness as Property," 1707; "The Philosophy of Democracy," *Austin, Texas State Gazette*, Nov. 13, 1858.

71. "Gonzales Convention," *Austin, Texas State Gazette*, Oct. 14, 1854. For examples of ads warning of slaves running to Mexico, see "Runaway Negroes," *Houston Telegraph and Texas Register*, Jan. 15, 1845; "Ranaway," *Austin, Texas State Gazette*, Oct. 8, 1859; "Negro Stealing," *San Augustine Red-Lander*, July 7, 1842.

72. *Hedgepeth v. Robertson*, 18 Tex. 858, 859, 862 (1857).

73. "Awful Tragedy," *Austin, Texas State Gazette*, July 12, 1851; "A Shocking Murder," *Austin, Texas State Gazette*, Mar. 28, 1854; "Negro Jake," *Houston Telegraph and Texas Register*, Sept. 1, 1841; "Awful Murder," *Clarksville Northern Standard*, Apr. 9, 1853; "Found Guilty," *Clarksville Northern Standard*, June 4, 1853; "Murder," *Clarksville Northern Standard*, Aug. 13, 1853; untitled, *Austin, Texas State Gazette*, Sept. 3, 1853. For more on Texas slaves and Mexico, see Kelley, "Mexico in His Head"; Nichols, "Line of Liberty"; Tyler, "Fugitive Slaves in Mexico."

74. "Excitement," *Marshall, Texas Republican*, Oct. 3, 1835; "Negroes," *Houston Telegraph and Texas Register*, Sept. 15, 1841; "Negro Insurrection," *Austin, Texas State Gazette*, Sept. 13, 1856; "The Late Plot," *Austin, Texas State Gazette*, Sept. 27, 1856.

75. See W. Johnson, "Inconsistency, Contradiction, and Complete Confusion"; Genovese, *Roll, Jordan, Roll*, 30.

76. Crocket, *Two Centuries in East Texas*, 257; "An Act to define the times for holding the District Courts in the fifth, sixth, and eighth Judicial Districts," *Laws Passed by the Second Legislature of the State of Texas* (1848), in Gammel, *Laws of Texas*, 3:1, 134–35; 1850 U.S. Census, Shelby Cty., Tex., Schedule 1—Free Inhabitants, s.v. "A. M. O. Hicks," accessed through Ancestry.com.

77. Jury list, *Brady v. Price*, no. 1132, p. 1.

78. 1850 U.S. Census, San Augustine Cty., Tex., Schedule 1—Free Inhabitants, s.v. "Wm. B. Shaw," accessed through Ancestry.com; verdict, *Brady v. Price*, no. 1132, p. 1 (listing Shaw as foreman).

79. 1850 U.S. Census, San Augustine Cty., Tex., Schedule 1—Free Inhabitants, s.v. "O. H. P. Bodine," accessed through Ancestry.com; ibid., s.v. "Wm. R. Bodine."

80. Ibid., s.v. "Burwell Eaves."

81. Ibid., s.v. "Wm. Norwood" (listing Thomas as fifteen in 1850 and a member of the household); ibid., s.v. "John Henry."

82. 1850 U.S. Census, San Augustine Cty., Tex., Schedule 1—Free Inhabitants, s.v. "James Higgins," accessed through Ancestry.com.

83. Ibid., s.v. "Adam J. Smith."

84. Ibid., s.v. "J. T. Childers;" ibid., Schedule 2—Slave Inhabitants, s.v. "J. T. Childers."

85. 1850 U.S. Census, San Augustine Cty., Tex., Schedule 1—Free Inhabitants, s.v. "T. G. Broocks," accessed through Ancestry.com (listing Moses as seventeen and a member of the household); ibid., Schedule 2—Slave Inhabitants, s.v. "Gen. T. G. Broocks"; "Our Celebration Yesterday," *San Augustine Red-Land Herald*, July 5, 1851; "Obituary Notice," Nov. 23, 1852 (noting Elijah's membership in the Masonic Fraternity).

86. "An Act Regulating Juries," *Laws Passed by the First Legislature of the State of Texas* (1846), in Gammel, *Laws of Texas*, 2:1307, 1476; "Constitution of the State of Texas (1845)," art. III, sec. 2," in ibid., 2:1275, 1280.

87. Charge to the jury, *Brady v. Price*, no. 1132, pp. 1–2.

88. "Cruel Treatment of Slaves," *General Laws of the Seventh Legislature of the State of Texas*, chap. 121, pt. 1, tit. 19, chap. 8 (1858), in Gammel, *Laws of Texas*, 4:1049; Stearlin Arnwine, in Rawick, *American Slave*, vol. 4, pt. 1, p. 32; Genovese, *Roll, Jordan, Roll*, 25–49. For additional discussions about what motivated courts to protect slaves from abuse, see Morris, *Southern Slavery and the Law*, 182–208; Fede, *People without Rights*; Higginbotham and Kopytoff, "Property First, Humanity Second." For Texas cases involving criminal liability of third parties for harm to slaves, see *Presley v. State*, 30 Tex. 160 (1867); *Wilson v. State*, 29 Tex. 240 (1867); *Bumpus v. Fisher*, 21 Tex. 561 (1858); *State v. Stephenson*, 20 Tex. 151 (1857); *Nix v. State*, 13 Tex. 575 (1855); *Chandler v. State*, 2 Tex. 305 (1847). For cases involving civil liability of third parties for harm to slaves, see *Callihan's Ex'r v. Johnson*, 22 Tex. 596 (1858); *Hedgepeth v. Robertson*, 18 Tex. 858 (1857); *Robinson v. Varnell*, 16 Tex. 382 (1856); *Phillips v. Wheeler*, 10 Tex. 536 (1853); *Mims v. Mitchell*, 1 Tex. 443 (1846).

89. Verdict, *Brady v. Price*, no. 1132, p. 1.

90. *Report and Treatise on Slavery*, 4. For more on the alleged slave insurrection, see Reynolds, *Texas Terror*; Addington, "Slave Insurrection in Texas"; W. White, "Texas Slave Insurrection of 1860."

91. "The Late Conflagrations," *Austin, Texas State Gazette*, July 28, 1860; untitled, *Houston Telegraph and Texas Register*, July 21, 1860.

92. "The Late Conflagrations," *Austin, Texas State Gazette*, July 28, 1860.

93. Ibid.; "The 6th Day of August," *Austin, Texas State Gazette*, Aug. 11, 1860; *Brady v. Price*, 19 Tex. 285, 288, 289 (1857).

94. "Another Negro Burned," *New York Times*, Feb. 2, 1893; Carol Marie Cropper, "Black Man Fatally Dragged in a Possible Racial Killing," *New York Times*, June 10, 1998.

95. Writ of garnishment, *Price v. Brady*, no. 1217, pp. 1–2 (Tex. Dist. Ct., San Augustine Cty., Nov. 1857), San Augustine County District Court Records, ETRC; Harry Noble, "Elijah Price Accumulated Fortunes and Friends," *San Augustine Tribune*, Dec. 1, 1994.

96. See generally W. Johnson, "Inconsistency, Contradiction, and Complete Confusion," 419–30. For Miles's estimated value and the notation that he was "diseased," see final partition, *Estate of Elijah and Tempe Price*, 3 (Dec. 1859).

CHAPTER 3. A Free Family of Color on the Borderland

1. "Another Murder," *Galveston Weekly News*, June 10, 1856. The precise year Samuel Deputy arrived in Orange County (then part of Jefferson County) is difficult to discern. He appears in the tax records in 1851 and every year after until his death in 1856. *Tax Assessment Rolls of Jefferson Cty., Tex., Made for the Year 1851, 1852*, s.v. "Samuel Deputy," Jefferson County Tax Rolls, THL; *Tax Assessment Rolls of Orange Cty., Tex., Made for the Year 1853, 1854, 1855, 1856*, s.v. "Samuel Deputy," Orange County Tax Rolls, SHLRC. There is also a "J. Deputy" in the 1850 census, but it is not known if this is Samuel or simply someone with the same last name. 1850 U.S. Census, Jefferson Cty., Tex., Schedule 1—Free Inhabitants, s.v. "J. Deputy," accessed through Ancestry.com.

2. "Disturbances in Orange County," *Houston Weekly Telegraph*, July 23, 1856; "Dis-

turbances in Orange County," *Galveston Weekly News*, July 15, 1856; see 1850 U.S. Census, Jefferson Cty., Tex., Schedule 1—Free Inhabitants, s.v. "Aaron Ashworth," accessed through Ancestry.com (listing Samuel as Aaron's son); ibid., s.v. "William Ashworth" (listing Clark as William's son); see also *Will of Abner Ashworth*, Cause 7, pp. 1–2 (Tex. Cty. Ct., Jefferson Cty., Mar. 18, 1851) (indicating that Aaron and William were brothers), Jefferson County Probate Records, JCC.

3. "Disturbances in Orange County," *Galveston Weekly News*, July 15, 1856.

4. U.S. Bureau of the Census, *Seventh Census of the United States*, Texas: Table 1—Population by Counties—Ages, Color, and Condition—Aggregates, 503–4 (identifying 63 free people of color in Jefferson in 1850, the most in any county). For an early article about the population of free people of color in the region, see Muir, "Free Negro in Jefferson and Orange Counties."

5. "Disturbances in Orange County," *Galveston Weekly News*, July 15, 1856.

6. Letter from A. Rigmaiden to McDonald Furman, May 6, 1893 (identifying the Ashworths and other families, who settled in what became Calcasieu Parish, as originating in South Carolina), Charles James McDonald Furman Papers, SCL. James Ashworth appears as the head of household in the Pendleton District, South Carolina, in the 1800 census. 1800 U.S. Census, Pendleton District, S.C., s.v. "James Ashworth," accessed through Ancestry.com. He appears as the head of household in Opelousas, Louisiana, in the 1810 census. Ibid., Opelousas, La., s.v. "James Ashworth." For populations of cities and counties in South Carolina in 1800, see U.S. Bureau of the Census, *Return of the Whole Number of Persons*, South Carolina, 2M. For an early history of the Pendleton District, see Simpson, *History of Old Pendleton District*, 10–44. For more on where the Ashworths and other related families settled, and the reasons why, see Mills, "Tracing Free People of Color," 264, 266.

7. Campbell, *Gone to Texas*, 86–87.

8. Olmsted, *Journey through Texas*, 220–22; "Lake Charles, Calcasieu, Louisiana," *Galveston Weekly News*, Feb. 24, 1857.

9. Olmsted, *Journey through Texas*, 220–22; see generally, Heinegg, *Free African Americans*; DeMarce, "Verry Slitly Mixt"; Gross, "Of Portuguese Origin." For more specific discussions on some of the origin myths and the reasons for them, see Estes et al., "Melungeons, a Multi-Ethnic Population"; DeMarce, "Looking at Legends."

10. Broussard and Gaddy, *Church at Lake Charles, Louisiana*, 27 ("In 1828 the Baptists built the first church in Calcasieu."); Swent, *Antioch Primitive Baptist Church*, 4–6 (listing members of the Ashworth, Perkins, Bunch, and Goins families as members of the first church); DeMarce, "Verry Slitly Mixt," 5 ("Anthropologists usually refer to them as *tri-racial isolates*."); Olmsted, *Journey through Texas*, 222 ("Sit up, stranger, take some fry!"). A. Rigmaiden, the treasurer of Calcasieu Parish in the 1890s, listed the Ashworths, the Goins, the Perkins, the Sweats, and the Dials as among some "of the principal & oldest families" identified as "Redbones." Letter from A. Rigmaiden to McDonald Furman, May 6, 1893, Charles James McDonald Furman Papers, SCL. For more on the name, see Marler, *Red Bones of Louisiana*, 1–11; E. Price, "Geographic Analysis," 143–44. Marler also offers a tentative list of Redbone surnames, including the Ashworths. Marler, *Red Bones of Louisiana*, 316–17.

11. 1850 U.S. Census, Jefferson Cty., Tex., Schedule 1—Free Inhabitants, s.v. "William Ashworth," accessed through Ancestry.com (listing William's age as 57 in 1850, meaning he was 38 in 1831); First Class Headright Certificate 111 for William Ashworth, 5 March 1838, Milam 1-710 (stating William arrived in Texas in 1831 and was married), Texas Land Grant Records, Archives and Records Program, GLO.

12. *Will of Abner Ashworth*, Cause 7, pp. 1-2 (listing siblings); Marriage Certificate of James Ashworth and Mary Perkins, St. Landry Parish, La. (Sept. 23, 1811), SLPC; Marriage Certificate of Jesse Ashworth and Sarah Perkins, St. Landry Parish, La. (Oct. 3, 1810), SLPC; Marriage Certificate of Polly Ashworth and George Perkins, St. Landry Parish, La. (Dec. 4, 1810), SLPC; Marriage Certificate of Moses Ashworth and Anna Bunch, St. Landry Parish, La. (Nov. 23, 1821), SLPC; Marriage Certificate of Aaron Ashworth and Mary Bunch, St. Landry Parish, La. (Sept. 16, 1829), SLPC. Abner's sister is listed in his will as Elizabeth Nelson. No probable marriage or census record was found for her.

13. Marriage Record of William Ashworth and Delaide Gallier, Jefferson County Marriage Book A-B, 11 (Feb. 2, 1838), JCC; 1820 U.S. Census, St. Landry Parish, La., s.v. "Francois Gallier," accessed through Ancestry.com (listing Gallier's name next to William's brother, "James Ashworth son"); Cott, *Public Vows*, 24-55 (noting how, in sparsely populated regions in the early United States, state laws on marriage often gave way to community values and practical realities, leading to flexibility in areas such as race); DeMarce, "Verry Slitly Mixt," 9 ("Throughout the eighteenth century and into the nineteenth century, members of all types of racially mixed families continued to intermarry with surrounding white communities, in spite of the fact that many states had passed laws forbidding such unions").

14. 1850 U.S. Census, Jefferson Cty., Tex., Schedule 1—Free Inhabitants, s.v. "William Ashworth," accessed through Ancestry.com (listing "Leide" as 46, eleven years younger than William); Olmsted, *Journey through Texas*, 216.

15. Cott, *Public Vows*, 24-55 (describing "informal" marriages and their role in the early United States); Character Certificate for William Ashworth, 24 November 1834 (noting that he was "a man of family consisting of six," which would include his wife), box 71, folder 12, Records of the Spanish Collection, Archives and Records Program, GLO.

16. 1850 U.S. Census, Jefferson Cty., Tex., Schedule 1—Free Inhabitants, s.v. "William Ashworth," accessed through Ancestry.com (marking box on census return indicating William and Delaide could not read or write); Ross, *Great New Orleans Kidnapping Case*, 25-39; Berlin, *Slaves without Masters*, 108-32.

17. Memorials and Petitions to Congress, Petition of William Goyens (May 5, 1838), TSLAC; ibid., Petition of Lewis B. Jones (Oct. 8, 1837); Lundy, *Life, Travels and Opinions*, 116 ("very respectable coloured man"); see also Treat, "William Goyens," 19-47.

18. Dillon, "Benjamin Lundy in Texas," 47-48.

19. Ibid., 46-62; Lundy, *Life, Travels and Opinions*, 116; Manuel Dublán and José Maria Lozano, eds., *Legislación mexicana ó colección completa de las disposiciones legislativas*, 2:239, cited in Howren, "Causes," 416.

20. First Class Headright Certificate 111 for William Ashworth, 5 March 1838, Milam 1-710, Texas Land Grant Records, Archives and Records Program, GLO.

21. Olmsted, *Journey through Texas*, 219-20.

22. *Inventory of the County Archives of Texas: Orange County*, 1–3; "Orange County," *Galveston Weekly News*, Jan. 20, 1857; 1830 U.S. Census, St. Landry Parish, La., s.v. "Jesse Dyson," accessed through Ancestry.com.

23. *Inventory of the County Archives of Texas: Orange County*, 4–7; "Orange" in *Texas Almanac for 1858*, 79; Olmsted, *Journey through Texas*, 208, 216.

24. *Inventory of the County Archives of Texas: Orange County*, 4; Olmsted, *Journey through Texas*, 216. In October 1835, William Ashworth and John Veatch purchased the front half of William Dyson's league along the Cow Bayou for $500. *Deed from William and Josephine Dyson to William Ashworth and John Veatch*, Jefferson County Deed Book C, 345 (Oct. 10, 1835), JCC. In March 1838, Ashworth bought the other half of Dyson's league for $1. *Deed from William and Josephine Dyson to William Ashworth*, Jefferson County Deed Book A, 100 (Mar. 6, 1838), JCC. In January 1840, Ashworth bought the quarter league owned by John Veatch for $500. *Deed from John Veatch to William Ashworth*, Jefferson County Deed Book C, 335 (Jan. 2, 1840), JCC. In 1843, William also purchased the west half of Gilbert Stephenson's league for $1,000. *Deed from Gilbert Stephenson to William Ashworth*, Jefferson County Deed Book E, 125 (Nov. 11, 1843), JCC. In 1849, he also acquired 200 acres of John Jett's league. *Deed from John Williams, dec'd, to William Ashworth*, Jefferson County Deed Book G, 208 (Aug. 1, 1849), JCC.

25. "Orange County," *Galveston Weekly News*, Jan. 20, 1857; First Class Headright Certificate 109 for Aaron Ashworth, 5 March 1838, Milam 1–302, Texas Land Grant Records, Archives and Records Program, GLO; First Class Headright Certificate 110 for Abner Ashworth, 5 March 1838, Milam 1–856, Texas Land Grant Records, Archives and Records Program, GLO; Duplicate Certificate 4181/4282 for Moses Ashworth, 26 November 1855, Milam 1–1522, Texas Land Grant Records, Archives and Records Program, GLO.

26. Jesse came over sometime before 1840. See letter from G. A. Patillo to Mirabeau Buonaparte Lamar, Feb. 24, 1840, in Gulick and Elliot, *Papers of Mirabeau Buonaparte Lamar*, 3:340 (referencing 1840 "petition of Jesse Ashworth to be allowed to stay in the Republic until the next meeting of Congress"). He was still in Jefferson County in 1846. Mullins, *Republic of Texas*, 6. By 1850, however, Jesse had moved back to Calcasieu Parish. 1850 U.S. Census, Calcasieu Parish, La., Schedule 1—Free Inhabitants, s.v. "Jesse Ashworth," accessed through Ancestry.com. He was still living there in 1860. 1860 U.S. Census, Calcasieu Parish, La., Schedule 1—Free Inhabitants, s.v. "Jesse Ashworth," accessed through Ancestry.com. As for James, it is not known precisely what year he came to Texas, but he eventually settled in nearby Angelina County. 1850 U.S. Census, Angelina Cty., Tex., Schedule 1—Free Inhabitants, s.v. "James Ashworth," accessed through Ancestry.com. He was still living in Angelina ten years later. 1860 U.S. Census, Angelina Cty., Tex., Schedule 1—Free Inhabitants, s.v. "Jesse Ashworth," accessed through Ancestry.com.

27. Mullins, *Republic of Texas*, 6 (imposing a poll tax—on males over 21 and females heading their own households—on Aaron, Aaron Jr., Abner, David, Henderson, Hetta, Jesse, Joshua, LeeRe, Louisa, Mary, William Jr., William Sr.); *Estate of Moses Ashworth*, Cause 245, p. 1 (Rep. of Tex. Cty. Ct., Jefferson Cty., Apr. 14, 1838) (indicating that Moses died in 1838), Jefferson County Probate Records, JCC; U.S. Bureau of the Census, *Seventh Census of the United States*, 503–4; U.S. Bureau of the Census, *Population of the*

United States in 1860, Texas: Table No. 2—Population by Color and Condition, 486; 1850 U.S. Census, Bexar Cty., Tex., Schedule 1—Free Inhabitants, s.v. "Jose Flores," accessed through Ancestry.com; U.S. Bureau of the Census, *Statistical View of the United States*, Table XLII—Free Colored Population of the United States, 63.

28. Olmsted, *Journey through Texas*, 208.

29. Character Certificate for William Ashworth, 24 November 1834, box 71, folder 12, Records of the Spanish Collection, Archives and Records Program, GLO; Character Certificate for Aaron Ashworth, 25 April 1835, box 71, folder 10, Records of the Spanish Collection, Archives and Records Program, GLO; Character Certificate for Abner Ashworth, 12 January 1835, box 71, folder 11, Records of the Spanish Collection, Archives and Records Program, GLO.

30. Unfinished Title for William Ashworth, 1834–1835, box 60, folder 24, Records of the Spanish Collection, Archives and Records Program, GLO; Unfinished Title for Abner Ashworth, 1834–1835, box 60, folder 23, Records of the Spanish Collection, Archives and Records Program, GLO; Unfinished Title for Aaron Ashworth, 1834–1835, box 60, folder 22, Records of the Spanish Collection, Archives and Records Program, GLO; *Inventory of the County Archives of Texas: Orange County*, 3 (indicating that only 26 titles were issued in present Orange County before the revolution); Olmsted, *Journey through Texas*, 218 ("reputation for great hospitality"); see Block, *History of Jefferson County*, 70–75 (describing cattle drives).

31. "General Austin's Order Book," 46 (listing William Ashworth as a member of Captain Garner's company and indicating that they arrived at a "Camp above Bexar" on November 17, 1835); Memorials and Petitions to Congress, Petition of Samuel McCulloch, Jr. (no date), TSLAC.

32. Campbell, *Gone to Texas*, 138; Application for Republic Donation Voucher for Deliade [*sic*] Ashworth, 5 May 1884, Republic Donation Voucher 1110 (affidavit of Delaide Ashworth) (stating that William was present at the grass fight), Texas Land Grant Records, Archives and Records Program, GLO.

33. Application for Republic Donation Voucher for Deliade [*sic*] Ashworth, 5 May 1884, Republic Donation Voucher 1110 (affidavit of John Turner); Application for Republic Donation Voucher for Mary Ashworth, 3 December 1881, Republic Donation Voucher 912 (Proof to Procure Land Certificate for Widow of Texas Veteran), Texas Land Grant Records, Archives and Records Program, GLO; Block, *History of Jefferson County*, 18–26. For insight into the cause of the Texas War for Independence, see Crisp, *Sleuthing the Alamo*, 27–60.

34. Memorials and Petitions to Congress, Petition of William Goyens (May 5, 1838), TSLAC; ibid., Petition of James Richardson (Oct. 19, 1840); ibid., Petition of Henry and John Bird (Dec. 1, 1836); ibid., Petition of Robert Thompson (Dec. 13, 1840); see generally Schoen, "Free Negro in the Republic," chap. 2.

35. Memorials and Petitions to Congress, Petition of Jefferson County Citizens for Relief of Free Blacks (Sept. 19, 1840), TSLAC; ibid., Petition of William Goyens (May 4, 1838).

36. Letter from Beaumont Committee to Henry Millard, Dec. 2, 1835, in Binkly, *Official Correspondence*, 1:160–61.

37. "Proceedings of the General Council, Council Hall, San Felipe de Austin, Janu-

ary 1st, 1836," in Gammel, *Laws of Texas*, 1:720–21. "Free Negroes Sent Off," *Marshall, Texas Republican*, Dec. 6, 1856.

38. "Free Colored Population in the South," *Marshall, Texas Republican*, Mar. 10, 1860; "Free Negroes—the Necessity of Reducing them to Slavery," *Austin, Texas State Gazette*, Sept. 12, 1857; see Fredrickson, *Black Image*, 43–96.

39. "Proceedings of the General Council," in Gammel, *Laws of Texas*, 1:720–21.

40. "Free Negroes Sent Off," *Marshall, Texas Republican*, Dec. 6, 1856.

41. 1860 U.S. Census, Travis County, Tex., Schedule 1—Free Inhabitants, s.v. "Sylvia Green," accessed through Ancestry.com (washerwoman); ibid., Cameron Cty., Tex., s.v. "Sarah Huey" (milkmaid); ibid., Galveston Cty., Tex., s.v. "Richard" (employee of wharf master); ibid., Maverick Cty., Tex., s.v. "Andrew Cox" (cook); ibid., Nacogdoches Cty., Tex., s.v. "A. J. Morrow" (day laborer); ibid., El Paso Cty., Tex., s.v. "Louis Hudson" (barber); ibid., Matagorda Cty., Tex., s.v. "Stephen Taylor" (carpenter); ibid., Washington Cty., Tex., s.v. "Henry" (wagoner); ibid., Jackson Cty., Tex., s.v. "Harriet Reynold" (stock raiser); Memorials and Petitions to Congress, Petition of Samuel McCulloch, Jr. (no date), TSLAC; ibid., Petition of Greenberry Logan & Wife Caroline (Mar. 13, 1837) (blacksmith); ibid., Petition of Juan Baptiste Maturin (Apr. 21, 1838) (landowner); ibid., Petition of William Goyens (Sept. 1840); Treat, "William Goyens," 29.

42. "Constitution of the Republic of Texas of 1836, General Provisions, sec. 9," in Gammel, *Laws of Texas*, 1:1069, 1079.

43. Memorials and Petitions to Congress, Petition of Greenberry Logan & Wife Caroline (Mar. 13, 1837), TSLAC.

44. Ibid.

45. "Joint Resolution for the relief of Free Persons of Color, June 5, 1837," in Gammel, *Laws of Texas*, 1:1292; "An Act to provide for the punishment of Crimes and Misdemeanors committed by slaves and free persons of color, Dec. 14, 1837, secs. 1, 2, 6," in ibid., 1:1385–86.

46. Block, *History of Jefferson County*, 27–32, 46–53.

47. "New Town," *San Felipe de Austin, Telegraph and Texas Register*, Oct. 26, 1835; Block, *History of Jefferson County*, 54–65; U.S. Bureau of the Census, *Manufactures of the United States in 1860*, Texas: Table No. 1—Manufactures, by Counties, 580–91.

48. Block, *History of Jefferson County*, 33–45.

49. Minutes of the County Court, Jefferson County, Tex., Minute Book A, 5–7 (Jan. 1838), JCC; ibid., Minute Book A-2, 3–4 (Feb. 27, 1838); see generally Olmsted, *Journey through Texas*, 213–16. William Fairfax Gray's recollections from the Runaway Scrape in the spring of 1836 indicate that Ashworth was operating his ferry before Texas gained independence from Mexico. Gray, *Diary of William Fairfax Gray*, 160 ("Arrived at Ashworth's ferry, we expected to find a boat, but there was none").

50. Minutes of the County Court, Jefferson County, Tex., Minute Book A, 1 (Jan. 1837) (listing freeholders subject to jury duty in 1837: James Stephenson, Wilson Gill, William T. Hatton, John Townsend, C. C. P. Welch, Benjamin Johnson, R. Ballew, William McFaddin, Uriah Gibson, David Garner, Joseph Ritchie, Stephen Simmons, Benjamin Allen, Robert Hatton, Isaac Garner, Thomas Rowe, Uriah Harris, Jacob Garner, D. St. Clair, Charles Cronier, Gilbert Stephenson, W. D. Smith, James Dyson, John Stephenson,

Elisha Stephenson, Abraham Winfrey, Marmaduke Hatton, B. Arthur, David Harmon, John Cole, William Hays, W. H. Irion, Elisha Allen, John Caruthers, William Clark, Clark Beach, John Bland, George Allen, Charles Meyers, Silas Parson, James Simmons, Joseph Young, William Hatton Jr., N. Holbert, James Ware, J. T. Robinson, James Jett, Peyton Bland, John Harmon, Thomas Heart, Elijah Allen, Charles Cohorn, C. West, S. N. Mathias, A. Jett, and Aaron Allen), JCC; G. White, *1840 Census*, 94–98; Jefferson County Marks and Brands Book A, 1–4, JCC.

51. Minutes of the County Court, Jefferson County, Tex., Minute Book A-2, 8–9 (July 3, 1838), JCC; Marriage Record of William Ashworth and Delilie [sic] Gallier, Jefferson County Marriage Book A-B, 11 (Feb. 2, 1838), JCC; Marriage Record of Abner Ashworth and "Rosale Collier" [sic], Jefferson County Marriage Book A-B, 9 (Jan. 16, 1838), JCC.

52. "An Act Concerning Free Persons of Color, Feb. 5, 1840," *Laws of the Republic of Texas Passed at the Sessions of the Fourth Congress* (1840), in Gammel, *Laws of Texas*, 2:325.

53. 1850 U.S. Census, Jefferson Cty., Tex., Schedule 1—Free Inhabitants, s.v. "William Ashworth," accessed through Ancestry.com (marking box on census return indicating William and Delaide could not read or write); Memorials and Petitions to Congress, Petition of Jefferson County Citizens for Relief of Free Blacks (Sept. 19, 1840), TSLAC; ibid., Petition of Jefferson County Citizen for Free Black man to remain in the Republic (Sept. 18, 1840).

54. Memorials and Petitions to Congress, Petition of Jefferson County Citizens for Relief of Free Blacks (Sept. 19, 1840), TSLAC.

55. Ibid., 1–5.

56. *Journals of the House of Representatives of the Republic of Texas: Fifth Congress, First Session*, 27, 33; "Report of Select Committee on Petition of Free Men of Color," appendix to the *Journals of the House of Representatives: Fifth Congress*, 262.

57. *Journals of the House of Representatives of the Republic of Texas: Fifth Congress, First Session*, 48, 52; *Journals of the Senate of the Republic of Texas: Fifth Congress—First Session*, 36–37; Memorials and Petitions to Congress, Petition of William Goyens (Nov. 25, 1840), TSLAC; ibid., Petition of John and Charity Bird (Jan. 3, 1841); ibid., Petition of Patsy (Dec. 31, 1840); ibid., Petition of Fanny McFarland (Oct. 30, 1840); ibid., Petition of Allen Dimery (Dec. 3, 1840); ibid., Petition of Diana Leonard (Dec. 14, 1840); ibid., Petition of James Richardson (Oct. 19, 1840); ibid., Petition of Robert Thompson (Dec. 13, 1840); ibid., Petition of Joseph Tate (Nov. 13, 1839); ibid., Petition of the Children of David and Sophia Towns (located in the Petition of William Goyens) (Nov. 25, 1840); ibid., Petition of Jefferson County Citizen for Free Black man to remain in the Republic (Sept. 18, 1840) (Elisha Thomas).

58. "An Act for the Relief of certain Free persons of Color, Dec. 12, 1840," *Laws of the Republic of Texas Passed at the Session of the Fifth Congress* (1840), in Gammel, *Laws of Texas*, 2:549–60.

59. Twenty-four people with the surname Ashworth lived in Calcasieu in 1850. Many other relatives with different surnames, like Perkins and Dial, also lived there. 1850 U.S. Census, Calcasieu Parish, La., Schedule 1—Free Inhabitants, s.v. "Ashworth," accessed through Ancestry.com.

60. *Journals of the House of Representatives of the Seventh Congress of the Republic of Texas*, 63; letter from A. Rigmaiden to McDonald Furman, May 6, 1893, Charles James McDonald Furman Papers, SCL.

61. *Tax Assessment Rolls of Jefferson Cty., Tex., Made for the Year 1837*, s.v. "Joshua Ashworth," Jefferson County Tax Rolls, THL; Minutes of the County Court, Jefferson County, Tex., Minute Book A-2, 8–9 (July 3, 1838), JCC; G. White, *1840 Census*, 94; *Tax Assessment Rolls of Jefferson Cty., Tex., Made for the Year 1846*, s.v. "Aaron Ashworth," "Abner Ashworth," and "William Ashworth," Jefferson County Tax Rolls, THL; 1850 U.S. Census, Jefferson Cty., Tex., Schedule 2—Slave Inhabitants, s.v. "Aaron Ashworth," "William Ashworth," "Abner Ashworth," and "Joshua Ashworth," accessed through Ancestry.com; ibid., Angelina Cty., Tex., Schedule 2—Slave Inhabitants, s.v. "James Ashworth;" ibid., Calcasieu Parish, La., Schedule 2—Slave Inhabitants, s.v. "Jesse Ashworth;" *Tax Assessment Rolls of Orange Cty., Tex., Made for the Year 1853*, s.v. "William Ashworth" and "Aaron Ashworth," Orange County Tax Rolls, SHLRC; 1860 U.S. Census, Calcasieu Parish, La., Schedule 2—Slave Inhabitants, s.v. "Jesse Ashworth," accessed through Ancestry.com.

62. "The Worst Enemies of Slavery," *Austin Southern Intelligencer*, Jan. 5, 1859; Berlin, *Slaves without Masters*, 269–73; Memorials and Petitions to Congress, Petition of Peter Allen (Feb. 2, 1863), TSLAC. Under- and over-reporting in the federal census make it difficult to determine the precise number of free people of color who owned slaves. Koger, *Black Slaveowners*, 5–7. Based on an analysis of the 1830 census, R. Halliburton Jr. puts the number of free black slaveholders in that year at 3,775. Halliburton, "Free Black Owners of Slaves," 135. Loren Schweninger gives the more conservative estimate of 2,128. Schweninger, *Black Property Owners*, 111.

63. Olmsted, *Journey through Texas*, 218; *Deed from Rachel Holden and Samuel Holden to Luke Ashworth*, Orange County Deed Book A, 90 (June 24, 1856), OCC.

64. *Deed from William Ashworth to Richard Baleu*, Jefferson County Deed Book D, 143 (Aug. 8, 1843), JCC; *Deed from John Williams to William Ashworth*, Jefferson County Deed Book D, 46 (Sept. 30, 1843), JCC; *Deed from William Ashworth and Delaide Ashworth to Charles Gamut*, Orange County Deed Book A, 32 (May 19, 1853), OCC; *Deed from Deliad [sic] Ashworth to Susan Barrow*, Orange County Deed Book A, 55 (Sept. 18, 1854), OCC.

65. *Deed from Abner Ashworth to William Carr*, Jefferson County Deed Book A, 39 (Nov. 8, 1843), JCC; *Deed from Nathan Bonner to Abner Ashworth*, Jefferson County Deed Book E, 360 (Jan. 17, 1846), JCC; *Deed from David Garner to Abner Ashworth*, Jefferson County Deed Book A, 1 (Nov. 30, 1846), JCC; *Deed from Emille Broussard to Abner Ashworth*, Jefferson County Deed Book B, 5 (Aug. 24, 1853), JCC; *Deed from Abner Ashworth to His Children*, Orange County Deed Book A, 123 (May 25, 1858), OCC; *Deed from Abner Ashworth & Wife to Their Children*, Orange County Deed Book A, 181 (Nov. 11, 1859), OCC.

66. Schoen, "State Census of 1847," 116–18; DeBow, "Texas—Character of the Country," 241.

67. "Constitution of the Republic of Texas of 1836, General Provisions, sec. 10," in Gammel, *Laws of Texas*, 1:1069, 1079–80; Hartley, *Digest of the Laws*, 668.

68. First Class Headright Certificate 111 for William Ashworth, 5 March 1838, Milam 1–710, Texas Land Grant Records, Archives and Records Program, GLO; First Class Headright Certificate 109 for Aaron Ashworth, 5 March 1838, Milam 1–302, Texas Land Grant Records, Archives and Records Program, GLO; First Class Headright Certificate 110 for Abner Ashworth, 5 March 1838, Milam 1–856, Texas Land Grant Records, Archives and Records Program, GLO; Duplicate Certificate 4181/4282 for Moses Ashworth, 26 November 1855, Milam 1–1522, Texas Land Grant Records, Archives and Records Program, GLO; Report of Commissioners to Detect Fraudulent Certificates Covering 15 Counties, 22 May 1841, box G713, p. 447, County Boards of Land Commissioners Records (AR.36.BLC), Archives and Records Program, GLO.

69. Report of Commissioners to Detect Fraudulent Certificates Covering 15 Counties, 22 May 1841; "Constitution of the Republic of Texas of 1836, General Provisions, sec. 10," in Gammel, *Laws of Texas*, 1:1069, 1079–80.

70. Memorials and Petitions to Congress, Petition of William Ashworth (Dec. 10, 1842), TSLAC.

71. *Journals of the House of Representatives of the Seventh Congress of the Republic of Texas*, 45.

72. Ibid., 63, 80; "Abstract of Private Acts and Joint Resolutions Passed by the Seventh Congress," *Laws Passed by the Seventh Congress of the Republic of Texas*, in Gammel, *Laws of Texas*, 2:875.

73. G. White, *1840 Census*, 94; Schedule of Adelaide Ashworth's Property, Orange County Deed Book A, 197 (May 21, 1860), OCC.

74. *Tax Assessment Rolls of Jefferson Cty., Tex., Made for the Years 1837, 1840, 1842, 1846, 1847, 1849, 1850, 1851* and *Tax Assessment Rolls of Orange Cty., Tex., Made for the Years 1852, 1853, 1854, 1855, 1856, 1857, 1858, 1859, 1860*, s.v. "Ashworth" (taxing 10 different family members on real estate over the periods covered—William, Aaron, Abner, Jesse, Joshua, Luke, David, Henderson, Aaron Jr., and Clarke), Jefferson County Tax Rolls, THL, and Orange County Tax Rolls, SHLRC; General Index, Orange County Deed Books B and E (listing 7 additional family members as deed holders of real estate—William's wife Delaide, Aaron's wife Mary, Abner's wife Rosalie and their children Lydia Ann, Phillippa, Sidney Jane, and Sublett Ashworth), OCC. 1850 U.S. Census, Jefferson Cty., Tex., Schedule 4—Production of Agriculture, s.v. "Ashworth," accessed through Ancestry.com (listing six members of the family in the agricultural reports—William, Aaron, Abner, Aaron Jr., David, and Joshua).

75. 1850 U.S. Census, Jefferson Cty., Tex., Schedule 4—Production of Agriculture, s.v. "Ashworth," accessed through Ancestry.com. There are forty-eight separate entries in Jefferson County records registering the cattle brands of members of the Ashworth family. A few names appear more than once, but, given the common practice of naming children after relatives, it is impossible to know whether this is the same person or someone else. Jefferson County Marks and Brands Book A, 1–4, JCC; Orange County Marks and Brands Book A, 1 (index), OCC.

76. H. Williams, *Gateway to Texas*, 237; petition, *Hutchinson v. Ashworth*, no. 34, pp. 1–2 (Rep. of Tex. Dist. Ct., Jefferson Cty., Jan. 1845), SHLRC; *Hutchinson v. Ashworth*, no. 34, Jefferson County District Court Minute Book A, 28–29 (1845) (costs), SHLRC; ibid., 46–47 (disposition); ibid., 58 (promise); 1850 U.S. Census, Jefferson Cty., Tex.,

NOTES TO CHAPTER THREE   211

Schedule 1—Free Inhabitants, s.v. "Aaron Ashworth," accessed through Ancestry.com (listing John Woods, schoolteacher, under household).

77. "Orange County," *Galveston Weekly News*, Jan. 20, 1857; "Our Lands and Stock," *Austin, Texas State Gazette*, Nov. 15, 1856; "Orange," *Texas Almanac for 1858*, 79; U.S. Bureau of the Census, *Population of the United States in 1860*, State of Texas, Table No. 2—Population by Color and Condition, 485.

78. "Texas and Her Destiny," *Austin, Texas State Gazette*, Nov. 4, 1854.

79. William and Henderson Ashworth were charged separately for gambling and given different case numbers. Both pled guilty. *State v. William Ashworth*, no. 35, Orange County District Court Minute Book A, 43, 58 (1854), SHLRC; *State v. Henderson Ashworth*, no. 33, Orange County District Court Minute Book A, 43, 58 (1854), SHLRC.

80. *State v. Clark Ashworth*, no. 2, Orange County District Court Minute Book A, 6, 17, 33, 36–37, 55, 74, 90, 121, 148, 180, 205, 226, 253, 278, 309, 331, 339, 359, 387, 408, 421 (1852–64), SHLRC; ibid., Orange County District Court Minute Book A½, 132 (1866); *State v. Henderson Ashworth*, no. 39, Orange County District Court Minute Book A, 60, 76 (1854–55), SHLRC; *State v. Moses Ashworth*, no. 130, Orange County District Court Minute Book A, 147, 182, 206, 227, 234, 279, 309, 341, 360, 388, 469 (1857–64), SHLRC.

81. *State v. William Ashworth*, no. 134, Orange County District Court Minute Book A, 155, 183, 207 (1857–58), SHLRC; *State v. William Ashworth*, no. 179, Orange County District Court Minute Book A, 313, 343, 362, 393–94, 409, 423 (1860–64), SHLRC. Case No. 179 was finally dismissed after William died. Ibid., Orange County District Court Minute Book A½, 133 (1866).

82. Transcript of trial, *Dark v. William Ashworth*, no. 51 (Tex. Dist. Ct., Orange Cty., Sept. 1856), Supreme Court Records and Briefs, no. M2937, TSLAC; *Ashworth v. Dark*, 20 Tex. 825 (1858).

83. Testimony of Harrington, transcript of trial, *Hillebrandt v. Abner Ashworth*, no. 206, p. 24 (Tex. Dist. Ct., Jefferson Cty., May 1855), Supreme Court Records and Briefs, no. M2687, TSLAC; testimony of J. P. Barnes, ibid., 26.

84. Petition, ibid., 1–2; answer of Ashworth, ibid., 14; judgment, ibid., 20.

85. Olmsted, *Journey through Texas*, 218; *State v. Gallier*, no. 4, Jefferson County District Court Minute Book A, 20, 23, 40, 76, 95 (1845–47), SHLRC; 1860 U.S. Census, Calcasieu Parish, La., Schedule 1—Free Inhabitants, s.v. "Celestine Gallin," accessed through Ancestry.com. Margarette and Sillistia were married in January 1845. Marriage Record of Sillistia Gallier and Margarette Ashworth, Jefferson County Marriage Book A–B, 55 (Jan. 8, 1845), JCC.

86. *State v. Henderson Ashworth*, no. 34, Jefferson County District Court Minute Book A, 76, 78, 97 (1847), SHLRC.

87. *State v. Henderson Ashworth*, no. 40, Jefferson County District Court Minute Book A, 98, 101 (1847), SHLRC; *State v. Letitia Stewart*, no. 41, Jefferson County District Court Minute Book A, 98, 101–2 (1847), SHLRC; *Ashworth v. State*, 9 Tex. 490 (1853).

88. *State v. Henderson Ashworth*, no. 40, Jefferson County District Court Minute Book A, 130 (1848), SHLRC.

89. Ibid., 146; *Ashworth v. State*, 9 Tex. at 490–91. For notations in the minute books while the case was pending before the Supreme Court, see *State v. Henderson Ashworth*,

no. 40, Jefferson County District Court Minute Book A, 187, 201, 221 (1849–50), SHLRC; ibid., Jefferson County District Court Minute Book B, 10, 41, 68, 107 (1851–52); *State v. Letitia Stewart*, no. 41, Jefferson County District Court Minute Book A, 163, 166, 183, 201, 221 (1849–50), SHLRC; ibid., Jefferson County District Court Minute Book B, 10, 41, 68, 107 (1851–52).

90. 1850 U.S. Census, Jefferson Cty., Tex., Schedule 1—Free Inhabitants, s.v. "Henderson Ashworth," accessed through Ancestry.com. For the first notations for 1853 indicating that judgment was entered against Henderson and that Letitia failed to appear, see *State v. Henderson Ashworth*, no. 40, Jefferson County District Court Minute Book B, 149, 150 (1853), SHLRC; *State v. Letitia Stewart*, no. 41, Jefferson County District Court Minute Book B, 149, 150 (1853), SHLRC. For subsequent entries indicating a failure to appear, see *State v. Letitia Stewart*, no. 41, Jefferson County District Court Minute Book B, 174, 179, 204. For Letitia's arrest, see ibid., 235–36. For the Orange County records, including the indictment and failure to appear, see *State v. Ashworth and Stewart*, no. 72, Orange County District Court Minute Book A, 10, 125 (1855–56), SHLRC.

91. The prosecutor first charged Willis and Keziah with adultery. *State v. Goodman*, no. 28, Jefferson County District Court Minute Book A, 74, 96 (1847), SHLRC. Because neither one was married to someone else, the prosecutor dismissed the charge and subsequently brought a charge of fornication, for which Willis was found guilty. *State v. Goodman*, no. 39, Jefferson County District Court Minute Book A, 98, 99–100 (1847), SHLRC. Willis escaped the custody of the sheriff and failed to show at subsequent appearances. Ibid., 128, 163, 201, 221; ibid., Minute Book B, 10, 41, 68. The prosecutor of Orange County also charged them with fornication. *State v. Goodman and Ashworth*, no. 68, Orange County District Court Minute Book A, 100, 124 (1855), SHLRC. Keziah was Aaron's daughter. *Estate of Aaron Ashworth*, 1 (Tex. Cty. Ct., Orange Cty., March 1862) (identifying Keziah Goodman among Aaron's heirs), Orange County Probate Records, OCC. Census records for Calcasieu in 1850 list Willis Goodman, a 35-year-old white man, married to Mary, a 30-year-old mulatto woman born in Louisiana. It is possible, though not certain, that Mary was in fact Keziah. 1850 U.S. Census, Calcasieu Parish, La., Schedule 1—Free Inhabitants, s.v. "Willis Goodman," accessed through Ancestry.com.

92. Two cases were brought against Martha and her husband. The first, in Jefferson County, was against Martha and "Peter Pinder." Peter was evidently not Martha's spouse, however, as the jury eventually found him not guilty and the prosecutor dismissed the case. *State v. Peter Pinder and Martha Ashworth*, no. 108, Jefferson County District Court Minute Book A, 44, 67–68, 84, 105–08, 132–33, 144, 146, 151–52, 179–80 (1851–54), SHLRC. The second case was in Orange County, and it was against Martha and "Jacob Pender." *State v. Jacob Pender*, no. 22, Orange County District Court Minute Book A, 23 (1853), SHLRC; *State v. Martha Ashworth*, no. 23, Orange County District Court Minute Book A, 23 (1853), SHLRC. The prosecutor dismissed the case against Martha and Jacob, as well as a number of other cases, in the spring of 1854. Ibid., 37–39. Martha was Aaron's daughter. *Estate of Aaron Ashworth*, 1 (identifying "Martha Ann Penders" among Aaron's heirs).

93. The prosecutor charged Sarah and her husband, William Burwick. *State v. Sarah Ashworth*, no. 13, Orange County District Court Minute Book A, 22 (1853), SHLRC; *State v. William Burwick*, no. 19, Orange County District Court Minute Book A, 23 (1853),

SHLRC. The prosecutor charged Clark and his wife, Sarah Arthur. *State v. Sarah Arthur*, no. 14, Orange County District Court Minute Book A, 22 (1853), SHLRC; *State v. Clark Ashworth*, no. 16, Orange County District Court Minute Book A, 22 (1853), SHLRC. The prosecutor charged Nancy and her husband, Jackson Stewart. *State v. Nancy Ashworth*, no. 10, Orange County District Court Minute Book A, 22 (1853), SHLRC; *State v. Jackson Stewart*, no. 15, Orange County District Court Minute Book A, 22 (1853), SHLRC. And the prosecutor charged Emily and her husband, Joseph Young. *State v. Joseph Young*, no. 17, Orange County District Court Minute Book A, 22 (1853), SHLRC; *State v. Emily Ashworth*, no. 20, Orange County District Court Minute Book A, 23 (1853), SHLRC. The prosecutor dismissed the charges against all of them in 1854. Ibid., 37–39. The following year, the prosecutor renewed the charges against Clark and Nancy, together with Henderson. *State v. Clark Ashworth and Sarah Arthur*, no. 71, Orange County District Court Minute Book A, 101 (1855), SHLRC; *State v. Henderson Ashworth and Letitia Stewart*, no. 72, Orange County District Court Minute Book A, 101 (1855), SHLRC; *State v. Jackson Stewart and Nancy Ashworth*, no. 73, Orange County District Court Minute Book A, 101 (1855), SHLRC. Emily, Clark, and Nancy were all William's children. 1850 U.S. Census, Jefferson Cty., Tex., Schedule 1—Free Inhabitants, s.v. "William Ashworth," accessed through Ancestry.com; *State v. Goodman*, no. 28., Jefferson County District Court Minute Book A, 74 (1847), SHLRC.

94. Olmsted, *Journey through Texas*, 218.

95. "Disturbances in Orange County," *Galveston Weekly News*, July 15, 1856; *Tax Assessment Rolls of Orange Cty., Tex., Made for the Year 1855*, s.v. "Henderson Ashworth," Orange County Tax Rolls, SHLRC. Henderson is occasionally identified as William's nephew, but court records indicate he was his son. Final decree, *Winfree v. Unknown Heirs of William Ashworth*, no. 4391, p. 4 (Tex. Dist. Ct., Orange Cty., 1922) (identifying Henderson as a "son of William Ashworth and Delaide Ashworth"). I am grateful to Verna Thompson for providing this document to me.

96. "Disturbances in Orange County," *Galveston Weekly News*, July 15, 1856; *Garnot v. William Ashworth*, no. 4, Orange County District Court Minute Book A, 16 (1852), SHLRC; Greenberg, *Honor & Slavery*; Wyatt-Brown, *Southern Honor*.

97. "Disturbances in Orange County," *Galveston Weekly News*, July 15, 1856; Olmsted, *Journey through Texas*, 218–19; Russell, *History of Orange*, 5–6.

98. "Disturbances in Orange County," *Galveston Weekly News*, July 15, 1856; Olmsted, *Journey through Texas*, 218–19.

99. "Disturbances in Orange County," *Galveston Weekly News*, July 15, 1856; Olmsted, *Journey through Texas*, 219.

100. Olmsted, *Journey through Texas*, 218–19; "Disturbances in Orange County," *Galveston Weekly News*, July 15, 1856. The events surrounding the killing were reported regularly in the newspapers through the summer of 1856. In addition to the articles cited, see "Another Murder," *Galveston Weekly News*, June 10, 1856; "Murder," *Houston Weekly Telegraph*, June 11, 1856; "Disturbances in Orange County," *Houston Weekly Telegraph*, June 25, 1856; "Murders," *Washington American*, July 2, 1856; "Orange County," *Galveston Weekly News*, July 8, 1856; "Madison, Orange Co., Texas," *Richmond Reporter*, July 12, 1856; "The Troubles on the Sabine," *Austin, Texas State Times*, July 12, 1856; "Letter

from General Henderson," *Austin, Texas State Times*, July 12, 1856; "The Orange County Disturbance," *Galveston Weekly News*, July 15, 1856; untitled, *Columbia Democrat and Planter*, July 15, 1856; "Disturbances in Orange County," *Houston Weekly Telegraph*, July 23, 1856; "More of the Orange County Difficulty," *Galveston Weekly News*, July 29, 1856; "Outlawry," *Galveston Weekly News*, August 16, 1856.

101. Olmsted, *Journey through Texas*, 219; Russell, *History of Orange*, 5–6; "The Troubles on the Sabine," *Austin, Texas State Times*, July 12, 1856; "Disturbances in Orange County," *Galveston Weekly News*, July 15, 1856.

102. "Disturbances in Orange County," *Galveston Weekly News*, July 15, 1856; Deed from Abner Ashworth to Charlton Midkiff, Orange County Deed Book B, 187–88 (August 11, 1856), OCC.

103. *State v. Sam Ashworth and Jack Bunch*, no. 124, Orange County District Court Minute Book A, 120 (1856), SHLRC; List of Grand Jurors in Fall 1856 Term, Orange County District Court Minute Book A, 115 (1856), SHLRC; Memorials and Petitions to Congress, Petition of William Poff (1858), TSLAC; "Communications," *Belton Independent*, Nov. 27, 1858; "Orange County," *Galveston Civilian and Gazette*, Nov. 16, 1858; Russell, *History of Orange*, 6. For additional notations on the case, see *State v. Sam Ashworth*, no. 124, Orange County District Court Minute Book A, 150, 181, 206, 226, 254, 279, 309, 341, 360, 388, 408, 422 (1857–64), SHLRC; *State v. Sam Ashworth*, no. 124, Orange County District Court Minute Book A½, 133 (1866), SHLRC. The case against him was dismissed following his death. *State v. Sam Ashworth*, no. 124, Orange County District Court Docket Book, 118–19.

104. *Galveston Weekly News*, Oct. 21, 1856 (noting sheriff had gone to retrieve Jack from Colorado County jail); untitled, *Houston Weekly Telegraph*, Oct. 22, 1856 (indicating that sheriff brought Jack through Harrisburg, near Houston, on way to Madison); untitled, *Galveston Weekly News*, Nov. 4, 1856 (commenting on arrival of Jack in Liberty); *State v. Jack Bunch*, no. 124, Jefferson County District Court Minute Book A, 138–39 (1856) (conviction), SHLRC; "To Be Hung," *Galveston Weekly News*, Nov. 25, 1856 (reporting verdict); "Jack Bunch," *Austin, Texas State Times*, Dec. 13, 1856 (describing day of execution).

105. "Disturbances in Orange County," *Galveston Weekly News*, July 15, 1856 (reporting Henderson's capture); *State v. Henderson Ashworth*, no. 126, Orange County District Court Minute Book A, 120 (1856), SHLRC; "Orange County," *Galveston Civilian and Gazette*, Nov. 16, 1858; *State v. Henderson Ashworth*, no. 126, Orange County District Court Docket Book, 140–41 (1867), SHLRC; untitled, *Columbia Democrat and Planter*, July 15, 1856. For additional notations on the case, see *State v. Henderson Ashworth*, no. 126, Orange County District Court Minute Book A, 151, 182, 206, 227, 279, 309, 341, 360, 388, 409, 422 (1857–64), SHLRC.

106. Charles James McDonald Furman Papers, University of South Carolina, https://library.sc.edu/socar/uscs/1997/furman97.html.

107. Letter from A. Rigmaiden to McDonald Furman, May 6, 1893, Charles James McDonald Furman Papers, SCL.

108. *Tax Assessment Rolls of Orange Cty., Tex., Made for the Years 1857, 1858, 1859, 1860*, s.v. "Ashworth," Orange County Tax Rolls, SHLRC; *Estate of Aaron Ashworth*, 1; 1860

U.S. Census, Orange Cty., Tex., Schedule 2—Slave Inhabitants, s.v. "Aaron Ashworth," accessed through Ancestry.com; ibid., s.v. "Rozella Ashworth."

109. Petition, *Jackson v. Ashworth*, no. 84, pp. 1–2 (Tex. Dist. Ct., Orange Cty., Fall 1857), SHLRC; ibid., Orange County District Court Minute Book A, 189 (1857) (verdict), SHLRC; *Deed from William Ashworth to Hugh Ochiltree*, Orange County Deed Book B, 297 (May 6, 1857), OCC; *Deed from William Ashworth to Moise LaBleu*, Orange County Deed Book B, 324, 336 (Sept. 10, 1857), OCC; *Deed from William Ashworth to Delaide Ashworth*, Orange County Deed Book B, 373 (Dec. 11, 1857), OCC; *Tax Assessment Rolls of Orange Cty., Tex., Made for the Year 1860*, s.v. "William Ashworth" (listing William as the owner of 200 acres and "Mrs. D. Ashworth" as the owner of 211 acres), Orange County Tax Rolls, SHLRC; *Deed from William Ashworth to Joseph Dark*, Jefferson County Deed Book B, 169 (Feb. 21, 1857), JCC; *Schedule of Adelaide Ashworth's Property*, Orange County Deed Book A, 197 (May 21, 1860), OCC; 1860 U.S. Census, Orange Cty., Tex., Schedule 2—Slave Inhabitants, s.v. "Delaide Ashworth," accessed through Ancestry.com (indicating Delaide—not William—owned the family's slaves).

110. U.S. Bureau of the Census, *Population of the United States in 1860*, State of Texas, Table No. 2—Population by Color and Condition, 485 (listing Jefferson County with 2 free people of color; Orange County with 29 free people of color); 1860 U.S. Census, Orange Cty., Tex., Schedule 1—Free Inhabitants, s.v. "William Ashworth," accessed through Ancestry.com (listing William's occupation as laborer); Application for Republic Donation Voucher for Deliade [sic] Ashworth, 5 May 1884, Republic Donation Voucher 1110 (affidavit of Delaide Ashworth), Texas Land Grant Records, Archives and Records Program, GLO.

111. *Hudgins v. Wrights*, 1 Hen. & M. 134, 140–41 (1806).

112. DeMarce, "Verry Slitly Mixt," 6 ("one of the major contentions of tri-racial Americans . . . has been that they were more likely bi-racial—that is, Indian and white," and not African American); answer of Ashworth, transcript of trial, *Hillebrandt v. Abner Ashworth*, no. 206, p. 14. For discussions of how law, human interactions, and societal factors influence the construction of race, see, e.g., Gross, *What Blood Won't Tell*; Haney-Lopez, *White by Law*; Roediger, *Wages of Whiteness*; Sharfstein, *Invisible Line*; Davis, "Identity Notes Part One"; M. Elliott, "Telling the Difference"; Gross, "Litigating Whiteness"; Haney-Lopez, "Social Construction of Race"; Sharfstein, "Crossing the Color Line." In researching families of color, Gary Mills cautions against drawing assumptions "of ethnicity on the basis of census data from a single year (or any other single document)." He observes, "Determining the ethnic identity of any family labeled *free people of color* (or f.p.c.) on any record invariably requires exhaustive research in the widest-possible variety of resources. This is especially so when treating the large number of southeastern families who traditionally paint their family tree red rather than black." Mills, "Tracing Free People of Color," 264.

113. Letter from A. Rigmaiden to McDonald Furman, May 6, 1893, Charles James McDonald Furman Papers, SCL.

114. *State v. Harrison*, 11 La. 722, 722 (1856) ("In the eye of the Louisiana law there is . . . all the difference between a free man of color and a slave, that there is between a white man and a slave."); letter from A. Rigmaiden to McDonald Furman, May 6, 1893; see,

e.g., 1870 U.S. Census, Calcasieu Parish, La., Schedule 1—Inhabitants, s.v. "Ashworth," "Perkins," and "Goins," accessed through Ancestry.com.

115. Application for Republic Donation Voucher for Deliade [sic] Ashworth, 5 May 1884, Republic Donation Voucher 1110 (affidavit of Delaide Ashworth), Texas Land Grant Records, Archives and Records Program, GLO.

116. In 1870 and 1880, census records list all the Ashworths living in Orange County as white. This includes members of the family who appeared in earlier records as "mulatto," including Aaron's son Sublett and Abner's daughter Sidney Jane in the 1860 census. 1860 U.S. Census, Orange Cty., Tex., Schedule 1—Free Inhabitants, s.v. "Sublett Ashworth" and "Sidney Ashworth," accessed through Ancestry.com. Sublett and Sidney married sometime during the decade and appear together in both the 1870 and 1880 census as white, with white children. 1870 U.S. Census, Orange Cty., Tex., Schedule 1—Inhabitants, s.v. "S. Ashworth" and "Sidney Ashworth," accessed through Ancestry.com; 1880 U.S. Census, Orange Cty., Tex., Schedule 1—Inhabitants, s.v. "Sublett Ashworth" and "S. Jane Ashworth," accessed through Ancestry.com.

117. *Will of Abner Ashworth*, Cause 7, pp. 1–2 (listing James, Jesse, William, Moses, Aaron, Mary, Elizabeth, and Sarah); Marriage Certificate of Aaron Ashworth and Mary Bunch, St. Landry Parish, La., (Sept. 23, 1811) (listing parents), SLPC; 1850 U.S. Census, Angelina Cty., Tex., Schedule 1—Free Inhabitants, s.v. "James Ashworth," accessed through Ancestry.com; ibid., Calcasieu Parish, La., s.v. "Jesse Ashworth;" ibid., Jefferson Cty., Tex., s.v. "William Ashworth;" ibid., Jefferson Cty., Tex., s.v. "Aaron Ashworth;" ibid., Jefferson Cty., Tex., s.v. "Abner Ashworth."

118. *Estate of Moses Ashworth*, Cause 245, p. 1; 1830 U.S. Census, St. Landry Parish, La., s.v. "Moses Ashworth," accessed through Ancestry.com.

119. Marriage Certificate of Polly Ashworth and George Perkins, St. Landry Parish, La. (Dec. 4, 1810), SLPC; 1850 U.S. Census, Calcasieu Parish, La., Schedule 1—Free Inhabitants, s.v. "Mary Perkins," accessed through Ancestry.com; *Estate of Sarah Ashworth*, Cause 54B, p. 1 (Rep. of Tex. Cty. Ct., Jefferson Cty., June 12, 1843), Jefferson County Probate Records, JCC.

CHAPTER 4. Lawyers and Slaves on Galveston Island

1. Will, transcript of trial, *Webster v. Heard*, no. 3088, pp. 38–40 (Tex. Dist. Ct., Galveston Cty., Feb. 1866), Supreme Court Records and Briefs, no. M6253, TSLAC; inventory, ibid., 46–51; testimony of W. P. Ballinger, ibid., 165.

2. "Death of Hon. M. M. Potter," *Houston Tri-Weekly Telegraph*, Oct. 21, 1863.

3. "The Worst Enemies of Slavery," *Austin Southern Intelligencer*, Jan. 5, 1859. On the role of honor in southern society, see Wyatt-Brown, *Southern Honor*; Greenberg, *Honor & Slavery*.

4. The four cases decided by the Supreme Court were *Webster v. Heard*, 32 Tex. 685 (1870); *Webster v. Corbett*, 34 Tex. 263 (1870–71); *Webster v. Mann*, 52 Tex. 416 (1880); and *Webster v. Mann*, 56 Tex. 119 (1881).

5. DeBow, "American Cities," 348–49; DeBow, "Commerce of American Cities," 403;

McComb, *Galveston*, 6. The 1850 census lists 4,177 residents of Galveston in 1850. U.S. Bureau of the Census, *Seventh Census of the United States*, Texas: Table II—Population of Cities and Towns, 504. David first appears in the Galveston tax records in 1847. *Tax Assessment Rolls of Galveston Cty., Tex., Made for the Year 1847*, s.v. "David Webster," Galveston County Tax Rolls, RL.

6. DeBow, "American Cities," 348–49; McComb, *Galveston*, 34–39, 68–70; Fornell, *Galveston Era*, 140–54.

7. Testimony of Marcia Paschal, transcript of trial, *Webster v. Heard*, no. 3088, pp. 236–38 (general background); testimony of Mary Hopkins, ibid., 230 (general background); inventory, ibid., 49 (listing telescope).

8. Testimony of Thomas Duval, transcript of trial, *Webster v. Heard*, no. 3088, p. 234 (estimating arrival in Florida in 1829 or 1830); testimony of Marcia Paschal, ibid., 238 (estimating arrival between 1820 and 1825); 1830 U.S. Census, Jackson Cty., Fla., s.v. "David Webster," accessed through Ancestry.com (listing David as a resident of Apalachicola); U.S. Bureau of the Census, *Abstract of the Returns of the Fifth Census*, 39; Knauss, "St. Joseph, Part I," 178–79.

9. *Mitchell v. United States*, 34 U.S. 711 (1835); Knauss, "St. Joseph, Part I," 178–80.

10. Knauss, "St. Joseph, Part I," 180; Porter, *Chronological History*, 25.

11. Testimony of Marcia Paschal, transcript of trial, *Webster v. Heard*, no. 3088, p. 236; 1840 U.S. Census, Calhoun Cty., Florida Territory, s.v. "David Webster," accessed through Ancestry.com (listing Webster as the owner of 84 slaves); Knauss, "St. Joseph, Part II," 3–15; testimony of Mary Hopkins, transcript of trial, *Webster v. Heard*, no. 3088, p. 231 ("My mother died with yellow fever in Florida at S. Joseph and Mr. Webster was very attentive during her last illness.").

12. U.S. Bureau of the Census, *Seventh Census of the United States*, Texas: Table II—Population of Cities and Towns, 504; "Shocking Murder," *Galveston Weekly Civilian and Gazette*, Jan. 5, 1858; untitled, *Galveston Weekly Civilian and Gazette*, Jan. 19, 1858.

13. Shelton, "On Empire's Shore," 717; Lack, "Dave," 2–3; untitled, *Galveston Weekly News*, Oct. 7, 1856.

14. *Charter and Revised Code of Ordinances of the City of Galveston, Passed in the Years 1856–57*, 88–93.

15. Gregory, *Records of Interments*, 30 (listing Betsy's age as 100); 1870 U.S. Census, Galveston Cty., Tex., Schedule 1—Inhabitants, s.v. "Betsy Webster," accessed through Ancestry.com (listing Betsy's age as 76 and her birthplace as Mississippi). Thomas Duval testified he had known David since 1830, and "ever since my first acquaintance with Mr. Webster he owned a negro woman named Betsy." Testimony of Thomas Duval, transcript of trial, *Webster v. Heard*, no. 3088, p. 232.

16. Testimony of Jane Hardin, transcript of trial, *Webster v. Heard*, no. 3088, p. 145; testimony of Oscar Farish, ibid., 157, 159; testimony of Mary Hopkins, ibid., 230; testimony of Marcia Paschal, ibid., 237.

17. Letter from Robert Meyers to Messrs. Potter & Ballinger, Sept. 23, 1858, William Pitt Ballinger Papers, CAH; McComb, *Galveston*, 151 ("To be sure, Galveston as a port city had always had a rough side."); Shelton, "On Empire's Shore," 721–23; "Local Intelligence," *Flake's Daily Bulletin*, Nov. 18, 1865.

218 NOTES TO CHAPTER FOUR

18. *Clements v. Crawford*, 42 Tex. 601 (1874); testimony of Mary Hopkins, transcript of trial, *Webster v. Heard*, no. 3088, pp. 230–31; testimony of Marcia Paschal, ibid., 238.

19. Inventory, transcript of trial, *Webster v. Heard*, no. 3088, pp. 46–47.

20. Menard and his associates began selling town lots on April 20, 1838. The following year the Texas legislature granted incorporation to the city of Galveston with the power to elect town officers. McComb, *Galveston*, 42–44; inventory, transcript of trial, *Webster v. Heard*, no. 3088, pp. 46–47.

21. Inventory, transcript of trial, *Webster v. Heard*, no. 3088, pp. 46–47; petition, ibid., 212 (identifying location of homestead); "An Interesting Case," *Galveston Daily News*, Oct. 20, 1878 (petition); *Webster v. Heard*, 32 Tex. 685, 707 (1870) (description of home); Fornell, *Galveston Era*, 92; inventory, transcript of trial, *Webster v. Heard*, no. 3088, pp. 48–51.

22. *Galveston Civilian and Gazette*, March 30, 1858. For more background on Ballinger and his theater reviews, see Moretta, *William Pitt Ballinger*, 94–95.

23. "Port of Galveston," *Texas Almanac for 1858*, 143–44; untitled, *Galveston Civilian*, Oct. 5, 1858; McComb, *Galveston*, 47; Fornell, *Galveston Era*, 23, 90.

24. Fornell, *Galveston Era*, 87–115; untitled, *Galveston Civilian and Gazette*, March 30, 1858.

25. Fornell, *Galveston Era*, 87–88; McComb, *Galveston*, 47–61; "Catalogue of the City Government," *Galveston Weekly News*, July 19, 1859.

26. Fornell, *Galveston Era*, 88; inventory, transcript of trial, *Webster v. Heard*, no. 3088, pp. 48–51.

27. *Tax Assessment Rolls of Galveston Cty., Tex., Made for the Year 1850*, s.v. "M. M. Potter" (indicating that Potter owned several lots on block 207, near David's property), Galveston County Tax Rolls, RL; 1850 U.S. Census, Galveston Cty., Tex., Schedule 1—Free Inhabitants, s.v. "Mark M. Potter," accessed through Ancestry.com (listing birthplace and birth year); "Catalogue of the City Government," *Galveston Weekly News*, July 19, 1859; "Mark Potter"; "Death of Hon. M. M. Potter," *Houston Tri-Weekly Telegraph*, Oct. 21, 1863; "Death of Hon. M. M. Potter," *Austin, Texas State Gazette*, Oct. 21, 1863.

28. "Questions Answered," *Galveston Civilian and Gazette*, July 14, 1857; "Democratic State Convention," *Austin Tri-Weekly State Times*, Jan. 17, 1854; 1850 U.S. Census, Galveston Cty., Tex., Schedule 2—Slave Inhabitants, s.v. "M. M. Potter," accessed through Ancestry.com.

29. Fornell, "Texans and Filibusters," 416 (identifying Potter as a contributor to effort); Fornell, *Galveston Era*, 193–215.

30. "African Slavery," *Texas Almanac for 1858*, 132–33; "An Act concerning offences committed by Negroes," *Laws of the Fourth Legislature of the State of Texas*, chap. 8, in Gammel, *Laws of Texas*, 3:1285, 1298–300; "Offences Against Slaves and Slave Property," *Laws of the Fifth Legislature of the State of Texas*, chap. 49, sec. 46–51, in ibid., 3:1445, 1511; "An Act to prevent slaves from carrying guns or other dangerous weapons," *General Laws of the Sixth Legislature of the State of Texas*, chap. 152, in ibid., 4:419, 499–500; chap. 4, 6–8 in *General Laws of the Seventh Legislature of the State of Texas*, chap. 121, pt. 1, tit. 19, chap. 4–8 (1858), in ibid., 4:873, 1048–49; "An Act to permit Free persons of African descent, to select their own Master and become Slaves," *General Laws of the Seventh Legislature of the State of Texas*, chap. 63, in ibid., 4: 873, 947–49.

31. "Died," *Galveston Weekly News*, May 13, 1856; will, transcript of trial, *Webster v. Heard*, no. 3088, pp. 38–40; testimony of Jane Hardin, ibid., 139–40. For more on clearing up the confusion in Hardin's name, see testimony of J. L. Hardin, transcript of trial, *Webster v. Corbett*, no. 3087, p. 115 (Tex. Dist. Ct., Galveston Cty., Feb. 1866), Supreme Court Records and Briefs, no. M5376, TSLAC.

32. *Hagerty v. Harwell*, 16 Tex. 663 (1856).

33. "Constitution of the Republic of Texas of 1836, General Provisions, sec. 9," in Gammel, *Laws of Texas*, 1:1069, 1079; "The Worst Enemies of Slavery," *Austin Southern Intelligencer*, Jan. 5, 1859.

34. "Sentence Pronounced by Judge Buckley on Anthony Hays," *Galveston Weekly News*, Feb. 10, 1852.

35. The thirty free people of color listed as living in the city of Galveston in the 1850 census are William Lynch, William Carter, Mary Madison, Winny Ervin, Tamor Townsend, Abby Townsend, William Townsend, Judy Jones, Richard Jones, Henry Jones, Ben Jones, Mary Jones, Luke Hall, Ben Cheesman, Celia Carey, Adaline Cooper, Nancy Gautier, George Cooper, Martha Cooper, Theodore Cooper, Ellen Cooper, George Cooper, Ofelia Cooper, Mary Ann Pell, Lucinda Green, William Green, Mary Green, Robert Green, Henry Siegler, and Celia Lee. One other free person of color lived outside the city but still in the county of Galveston. Her name was Eliza Henry. 1850 U.S. Census, Galveston Cty., Tex., Schedule 1—Free Inhabitants, accessed through Ancestry.com.

36. "An Interesting Case," *Galveston Daily News*, Oct. 20, 1878; testimony of Oscar Farish, transcript of trial, *Webster v. Heard*, no. 3088, p. 159; *Webster v. Heard*, 32 Tex. 685, 707 (1870).

37. Testimony of L. A. Thompson, transcript of trial, *Webster v. Heard*, no. 3088, p. 264; petition for probate of will, ibid., 36–38; 1860 U.S. Census, Galveston Cty., Tex., Schedule 2—Slave Inhabitants, s.v. "L. A. Thompson," accessed through Ancestry.com.

38. Petition of Martha Greenwood, transcript of trial, *Webster v. Heard*, no. 3088, pp. 210–22.

39. Ibid. For manumission cases, see *Hunt v. White*, 24 Tex. 643 (1860); *Philleo v. Holliday*, 24 Tex. 38 (1859); *Armstrong v. Jowell*, 24 Tex. 58 (1859); *Purvis v. Sherrod*, 12 Tex. 140 (1854).

40. Testimony of L. A. Thompson, transcript of trial, *Webster v. Heard*, no. 3088, p. 264.

41. Testimony of Jane Hardin, transcript of trial, *Webster v. Heard*, no. 3088, p. 186; testimony of Martin Hardin, ibid., 190; *Purvis v. Sherrod*, 12 Tex. 140 (1854).

42. "Death of Judge Ballinger," *Galveston Daily News*, Jan. 21, 1888. For general background on Ballinger, see Moretta, *William Pitt Ballinger*; Curtsinger, "Career of Judge William P. Ballinger"; King, "William Pitt Ballinger."

43. *City of Galveston v. Menard*, 23 Tex. 349 (1859); "Death of Judge Ballinger," *Galveston Daily News*, Jan. 21, 1888; Moretta, *William Pitt Ballinger*, 72–77; Curtsinger, "Career of Judge William P. Ballinger," 56–58.

44. Diary of William Pitt Ballinger, Dec. 31, 1860, William Pitt Ballinger Papers, CAH; ibid., Nov. 14, 1860; Moretta, *William Pitt Ballinger*, 111–32.

NOTES TO CHAPTER FOUR

45. "Death of Judge Ballinger," *Galveston Daily News*, Jan. 21, 1888; Moretta, *William Pitt Ballinger*, 134–37, 170, 211–20; Curtsinger, "Career of Judge William P. Ballinger," 60, 62.

46. "Death of Judge Ballinger," *Galveston Daily News*, Jan. 21, 1888; Moretta, *William Pitt Ballinger*, 207–9, 223–27; Curtsinger, "Career of Judge William P. Ballinger," 64–69.

47. "Death of Judge Ballinger," *Galveston Daily News*, Jan. 21, 1888; "Judge Ballinger," *Fort Worth Daily Gazette*, Jan. 21, 1888; "W. P. Ballinger," *Waco Daily Examiner*, Jan. 21, 1888; Moretta, *William Pitt Ballinger*, 78, 241–42.

48. *Bryan's Adm'r v. Harvey's Adm'r*, 11 Tex. 311 (1854); *City of Galveston v. Menard*, 23 Tex. 349 (1859); Diary of William Pitt Ballinger, Nov. 14, 1860 ("Potter took half way ground"), William Pitt Ballinger Papers, CAH; letter from William Pitt Ballinger to Lucy Ballinger (daughter), Oct. 11, 1863 (referencing visit to "Mr. Potter, who is extremely ill"), William Pitt Ballinger Papers, RL.

49. Diary of William Pitt Ballinger, May 2, 1857, William Pitt Ballinger Papers, CAH; testimony of W. P. Ballinger, transcript of trial, *Webster v. Heard*, no. 3088, p. 166.

50. Testimony of W. P. Ballinger, transcript of trial, *Webster v. Heard*, no. 3088, p. 165; "Death of Judge Ballinger," *Galveston Daily News*, Jan. 21, 1888; Moretta, *William Pitt Ballinger*, 98–105; Curtsinger, "Career of Judge William P. Ballinger," 58–59.

51. Testimony of W. P. Ballinger, transcript of trial, *Webster v. Heard*, no. 3088, p. 165.

52. Inventory, ibid., 51; testimony of W. P. Ballinger, ibid., 165; Moretta, *William Pitt Ballinger*, 106 (annual income).

53. Diary of William Pitt Ballinger, Jan. 21, 1860, William Pitt Ballinger Papers, CAH.

54. 1860 U.S. Census, Galveston Cty., Tex., Schedule 2—Slave Inhabitants, s.v. "W. P. Ballinger," accessed through Ancestry.com; Diary of William Pitt Ballinger, July 28, 1860 ("Went . . . to look at negroes"), William Pitt Ballinger Papers, CAH; ibid., Jan. 13, 1860 ("Hally took her out home to try her"); ibid., Jan. 24, 1860 ("untruthful negro"); ibid., Aug. 11, 1860 ("liked her face" and "is in a family way"); ibid., Aug. 12, 1860 ("some fault" and the "girls name is Agnes").

55. Letter from William Pitt Ballinger to Hally (wife), Nov. 26, 1864, William Pitt Ballinger Papers, RL; letter from William Pitt Ballinger to Hally (wife), Nov. 28, 1864, William Pitt Ballinger Papers, RL. For a discussion of Dave's case and the larger context of urban slavery, see Lack, "Dave," 1–18.

56. "The Worst Enemies of Slavery," *Austin Southern Intelligencer*, Jan. 5, 1859.

57. James Love to William Pitt Ballinger, June 5, 1858 (quoted in Moretta, *William Pitt Ballinger*, 115). Moretta quotes a handful of other notes and letters to Ballinger from residents of Galveston opposed to his decision to represent Betsy. Ibid.

58. *Webster v. Heard*, 32 Tex. 685, 706 (1870); testimony of A. H. Cleveland, transcript of trial, *Webster v. Heard*, no. 3088, p. 154.

59. Mrs. Hardin's letter to Messr. Potter, transcript of trial, *Webster v. Heard*, no. 3088, p. 137; testimony of John Jones, ibid., 161 ("sensible"); testimony of Granger, ibid., 160 ("quiet peaceable inoffensive person"); Memorials and Petitions to Congress, Petition of Betsy Webster (July 1, 1856), TSLAC.

60. Testimony of John James, transcript of trial, *Webster v. Heard*, no. 3088, p. 161; testimony of W. P. Ballinger, ibid., 166.

61. Testimony of W. P. Ballinger, *Webster v. Heard*, no. 3088, p. 169; 1850 U.S. Census, Galveston Cty., Tex., Schedule 1—Free Inhabitants, s.v. "Ebenezer Allen," accessed through Ancestry.com; ibid., Schedule 2—Slave Inhabitants, s.v. "Ebenezer Allen" (five slaves); 1860 U.S. Census, Galveston Cty., Tex., Schedule 1—Free Inhabitants, s.v. "W Allen," accessed through Ancestry.com.

62. Letter from H. R. Taylor to J. G. Ruau, Sept. 23, 1858, William Pitt Ballinger Papers, CAH; letter from Robert Meyers to Messrs. Potter & Ballinger, Sept. 23, 1858, William Pitt Ballinger Papers, CAH.

63. Letter from Nancy L. Thomson to Mr. M. M. Potter, Apr. 24, 1857, William Pitt Ballinger Papers, CAH; letter from [name illegible] of Henry County, Alabama, to unnamed recipient, May 13, 1857, William Pitt Ballinger Papers, CAH; letter from [name illegible] to Mr. Potter, Apr. 24, 1857, William Pitt Ballinger Papers, CAH.

64. Letter from H. R. Taylor to J. G. Ruau, Sept. 23, 1858, William Pitt Ballinger Papers, CAH; *Jones v. Laney*, 2 Tex. 342, 349 (1847). In addition to *Laney*, for an example of case from Texas upholding the right of an owner to free his slaves with whom he had a personal or sexual relationship, see *Moore v. Mary Minerva and Her Children*, 17 Tex. 20 (1856) and *Moore v. Francis and Her Children*, 17 Tex. 28 (1856). For an analysis contextualizing will disputes and the rights of property during the antebellum period, see Davis, "Private Law."

65. Testimony of John James, transcript of trial, *Webster v. Heard*, no. 3088, p. 161; *Purvis v. Sherrod*, 12 Tex. 140, 141 (1854).

66. *Purvis v. Sherrod*, 12 Tex. at 165, 166.

67. Ibid., 171, 141.

68. Testimony of W. P. Ballinger, transcript of trial, *Webster v. Heard*, no. 3088, p. 168.

69. *Webster v. Heard*, 32 Tex. 685, 700 (1870); see also *Hunt v. White*, 24 Tex. 643 (1860) (finding that will purporting to free slaves was invalid because it did not expressly provide for the manumissions to take place outside of the state).

70. *Webster v. Heard*, 32 Tex. at 700–701; will, transcript of trial, *Webster v. Heard*, no. 3088, p. 39; testimony of W. P. Ballinger, ibid., 169.

71. Letter from H. R. Taylor to J. G. Ruau, Sept. 23, 1858, William Pitt Ballinger Papers, CAH; letter from Robert Meyers to Messrs. Potter & Ballinger, Sept. 23, 1858, William Pitt Ballinger Papers, CAH; letter from John Ruau to Messrs. Potter & Ballinger, Sept. 23, 1858, William Pitt Ballinger Papers, CAH.

72. Testimony of Mary Hopkins, transcript of trial, *Webster v. Heard*, no. 3088, pp. 229–31; testimony of Thomas Duval, ibid., 232; testimony of Marcia Paschal, ibid., 235–36.

73. Affidavit of petitioner for continuance, transcript of trial, *Webster v. Heard*, no. 3088, pp. 240, 241 (stating belief that "said letters must have been lost or miscarried and never came to the hands of the Plf"); final dismissing of *Greenwood v. Martin & Whiting* suit, ibid., 263.

74. Moretta, *William Pitt Ballinger*, 134–39; Campbell, *Gone to Texas*, 253–54, 259–60.

75. Testimony of W. P. Ballinger, transcript of trial, *Webster v. Heard*, no. 3088, pp. 165, 169.

76. Testimony of W. P. Ballinger, ibid., 166; final act and petition for discharge by

admrs, ibid., 68; petition for order of sale of negro Harry, ibid., 54; final accounting, 72–73; decree of court, ibid., 87.

77. Opposition, transcript of trial, *Webster v. Heard*, no. 3088, pp. 78–79; decree of court, ibid., 86; order of sale of land, ibid., 77–78; decree of court, ibid., 87–88.

78. Felix Haywood, in Rawick, *American Slave*, vol. 4, pt. 2, pp. 130–34.

79. Testimony of John Jones, transcript of trial, *Webster v. Heard*, no. 3088, p. 161; testimony of Oscar Farish, ibid., 155–57.

80. Testimony of Col. J. S. Sydnor, transcript of trial, *Webster v. Corbett*, no. 3087, p. 152; testimony of W. P. Ballinger, transcript of trial, *Webster v. Heard*, no. 3088, p. 172; testimony of Oscar Farish, ibid., 156; exhibits A, B, C, D, F to plaintiff's exceptions, ibid., 276–91, 295–98.

81. Second amended petition, transcript of trial, *Webster v. Corbett*, no. 3087, p. 10 ("agent or guardian"); testimony of Oscar Farish, ibid., 91–92 (use of agents, including Corbett, and location of homes); testimony of John Corbett, transcript of trial, *Webster v. Heard*, no. 3088, p. 208 ("Potter advised it"); exhibit B to plaintiff's exceptions, ibid., 280–83 (deed for homestead); testimony of Oscar Farish, ibid., 157 ("hold property for her benefit"); testimony of J. M. Hill, transcript of trial, *Webster v. Corbett*, no. 3087, p. 141 (banana plants); deed, ibid., 121–22; testimony of John S. Jones, ibid., 124 ("never worth more than fourteen hundred dollars in witnesses opinion—if Corbett paid more he paid too much for them"); testimony of Sydney Fontaine, ibid., 136 (signing of deed); testimony of Oscar Farish, transcript of trial, *Webster v. Heard*, no. 3088, 158 ($6,000).

82. Testimony of Oscar Farish, transcript of trial, *Webster v. Heard*, no. 3088, pp. 158–59; testimony of W. P. Ballinger, ibid., 168.

83. Testimony of A. H. Cleveland, transcript of trial, *Webster v. Heard*, no. 3088, pp. 154–55; testimony of Granger, ibid., 160; testimony of Oscar Farish, transcript of trial, *Webster v. Corbett*, no. 3087, p. 92; testimony of Balderdice, transcript of trial, *Webster v. Heard*, no. 3088, p. 160.

84. *Webster v. Heard*, 32 Tex. 685, 708 (1870).

85. *Webster v. Mann*, 52 Tex. 416, 417–19 (1880) (quoting testimony that Betsy was "of sound mind" and referencing documents referring to Baker as Betsy's "adopted son" and stating his obligation to "keep up the ground as a garden"); 1870 U.S. Census, Galveston Cty., Tex., Schedule 1—Inhabitants, s.v. "Thomas Baker," accessed through Ancestry.com (identifying Baker as a "mulatto" and stating his occupation as a gardener).

86. Untitled, *Austin, Texas State Gazette*, Dec. 28, 1861; untitled, *Flake's Weekly Bulletin*, Sept. 6, 1865; untitled, *Flake's Weekly Bulletin*, Sept. 27, 1865. Jesse's brother, G. W. Stancel, appears in the 1870 census records for Galveston as a thirty-five-year-old attorney from Alabama. 1870 U.S. Census, Galveston Cty., Tex., Schedule 1—Inhabitants, s.v. "G. W. Stancel," accessed through Ancestry.com. Jesse cannot be located. A person with the name Jesse "Stenzel," however, begins appearing in the Galveston tax records in 1868, and is likely him. *Tax Assessment Rolls of Galveston Cty., Tex., Made for the Year 1868*, s.v. "Jesse Stenzel," Galveston County Tax Rolls, RL. A newspaper report indicates that he was still living in Galveston in 1874, when he shows up as an officer in a memorial for Charles Sumner. "Sumner," *Galveston Daily News*, Mar. 20, 1874.

87. *Tax Assessment Rolls of Galveston Cty., Tex., Made for the Year 1868*, s.v. "Jesse

Stenzel" (listing net income of $200), Galveston County Tax Rolls, RL; ibid., *Made for the Year 1869*, s.v. "Jesse Stenzel" (listing annual income of $225); ibid., *Made for the Year 1870*, s.v. "Jesse Stenzel" (listing annual income of $900); 1880 U.S. Census, Huntsville, Walker Cty., Tex., Schedule 6—Inhabitants in Prison, s.v. "Jesse Stancel," accessed through Ancestry.com; "Great Texas Land Theft," *Galveston Daily News*, Nov. 7, 1879; "An Old Acquaintance," *Galveston Daily News*, June 5, 1879; "State News," *Galveston Daily News*, Feb. 19, 1876; *Stancel v. State*, 6 Tex. Ct. App. 460 (1879); "Attempt to Assassinate—Stabbed, Etc.," *Galveston Daily News*, June 3, 1879; "Not a Partner," *Galveston Daily News*, June 8, 1879; "Attempt to Rob the Deaf and Dumb Asylum—Lively Skirmish," *Galveston Daily News*, Mar. 27, 1880; *A. H. Belo & Co. v. Wren*, 63 Tex. 686 (1884).

88. Diary of William Pitt Ballinger, Jan. 6, 1859, William Pitt Ballinger Papers, CAH; testimony of W. P. Ballinger, transcript of trial, *Webster v. Heard*, no. 3088, p. 170.

89. Petition, transcript of trial, *Webster v. Heard*, no. 3088, pp. 1, 3; *Webster v. Heard*, 32 Tex. at 689.

90. *Webster*, 32 Tex. at 695; *Webster to Stancel & Wiley*, Galveston County Deed Book 8, p. 62 (Sept. 3, 1868), GCC; judgment, transcript of trial, *Webster v. Heard*, no. 3088, p. 1.

91. *Webster*, 32 Tex. at 710–11.

92. Ibid., 711. For background on Chief Justice Amos Morrill, see "Morrill, Amos," *Handbook of Texas Online*, http://www.tshaonline.org/handbook/online/articles/fm054, accessed Sept. 11, 2015, uploaded June 15, 2010, published by the Texas State Historical Association.

93. Testimony of Oscar Farish, transcript of trial, *Webster v. Corbett*, no. 3087, p. 92 ("Betsy was very suspicious"); testimony of Col. J. S. Sydnor, ibid., 155 ("very smart"); exhibit B to plaintiff's exceptions, transcript of trial, *Webster v. Heard*, no. 3088, pp. 280–83 (deed to Corbett); testimony of John Corbett, ibid., 208 ("she made the trouble" and "had her arrested for assault"); exhibit E to plaintiff's exceptions, ibid., 291–94 (deed to Farish); amended answer, transcript of trial, *Webster v. Corbett*, no. 3087, p. 19 ("with force and arms"); testimony of John S. Jones, ibid., 125 ("it was understood that Gen'l Gregory of the Freedman's Bureau took possession of the lots"); petition, ibid., 3. For more on the Freedmen's Bureau, see Crouch, "Guardian of the Freedpeople"; C. Elliott, "Freedmen's Bureau in Texas."

94. Petition, transcript of trial, *Webster v. Corbett*, no. 3087, p. 5; amended petition, ibid., 8; second amended petition, ibid., 9–10. For testimony surrounding the sale of lots to Corbett, see testimony of Oscar Farish, ibid., 89–91; testimony of John S. Jones, ibid., 123; testimony of J. M. Hill, ibid., 141; testimony of Col. J. S. Sydnor, ibid., 152–53; testimony of Frengat Schalter, ibid., 158.

95. Verdict, transcript of trial, *Webster v. Corbett*, no. 3087, p. 1; *Webster v. Corbett*, 34 Tex. 263, 266 (1870–71).

96. Norvell, "Reconstruction Courts of Texas." For a discussion of the Court's opinion in *Honey v. Clark* and more on the Semicolon Court, see chap. 1.

97. *Webster v. Mann*, 52 Tex. 416, 417–20 (1880); see also "An Interesting Case," *Galveston Daily News*, Oct. 20, 1878. For later stages of the case, including an amended petition filed by reputed heirs, see transcript of trial, *Webster v. Mann*, no. 9462 (Tex. Dist. Ct., Galveston Cty., Dec. 1880), Supreme Court Records and Briefs, no. M7970, TSLAC.

98. *Webster v. Mann*, 52 Tex. at 420; sixth amended petition, transcript of trial, *Webster v. Mann*, no. 9462, p. 17; testimony of Col. J. S. Sydnor, transcript of trial, *Webster v. Corbett*, no. 3087, p. 155 ("woman of most excellent judgment"); testimony of Frengat Schalter, ibid., 158 ("desired us to act for her"); testimony of John S. Jones, ibid., 124 ("sharp in a trade" and "competent to act for herself"). The case reached the Texas Supreme Court twice. Betsy lost both. The citation to the first is *Webster v. Mann*, 52 Tex. 416 (1880). The citation to the second is *Webster v. Mann*, 56 Tex. 119 (1881).

99. Gregory, *Records of Interments*, 30.

CONCLUSION. Telling Stories of Slavery and Freedom

1. Transcript from Limestone County, jury verdict, *Gaines v. Thomas*, no. 426, p. 5 (Tex. Dist. Ct., McLennan Cty., Apr. 1857), McLennan County District Court Records, MCC; statement of facts, testimony of Dr. Slater, *Gaines v. Thomas*, no. 175, pp. 5–6 (Tex. Dist. Ct., Limestone Cty., Aug. 1855), McLennan County District Court Records, MCC; *Gaines v. Ann*, 17 Tex. 211, 215 (1856).

2. Transcript from Limestone County, *Gaines v. Thomas*, no. 426, pp. 7–8; ibid., 8–9; amended petition, ibid., 1; "McLennan," *Texas Almanac for 1859*, 178–79. There were 663 families in McLennan County in 1860. U.S. Bureau of the Census, *Statistics of the United States*, Miscellaneous Statistics: Number of Families and Free Population, 1860, 349. Two hundred seventy, or 40 percent, owned at least one slave. Twenty-seven families owned twenty or more. U.S. Bureau of the Census, *Agriculture of the United States in 1860*, Texas: Slaveholders and Slaves, 241.

3. Statement of facts, testimony of Louis Vanlandingham, *Gaines v. Thomas*, no. 426, pp. 1–3; testimony of Mary Vanlandingham, ibid., 3–4; testimony of Dr. Samuel Rhodes, ibid., 5–7; Chesnut, *Mary Chesnut's Civil War*, 29.

4. Statement of facts, testimony of Louis Vanlandingham, *Gaines v. Thomas*, no. 426, pp. 1–3; testimony of Mary Vanlandingham, ibid., 3–5; testimony of Dr. Samuel Rhodes, ibid., 5–7; testimony of Strother M. Hawkins, ibid., 7–8.

5. Statement of facts, testimony of Dr. Samuel Rhodes, *Gaines v. Thomas*, no. 426, p. 6; testimony of Mary Vanlandingham, ibid., 4 ("it was impossible for any exchange of children to have taken place").

6. Statement of facts, testimony of Dr. [name illegible], *Gaines v. Thomas*, no. 426, p. 8; testimony of Mrs. McLennan, ibid., 9; verdict, ibid., 1; see Gross, *What Blood Won't Tell*.

7. *Gaines v. Ann*, 26 Tex. 340, 342 (1862).

8. Statement of facts, testimony of Strother M. Hawkins, *Gaines v. Thomas*, no. 426, p. 7.

9. *Gaines v. Ann*, 17 Tex. at 215–16.

BIBLIOGRAPHY

Primary Sources
UNPUBLISHED DOCUMENTS
Colorado County Courthouse, Columbus, Texas
Colorado County Deed Book.
Colorado County Spanish Translations Deed Book.

Dolph Briscoe Center for American History, University of Texas, Austin, Texas
Charles William Tait Papers.
William Pitt Ballinger Papers.

East Texas Research Center, Stephen F. Austin University, Nacogdoches, Texas
San Augustine County Deed Book.
San Augustine County District Court Records.
San Augustine County Probate Records.
San Augustine County Tax Rolls.
San Augustine County, Texas Records.
William F. Price Collection.

Galveston County Courthouse, Galveston, Texas
Galveston County Deed Book.

Jefferson County Courthouse, Beaumont, Texas
Jefferson County Court Minute Book.
Jefferson County Marriage Book.
Jefferson County Marks and Brands Book.
Jefferson County Probate Records.

McLennan County Courthouse, Waco, Texas
McLennan County District Court Records.

Orange County Courthouse, Orange, Texas
Orange County Deed Book.
Orange County Marks and Brands Book.
Orange County Probate Records.

Rosenberg Library, Galveston, Texas
Galveston County Tax Rolls.
William Pitt Ballinger Papers.

Sam Houston Regional Library and Research Center, Liberty, Texas
Jefferson County District Court Minute Book.
Orange County District Court Docket Book.
Orange County District Court Minute Book.
Orange County District Court Records.
Orange County Tax Rolls.

South Caroliniana Library, University of South Carolina, Columbia, South Carolina
Charles James McDonald Furman Papers.

St. Landry Parish Courthouse, Opelousas, Louisiana
Marriage Licenses.

Texas State Library and Archives Commission, Austin, Texas
Memorials and Petitions to Congress.
Supreme Court Records and Briefs.

Texas General Land Office, Austin, Texas
Padrón a la Colonia de Austin.
Texas Land Grant Records.
Mexican Land Grant Records.

Tyrrell Historical Library, Beaumont, Texas
Jefferson County Tax Rolls.

Wharton County Courthouse, Wharton, Texas
Wharton County District Court Minute Book.

Wharton County Courthouse Annex, Wharton, Texas
Wharton County Deed Book.
Wharton County Probate Book.

Wharton County Historical Museum, Wharton, Texas
Wharton County District Court Records.
Miscellaneous Papers.

PUBLISHED GOVERNMENT DOCUMENTS AND OFFICIAL SOURCES

Appendix to the Journals of the House of Representatives: Fifth Congress. Austin: Printed at the Gazette Office, 1841.

Bugbee, Lester G. "The Old Three Hundred: A List of Settlers in Austin's First Colony," *Quart. of the Texas State Hist. Assoc.* 1, no. 2 (1897): 108–17.

Campbell, Randolph B., ed. *The Laws of Slavery in Texas.* Austin: University of Texas Press, 2010.

Charter and Revised Code of Ordinances of the City of Galveston, Passed in the Years 1856–57. Galveston: Printed at the Civilian Book and Job Office, 1857.

Gammel, H. P. N., comp. *The Laws of Texas, 1822–1897*. 10 vols. Austin: Gammel Book Co., 1898–1902.

"General Austin's Order Book for the Campaign of 1835." *Quart. of the Texas State Hist. Assoc.* 11, no. 1 (1907): 1–55.

Gregory, Peggy H. *Records of Interments of the City of Galveston, 1859–1872*. Houston: N.p., 1976.

Hartley, Oliver Cromwell. *A Digest of the Laws of Texas: To which is Subjoined an Appendix Containing the Acts of the Congress of the United States on the Subjects of the Naturalization of Aliens, and the Authentication of Records, Etc.* Philadelphia: Thomas, Cowperthwait & Co., 1850.

Inventory of the County Archives of Texas: Orange County. San Antonio: Texas Historical Records Survey, 1941.

Journals of the House of Representatives of the Republic of Texas: Fifth Congress, First Session, 1840–1841. Austin: Cruger and Wing, Public Printers, 1841.

Journals of the House of Representatives of the Seventh Congress of the Republic of Texas. Washington, D.C.: Thomas Johnson, Public Printer, 1843.

Journals of the Senate of the Republic of Texas: Fifth Congress—First Session. Houston: Printed at the Telegraph Office, 1841.

Mullins, Marion Day, comp. *Republic of Texas: Poll Lists for 1846*. Baltimore, Md.: Genealogical Publishing Co., 1974.

A Report and Treatise on Slavery and the Slavery Agitation. Austin: John Marshall & Co., 1857.

Schoen, Harold. "State Census of 1847." *Southwestern Hist. Quart.* 50 (1946): 116–18.

Swent, Vivian Hébert. *Antioch Primitive Baptist Church, Big Wood Louisiana: Church Records 1827–1903*. San Francisco: N.p., 1966.

United States Bureau of the Census, Washington, D.C. *Abstract of the Returns of the Fifth Census: 1830. Showing the Number of Free People, the Number of Slaves, the Federal or Representative Number, and the Aggregate of Each County of Each State of the United States*. Washington, D.C.: Duff Green, 1832.

———. *Agriculture of the United States in 1860; Compiled from the Original Returns of the Eighth Census*. Washington, D.C.: Government Printing Office, 1864.

———. *Manufactures of the United States in 1860; Compiled from the Original Returns of the Eighth Census*. Washington, D.C.: Government Printing Office, 1865.

———. *Population of the United States in 1860; Compiled from the Original Returns of the Eighth Census*. Washington, D.C.: Government Printing Office, 1864.

———. *Return of the Whole Number of Persons within the Several Districts of the United States*. Washington, D.C.: Government Printing Office, 1800.

———. *The Seventh Census of the United States: 1850. Embracing a Statistical View of Each of the States and Territories*. Washington, D.C.: Robert Armstrong, 1853.

———. *Statistical View of the United States, Being a Compendium of the Seventh Census*. Washington, D.C.: Beverley Tucker, Senate Printer, 1854.

———. *The Statistics of the Population of the United States; Compiled from the Original Returns of the Ninth Census.* Washington, D.C.: Government Printing Office, 1872.

———. *Statistics of the United States (Including Mortality, Property, &c.,) in 1860; Compiled from the Original Returns and Being the Final Exhibit of the Eighth Census.* Washington, D.C.: Government Printing Office, 1866.

———. United States Federal Census for the Years 1790 through 1880, accessed through Ancestry.com.

White, Gifford, ed. *The 1840 Census of the Republic of Texas.* Austin: Pemberton Press, 1966.

PUBLISHED CORRESPONDENCE AND CONTEMPORARY ACCOUNTS

Barker, Eugene C., ed. *The Papers of Stephen F. Austin.* 3 vols. Washington, D.C.: U.S. Government Printing Office, 1924–1928.

Binkley, William C., ed. *Official Correspondence of the Texas Revolution, 1835–1836.* 2 vols. New York: D. Appleton-Century Co., 1936.

Chesnut, Mary. *Mary Chesnut's Civil War.* Edited by C. Vann Woodward. New Haven, Conn.: Yale University Press, 1981.

DeBow, James D. B. "American Cities: The City of Galveston." *DeBow's Review* 3, no. 4 (1847): 345–50.

———. "Commerce of American Cities: Galveston, Texas." *DeBow's Review* 4, no. 3 (1847): 391–404.

———. "Overseers at the South." *DeBow's Review* 21, no. 3 (1856): 277–79.

———. "Texas." *DeBow's Review* 10, no. 6 (1851): 627–45.

———. "Texas—Character of the Country, Emigrants, Etc." *DeBow's Review* 20, no. 2 (1856): 241a–248a.

Faust, Drew Gilpin, ed. *The Ideology of Slavery: Proslavery Thought in the Antebellum South, 1830–1860.* Baton Rouge: LSU Press, 1981.

Gray, William Fairfax. *The Diary of William Fairfax Gray, from Virginia to Texas, 1835.* Edited by Paul D. Lack. Dallas: DeGolyer Library & William P. Clements Center for Southwest Studies, Southern Methodist University, 1997.

Gulick, Charles Adam, Jr., and Katherine Elliot, eds. *The Papers of Mirabeau Buonaparte Lamar.* 6 vols. Austin: A. C. Baldwin Printers, 1922.

Harris, Dilue. "The Reminiscences of Mrs. Dilue Harris I." *Quart. of the Texas State Hist. Assoc.* 4, no. 2 (1900): 85–127.

———. "The Reminiscences of Mrs. Dilue Harris II." *Quart. of the Texas State Hist. Assoc.* 4, no. 3 (1901): 155–89.

Hodges, Willis Augustus. *Free Man of Color: The Autobiography of Willis Augustus Hodges.* Edited by Willard B. Gatewood Jr. Knoxville: University of Tennessee Press, 1982.

Hogan, William Ransom, and Edwin Adams Davis, eds. *William Johnson's Natchez: The Ante-Bellum Diary of a Free Negro.* Baton Rouge: Louisiana State University Press, 1993.

Holly, Mary Austin. *Texas: Observations, Historical, Geographical and Descriptive, in a*

Series of Letters; Written During a Visit to Austin's Colony With a View to Permanent Settlement in That Country in the Autumn of 1831. London: Forgotten Books, 2013.

Horton, Albert. "Life of A. Horton and Early Settlement of San Augustine County." *Quart. of the Texas Hist. Assoc.* 14, no. 4 (1911): 305–8.

"Isaac N. Baughman," *RootsWeb*. Last accessed August 26, 2016. http://freepages.history.rootsweb.ancestry.com/~barrettbranches/sherriff/isaacnbaughman.html.

Jacobs, Harriet A. *Incidents in the Life of a Slave Girl*. Edited by Jean Fagan Yellin. Cambridge, Mass.: Harvard University Press, 2000.

"Journal of William F. S. Alexander," *RootsWeb*. Last accessed August 26, 2016. http://freepages.history.rootsweb.ancestry.com/~barrettbranches/plantations/fleetwood/alexanderjournal.html).

Kuykendall, J. H. "Reminiscences of Early Texans." *Quart. of the Texas State Hist. Assoc.* 6, no. 3 (1903): 236–53.

———. "Reminiscences of Early Texans." *Quart. of the Texas State Hist. Assoc.* 6, no. 4 (1903): 311–30.

———. "Reminiscences of Early Texans." *Quart. of the Texas State Hist. Assoc.* 7, no. 1 (1903): 29–64.

Lane, Lunsford. *The Narrative of Lunsford Lane, formerly of Raleigh, N.C., embracing an account of his early life, the redemption by purchase of himself and family from slavery, and his banishment from the place of his birth for the crime of wearing a colored skin*. 2nd ed. Boston: Lunsford Lane, 1842.

Lundy, Benjamin. *The Life, Travels and Opinions of Benjamin Lundy, Including His Journeys to Texas and Mexico; with a Sketch of Contemporary Events, and a Notice of the Revolution in Hayti*. Philadelphia: William D. Parrish, 1847.

Olmsted, Frederick Law. *A Journey through Texas: Or, a Saddle-Trip on the Southwestern Frontier*. Edited by Randolph B. Campbell. Dallas: Southern Methodist University Press, 2004.

Parker, Amos Andrew. *Trip to the West and Texas*. 1835. Reprint, New York: Arno Press, 1973.

Rawick, George P., ed. *The American Slave: A Composite Autobiography*. Series 1 (7 vols.) and supplement, series 2 (10 vols.). Westport, Conn.: Greenwood Press, 1972.

Russell, Robert E. *A History of Orange*. Edited by Loren LeBlanc. Orange, Tex.: Orange County Historical Society, 1911.

Shindler, Emma B. "San Augustine." *Quart. of the Texas State Hist. Assoc.* 3, no. 1 (1899): 41–43.

The Texas Almanac for 1858. Galveston: Richardson & Co., 1857.

The Texas Almanac for 1859. Galveston: Richardson & Co., 1858.

The Texas Almanac for 1871, and Emigrant's Guide to Texas. Galveston: Richardson & Co., 1871.

Secondary Sources

Addington, Wendell G. "Slave Insurrections in Texas." *Journal of Negro History* 35, no. 4 (1950): 408–34.

Ariens, Michael. *Lone Star Law: A Legal History of Texas.* Lubbock: Texas Tech University Press, 2011.

Barker, Eugene C. "The African Slave Trade in Texas." *Quart. of the Texas State Hist. Assoc.* 6, no. 2 (1902): 145–58.

———. "The Influence of Slavery in the Colonization of Texas." *Mississippi Valley Hist. Rev.* 11, no. 1 (1924): 3–36.

Barr, Alwyn. *Black Texans: A History of African Americans in Texas, 1528–1995.* 2nd ed. Norman: University of Oklahoma Press, 1996.

———, and Robert A. Calvert, eds. *Black Leaders: Texans for Their Times.* Austin: Texas State Historical Association, 1981.

Barrett, Faydell Lomma. "Slavery in the Economy of San Augustine County, Texas 1837–1860." Master's thesis, Prairie View Agricultural and Mechanical College, 1963.

Baum, Dale. *Counterfeit Justice: The Judicial Odyssey of Texas Freedwoman Azeline Hearne.* Baton Rouge: Louisiana State University Press, 2009.

Bertleth, Rosa Groce. "Jared Ellison Groce." *Southwestern Hist. Quart.* 20, no. 4 (1917): 358–68.

Berlin, Ira. *Slaves without Masters: The Free Negro in the Antebellum South.* New York: Pantheon Books, 1974.

Block, W. T. *A History of Jefferson County, Texas, from Wilderness to Reconstruction.* Nederland, Tex.: Nederland Publishing Company, 1976.

Breen, T. H., and Stephen Innes. *"Myne Owne Ground": Race and Freedom on Virginia's Eastern Shore, 1640–1676.* 25th anniv. ed. New York: Oxford University Press, 2005.

Broussard, James R., and James Michael Gaddy. *The Church at Lake Charles, Louisiana, 1850's to 1910.* Edited by Donald J. Herbert. N.p.: D. J. Herbert, 1976.

Bugbee, Lester G. "Slavery in Early Texas I." *Political Science Quart.* 13, no. 3 (1898): 389–412.

———. "Slavery in Early Texas II." *Political Science Quart.* 13, no. 4 (1898): 648–68.

Campbell, Randolph B. *An Empire for Slavery: The Peculiar Institution in Texas, 1821–1865.* Baton Rouge: Louisiana State University Press, 1989.

———. *Gone to Texas: A History of the Lone Star State.* New York: Oxford University Press, 2003.

———. "Intermittent Slave Ownership: Texas as a Test Case." *Journal of Southern History* 51, no. 1 (1985): 15–23.

———. "Political Conflict within the Southern Consensus: Harrison County, Texas, 1850–1880." *Civil War History* 26, no. 3 (1980): 218–39.

———. "Research Note: Slave Hiring in Texas." *American Hist. Rev.* 93, no. 1 (1988): 107–14.

———. *A Southern Community in Crisis: Harris County, Texas, 1850–1880.* Austin: Texas State Historical Association, 1983.

———, and Richard G. Lowe. *Wealth and Power in Antebellum Texas.* College Station: Texas A&M University Press, 1977.

Carroll, Mark M. *Homesteads Ungovernable: Families, Sex, Race, and the Law in Frontier Texas, 1823–1860.* Austin: University of Texas Press, 2001.

Clinton, Catherine. *The Plantation Mistress: Woman's World in the Old South*. New York: Pantheon, 1982.
Coontz, Stephanie. *Marriage, a History: How Love Conquered Marriage*. New York: Penguin, 2006.
Cott, Nancy. *Public Vows: A History of Marriage and the Nation*. Cambridge, Mass.: Harvard University Press, 2000.
Crisp, James E. *Sleuthing the Alamo: Davy Crockett's Last Stand and Other Mysteries of the Texas Revolution*. New York: Oxford University Press, 2005.
Crocket, George Louis. *Two Centuries in East Texas: A History of San Augustine County and Surrounding Territory from 1685 to the Present Time*. Dallas: Southwest Press, 1932.
Crouch, Barry A. "The 'Chords of Love': Legalizing Black Marital and Family Rights in Postwar Texas." *Journal of Negro History* 79, no. 4 (1994): 334–51.
———. *Dance of Freedom: Texas African Americans during Reconstruction*. Ed. Larry Madaras. Austin: University of Texas Press, 2007.
———. *The Freedmen's Bureau and Black Texans*. Austin: University of Texas Press, 1992.
Curlee, Abigail. "The History of a Texas Slave Plantation, 1831–1863." *Southwestern Hist. Quart.* 26, no. 2 (1922): 79–127.
———. "Study of Texas Slave Plantations, 1822–1865." PhD diss., University of Texas, 1932.
Curtsinger, Louise C. "The Career of Judge William P. Ballinger." *West Texas Hist. Association Year Book* 18 (1942): 54–71.
Davis, Adrienne D. "Identity Notes Part One: Playing in the Light." *American Univ. Law Rev.* 45, no. 3 (1996): 695–720.
———. "The Private Law of Race and Sex: An Antebellum Perspective." *Stanford Law Rev.* 51, no. 2 (1999): 221–88.
DeMarce, Virginia Easley. "Looking at Legends—Lumbee and Melungeon: Applied Genealogy and the Origins of Tri-racial Isolate Settlements." *Nat'l Genealogical Soc'y Quart.* 81, no. 1 (1993): 24–39.
———. "'Verry Slitly Mixt': Tri-racial Isolate Families of the Upper South—A Genealogical Study." *Nat'l Genealogical Soc'y Quart.* 80, no. 1 (1992): 5–35.
Dickens, Charles. *Bleak House*. 1852. Reprint, New York: Bantam Books, 1992.
Dillon, Merton L. "Benjamin Lundy in Texas." *Southwestern Hist. Quart.* 63, no. 1 (1960): 46–62.
Elliott, Claude. "The Freedmen's Bureau in Texas." *Southwestern Hist. Quart.* 56, no. 1 (1952): 1–24.
Elliott, Michael A. "Telling the Difference: Nineteenth-Century Legal Narratives of Racial Taxonomy." *Law & Social Inquiry* 24, no. 3 (1999): 611–36.
Ely, Melvin Patrick. *Israel on the Appomattox: A Southern Experiment in Black Freedom from the 1790s through the Civil War*. New York: Vintage Books, 2004.
Estes, Roberta J., Jack H. Goins, Penny Ferguson, and Janet Lewis Crain. "Melungeons, A Multi-Ethnic Population." *Journal of Genetic Genealogy* 7 (2011), 1–108. http://www.jogg.info/72/files/Estes.pdf.

Exley, Jo Ella Powell. *Frontier Blood: The Saga of the Parker Family*. College Station: Texas A&M University Press, 2001.

Fede, Andrew. *People without Rights: An Interpretation of the Fundamentals of the Law of Slavery in the U.S. South*. New York: Garland Publishing, 1992.

Fehrenbach, T. R. *Lone Star: A History of Texas and the Texans*. Boulder, Colo.: Da Capo Press, 2000.

Fields, Barbara Jeanne. *Slavery and Freedom on the Middle Ground: Maryland during the Nineteenth Century*. New Haven, Conn.: Yale University Press, 1985.

Fisher, John E. "The Legal Status of Free Blacks in Texas, 1836–1861." *Texas Southern Univ. L. Rev.* 4, no. 3 (1976): 342–62.

Fornell, Earl Wesley. "The Abduction of Free Negroes and Slaves in Texas." *Southwestern Hist. Quart.* 60, no. 3 (1957): 369–80.

———. "Agitation in Texas for Reopening the Slave Trade." *Southwestern Hist. Quart.* 60, no. 2 (1956): 245–59.

———. *The Galveston Era: The Texas Crescent on the Eve of Secession*. Austin: University of Texas Press, 1961.

———. "Texans and Filibusters in the 1850s." *Southwestern Hist. Quart.* 59, no. 4 (1956): 411–28.

"Francis Franks." *Legislative Reference Library of Texas*. Last accessed August 26, 2016. http://www.lrl.state.tx.us/legeLeaders/members/memberDisplay.cfm?memberID=4433&searchparams=chamber=~city=~countyID=0~RcountyID=~district=~first=~gender=~last=franks~leaderNote=~leg=~party=~roleDesc=~Committee=.

Franklin, John Hope. *The Free Negro in North Carolina, 1790–1860*. 2nd ed. Chapel Hill: University of North Carolina Press, 1995.

Fredrickson, George M. *The Black Image in the White Mind: The Debate on Afro-American Character and Destiny, 1817–1914*. New York: Harper & Row, 1971.

Genovese, Eugene. *Roll, Jordan, Roll: The World the Slaves Made*. New York: Vintage Books, 1972.

Glasrud, Bruce A., ed. *African Americans in South Texas History*. College Station: Texas A&M University Press, 2001.

Gordon-Reed, Annette. *The Hemingses of Monticello: An American Family*. New York: Norton, 2008.

Greenberg, Kenneth S. *Honor & Slavery: Lies, Duels, Noses, Masks, Dressing as a Woman, Gifts, Strangers, Humanitarianism, Death, Slave Rebellions, the Proslavery Argument, Baseball, Hunting, and Gambling in the Old South*. Princeton, N.J.: Princeton University Press, 1996.

Gross, Ariela J. "Beyond Black and White: Cultural Approaches to Race and Slavery." *Columbia Law Rev.* 101, no. 3 (2001): 640–89.

———. *Double Character: Slavery and Mastery in the Antebellum Southern Courtroom*. Princeton, N.J.: Princeton University Press, 2000.

———. "Litigating Whiteness: Trials of Racial Determination in the Nineteenth Century South." *Yale Law Journal* 108, no. 1 (1998): 109–88.

———. "'Of Portuguese Origin': Litigating Identity and Citizenship among the 'Little Races' in Nineteenth-Century America." *Law and History Rev.* 25, no. 3 (2007): 467–512.

———. *What Blood Won't Tell: A History of Race on Trial in America.* Cambridge, Mass.: Harvard University Press, 2008.

Hales, Douglas. *A Southern Family in White & Black: The Cuneys of Texas.* College Station: Texas A&M University Press, 2003.

Halliburton, R., Jr. "Free Black Owners of Slaves: A Reappraisal of the Woodson Thesis." *S.C. Hist. Magazine* 76, no. 3 (1975): 129–42.

Haney-Lopez, Ian F. "The Social Construction of Race: Some Observations on Illusion, Fabrication, and Choice." *Harvard Civil Rights–Civil Liberties Law Rev.* 29, no. 1 (1994): 1–62.

———. *White by Law: The Legal Construction of Race.* New York: New York University Press, 1996.

Harper, Cecil, Jr. "Slavery without Cotton: Hunt County, Texas, 1846–1864." *Southwestern Hist. Quart.* 88, no. 4 (1985): 387–405.

Harris, Cheryl. "Whiteness as Property." *Harvard Law Rev.* 106, no. 8 (1993): 1707–91.

Hartog, Hendrik. *Man and Wife in America: A History.* Cambridge, Mass.: Harvard University Press, 2000.

Haynes, Sam W., and Cary D. Wintz, eds. *Major Problems in Texas History.* Boston: Wadsworth, 2002.

Heinegg, Paul. *Free African Americans of North Carolina and Virginia.* Genealogical Publishing, 1999. http://www.freeafricanamericans.com.

Higginbotham, A. Leon, Jr., and Barbara K. Kopytoff. "Property First, Humanity Second: The Recognition of the Slave's Human Nature in Virginia Civil Law." *Ohio State Law Journal* 50, no. 3 (1989): 511–40.

Hodes, Martha. *White Women, Black Men: Illicit Sex in the 19th-Century South.* New Haven, Conn.: Yale University Press, 1997.

Howren, Alleine, "Causes and Origins of the Decree of April 6, 1830." *Southwestern Hist. Quart.* 16, no. 4 (1913): 378–422.

Ivan, Adrien D. "Masters No More: Abolition and Texas Planters, 1860–1890." PhD diss., University of North Texas, 2010.

Jackson, Susan. "Slavery in Houston: The 1850s." *Houston Rev.* 2 (1980): 66–82.

Johnson, Michael P., and James L. Roark. *Black Masters: A Free Family of Color in the Old South.* New York: W. W. Norton, 1984.

Johnson, Walter. "Inconsistency, Contradiction, and Complete Confusion: The Everyday Life of the Law of Slavery." *Law & Social Inquiry* 22, no. 2 (1997): 405–33.

———. *Soul by Soul: Life Inside the Antebellum Slave Market.* Cambridge, Mass.: Harvard University Press, 1999.

Jordan, Winthrop. *White over Black: American Attitudes Toward the Negro, 1550–1812.* New York: W. W. Norton, 1968.

Kelley, Sean. "'Mexico in His Head': Slavery and the Texas-Mexico Border, 1810–1860." *Journal of Social History* 37, no. 3 (2004): 709–23.

King, C. Richard. "William Pitt Ballinger: Texas Bibliophile." *Texas Libraries* 31 (1969): 154–61.

Knauss, James Owen. "St. Joseph, an Episode of the Economic and Political History of Florida, Part I." *Florida Hist. Soc'y Quart.* 5, no. 4 (1927): 177–95.

———. "St. Joseph, an Episode of the Economic and Political History of Florida, Part II." *Florida Hist. Soc'y Quart.* 6, no. 1 (1927): 3–20.

Koger, Larry. *Black Slaveowners: Free Black Slave Masters in South Carolina.* Jefferson, N.C.: McFarland, 1985.

Kosary, Rebecca A. "'Wantonly Maltreated and Slain, Simply Because They Are Free': Racial Violence during Reconstruction in South Texas." In *African Americans in South Texas History*, edited by Bruce A. Glasrud. College Station: Texas A&M University Press, 2001.

Lack, Paul D. "Dave: A Rebellious Slave." In *Black Leaders: Texans for Their Times*, edited by Alwyn Barr and Robert A. Calvert. Austin: Texas State Historical Association, 1981: 1–18.

———. "Slavery and the Texas Revolution." *Southwestern Hist. Quart.* 89, no. 2 (1985): 181–202.

———. "Slavery and Vigilantism in Austin, Texas, 1840–1860." *Southwestern Hist. Quart.* 85, no. 1 (1981): 1–20.

Ledbetter, Billy D. "White over Black in Texas: Racial Attitudes in the Ante-Bellum Period." *Phylon* 34, no. 4 (1973): 406–18.

Lowe, Richard G., and Randolph B. Campbell. *Planters and Plain Folk: Agriculture in Antebellum Texas.* Dallas: Southern Methodist University Press, 1987.

———. "Slave Property and the Distribution of Wealth in Texas, 1860." *Journal of American History* 63, no. 2 (1976): 316–24.

Malone, Ann Patton. *Women on the Texas Frontier: A Cross-Cultural Perspective.* El Paso: Texas Western Press, University of Texas at El Paso, 1983.

"Mark Potter," *Legislative Reference Library of Texas.* Last accessed August 26, 2016. http://www.lrl.state.tx.us/legeleaders/members/memberdisplay.cfm?memberID=4950.

Marks, John Garrison. "Community Bonds in the Bayou City: Free Blacks and Local Reputation in Early Houston." *Southwestern Hist. Quart.* 117, no. 3 (2014): 267–82.

Marler, Don C. *Red Bones of Louisiana.* Hemphill, Tex.: Dogwood Press, 2003.

McComb, David G. *Galveston: A History.* Austin: University of Texas Press, 1986.

McKnight, Joseph W. "Stephen Austin's Legalistic Concerns." *Southwestern Hist. Quart.* 89, no. 3 (1986): 239–68.

McLaurin, Melton A. *Celia: A Slave.* Athens: University of Georgia Press, 1991.

Mills, Gary B. *The Forgotten People: Cane River's Creoles of Color.* Baton Rouge: Louisiana State University Press, 1977.

———. "Tracing Free People of Color in the Antebellum South: Methods, Sources, and Perspectives," *Nat'l Genealogical Soc'y Quart.* 78, no. 4 (1990): 262–78.

Moneyhon, Carl H. *Edmund J. Davis: Civil War General, Republican Leader, Reconstruction Governor.* Fort Worth: Texas Christian University Press, 2010.

———. *Republicanism in Reconstruction Texas*. Austin: University of Texas Press, 1980.

———. *Texas after the Civil War: The Struggle of Reconstruction*. College Station: Texas A&M University Press, 2004.

Moretta, John Anthony. *William Pitt Ballinger: Texas Lawyer, Southern Statesman, 1825–1888*. Austin: Texas State Historical Association, 2000.

Morgan, Edmund S. *American Slavery, American Freedom: The Ordeal of Colonial Virginia*. New York: W. W. Norton & Co., 1975.

Morris, Thomas D. *Southern Slavery and the Law: 1619–1860*. Chapel Hill: University of North Carolina Press, 1996.

Muir, Andrew Forest. "The Free Negro in Fort Bend County, Texas." *Journal of Negro History* 33, no. 1 (1948): 79–85.

———. "The Free Negro in Galveston County, Texas." *Negro History Bulletin*, 22 (1958): 68–71.

———. "The Free Negro in Harris County, Texas." *Southwestern Hist. Quart.* 46, no. 3 (1943): 214–38.

———. "The Free Negro in Jefferson and Orange Counties, Texas." *Journal of Negro History* 35, no. 2 (1950): 183–206.

Nash, A. E. Keir. "The Texas Supreme Court and Trial Rights of Blacks, 1845–1860." *Journal of American History* 58, no. 3 (1971): 622–42.

Nichols, James David. "The Line of Liberty: Runaway Slaves and Fugitive Peons in the Texas-Mexico Borderlands." *Western Hist. Quart.* 44, no. 4 (2013): 413–33.

Norvell, James R. "The Reconstruction Courts of Texas, 1867–1873." *Southwestern Hist. Quart.* 62, no. 2 (1958): 141–63.

Oakes, James. *The Ruling Race: A History of American Slaveholders*. New York: Alfred A. Knopf, 1982.

Parish, Peter J. *Slavery: History and Historians*. New York: Westview Press, 1989.

Pascoe, Peggy. *What Comes Naturally: Miscegenation Law and the Making of Race in America*. New York: Oxford University Press, 2009.

Paulsen, James W. "The Judges of the Supreme Court of the Republic of Texas." *Texas Law Rev.* 65, no. 2 (1986): 305–71.

———. "A Short History of the Supreme Court of the Republic of Texas." *Texas Law Rev.* 65, no. 2 (1986): 237–304.

Pitre, Merline. "A Note on the Historiography of Blacks in the Reconstruction of Texas." *Journal of Negro History* 66, no. 4 (1981–1982): 340–48.

Porter, Louise M. *The Chronological History of the Lives of St. Joseph*. Chattanooga, Tenn.: Great American, 1975.

Pratt, Alexander Thomas Martin. "The Free Negro in Texas to 1860." Master's thesis, Prairie View Agricultural and Mechanical College, 1963.

Price, Edward T. "A Geographic Analysis of White-Negro-Indian Racial Mixtures in Eastern United States." *Annals of the Assoc. of Am. Geographers* 43, no. 2 (1953): 138–55.

Prince, Diane Elizabeth. "William Goyens, Free Negro on the Texas Frontier." Master's thesis, Stephen F. Austin State College, 1967.

Reynolds, Donald E. *Texas Terror: The Slave Insurrection Panic of 1860 and the Secession of the Lower South*. Baton Rouge: Louisiana State University Press, 2007.
Roberts, Oran M. "The Political, Legislative, and Judicial History of Texas for Its Fifty Years of Statehood." In *Comprehensive History of Texas, 1685–1897*, edited by Dudley G. Wooten. 2 vols. Goliad, Tex.: W. G. Scarff, 1898.
Roediger, David. *The Wages of Whiteness: Race and the Making of the American Working Class*. London: Verso, 1991.
Ross, Michael A. *The Great New Orleans Kidnapping Case: Race, Law, and Justice in the Reconstruction Era*. New York: Oxford University Press, 2015.
Rothman, Adam. *Beyond Freedom's Reach: A Kidnapping in the Twilight of Slavery*. Cambridge, Mass.: Harvard University Press, 2015.
Rothman, Joshua D. *Flush Times and Fever Dreams: A Story of Capitalism and Slavery in the Age of Jackson*. Athens: University of Georgia Press, 2012.
Schoen, Harold. "The Free Negro in the Republic of Texas, Chapter I: Origins of the Free Negro in the Republic of Texas." *Southwestern Hist. Quart.* 39, no. 4 (1936): 292–308.
———. "The Free Negro in the Republic of Texas, Chapter II: The Free Negro and the Texas Revolution." *Southwestern Hist. Quart.* 40, no. 1 (1936): 26–34.
———. "The Free Negro in the Republic of Texas, Chapter III: Manumissions." *Southwestern Hist. Quart.* 40, no. 2 (1936): 85–113.
———. "The Free Negro in the Republic of Texas, Chapter IV: Legal Status." *Southwestern Hist. Quart.* 40, no. 3 (1937): 169–99.
———. "The Free Negro in the Republic of Texas, Chapter V: The Law in Practice." *Southwestern Hist. Quart.* 40, no. 4 (1937): 267–89.
———. "The Free Negro in the Republic of Texas, Chapter VI: The Extent of Discrimination and Its Effects." *Southwestern Hist. Quart.* 41, no. 1 (1937): 83–108.
Schweninger, Loren. *Black Property Owners in the South, 1790–1915*. Urbana: University of Illinois Press, 1990.
Scott, Rebecca, and Jean M. Hébrard, *Freedom Papers: An Atlantic Odyssey in the Age of Emancipation*. Cambridge, Mass.: Harvard University Press, 2012.
Sharfstein, Daniel J. "Crossing the Color Line: Racial Migration and the One-Drop Rule, 1600–1860." *Minnesota Law Rev.* 91, no. 3 (2007): 592–656.
———. *The Invisible Line: A Secret History of Race in America*. New York: Penguin Books, 2011.
Shelton, Robert S. "On Empire's Shore: Free and Unfree Workers in Galveston, Texas, 1840–1860." *Journal of Social History* 40, no. 3 (2007): 717–30.
Shively, Charles. "An Option for Freedom in Texas, 1840–1844." *Journal of Negro History* 50, no. 2 (1965): 77–96.
Sibley, Marilyn McAdams. *Lone Stars and State Gazettes: Texas Newspapers before the Civil War*. College Station: Texas A&M University Press, 1983.
Silbey, Joel H. *Storm over Texas: The Annexation Controversy and the Road to Civil War*. New York: Oxford University Press, 2005.
Simpson, R. W. *History of Old Pendleton District*. Anderson, S.C.: Oulla Printing & Binding Co., 1913.

Sterkx, H. E. *The Free Negro in Ante-Bellum Louisiana*. Rutherford, N.J.: Fairleigh Dickinson University Press, 1972.

Teja, Jesus F. de la, Paula Marks, and Ron Tyler. *Texas Crossroads of North America*. Boston: Houghton Mifflin, 2004.

Texas State Library and Archives Commission. "Stolen Texas Supreme Court Records Cache Recovered by Texas State Library and Archives Commission." Press Release, February 27, 2012. https://www.tsl.texas.gov/sites/default/files/public/tslac/news/docs/2012releases/02.27.12%20TSLAC%20SUPREME%20COURT%20CASES%20RECOVERED%20TSLAC.pdf.

Torget, Andrew J. *Seeds of Empire: Cotton, Slavery, and the Transformation of the Texas Borderlands, 1800–1850*. Chapel Hill: University of North Carolina Press, 2015.

Treat, Victor H. "William Goyens: Free Negro Entrepreneur." In *Black Leaders: Texans for Their Times*, edited by Alwyn Barr and Robert A. Calvert. Austin: Texas State Historical Association, 1981.

Tyler, Ronnie C. "Fugitive Slaves in Mexico." *Journal of Negro History* 57, no. 1 (1972): 1–12.

Walter, Ray A. *A History of Limestone County*. Austin: Von Boeckmann-Jones, 1959.

White, William W. "The Texas Slave Insurrection of 1860." *Southwestern Hist. Quart.* 52, no. 3 (1949): 259–85.

Wiecek, William M. "The Statutory Law of Slavery and Race in the Thirteen Mainland Colonies of British America." *William & Mary Quart.* 34, no. 2 (1977): 258–80.

Wikramanayake, Marina. *A World in Shadow: The Free Black in Antebellum South Carolina*. Columbia: University of South Carolina Press, 1973.

Williams, Annie Lee. *A History of Wharton County, 1846–1961*. Austin: Von Boeckmann-Jones, 1964.

Williams, Howard C., ed. *Gateway to Texas: The History of Orange and Orange County*. 2nd ed. Orange, Tex.: Heritage House Museum of Orange, 1988.

Woolfolk, George Ruble. "Cotton Capitalism and Slave Labor in Texas." *Southwestern Social Science Quart.* 37, no. 1 (1956): 43–52.

———. *The Free Negro in Texas, 1800–1860: A Study in Cultural Compromise*. Ann Arbor, Mich.: Published for the Journal of Mexican American History by University Microfilms International, 1976.

Wooster, Ralph A. "Notes on Texas' Largest Slaveholders, 1860." *Southwestern Hist. Quart.* 65, no. 1 (1961): 72–79.

Wortham, Louis J. *A History of Texas: From Wilderness to Commonwealth*. 5 vols. Fort Worth: Worthan-Molyneaux Cty., 1924.

Wyatt-Brown, Bertram. *Southern Honor: Ethics and Behavior in the Old South*. New York: Oxford University Press, 1982.

Yoakum, H. *History of Texas: From Its First Settlement in 1685 to Its Annexation to the United States in 1846*. 2 vols. New York: Redfield, 1855.

INDEX

Page numbers in italics indicate illustrations.

Alamo, Battle of, 23, 79
Alexander, Burwell, 125
Alexander, William, 46
Allen, Ebenezer, 158–59, 163, 165
Allen, Peter, 114
American Indians, 17–18, 129; Cherokee, 91, 103; Choctaw, 3; "Civilized Tribes" of, 3; Comanche, 3; Karankawa, 17, 18; settler marriages with, 3, 93
Anderson, Andy, 64, 66
Anderson, Joseph, 37, 41
Anderson, William, 63
Ann (slave), 1–6, 11, 175–79
Apalachicola Land Company, 137
Arthur, Sarah, 213n93
Ashworth, Aaron, 94, 101, 103, 110, 112, 131; as cattle rancher, 108, 118; death of, 129; slaves of, 113
Ashworth, Abner, 94, 101, 110, 112, 130, 131; as cattle rancher, 118; death of, 129; slander suit of, 120–21; slaves of, 113–15
Ashworth, Clark, 89, 123, 213n93
Ashworth, David, 110, 112
Ashworth, Elizabeth, 94
Ashworth, Emily, 123, 213n93
Ashworth, Henderson, 120, 121–24; marriage of, 121–22, 213n93; near lynching of, 126–27
Ashworth, James (father), 91–94, 97
Ashworth, James (son), 94, 100, 131
Ashworth, Jesse, 94, 100, 113, 131, 205n26
Ashworth, Joshua, 109, 110, 113, 118
Ashworth, Luke, 114, 128
Ashworth, Margarette, 121
Ashworth, Mary "Polly," 94, 132
Ashworth, Moses, 94, 100, 131
Ashworth, Nancy, 123, 213n93
Ashworth, Sam, 89–91, 123–24, 126
Ashworth, Sarah, 94, 212n93

Ashworth, William, 94–101, 106, 108–10, 112; as cattle rancher, 108, 118; gambling fine of, 120; marriage of, 95 (see also Gallier, Delaide); slaves of, 113–14; as Texas immigrant, 95–101; during Texas War for Independence, 101–3
Ashworth Act (1840), 112, 113, 115, 117
Ashworth family, 91–96, 100–103, 127–28, 130–31, 148, 208n59; as cattle ranchers, 108, 118, 119; discrimination against, 109–13, 116–17, 120–24; slaves of, 113–15
Austin, Moses, 16, 96
Austin, Stephen F., 16–18, 96, 106; Haden Edwards and, 59; as slavery advocate, 21–23, 30
Austin, Texas State Gazette, 40, 65; on free people of color, 104; on Potter's death, 145; on runaway slaves, 79–80; on white privilege, 78
Austin Southern Intelligencer, 113, 147, 157

Baker, Thomas, 168, 173–74
Baker, William, 79–80
Ballard, Lourinda, 24; death of, 52; inheritance trial of, 13–16, 31–45; sale of, 43–44; during Texas War for Independence, 29–30; trial aftermath for, 48–50
Ballard, Pleasant, 24, 34–35, 48, 52
Ballew, Richard, 99, 108, 111, 114
Ballew's Ferry, 90, 108, 113
Ballinger, Hally, 156
Ballinger, William Pitt, 133–35, 150–58, 169–71; income of, 155; portrait of, *152*; Potter and, 133, 153–55, 163; on *Purvis v. Sherrod*, 161–62; on secession, 151–52; slaves of, 156–57; on theatrical shows, 143–44
Barden, Tilson, 48–49
Barnes, J. P., 120–21

Baughman, Isaac "Newt," 45–46
Bean, Ellis H., 185n22
Beaumont, 107–8; maps of, 2, *90*; racial conflicts in, 103–5
Bell, Peter Hansbrough, 159
Bell, Thomas, 103
Beverly, Charlotte, 67
Bird, Clarisa, 25–26, 188n39; at Clark children's trial, 32–34, 36, 191n68; during Texas War for Independence, 29–30
Bird, Henry, 103, 116, 118
Bird, John, 112, 116, 118
Blake, William (British poet), 9
Blake, William (Orange County resident), 123, 126
Blount, Stephen, 68
Bodine, O. H. P., 81–82
Boles, Elvira, 26
Bolton, Charles, 35
Bowie, Jim, 23, 102
Brady, Charles, 53–55, 69–88
Brady v. Price, 55, 78, 81–88
Brandon, Joel, 125
Brazoria County, 28–29, 106; demographics of, 62; maps of, *14*, *134*
Broocks, Moses, 83
Broocks, Travis G., 83
Bunch, Drury, 94
Bunch, Hiram, 116
Bunch, Jack, 124, 126
Bunch family, 93–94
Burell, David, 108
Burkhart, William, 39, 44–45
Burwick, William, 212n93
Byrd, James, 87
Byrne, Reason, 19–20, 37, 43

carpetbaggers, 28, 47. *See also* Reconstruction era
Catchings, Augustus, 39–40
Catchings, Sally, 40
Cayce, H. P., 42
Central American filibusters, 145
Chavis, Jesse, 109
Cherokees, 91, 103
Chesnut, Mary, 176
Childers, J. T., 83
Choctaws, 3

cholera, 35
Clarisa (slave). *See* Bird, Clarisa
Clark, Bishop, 42; death of, 52; inheritance trial of, 13–16, 31–45; marriage of, 52; sale of, 43–44; trial aftermath for, 48–50
Clark, John C., 13–16, 45; Byrne on, 19–20; death of, 37; early years of, 13, 16–20, 38; family life of, 13, 15, 31–34, 36–37, 41–43; as Indian fighter, 17–18; landholdings of, 18, *19*, 24; slaves of, 15, 20–21, 23–25, 186n27
Clark, Richard, 38
Clark, Warren, 49, 52
Clarksville Northern Standard, 80
Clark v. Honey, 13–16, 31–45. See also *Honey v. Clark*
Clements, Mary, 52, 140
Clements v. Crawford, 52
Cleveland, A. H., 157–58, 167
Coke, Richard, 51, 153
Collier, Edward, 40–42
Colorado County, *14*, 80
Colorado River, in Texas, 2, *14*, 17–18
Colten, Samuel, 74
Comanches, 3
Cook, R. V., 40
Copeland, John, 27–28
Corbett, John, 166, 169–72
cotton, 16, 56; slave trade and, 145; in Texas, 8, 57, 67–68, 78, 143
Cox, Joseph, 5, 179
Croatans, 93
Cross, Jack, 125
Cuba, 145

Dallas Herald, 38, 85–86
Danagh, John, 166
Dark, Joseph, 120
Davis, Edmund J., 28, 46, 51, 153, 173
DeBow's Review, 5, 68, 70; on land availability, 115; on slavery, 196n21
Dennis, Isaac, 41, 42, 43–44
Deputy, Samuel, 89–91, 123, 124, 202n1
Dial, Keziah, 94, 108, 131
Dial family, 91–94, 127–28, 208n59
Dickens, Charles, 43
Dimery, Allen, 112
Duval, Thomas, 163

Dyson, James, 99
Dyson, Jesse, 98, 100
Dyson, William, 99, 100

Eaves, Burwell, 82
Edwards, Haden, 59
Ellison, Elisha, 63
Evans, Lemuel D., 46

Farish, Oscar, 148, 158, 165–67, 171, 172
filibusters (soldiers of fortune), 145
Flake, Ferdinand, 136
Fleming, Henry, 44, 45
Florida Territory, 136–37
Fontaine, Sydney, 166
Fort Bend County, 14, 134
Fort Parker, 3
Foster, A. H., 28
Franks, F. Gray, 27–29; attorney fees of, 48–49; during Clark children's trial, 31–35, 38–45; death of, 45–46
Fraulis, Mary Ann, 28–29
Frazer, C. A., 64
Fredonia, Republic of, 59
free people of color, 7, 44; discrimination against, 51, 91–96, 103–6, 109–13, 116–17, 130; in Galveston, 138, 219n35; jury duty by, 108, 119; re-enslavement of, 148; slaves of, 113–15, 128; terms used for, 93, 130; Texas immigration by, 96–97, 100, 109–10, 115–16; during Texas War for Independence, 101–3; trial testimony from, 34; voting rights of, 96, 108, 110. *See also* mixed race
Furman, Richard, 127

Gaffeney, William, 80
Gaines, George, 3–5, 175, 179
Gaines Ferry, 54, 58
Gaines v. Thomas, 3–6, 11, 175–79
Gallier, Delaide, 95–99, 108–9, 121; later years of, 128–31; marriage of, 95 (*see also* Ashworth, William); slaves of, 114, 128; as Texas immigrant, 95–101
Gallier, Sillistia, 121
Galveston, 133–36; during Civil War, 164; demographics of, 138, 219n35; German immigrants of, 136, 144; maps of, 2, 134, 142; slavery in, 138–39; theatrical shows in, 143–44
Galveston News, 77, 136, 146, 153, 169
Galveston Wharf Company, 151, 153
Garner, David, 101, 102, 111
Garner family, 98
Gilbert, Preston, 26
Glover, E. C., 124
Going, Jeremiah, 116
Goins, William, 96, 104, 109, 112; estate of, 105; as Indian agent, 103; Lundy and, 97
Goins family, 91–92, 96, 127–28, 130
"Gone to Texas" migrants, 5, 56–57, 91–92
Gonzales County, 79
Goodman, Keziah, 122, 212n91
Goodman, Willis, 122, 212n91
Gould, Jay, 153
Graham, Malcolm, 167
Gray, William Fairfax, 188n39, 207n49
Green's Bluff, 90, 98, 119
Greenwood, Martha, 149, 158–59, 163, 165
Greer, Louis, 87–88
Gregory, Edgar, 172
Grigsby, Joseph, 107, 109–13, 116, 117
Grigsby's Bluff, 90, 107
Groce, Jared, 22

Hagerty, Spire, 147
Hall, Timothy, 36
Hamblin, W. P., 46
Hamilton, Andrew Jackson, 28, 168
Hammond, James Henry, 21
Hannah (slave), 25
Hardin, Jane, 146, 158, 166, 170
Hardin, Martin B., 146, 165
Hardin, William, 101
Harmon, David, 109
Harmon, John, 111
Harmon, Joshua, 124
Harmon family, 98
Harper, B. J., 102–3
Harris, Dilue, 23–24
Harris County, 134
Hawkins, Joseph, 5, 176
Hawkins, Strother, 5, 177
Hays, Anthony, 147–48
Haywood, Felix, 165
Heard, Nelson, 40

Heard, Q. M., 41, 43
Heard, Stephen, 40, 41
Heard, Thomas, 170–71, 172, 173
Heard, William J. E., 20, 27, 185n17
Hedgepeth, Henry, 79
Henderson, James Pinckney, 55, 61, 75–79, 85, 87; law partner of, 65, 75; portrait of, 76; wife of, 74
Henry, John, 82
Herbert, Paul, 164
Hicks, Archibald, 81, 84
Higgins, James, 82
Hillebrandt, Christian, 107, 108, 121
Honey, George W., 13–16
Honey v. Clark, 47–48, 50, 52, 173; *Clark v. Honey*, 13–16, 31–45
Hopkins, Mary, 163
Horton, A. C., 186n27
Horton, Albert, 34, 37, 43
Horton, Alexander, 61
Horton, J. P., 40
Houston, 51, 144; maps of, 2, 134
Houston, Sam, 60–61, 118
Howard, Josephine, 67
Hutchinson, Nancy, 119

Imperial Colonization Law of 1823 (Mexico), 21
"indentured servants," 22, 185n22
Ingram, Wash, 57
interracial marriage. *See* mixed-race marriage

Jack, Thomas, 151
Jackson, Alexander, 17, 27; as Indian fighter, 18; landholdings of, 19
Jackson, Charles, 60–61
Jackson, Jim, 27
Jackson, Sharp, 26, 34
Jacobs, Harriet, 26, 68
Jasper County, 90
Jefferson, Thomas, 92
Jefferson County, 90, 92, 98, 100, 107–8
Jett family, 98
Johnson, Bob, 98
Jones, Anson, 159
Jones, Lewis B., 96
jury duty, 84, 108, 119

Kansas-Nebraska Act, 65
Karankawas, 17, 18
Kichoe, Jacob, 166
Kincheloe, Abraham, 8, 37
Kincheloe, William, 17, 27; family of, 20; landholdings of, 19; slaves of, 20, 21
Kinsey, H. M., 55, 71–78, 81, 86–87
Kuykendall, Robert, 18, 19

LaBleu, Moise, 128
Lacy, Lee, 46
Lafitte, Jean, 23, 136
Lamar, Mirabeau, 112
land prices, 18, 20–21, 48, 115
Leonard, Diana, 112
Liberty County, 90, 134
Limestone County, 1, 3, 175, 181n1
Logan, Greenberry, 106, 109
Lost Colony of Roanoke Island, 93
Louisiana, 92; free people of color in, 91–94, 100, 101, 130; mixed race as separate caste in, 96, 130; "one drop" rule of, 128
Louisiana Purchase, 91–93, 92
Lourinda (John Clark's daughter). *See* Ballard, Lourinda
Love, James, 151
Lumbees, 93
Lundy, Benjamin, 96–97, 103–4
lynchings, 87, 126–27

Maddox, Rosa, 26
Madison (Orange), 80, 89, 98, 119; maps of, 2, 90, 99
Magruder, John B., 164, 167
malaria, 35
Mann, George, 173, 174
manumission, 44, 147, 150, 157, 162, 165
marriage, 15, 204n13; with American Indians, 3, 93; cohabiting versus, 41–42, 44; common-law, 32, 44–45; of convenience, 37; Mexican laws on, 44–45; on plantations, 67. *See also* mixed-race marriage
Marshall, Adeline, 57
Marshall, Texas Republican, 21, 77, 105
Martin, Henry, 146, 149, 158
Maturin, Juan Baptiste, 105
McCulloch, Samuel, Jr., 101–2, 104, 105, 109

McDonald Furman, Charles James, 127, 130
McFarland, Fanny, 112
McLennan County, 175, 224n2
Melungeons, 93
Menard, Michel, 151
Merriman, A. C., 124, 126
Merriman, John, 126
Merritt, Susan, 64
Mexico: antislavery laws of, 8, 21–23, 79, 96; Louisiana Purchase and, 92; marriage laws of, 44–45; Texas independence from, 29–31, 56, 80, 101–3; Texas territory of, 5, 18, 21–23, 59, 96–97, 100
Meyers, Robert, 159, 163
Midkiff, Charlton, 125–26
Milam (city), 54
Milam, Ben, 106
Miles (slave), 53–56, 66–69, 71–80, 84–88, 194n1
Miller, Mintie Maria, 64
Mills, Robert, 144
mixed race, 3, 100, 124; John Clark's children as, 15, 35; cultural negotiation of, 7–10, 35, 93, 127–30, 175–79; marriage and, 28–29, 34–36, 39–40, 44; as separate caste, 96, 130; Sobrina as, 26; South Carolinian families of, 127; terms used for, 93, 130; "tri-racial isolates" of, 93, 94, 127, 130. *See also* free people of color; race
mixed-race marriage, 28–29, 34–36, 39–40, 188n37; banning of, 44, 47–48, 52; discouraging of, 121–22; recognition of, 140. *See also* marriage
Moderators, 60, 78, 83, 124–25
Montgomery, James, 30, 34, 35
Moore, Jack, 125
Moore, Van, 64
Moore, William, 63–64
Morrill, Amos, 171
"mulattos." *See* mixed race
Murrah, Pendleton, 153–54
Myers, D. V., 40, 42

Nacogdoches, 58, 80; maps of, 2, 54
Nancy (John Clark's daughter). *See* Townsend, Nancy
Native Americans. *See* American Indians

Neches Steam Milling Company, 107
Nelson, Aaron, 109, 116, 118
Nelson, Moses, 109
Nelson family, 94
Neutral Ground, 92
Newton County, *90*
Nicaragua, 145
Norwood, Thomas, 82

Ochiltree, Hugh, 125, 128
Ogden, Wesley, 46
Oldham, Phillis, 39, 52
Oldham, William, 39
Oldham v. McIver, 52
Old Three Hundred (first settler families), 18, 26, 94
Olmsted, Frederick, 20, 25, 37, 114; in Louisiana, 95; in Orange County, 121, 124–25; in San Augustine, 62, 65
Orange County, 89–91; "civil war" in, 124–25; maps of, *90, 99*
overseers, 70–73, 84. *See also* slavery
Owens, Dan, 35

Pardo, Juan, 93
Parker, Cynthia Ann, 3
Paschal, Marcia, 163
Patillo, George A., 98, 99
Patton, S. G., 40–42
Pender, Jacob, 122–23, 212n92
Perkins, George, 132
Perkins, Mary "Polly" Ashworth, 131–32
Perkins family, 91–94, 127–28, 130, 208n59
Peticolas, Alfred B., 46
Plummer, Rachel, 3
Poff, William, 126
Potter, Mark M., 135, 144–46, 169–71; Ballinger and, 133, 153–55, 163; death of, 145; Webster's will and, 133, 150
Powers, Betty, 26
Price, Albert, 56, 57, 71, 76–77, 88
Price, Benjamin, 56, 57, 62, 76–77, 88
Price, Cornelia, 57, 195n8
Price, Elijah, 56–59, 66, 83, 198n40; children of, 195n8; death of, 53, 69
Price, Mary, 57, 195n8
Price, Susan, 57, 195n8
Price, Temperance (daughter), 53–58, 195n8

Price, Temperance "Tempe" (mother), 53–57, 59, 74–78; Brady suit against, 55, 71, 78–88; children of, 195n8; death of, 88
Price, William, 163
Prophet, David, 33, 34, 35
Pryor, Charles, 85–86
Purvis v. Sherrod, 150, 160–62, 170

race, 46, 52, 103–5; class conflict and, 85, 87, 124, 128, 130; social construction of, 129–30, 215n112. *See also* mixed race
racial discrimination: against free people of color, 51, 91–96, 103–6, 109–13, 116–17, 130; in jury duty, 84, 108, 119; in Texas Constitution, 105–6; in voting, 28, 51, 96, 108, 110
rape, of slaves, 26, 41–42, 177, 179
Reconstruction era, 6–7, 28, 44, 47, 153
"Redbones," 94, 127
Red-Lander, 62, 83, 88
Red River County, 62
Regulators, 60, 78, 83, 124–25
Reynolds family, 105
Rhodes, Samuel, 176, 177
Richardson, James, 103, 112
Richardson, Willard, 136, 146
Richmond, *14*, 134
Rigmaiden, A., 127–28, 130
Roberts, J. J., 77
Roberts, Oran M., 51–52, 61
Ruau, John, 146, 163
Runaway Scrape of 1836, 29–31, 188n39
Rusk, Thomas, 65, 75
Rust, Jackson, 48–49

Sabine County, 54, 58
San Antonio, 2, 58, 102
San Augustine, 53, 56–61; cotton production in, 68; demographics of, 62; maps of, *2*, *54*; Olmsted on, 62, 65
San Augustine Tribune, 88
San Augustine University, 62
San Felipe, *14*
San Jacinto, Battle of, 30, 79
Santa Anna, Antonio López de, 29–30
Second Middle Passage, 57

Semicolon Court, 51, 173
Shaw, William, 81
Shelby County, *54*, 60
Simpson, Ben, 58, 64
slave rebellions, 63, 74, 75; conspiracy theories of, 85–87, 148
slavery, 5–9, 21–25; as "benign" institution, 64–66, 76, 196n21; children born into, 4, 15, 22, 40; contract law and, 155; cultural negotiations of, 4, 7–10, 35, 176–77; daily life of, 66–69, 79; free people of color and, 113–15, 128; in Galveston, 138–39; legal protections in, 84; manumission and, 147, 150, 157, 162, 165; Mexican laws against, 8, 21–23, 96; murdered masters and, 80, 138; narratives of, 62–66; overseers' role in, 70–73, 84; runaways from, 79–80; sexual assault in, 26, 41–42, 177, 179; violence in, 63–64, 84
slave trade, 23–24, 66, 145, 185n21
Smelser, John, 28–29
Smith, Adam (German immigrant), 82–83
Smith, Ben Fort, 24
Smith, Billy, 124
Smith, Henry, 87
Smith, R. W., 40
Smith, William, 128
Sobrina, 15–16, 26, 45; children of, before John Clark, 187n30; death of, 28; family life of, 31–33, 35–37, 41–43; sale of, 43–44; during Texas War for Independence, 30. *See also* Clark, John C.
Sorrel, R. D., 186n27
Spain: Louisiana Purchase and, 92; marriage laws of, 44
Stancel, Jesse, 168–72, 222n86
State v. Wygall, 50
Steddham, Samuel, 66
Stephenson, George, 109
Stephenson, Gilbert, 98, *99*
Stephenson, William, 98, *99*, 107
Stephenson family, 111
Stevens, David T., 186n27
Stewart, Jackson, 213n93
Stewart, John, 101
Stewart, Letitia, 121–22, 213n93
Stewart, Mart, 126

Stith, M. S., 186n27
storytelling skills, of trial lawyers, 9, 177–78
Stuart, Hamilton, 136
Sublett, Philip, 63
Sweat family, 91–92

Tait, Charles William, 70
Tate, Joseph, 112
Taylor, George, 83
Taylor, H. R., 159, 160, 163
Teal, George, 66, 70, 71
Telegraph and Texas Register, 107
Tevis, Nancy, 107
Texas Almanac, 27, 145–46, 175
Texas Constitution of 1836, 62, 63, 105, 106, 196n22
Texas Constitution of 1845, 160–61, 196n22
Texas Declaration of Independence, 98, 105
Texas State Library and Archives Commission (TSLAC), 10–11
Texas War for Independence, 29–31, 56, 80, 101–3
Thomas, Elijah, 116
Thomas, Elisha, 109, 112, 116
Thomas, Ichabod, 74
Thomas, William, 3–5, 11, 176
Thompson, Leslie, 149–50
Thompson, Robert, 103, 112
Thompson, Thomas, 82
Thomson, Nancy, 160
Townsend, Joseph, 48
Townsend, Nancy: death of, 52; inheritance trial of, 13–16, 31–45; sale of, 43–44; during Texas War for Independence, 29–30; trial aftermath for, 48–50
Townsend family, 148
Towns family, 28, 112
"tri-racial isolates," 93, 94, 127, 130
Tucker, Philip, 149
Turner, Nat, 74, 86, 148. *See also* slave rebellions
Twain, Mark, 177
Tyler County, 90

Vanlandingham, Louis, 176
Vanlandingham, Mary, 176
Veatch, John, 205n24
voting rights, 28, 51, 96, 108, 110

Waco, 1, 2, 175
Waco Examiner, 153
Walker, Moses B., 46–47, 50, 173
Washington-on-the Brazos, 2, 30, 36
Webster, Betsy, 133–35, 138–41; during Civil War, 164, 167; emancipation of, 146–47; Jane Hardin and, 166
Webster, David, 140–41; as city planner, 144; competency of, 159–60; death of, 146; as Florida land speculator, 136–38; slaves of, 144, 164–65; as Texas land speculator, 141; will of, 133, 135, 146–50
Webster v. Corbett, 172–73, 224n98
Webster v. Heard, 170–71, 172, 173
Webster v. Mann, 223n97, 224n98
Wesleyan College (San Augustine), 62
West, Claiborne, 98, 99, 101, 107
Wharton County, 18, 165; after Civil War, 15; demographics of, 27, 44, 51, 186n27; landholders in, 19; map of, 14; racial strife in, 46, 52; voting irregularities in, 51
Wheeler, Royall T., 61
Whiting, Francis, 146, 149, 158
Whitten, James, 43
Wilhelm, Dietrich, 166
Williams, Annie Lee, 52
Williams, Rose, 67
Willis, John, 116
Wilson, William, 63
Woods, John, 119
Wygall, John, 38
Wygall, Joseph, 38–39, 49–50, 52
Wygall, Mildred Ann, 38

yellow fever, 35, 138, 167
Young, Joseph, 213n93